THE **BIG** BOOK OF **CAKES** **& COOKIES**

HANNAH MILES

FOREWORD BY GREGG WALLACE
FROM BBC'S MASTERCHEF

THE **BIG** BOOK OF
CAKES
& COOKIES

365 MUCH-LOVED CLASSICS
AND NEW FAVOURITES

DUNCAN BAIRD PUBLISHERS

LONDON

*To my Grandma, Marjorie Goodwin, who never saw the publication
of this book but would have been so proud if she had.*

The Big Book of Cakes & Cookies
Hannah Miles

First published in the United Kingdom and Ireland in 2009 by
Duncan Baird Publishers Ltd
Sixth Floor, Castle House
75–76 Wells Street
London W1T 3QH

Conceived, created and designed by Duncan Baird Publishers

Managing Editors: Grace Cheetham, Deirdre Headon
Editor: Alison Bolus
Managing Designer: Suzanne Tuhrim
Studio photography: William Lingwood
Photography Assistant: Sally Hamer
Food Stylist: Bridget Sargeson
Assistant Food Stylists: Stella Sargeson, Jack Sargeson
Prop Stylist: Rachel Jukes

British Library Cataloguing-in-Publication Data:
A CIP record for this book is available from the British Library

ISBN: 978-1-84483-834-9

10 9 8 7 6 5 4 3 2

Typeset in News Gothic
Colour reproduction by Scanhouse, Malaysia
Printed in China by Imago

Publisher's Note: While every care has been taken in compiling the recipes for this book, Duncan Baird
Publishers, or any other persons who have been involved in working on this publication, cannot accept
responsibility for any errors or omissions, inadvertent or not, that may be found in the recipes or text, nor for
any problems that may arise as a result of preparing one of these recipes. If you are pregnant or breastfeeding
or have any special dietary requirements or medical conditions, it is advisable to consult a medical professional
before following any of the recipes contained in this book. Ill or elderly people, babies, young children and
women who are pregnant or breastfeeding should avoid any recipes containing uncooked egg whites.

Notes on the recipes
Unless otherwise stated:
• Use whole milk
• Do not mix metric and imperial measurements
• Pack brown and muscovado sugar firmly into cups, if using
• 1 tsp = 5ml • 1 tbsp = 15ml • 1 cup = 250ml

Author's acknowledgments:
Thanks to Sacha, Mum, Dad, Liz, Mike, Gareth, Amy, Jane, Geoff, the Patel family, Aunty Sylvie and my
friends and readers of Hannah's Country Kitchen for their love, support and endless baking. Heartfelt gratitude
to those who have made this book possible: Heather and Elly at HHB; Grace, Deirdre, Suzanne and all at
DBP, including Alison Bolus for her unending patience during editing; William Lingwood and his team for the
beautiful photographs; Bridget Sargeson and her team for making and displaying the cakes and cookies so
elegantly; Gregg Wallace, particularly for the kind foreword and support during the writing of this book,
John Torode, Karen Ross and all at Shine/Masterchef; Giancarlo and Katie Caldesi; Kathy and Simon Brown;
Chris Lee at the Bildeston Crown; Fitzbillies in Cambridge and my wonderful recipe testers: Tina, Maren, Jess,
Josh, Rosie, Miles, Nick, Sophie, Henry, Alfred, Abena, Amelia, Zara, Deidre, Charlotte, Freddie, Elaine, Fay,
Lisa, Tommy, Mags, Ishan, Sonya, Jane, Jenny, Jo, Kath, Louisa, Madeleine, Sarah, Jonathan, Susan, Pam,
Clare, Mark, William, Anna, Bree, Alison, Ella, Torin, Jackie, Linda, Rita, Premela, Sheila, Tania, Steven,
William, Ben, Charlotte, Kathy, Lucy, David, Cerys, Vanessa, Rachael, Anna, Liz, Joanne, Premala, Helen, Ed,
Kate, Marian, Ros, the Teesdale boys and our village sewing circle.

CONTENTS

FOREWORD

Hannah impressed me from the moment I met her. She has a winning smile and she bakes like an angel. For a man like me with a well-documented sweet tooth, she is simply irresistible!

From the first time she walked into the MasterChef kitchen it was obvious she was a special kind of cook. In the first round, the Invention test, she was half way into a dish when she realized she didn't have all the ingredients to complete the dish. Falling back on her enormous repertoire of sweet things, she managed to knock up the best-tasting cheesecake I've sampled on MasterChef, in less than 12 minutes!

Hannah and I obviously both share a passion for all things sweet and gooey. Hannah is one of the best pastry cooks that I have met, with such generosity of spirit. She wants to make a cake for everybody she meets. She gets real pleasure out of feeding people. I think she takes a naughty delight in watching people indulge themselves. She has presented me with some truly wonderful creations, and I think that everybody should regularly treat themselves to a Hannah work of art.

This book is an absolute joy, as it works on two fronts: it has hundreds of really, really good recipes, but also lots of practical advice from a master of the art. Using this book is like having Hannah standing beside you in the kitchen as you work.

Anybody for another slice? Save me the big bit!

Gregg Wallace, MasterChef

INTRODUCTION

I have enjoyed baking since I was very young, when I baked with my mum, tugging at her apron strings and asking for pieces of dough to make mini loaves for dolls' tea parties. It is no surprise that I enjoy baking – it is a skill I inherited from my Welsh grandpa, who as a baker in the army used to bake loaves in a mobile bake oven. From him I learned how to make perfect loaves of bread and crisp pastry for fruit tarts. During my time on MasterChef, I worked under talented pastry chefs and patissiers at La Cucina Caldesi, at the Savoy and in Paris and have since worked with the wonderful bakers at Fitzbillies in Cambridge and the Bildeston Crown, swapping ideas for unusual flavours and learning secrets of the baking trade.

There is no place I would rather be than in my kitchen, with cakes or biscuits in the oven and a warm scent of baking filling the air. Baking is a skill that can be learnt by anyone of virtually any age, and with a little practice, good-quality ingredients and the right equipment, you will easily be able to make delicious home-baked cakes and cookies for family and friends. In this book I have included a wide variety of my favourite cakes and biscuits. In chapters 1 and 2 you will find quick all-in-one cakes, perfect if you are short of time or have unexpected visitors, smalls cakes for packed lunches and picnics as well as Swiss rolls and desserts. There are also traditional favourites such as Lemon Drizzle Cake, Devil's Food Cake, Country Fruitcake and more unusual combinations such as Chocolate & Chilli Cake, Carrot & Courgette Cake and Peshwari Cupcakes. A selection of heavenly desserts make up Chapter 3, most of which can be prepared in advance, which makes them perfect for suppers or dinner parties with friends. Recipes include luscious mousse cakes, cloud cakes with crisp meringue shells and family favourites such as Pineapple Upside-Down Cake. Chapter 4 contains biscuits and cookies of all descriptions – refrigerator cookies that are either rolled and stamped-out or sliced, drops, thins and family favourites such as Melting Moments, Vanilla Shortbread and Coconut Macaroons – as well as delicate meringues, tray bakes and brownies. For birthdays, special events and seasonal celebrations, chapter 5 contains easy-to-assemble but stunning cakes, Ribboned Christmas Tree Biscuits, a Giant Birthday Cookie and party cupcakes. Introducing children to baking at a young age is so important if the tradition of baking is to be carried on from generation to generation. Chapter 6 does just that, containing simple recipes that you can help children to make and also novel ideas for cakes and biscuits for children's parties. (The Magnifying Glass Biscuits with peppermint 'glass' are my particular favourite.) Whatever the occasion, I hope that you will find something in this book to delight you and to encourage you to keep baking.

TOP TIPS FOR BAKING SUCCESS

- Use the best baking ingredients you can afford, such as organic/free-range eggs and high cocoa-percentage chocolate, as they will improve the flavour of your baking.

- Use eggs at room temperature.

- When making pastry or scones, use chilled butter for easy rubbing in. When creaming, use butter at room temperature, as this will allow you to put more air into the mixture.

- Beat lots of air in when creaming butter and sugar, as this will help your cakes to rise.

- Make sure raising agents such as baking powder, bicarbonate of soda and self-raising flour are not out of date, as this could affect the rising of your cakes.

- Sift flour, icing sugar and other powdered ingredients to remove lumps and to add as much air as possible.

- Smooth out cake mixture in the tins evenly with a spatula or metal spoon so that the cakes rise evenly.

- Roll cookie dough out evenly to ensure even cooking results.

- Preheat your oven so that it comes to the required temperature before the food goes in, otherwise more cooking time may be required. Check the temperature of your oven with an oven thermometer – some ovens can vary as much as 50°C/100°F from their stated dials.

- Use the tin size specified in the recipe. Using a smaller or larger tin will mean the cooking time needs to be adjusted.

- Grease your baking tins and trays well with butter to prevent cakes and biscuits sticking. Once you have greased a tin, you can choose to add a little flour to the tin and shake. This will enable you to spot any areas that are not greased as the flour will not stick. The flour also helps the cake not to stick to the tin.

- Line the tins as recommended. Although lining takes a little time, it will ensure that your cakes do not get stuck in the tin.

- Place your cake tin or tray in the centre of the oven to ensure even baking (unless you have a fan oven, in which case the position is unimportant).

- Try to avoid opening the oven door during the early stages when a cake is cooking, as this could cause the cake to sink in the middle. If you are cooking more than one cake with different cooking times, however, and so do need to test a cake, remove the cake and shut the oven door while testing it, to minimize heat loss.

- When nearing the end of the cooking time, check to see if cakes are done at 5-minute intervals to prevent over-cooking or burning. If a cake has not finished cooking and is starting to brown too much on top, cover the top loosely with baking parchment.

- Use two different methods to check a cake is done, as just one method may not always be accurate. First, insert a skewer into the centre of the cake. If the skewer comes out with cake mixture on it, put the cake back in the oven for 5 minutes. If it comes out clean, press the middle of the cake lightly with a finger. If the cake does not spring back to your touch, cook the cake for a little longer, then retest until it does spring back.

- Do not fill or ice your cakes or cookies until they are completely cold, otherwise the icing and/or filling will melt.

- Store uneaten cakes and cookies in tins or other airtight containers to prolong their life. If they have fresh cream in them, store in a lidded container in the fridge.

BAKING INGREDIENTS

Here is a basic list of ingredients to get you started:

- plain and self-raising flour
- baking powder
- bicarbonate of soda
- butter
- eggs
- caster sugar
- brown sugar
- muscavodo sugar
- icing sugar
- porridge oats
- chocolate chips
- a selection of food colourings

Set out below are the types of different ingredients that appear in this book, their main uses and any possible substitutions. Other than the dairy products, which need to be stored in a fridge, many of these ingredients have long sell-by dates and can be kept in the store cupboard so that you can make cakes or biscuits for any unexpected visitors.

FLOURS

Bread flour/Strong flour – Used for making breads and rolls. This flour has a higher gluten content than other flours, making it ideal for bread because it enables the bread to rise evenly. It comes in white or wholemeal as well as in a wide range of more interesting types, such as Granary, seeded and mixed grain.

Plain flour – Used in cookies, biscuits and pastry. This flour does not contain any raising agent and should not be used in cakes without an additional raising agent, such as baking powder, being added.

Self-raising flour – Used for cakes and in some cookies. This flour contains baking powder and will allow your baking to rise without the addition of any additional raising agent. If you do not have self-raising flour, add 2 tsp baking powder to every 100g/3½oz plain flour to make your own.

Wholemeal flour – This is used for scones and pastry. This flour contains a higher percentage of the grain than white flour, giving it a browner colour and more nutty flavour.

00 Flour – This very fine flour is ideal for sauces, shortbread and biscuits. It does not contain any raising agent.

RAISING AGENTS & STABILIZERS

Baking powder – This is a raising agent that can be added to plain or self-raising flour to make cakes rise. It can also be used together with bicarbonate of soda, especially in muffins, to ensure a soft crumb.

Bicarbonate of soda – This is a raising agent that can be added to plain or self-raising flour to make cakes, biscuits or cookies rise. It has an alkaline taste and should be used sparingly otherwise it can taint the flavour of your cakes or cookies.

Cream of tartar – This is used to stabilize whipped egg whites and give them volume.

Yeast – This can be either fresh or dried. There is much debate about which gives the better flavour, but from personal experience I would say there is little to choose between the two. Supermarkets with in-store bakeries will often offer fresh yeast to customers for free or for a nominal charge. If you do manage to buy fresh yeast, cut it into small 30g/1oz blocks, wrap in cling film and freeze for up to 3 months so that you have a ready supply. The recipes in this book are made with fast action dried yeast, which can be replaced with fresh yeast if available and if desired. (As a rough guide, use twice the amount of fresh yeast to dried yeast and crumble the fresh yeast before use.) Note that I do not add the fast action yeast directly to the dry ingredients, as instructed on the packet, but prefer to reconstitute it with water first, as explained in the recipes.

DAIRY PRODUCTS

Butter (salted) – Commonly used in cakes and cookies and gives a rich taste to baking. It is preferable to use butter in biscuit recipes and also essential to use butter in recipes that call for melted butter.

Butter (unsalted) – Butter that has had no salt added to it. This is frequently used in baking and can be substituted for salted butter in recipes if you wish to reduce the salt content of your baking.

Butter substitutes/margarines – Many spreads and butter substitutes are not suitable for baking, so always check the information on them. Some margarines are suitable for cooking and can be used instead of butter in some cake recipes if you wish.

Buttermilk – This milk does not actually contain any butter but is thicker than normal milk and has a slightly sour taste. It can be added to cake mixtures or used in place of milk to make buttermilk pancakes.

Clotted cream – This rich, thick, yellow cream is made by heating unpasteurized cow's milk. It is the perfect accompaniment to scones and jam and is also used in cheesecakes and to fill sandwich cakes. The cream is very rich and therefore should be saved for special occasions or treats.

Double cream – This is a thick cream, which is often whisked to soft or stiff peaks. It is a common ingredient in cheesecakes. It can be piped into decorations on cakes and used to fill meringues, cakes and choux pastry. Take care not to overwhip double cream or it will end up curdling and having buttery lumps in it.

Greek yogurt – A very thick, rich, natural yogurt that can be added to cakes to keep them moist.

Natural yogurt – A plain thin yogurt that can be added to cakes to keep them moist.

Single cream – This thin cream cannot be whipped to a thicker texture. It can be served to pour over puddings.

Soured cream – This cream has a slightly sour taste and can be used in baking. It is excellent added to cake mixtures, resulting in a moist cake when baked. If you do not have soured cream, you can make your own by adding 1 tablespoon lemon juice to 250ml/9fl oz/1 cup double, single or whipping cream. The cream will thicken when the lemon juice is added and stirred.

Whipping cream – Thicker than single cream but lighter in texture than double cream, this cream can be whipped only to soft peaks. It can be piped into decorations on cakes and used to fill meringues, cakes and choux pastry.

EGGS

Unless otherwise stated, all the recipes in this book use large hens' eggs. Use the freshest eggs available, ideally organic or free-range. Eggs from chickens that have had a better diet will have golden yolks, and you will really notice the difference in the colour of sponge cakes if you use top-quality eggs. Use eggs at room temperature rather than straight from the fridge for the best results.

Duck eggs can be substituted in recipes but are generally larger and richer than hens' eggs. Generally speaking, substitute two duck eggs for three large hens' eggs.

SUGARS & OTHER SWEETENERS

Brown sugar – This is either a light (a golden-coloured) or a dark (a rich dark brown) soft sugar that contains molasses. The difference in colour is determined by the quantity of molasses the sugar contains. Store in an airtight container to stop it drying out.

Caster sugar – A fine white granular sugar, ideal for cakes and biscuits.

Fondant icing sugar – This icing sugar has added glucose and sets with a glossy finish, making it perfect for icing cupcakes and fondant fancies.

Golden icing sugar – This has the same uses as icing sugar but is unrefined and is therefore a pale brown colour, rather than pure white. It has a slightly caramel taste and can be substituted in place of icing sugar.

Granulated sugar – This is a coarse white sugar. It is mainly used in drinks. It can be used in baking recipes, but best results are obtained by using finer caster sugar.

Honey – A natural sweetner that can be used to sweeten cakes and biscuits. It can be opaque (set) or clear.

Icing sugar – A fine powdered sugar that can be mixed with water to make a runny icing to decorate cakes and biscuits. This sugar is often sifted over cakes in a light dusting to decorate them.

Muscovado sugar – A brown sugar with a molasses flavour, also known as Barbados or moist sugar. It comes in light and dark versions and can be a bit lumpy, so crush any lumps before using. Store in an airtight container to prevent it drying out.

Substitute sugars – There are a variety of sugar substitutes available for people suffering from illnesses such as diabetes. They vary in quality and taste. Some have a very strong taste and can taint the delicate flavour of cakes. There are varying opinions on whether sugar substitutes are better or worse than simply using a lesser quantity of ordinary sugar in recipes. Not all sugar substitutes are suitable for baking and you should check the packaging. Always seek medical advice on whether sugar substitutes are suitable for you.

FLAVOURINGS, DRIED FRUITS & NUTS

Chocolate – It is always preferable to use good-quality chocolate for its intensity of flavour. However, dark chocolate with a high cocoa content such as 70 per cent is not cheap, and so is best reserved for those recipes in which it will really make a difference. For other recipes, plain chocolate with a cocoa content of around 40 per cent is fine and will still give a wonderful result.

To make chocolate curls for decoration, rub a bar of chocolate against a coarse cheese grater for short curls; alternatively, shave a vegetable peeler along a bar of chocolate for longer curls. White, milk and dark chocolate can be chopped and added to cake mixtures and biscuit dough for extra flavour and texture.

Citrus – Juices and zests of lemons, limes and oranges are used frequently in this book. The finely grated zest can be added to cake mixture or biscuit dough and the juice can be heated with icing sugar to make a tangy drizzle to pour over cakes.

Culinary lavender – Dried lavender buds (stalks removed) that are pesticide free can be used to add a wonderful floral scent to cakes and biscuits. Buy in delis or on the internet.

Dried fruits – Dried apricots, sultanas, raisins and currants can be added to cake mixtures to give a rich fruity flavour. They can either be used in their dried form or can be rehydrated in water, tea or alcohol. Generally, soaked fruits will increase the cooking time required as they add extra moisture to the cake.

Glacé cherries – These come in two colours: either bright red or a natural dark red. They can be added to cake mixtures or be used as decoration.

Nuts – A wide variety of nuts are used throughout this book. Nuts can be used whole, chopped or even ground into nut pastes. They can be added to cake mixtures to add flavour and texture and also to biscuits. Ground almonds can be used in place of plain flour in some recipes and a few drops of almond essence will add a wonderful flavour to cakes. Nuts keep well if stored in airtight containers. Use by their best-before date.

Spices – A variety of spices, both whole and ground, are used throughout this book. Cinnamon, mixed spice, cardamom, nutmeg and ginger are all wonderful for adding flavour to cakes, biscuits and desserts. These spices are available from supermarkets and wholefood shops. They should be stored in airtight containers and used before the best-before date, otherwise they can lose the intensity of their flavour.

Vanilla – Vanilla extract or essence will give a good vanilla flavour in baking and can be added to cake mixtures and cookie doughs. However, the flavour you get from using vanilla pods is far better. To remove the seeds from a vanilla pod, place the pod on a chopping board and use a sharp knife to cut the pod in half lengthways. Scrape out the seeds from the inside of each half of the pod using a teaspoon. The leftover pod, if not needed for the recipe, can be placed in a jar of caster sugar to make vanilla sugar or can be added to fruit sauces for a wonderful vanilla aroma.

Violet syrup and liqueur, and rose syrup – Violet and rose flavourings give cakes and biscuits a delicate floral perfume and can be added to cake mixtures or to whipped creams, icings or buttercreams to fill cakes, biscuits or choux pastry. Rose and violet syrups are available in specialist food stores and violet liqueur can be found on the internet.

BAKING EQUIPMENT

Here is a basic list of the kitchen equipment you will need to make most of the cakes and cookies in this book.

- 2 sandwich cake tins
- loaf tin
- 20cm/8in or 23cm/9in springform cake tin
- 12-hole bun tin and/or muffin tin
- paper cake/muffin cases
- mixing bowl
- scissors
- baking parchment
- kitchen foil
- electric hand mixer or wooden spoon (to use for beating)/balloon whisk (to use for whisking)
- fine-mesh sieve
- weighing scales or cups
- wire rack
- spatula
- large metal spoon
- oven gloves
- pastry brush
- citrus peeler, zester and grater
- lemon squeezer
- icing bag and nozzles

CAKE TINS & BAKING TRAYS

There is a wide variety of cake tins and baking trays available from kitchen shops or on the internet. The following types are used in this book:

Angel food cake tin – A very deep ring pan with sloping sides and a narrow hole in the centre used for making angel food cake: a light, tall, meringue-like sponge cake.

Baking tin – A rectangular tin with deep sides, perfect for tray bakes and slices.

Baking tray – A rectangular tray used for baking cookies and meringues.

Bun tin – A baking tray with 12 round holes to take cake cases for cupcakes.

Bundt tin – A ring tin with a decorative pattern embossed in it, which creates a patterned cake. A ring tin can be substituted for a bundt tin.

Flan tin – A round tin with a fluted edge, deep sides and a removable base.

Flowerpots – Clean, new mini terracotta flowerpots make novel cake tins. Wash before use and line with cake cases or parchment paper.

Friand tin – A small oval tin (about 6cm/2¼in in length), often with a decorative pattern in the base.

Heart-shaped cake tin – Either deep with straight sides or shallow with a fluted edge like a flan tin. Either version is suitable for the heart cake in this book.

Loaf tin/mini loaf tin – Small, deep rectangular tins used for making loaf cakes or mini loaf cakes, depending on the size. These pans can also be used to make bread.

Madeleine tin – A tin with usually 12 shell-shaped depressions.

Muffin tin/mini muffin tin – A baking tray with 12 large deep or small shallow round holes to take muffin or mini muffin cases.

Rectangular cake tin – A rectangular deep tin, similar to a baking tin.

Ring tin – Either a one-piece tube-shaped tin, as used for a savarin, or a springform tin with a separate funnel centre, which can be used together to create a ring shape.

Sandwich cake tins – Shallow round cake tins used in pairs to make sandwich cakes, such as Victoria sponges.

Sponge flan tin – A round tin with a fluted edge, deep sides and a raised base in the centre. When the cake is turned out you have a cake with high sides and a cut-away section in the centre which you can fill with a variety of fruits and creamy fillings.

Springform cake tin – A cake tin with sides that clip around a base. This type of tin is useful for a wide variety of cakes, including cheesecakes.

Square cake tin – A deep square tin, usually with a loose bottom.

Swiss roll tin – A rectangular cake tin with shallow sides used for Swiss rolls and roulades.

LINING TINS & TRAYS

Most tins will need to be lined as well as greased to stop food sticking to them. Sometimes just the base needs covering with baking parchment ('base-lined'), for which you simply need to stand the tin on a sheet of baking parchment and draw around it with a pencil, then cut out the marked shape. Grease the base of the tin (see page 14) and place the piece of paper on the greased surface, smoothing it into position. If you are using a raised-base flan tin, only the raised area needs to be covered.

At other times the sides of cake tins will also need to be covered ('lined'). The technique for this varies according to the type of tin or tray, as follows:

Shallow square or rectangular tins – Cut a sheet of baking parchment slightly larger than the size of your tin. Grease the base and sides of the tin with butter. Place the tin in the centre of the paper and, using small scissors, cut diagonally from the corners of the paper to the corresponding corners of the tin. Place the paper in the greased tin and overlap the cut corners so that the paper fits neatly.

Round tins/deep square and rectangular tins – Cut a long strip of baking parchment 2.5cm/1in deeper than the tin and long enough to go all around the sides. Fold the strip along its length so that the extra 2.5cm/1in is on one side of the fold. Snip small incisions at frequent intervals along this side of the strip up to the fold line. Cut a circle or square/rectangle of baking parchment the size of the bottom of the tin. Grease the base and sides of the tin with butter. Press the strip of baking parchment around the inside of the sides of the tin so that the snipped fringe lies flat on the base of the tin. Continue until all the paper is in place and the paper overlaps slightly at the join. Place the baking parchment circle or square over the fringe to cover the base.

OTHER EQUIPMENT

In addition to a good supply of tins and trays, the following items will be of help.

Bain marie – This is a water bath, which enables you to cook delicate dishes such as cheesecakes in the oven without the dish receiving direct heat. Wrap the cheesecake in its tin in cling film to make sure it is water tight, then place the tin in a baking tin half-filled with water. The cheesecake in its bain marie can then be placed in the oven to cook.

Baking parchment – Culinary paper with a non-stick finish, which eliminates the need to grease the paper. Use for lining tins and trays.

Double boiler – A set of two saucepans, one containing the ingredient to be melted on top of the other containing simmering water. Ideal for melting chocolate and butter.

BASIC BAKING METHODS

Different types of cakes and cookies use different methods, which are explained below.

All-in-one method – All the ingredients are placed in a bowl and mixed together, making these the easiest types of cakes and cookies to make.

Creaming method – This can be used for either cakes or cookies. At the start of preparing the cake or cookie mixture, the butter and sugar are beaten together with an electric hand mixer or wooden spoon until they are light and creamy. This process adds air to the mixture, which helps cakes to rise and binds biscuit dough together well.

Melted method – In this method, the 'wet' ingredients (butters and fats, syrups, etc.) are heated together until the butter or fat has melted. This liquid is then stirred into the dry ingredients (flours, sugars, spices and raising agents). This method makes chewy cookies and is also used for making gingerbread.

Refrigerator dough – This cookie dough is made either using the creaming method or the rubbing-in method. The dough is then chilled in the refrigerator before being either cut into slices (from a preformed cylinder of the dough) or rolled out and the cookies stamped out with cutters.

Rubbing-in method – This method requires you to rub the fat into the dry ingredients with your fingertips until the mixture resembles fine breadcrumbs. The mixture is then bound together with liquid, usually milk, for scones, some biscuits and pastry or left dry for crumble toppings.

Whisked egg-white method – Eggs are separated and the whites are whisked to stiff peaks and then folded into the cake or biscuit mixture to add air to the mixture. This method is used for flourless cakes, some extra-light sponge cakes and drop biscuits.

Whisking-in method – Air is added to the mixture by whisking whole eggs and sugar together until they have doubled in size and are light and creamy. Flour and flavourings are then folded into the mixture. This method is mainly used in Swiss rolls and roulades and other fatless sponges to give a light result. The whisking is best done with an electric mixer, as whisking with a hand whisk can take some time.

OTHER COOKING TERMS

Greasing – This is rubbing the inside of a cake tin or baking tray with butter. It is important that every part of the tin's surface is covered, otherwise your cakes or cookies may stick. If you are greasing a decorative tin, such as a bundt tin, it is best to melt the butter and apply it with a pastry brush. Note that even when a tin has been greased it is still a good idea to slide a knife around the edge of the tin before turning the cake out or, in the case of a springform tin, releasing the clip and removing the cake.

Melting chocolate – Put pieces of broken chocolate in the top part of a double boiler or in a heatproof bowl set over a pan of simmering water (but not touching the water) and stir occasionally until they have melted into a thick cream. Chocolate can also be melted in a microwave: put the broken pieces of chocolate in a microwave-proof bowl and cook on full power for 1–1½ minutes, stopping every 10–20 seconds to stir the chocolate to prevent it burning. (You may need longer than this time depending on the quantity of chocolate you are melting or on the power of your microwave.) Note that the microwave method is unsuited to white chocolate.

If you have a range cooker, you can melt chocolate by placing it in a heatproof bowl and placing it at the back of the range for 30 minutes.

Melting butter – This can be done as for chocolate. If using a microwave, allow about 1 minute on full power, depending on quantity.

Melting butter and chocolate – This can be done as for chocolate. If using a microwave, allow 1–1½ minutes on medium power, stirring every 10–20 seconds.

Preheating – It is important that an oven is allowed to heat up to the correct temperature before food is put inside to bake. If it is not at full temperature, this may affect the baking time. An oven will usually take about 10 minutes to come to the set temperature.

Softened – This term is primarily used to refer to butter, and it means that the product should be brought to room temperature before being used. This is essential when creaming butter, because cold butter from the fridge is difficult to cream and may result in lumps of butter in your cake mixture or icing.

Whipping cream to peaks – Double cream can be whipped to soft or stiff peaks and is perfect as a filling for pavlovas and flans with fresh fruit. Whipping cream, which has a slightly lower fat content, gives similar, but lighter, results. To whip cream, put the cream in a clean, dry bowl and whip with an electric hand mixer or a whisk until the cream is stiff enough to stand in soft peaks (which flop slightly) or stiff peaks (which are very firm) when you lift the beaters or whisk out of the mixture.

Whisking egg whites to peaks – To whisk egg whites, put the whites in a clean, dry bowl and whisk with an electric hand mixer or a whisk until the whites are stiff enough to stand in soft peaks (which flop slightly) or stiff peaks (which are very firm) when you lift the beaters or whisk out of the mixture. Note that if you have used the mixer or whisk earlier in the recipe, you must wash and dry it thoroughly before using it to whisk the whites.

TROUBLE SHOOTING

If your cakes or cookes don't look or taste quite right, it may be there was a problem in their making or baking. Use the list below to identify and remedy the problem.

Cookie/biscuit dough is too sticky or wet – Add extra sifted flour, a little at a time, until the dough becomes firmer and easier to handle. Alternatively, wrap the dough in cling film and place it in the fridge for 30 minutes before cooking.

Cookie/biscuit dough is too crumbly – Add 1–2 tablespoons milk or water gradually until the dough comes together and can be formed into a ball.

Cake mixture curdles when you add the eggs – Curdling is the separating of eggs and the butter not mixing together properly. Although this can look serious, it will not generally affect the finished product and is easy to remedy: just whisk in 1–2 tablespoons flour.

Cake starts to brown too much – Cover the top with a piece of baking parchment or turn the temperature down and cook for a little longer than the stated time.

Cake sinks when you take it out of the oven – There are several potential causes of a sinking cake: the cake may not have been baked for long enough; the oven temperature may be too low; the cake tin may be too small, meaning that the mixture will be deeper and so may require more cooking; any rising agent used, such as self-raising flour or baking powder, may have been out of date.

Cake doesn't rise – There are several potential causes of a flat cake: the cake tin may be too large, which will give a flatter-than-expected cake; the mixture may have been over-beaten; the air may have been knocked out of the mixture when the flour was folded in; any rising agent, such as self-raising flour or baking powder, may have been out of date.

Cake sticks in the tin – The cake tin was not greased properly. Make sure that every part of the tin is covered with a thin layer of butter.

Cake has a crumbly or dry texture – The cake does not contain enough liquid or the eggs and sugar have not been creamed together for long enough. Creaming should take 3–4 minutes with an electric hand mixer and longer with a wooden spoon.

Icing melts when applied – Icing must be applied to completely cooled cakes and biscuits. If you are in a hurry to ice and the weather is fine, place the cake or biscuits on a wire rack in the garden under a mesh food cover, which will speed up the cooling.

OVEN TYPES & RANGE COOKERS

There is a large selection of ovens available, all of which will have slightly different cooking styles. Over time, you will get to know your oven and how best to use it for baking.

OVEN TYPES

Even within the same type of oven, temperatures, cooking styles and heat distribution can vary. For best results you should buy an oven temperature thermometer, which will enable you to check the actual temperature of your oven and so that you can adjust your dials accordingly if they are not at the correct temperatures.

Whatever oven type you use, towards the end of the specified cooking time you should regularly check to see whether the cake or cookies are done. The more you cook with your oven, the more familiar you will become with its temperature and where to position cakes and biscuits within the oven to achieve the best results.

Electric ovens have a more consistent heat within the oven itself.

Fan-assisted ovens generally cook at a higher temperature then regular ovens, so when using them it is advisable to reduce the oven temperature by 10°C/50°F.

Gas ovens cook with a flame and, depending on the location of the flame, are generally hotter at the bottom of the oven than the top.

RANGE COOKERS

With a range cooker you have very limited control over the temperature, and if your range cooker is like mine, the oven temperature varies from day to day depending on how much I have cooked and the weather outside. It is worth investing in an oven thermometer so that you can know the actual temperature of each of the ovens.

A four-door range cooker has a designated baking oven. This is a moderately hot oven that is ideal for baking cakes and cookies and can be used in the same way as a regular oven. If you have a two-door range cooker, you will need to invest in a cool shelf to use in the roasting oven. The roasting oven is generally very hot (about 200°C/400°F) and without using a cool shelf it will harm cakes. Inserting the cool shelf will lower the temperature in the roasting oven below the shelf. Although you can buy specialist cake baking kits for range cookers, I usually bake using normal cake tins without any difficulties. It is best to buy good-quality tins, however, as cheaper tins will warp in the heat of a range cooker. The side of the cooker that is nearest to the burner will be hotter, and therefore it is important to rotate your cake tin or baking tray 180 degrees halfway through cooking to ensure even browning.

For cakes that take over 1 hour to cook, it is advisable to bake them in the roasting oven for 15–20 minutes and then transfer them to the simmering oven for 1–2 hours until the cake is cooked, testing with both the skewer and finger-pressing tests (see page 7).

For quick-cooking cakes, bake in the roasting oven below a cool shelf. Watch the cakes carefully and rotate if they start to brown too much on one side or cover with baking parchment. Depending on the temperature of your range cooker, you may need to reduce the cooking time.

Range cooker temperatures do not drop when you open the oven doors, so until you are familiar with the temperatures of your oven it is best to check the the progress of cakes or biscuits on a regular basis. Each range cooker is different and you will need to get to know where it cooks hottest. In my range cooker, if I am making a pair of sponge cakes, I bake both on the same shelf and swap over from front to back half way through.

Although you can vary the temperature of your range cooker by controlling the flow of fuel to the cooker, the temperature increase will not usually be instant. With my cooker, it takes at least 2 hours to boost the temperature, so forward planning is required.

Range cookers can be temperamental, and in the summer you may need a second cooker to cook on to avoid having a boiling hot kitchen, but they are very much part of a home and can be used for drying cloths and warming mugs of tea, as well as providing cosy warmth for a sleepy cat. It is said that once you have owned a range cooker you will never be without one, and I think that is probably true.

FREEZING CAKES & COOKIES

To freeze cakes, leave them to cool completely and then double-wrap in cling film and place in the freezer. Most cakes can be frozen for up to 3 months. For best results, prepare the cake filling after defrosting, rather than icing and filling before freezing.

Freeze brownies or slices in one piece. Wrap in cling film and then cover in foil. They will freeze for up to 3 months. Defrost completely and then cut into slices to serve.

Freeze cookies at the uncooked stage, rather than when cooked. The dough will freeze for about 1 month. Once the dough has defrosted, follow the cooking instructions.

- For refrigerator cookies, roll the dough into a cylinder and double-wrap in cling film before freezing. Defrost completely, then cut into slices and cook.
- For drop cookies or ball cookies, form the dough into balls and wrap individually in cling film before freezing. When ready to cook, defrost completely and place the balls on a tray, then cook according to the recipe instructions.
- For cut-out cookies, roll the prepared dough into a ball and double-wrap in cling film before freezing. To use, defrost completely, then roll out to the required thickness using a rolling pin, cut out your cookies and bake.

STORAGE

Apart from fruit cakes, which keep well and improve with age, cakes are best eaten on the day or day after you make them. However, if you do want to store a cake for a little longer (though 2–3 days is the maxiumum I would recommend for freshness), note:

- Leave cakes to cool completely before storing or wrapping them.
- Wrap un-iced cakes in greaseproof paper or cling film.
- Place iced cakes in cake tins or other containers with tight-fitting lids.
- Store any cakes or biscuits containing fresh cream or fresh dairy products such as cream cheese in the fridge.
- Store biscuits in an airtight container; they will generally keep for at least 1 week.

PACKAGING

Cakes and cookies make perfect gifts for friends and family. Cakes can be packaged in tins tied with ribbons or be placed in wicker baskets lined with a napkin and wrapped in clear florist's wrap tied with a bow. A wide variety of clear and coloured plastic bags are available, which can be filled with freshly baked cookies and tied with a ribbon.

Why not give a tin filled with your favourite cookies and small cakes as a present? Cookies can also be used to decorate presents, so try some Gift Tag Cookies on page 175.

FINISHING TECHNIQUES

While most cakes and cookies are delicious on their own with a cup of tea, adding a finishing touch in the form of icing or just a simple dusting of icing sugar can transform many of the cakes and cookies in this book.

Drizzling – Using either melted chocolate or a runny icing made with icing sugar, water and any flavouring of your choice, drizzle over the cookie or biscuit using a fork to make thin lines, flicking the fork backwards and forwards between your fingers quickly to make thin and dainty patterns. Alternatively, put the chocolate or icing in a piping bag with a small plain nozzle and pipe backwards and forwards over your cake or biscuits to make a more regular pattern than with a fork. Allow the icing or chocolate to set before serving.

Dusting – This is the simplest method of decorating. Place icing sugar in a sieve and tap the side of the sieve gently over the cake or biscuits so that they are covered in a light and even layer of icing sugar. For a cake containing spices, you can sift icing sugar with 2 teaspoons cinnamon added, while for a chocolate cake combine equal quantities of cocoa powder and icing sugar to dust over. For more fancy dusting decoration, place a doily or a cake decoration template on top of your cake, dust with icing sugar and then carefully remove the doily or template to leave a pretty pattern on the top of the cake.

Icing – Plain biscuits such as simple shortbread and rolled-out cookies that do not spread during cooking have a flat surface, as do cupcakes and muffins, which are ideal for covering with a runny icing. Use a thick but not too stiff icing made with icing sugar, water and liquid food colouring or use fondant icing sugar for a shiny, glossy icing. Place 1 teaspoon of the icing in the centre of the biscuit or cake and spread it out to the edges using a round-bladed knife, adding more icing if you need it. Decorate with sprinkles, glitter or sweets for an effective but simple finish. Allow the icing to set before serving.

Piping – Whether you are piping fresh cream, buttercream or royal icing, place the icing bag in the palm of your hand with the nozzle pointing towards the base of your wrist. Fold 2.5cm/1in around the top of the bag over your fingers. Use a spatula or spoon to fill the bag with icing. Once filled, pull the folded-over top of the bag up and twist together to squeeze the icing into the bag tightly. This will ensure that you have even pressure when you ice. Using a large star or plain nozzle, you can easily cover the top of a cupcake with a large swirl of icing, then decorate it with some sugar sprinkles to create a very impressive effect that is actually easy to achieve. Different shaped nozzles will create different patterns of icing. The best idea is to make some buttercream and then experiment with each of your nozzles, using them upright and at an angle to see the different effects you can achieve. There are many wonderful books on icing techniques and you will find local courses on cake decorating if you wish to develop your skills further. Piped icing can be used to decorate both cakes and biscuits.

ICINGS & DECORATIONS

Buttercream icing – Cakes can be sandwiched and topped (or even completely coated) with many varieties of buttercream or cream cheese icing. You can vary the flavours easily by adding dissolved coffee, cocoa powder or citrus zest and juice.

Rolled fondant icing/Marzipan – Traditional celebration fruit cakes are covered with marzipan and rolled fondant icing (sold as ready-to-roll or in pre-rolled-out sheets) and then decorated. For best results, the cake will need to be covered with a thin layer of warm apricot jam to allow the marzipan to stick; the jam layer is then repeated on the marzipan so that the rolled icing sticks when laid on top of the marzipan. Roll out the marzipan and icing on an icing sugar-dusted surface. To lift the marzipan or rolled icing onto the cake, place your cake as close as possible to where you have rolled out your icing to reduce the lifting distance, place the rolling pin in the centre of the icing and then fold the icing in half over the rolling pin. Lift the rolling pin and position it over the centre of the cake, then gently unfold the icing so that it covers the top and sides of the cake. Using the palms of your hands, gently flatten and smooth the icing around the sides. Any excess icing sugar can simply be brushed away with your hands.

Royal icing – This icing is made from icing sugar and egg whites and will set hard. It is usually used over a layer of marzipan, particularly for Christmas and wedding cakes because it preserves both well. The icing is spread over the sides and top of the cake and then can either be smoothed with a spatula or rubber scraper or, for Christmas cakes, can be lifted into snow peaks using a fork. This icing can also be used in piping bags to pipe decoration on to cakes and cookies and is good for writing celebration messages on cakes or cookies.

Whipped cream – A simple method of finishing cakes is to fill them with fresh cream and fruit, such as strawberries or raspberries, or with a good-quality jam or lemon curd.

Decorations – Even the most plainly iced cake can be transformed into something spectacular with just a few decorations. Most supermarkets and cake-decorating shops have a wide selection of cake decorations, including edible silver balls, hundreds and thousands, chocolate sprinkles and chocolate chips. In addition, sweets can form ideal cake decorations, and are very popular with children. Plastic-backed floral foam pads can be filled with fresh flowers and placed on top of a fondant-iced cake, though it is important to ensure that the foam does not touch the icing itself. Brightly coloured ribbons can be wrapped around cakes and tied in bows or threaded through holes made in cookies before baking, while edible glitter adds the perfect twinkling finish to any cake or cookie. Ideal for a finishing touch on cakes or desserts, chocolate curls can be made easily by grating the chocolate on a coarse grater for short curls or by pulling a vegetable peeler along the side of the chocolate for longer curls.

DECORATING EQUIPMENT

Often the prospect of decorating a cake can seem daunting, but with a few simple pieces of equipment and some practice you will be amazed by the results you can achieve. If you are not used to icing, prepare a batch of buttercream or royal icing and spend some time experimenting with piping different shapes, piping patterns around the edge of a plate and writing words and names. Do not worry if you cannot master all types of icing skills – just find a method that you feel comfortable with and use that for your cakes.

Cake boards – These silver or gold boards come in rounds, squares or rectangles of many sizes. These are ideal for serving cakes. A plate can be used as an alternative.

Cake turntable – Although not essential, it can be useful to have a turntable to place your cake on when decorating. This enables you to rotate your cake and ice evenly.

Candles – It is always useful to have a pack of birthday candles in your store cupboard.

Food colourings and food pastes – Liquid food colourings are available in most supermarkets. As a minimum, blue, yellow and red colourings are required, which you can combine to make other colours. The colours from food colourings are not as vibrant as the colour you will obtain from using colouring pastes, which are available from most cake decorating shops. Food colouring pastes are best for colouring rolled fondant icing as they are easier to mix in than liquid colourings.

Icing bags – Fabric icing bags come in several different sizes and can be used with large icing nozzles directly or with small icing nozzles fitted to the bag with a coupler (normally sold with the bag). Fabric bags can retain some moisture when washed and should be used only when they are completely dry, otherwise the icing can be affected. Disposable icing bags are plastic bags that you fill with icing and can then dispose of when you have finished decorating. They are ideal when you are icing with several different colours of icing, as it saves washing and drying a fabric bag between uses. You can also make icing bags yourself using folded greaseproof paper or baking parchment.

Icing nozzles – It is worth investing in a set of icing nozzles as these will enable you to decorate in many different ways. The sizes and styles of nozzles required for decoration in this book are: 3mm/⅛in, 13mm/½in, 15mm/⅝in and 2cm/¾in plain and 6mm/¼in, 13mm/½in and 15mm/⅝in star.

Palette knife – Palette knives are used to spread out icing smoothly on cakes and biscuits. If you do not have one of these, you can use a round-bladed knife.

Rolling pin – For rolling out ready-to-roll fondant icing.

HINTS & TIPS FOR CUTTING & FILLING CAKES

- Always slice on a level surface using a sharp serrated knife. Specific cake slices with a blade and handle on each side are available and ensure level cutting.

- If your cake is not level, use a sharp knife to cut the top of the cake level if you are going to ice it. The icing will cover the cut-away part of the cake and leave you with a perfect finish.

- When cutting cakes to serve, the first slice is always the most difficult to remove. Cut two lines meeting in the centre of the cake. Slide the knife or a palette knife under the slice of cake and gently lift away.

- Before filling a cake, place the bottom layer of the cake on your desired serving plate or cake board. Place a little of the filling on the plate and place the bottom cake on top. This will secure your cake in place and will ensure that it does not move if you need to transport the cake.

- When filling a cake, place the filling in the centre of the cake and, using a palete knife or spatula, gently work the filling out to the edges of the cake.

- When icing the sides of a cake, place the icing on top of the cake and, using a palette knife, smooth small amounts of icing from the top of the cake and down the sides, working quickly so that you cover as much of the sides of the cake as possible.

- When icing a cake on top of a wire rack, place a sheet of kitchen foil or baking parchment under the wire rack to collect the icing that runs off. If there are no crumbs in it, the icing can be reused on the cake if necessary.

BASIC RECIPES

Vanilla Buttercream

MAKES 350g/12oz   PREPARATION TIME 10 minutes

225g/8oz/1½ cups icing sugar, sifted
125g/4½oz butter, softened

1 tsp vanilla extract
2 tbsp milk

Place all the ingredients in a mixing bowl and beat with an electric hand mixer or wooden spoon for 4–5 minutes to form a light and creamy icing.

VARIATIONS To make Chocolate Buttercream, replace 30g/1oz icing sugar with the same amount of sifted cocoa powder.
To make Coffee Buttercream, replace the vanilla extract with 1 tablespoon instant coffee granules dissolved in 1 tablespoon hot water and cooled.
To make Rose or Violet Buttercream, replace the vanilla extract with 1 tablespoon rose or violet syrup.

Royal Icing

MAKES 900g/2lb   PREPARATION TIME 15 minutes

900g/2lb/6 cups icing sugar, sifted
4 large egg whites
1 tsp glycerine

Place the sifted icing sugar and egg whites in a large bowl and whisk with an electric hand whisk for 10 minutes until you have a stiff icing. Add the glycerine and whisk again.

Glacé Icing

MAKES 200g/7oz   PREPARATION TIME 5 minutes

200g/7oz/1⅓ cups icing sugar, sifted

Place the sifted icing sugar in a bowl. Gradually add 1–2 tablespoons cold water, while stirring with a large metal spoon, until you have a smooth, thick icing. Add a few drops of liquid food colouring, if you wish.

Chocolate Ganache

MAKES 250g/9oz   PREPARATION TIME 10 minutes

200g/7oz plain chocolate
75ml/2½fl oz/⅓ cup double cream
30g/1oz butter

Place all the ingredients in a double boiler or a bowl set over (but not touching) a pan of simmering water and stir until melted. Alternatively, place the ingredients in a microwave-proof bowl and melt on high power for 1 minute, then stir and heat again at 10-second intervals until the chocolate has melted.

Nut Butters

MAKES 100g/3½oz   PREPARATION TIME 15 minutes

90g/3¼oz/⅔ cup pistachio nuts or hazelnuts, toasted
2 tbsp sunflower or coconut oil
3 heaped tbsp icing sugar

Place the nuts, oil and icing sugar in a blender and grind to a smooth paste. Store in a sterilized jar in the fridge for up to 1 week.

Frosted Rose Petals

MAKES 20   PREPARATION TIME 30 minutes

20 unblemished, fresh and pesticide-free rose petals
1 large egg white
5 tbsp caster sugar

1   Remove the bottom point of each petal, where it joins the stem, as this has a rather
    bitter flavour.
2   Whisk the egg white well with a whisk in a shallow bowl. Place the caster sugar on a
    plate. Using a paintbrush, brush the egg white over the rose petals one at a time. Place
    the petals in the caster sugar and cover lightly, ensuring that each petal is completely
    covered in sugar.
3   Transfer to a wire rack or a sheet of baking parchment and repeat with all the remaining
    petals. Leave to dry in a warm place for 24 hours. These can be stored for 2 days in a tin.

Rose Petal Paste

MAKES 2–3 tbsp   PREPARATION TIME 10 minutes

40–50 fresh and pesticide-free rose petals
1 tbsp rose syrup or rosewater
2 tbsp icing sugar

Remove the bottom point of each petal where it joins the stem, as this has a rather bitter
flavour. Place the petals in a blender and chop finely. Add the rose syrup and sugar and
blitz again. Use this paste soon after making it, as the petals will discolour over time.

Shortcrust Pastry

MAKES 550g/1lb 4oz   PREPARATION TIME 10 minutes, plus chilling

350g/12oz/2¼ cups plain flour, sifted
1 tsp salt
175g/6oz chilled butter, chopped

1   Place the flour and salt in a large mixing bowl and rub the butter into the flour with your
    fingertips until the mixture resembles fine breadcrumbs. Add 2–3 tablespoons chilled
    water a little at a time, mixing with a flat-bladed knife until you have a soft dough.
2   Bring the dough together in a ball with your hands and wrap in baking parchment or
    cling film. Chill in the fridge for at least 1 hour.

Lavender Sugar

MAKES 1 jar   PREPARATION TIME 10 minutes

Layer caster sugar with pesticide-free lavender flowers in a jam jar in alternate layers.
Seal the jar and leave for 2 weeks to infuse. You can use the sugar with the lavender still
in or sieve the flowers out if you prefer. (For a more intense lavender flavour, grind the
sugar and flowers using a pestle and mortar.)

CHAPTER 1

LARGE CAKES

There is something very special about being able to offer family, friends and visitors a slice of homemade cake still warm from the oven, and it always amazes me that something so delicious can be created so quickly and easily with the simple ingredients of flour, eggs, butter and sugar. Everyone loves cake – whether a traditional Dundee or Battenberg, an indulgent chocolate creation or a refreshing gateau covered with fresh seasonal fruits. From classic favourites, such as Victoria Sandwich, Strawberry & Vanilla Swiss Roll and Lemon Drizzle Cake, to more unusual modern recipes, such as Chocolate & Chilli Pound Cake, Carrot & Courgette Cake and Caramelized Mango Upside-Down Cake and a wide assortment of cakes containing nuts, such as Sticky Toffee Nut Upside-Down Cake and delicious Pistachio Marzipan Ring, there is a cake for everyone in this chapter. So put on your apron and bake a cake today.

WHITE CHOCOLATE, APRICOT & PISTACHIO CAKE *(SEE PAGE 37)*

001 Lemon Drizzle Cake

PREPARATION TIME 20 minutes   COOKING TIME 25–30 minutes   SERVES 8

225g/8oz butter, softened, plus extra
   for greasing
225g/8oz/scant 1 cup caster sugar
4 large eggs, lightly beaten

225g/8oz/1½ cups self-raising flour,
   sifted
juice and finely grated zest of 2 lemons
1 heaped tbsp icing sugar

1   Preheat the oven to 180°C/350°F/gas 4. Grease and line a 20cm/8in springform cake tin.
2   Put the butter and caster sugar in a mixing bowl and beat using an electric hand mixer
    or wooden spoo   until the mixture is light and creamy. Add the eggs gradually, beating
    after each addition. Add the flour and lemon zest and gently fold them into the mixture,
    using a large metal spoon. Scrape the mixture into the tin using a spatula.
3   Bake for 25–30 minutes until the cake springs back when pressed lightly and a skewer
    inserted into the middle of the cake comes out clean.
4   Just before the cake comes out of the oven, heat the lemon juice with the icing sugar
    in a saucepan until the sugar has dissolved, then boil for 1 minute to create a syrup.
    Remove the cake from the oven and pour the syrup over the cake. Leave the cake to
    cool in the tin, then turn out on to a serving plate.

002 Lime & Cardamom Drizzle Cake

PREPARATION TIME 20 minutes   COOKING TIME 25–30 minutes   SERVES 8

225g/8oz butter, softened, plus extra
   for greasing
225g/8oz/scant 1 cup caster sugar
4 large eggs, lightly beaten

225g/8oz/1½ cups self-raising flour
1 tsp ground cardamom
juice and finely grated zest of 4 limes
2 tbsp icing sugar, sifted

1   Preheat the oven to 180°C/350°F/gas 4. Grease and line a 20cm/8in springform cake tin.
2   Put the butter and caster sugar in a mixing bowl and beat using an electric hand mixer
    or wooden spoon until the mixture is light and creamy. Add the eggs gradually, beating
    after each addition. Sift in the flour and cardamom and fold them into the mixture with
    the lime zest, using a large metal spoon. Scrape the mixture into the tin using a spatula.
3   Bake for 25–30 minutes until the cake springs back when pressed lightly and a skewer
    inserted into the middle of the cake comes out clean.
4   Just before the cake comes out of the oven, heat the lime juice with the icing sugar in a
    saucepan until the sugar has dissolved, then boil for 1 minute to create a syrup. Remove
    the cake from the oven and pour the syrup over the cake. Leave the cake to cool in the
    tin, then turn out on to a serving plate.

003 Madeira Cake

PREPARATION TIME 20 minutes   COOKING TIME 45–50 minutes   SERVES 8

225g/8oz butter, softened, plus extra
   for greasing
1 pinch saffron stamens
1 tbsp warm milk
115g/4oz/scant ½ cup caster sugar
115g/4oz/½ cup light soft brown sugar

4 large eggs, lightly beaten
225g/8oz/1½ cups plain flour
2 tsp baking powder
finely grated zest of 1 lemon, 1 lime
   and 1 orange
100g/3½oz/scant ⅔ cup mixed peel

1   Preheat the oven to 180°C/350°F/gas 4. Grease and line a deep 23cm/9in springform
    cake tin. Put the saffron stamens and the milk in a bowl and leave to infuse for 5 minutes.
2   Put the butter, caster sugar and light brown sugar in a mixing bowl and beat using an
    electric hand mixer or wooden spoon until the mixture is light and creamy. Add the eggs
    gradually, beating after each addition. Sift in the flour and baking powder and gently fold
    them into the mixture with the lemon, lime and orange zests, mixed peel and soaked
    saffron and milk, using a large metal spoon. Scrape the mixture into the tin using a spatula.
3   Bake for 30 minutes, then turn the temperature down to 170°C/325°F/gas 3 for a
    further 15–20 minutes until the cake springs back when pressed lightly and a skewer
    inserted into the middle of the cake comes out clean. Remove the cake from the oven
    and leave to stand for 5 minutes, then turn out on to a wire rack and leave to cool.

004 Marmalade & Whisky Cake

PREPARATION TIME 20 minutes, plus soaking **COOKING TIME** 35–40 minutes **SERVES** 8

100g/3½oz/heaped ½ cup sultanas
3 tbsp whisky
240g/8½oz butter, softened, plus extra
   for greasing
115g/4oz/scant ½ cup caster sugar
115g/4oz/½ cup dark soft brown sugar

4 large eggs, lightly beaten
225g/8oz/1½ cups self-raising flour, sifted
3 tbsp thin-shred marmalade
finely grated zest of 1 orange
2 tbsp demerara sugar
4 tbsp plain flour, sifted

1. Soak the sultanas in the whisky overnight.
2. Preheat the oven to 180°C/350°F/gas 4. Grease and line a deep 23cm/9in springform cake tin.
3. Put 225g/8oz of the butter, the caster sugar and dark brown sugar in a mixing bowl and beat using an electric hand mixer or wooden spoon until the mixture is light and creamy. Add the eggs gradually, beating after each addition. Add the self-raising flour, marmalade and the soaked sultanas and whisky and gently fold them into the mixture, using a large metal spoon. Scrape the mixture into the tin using a spatula.
4. Put the orange zest, remaining butter, the demerara sugar and plain flour in a mixing bowl and rub together with your fingertips to form a crumble topping. Sprinkle the crumble over the cake mixture.
5. Bake for 35–40 minutes until the cake springs back when pressed lightly and a skewer inserted into the middle of the cake comes out clean. Remove the cake from the oven and leave to stand for 5 minutes, then turn out on to a wire rack and leave to cool.

005 Cherry Cake

PREPARATION TIME 20 minutes **COOKING TIME** 35–40 minutes **SERVES** 8

225g/8oz butter, softened, plus extra
   for greasing
225g/8oz/scant 1 cup caster sugar
4 large eggs, lightly beaten
225g/8oz/1½ cups self-raising flour,
   sifted

1 tsp vanilla extract
200g/7oz/1 cup glacé cherries, halved
200g/7oz/1⅓ cups icing sugar, sifted
1–2 tbsp cherry juice

1. Preheat the oven to 180°C/350°F/gas 4. Grease and line a 20cm/8in springform cake tin.
2. Put the butter and caster sugar in a mixing bowl and beat using an electric hand mixer or wooden spoon until the mixture is light and creamy. Add the eggs gradually, beating after each addition. Add the flour, vanilla extract and cherries and gently fold them into the mixture, using a large metal spoon. Scrape the mixture into the tin using a spatula.
3. Bake for 35–40 minutes until the cake springs back when pressed lightly and a skewer inserted into the middle of the cake comes out clean. Remove the cake from the oven and leave to stand for 5 minutes, then turn out on to a wire rack and leave to cool.
4. Put the icing sugar in a bowl and gradually stir in the cherry juice, adding a little at a time until you have a smooth thick icing. You may not need all of the cherry juice. Spoon the icing over the top of the cake, smoothing it out with a palette knife or round-bladed knife. Leave the icing to set before serving.

006 Apple Streusel Cake

PREPARATION TIME 25 minutes   **COOKING TIME** 1 hour 5 minutes–1 hour 10 minutes   **SERVES** 8

2 large cooking apples, peeled, cored
  and chopped
2 tbsp light soft brown sugar
115g/4oz butter, softened, plus extra
  for greasing
115g/4oz/scant ½ cup caster sugar
2 large eggs, lightly beaten
115g/4oz/¾ cup self-raising flour
1 tsp baking powder

2 tsp cinnamon
custard, to serve

FOR THE STREUSEL
175g/6oz/heaped 1 cup plain flour, sifted
115g/4oz chilled butter, chopped
85g/3oz/⅓ cup caster sugar
1 tsp cinnamon

1   Put the apples, light brown sugar and 100ml/3½fl oz/scant ½ cup water in a saucepan and
    simmer for 10 minutes until the apples are very soft. Drain off any water and set aside to cool.
2   Preheat the oven to 180°C/350°F/gas 4. Grease and line a 20cm/8in springform cake tin.
3   Put the butter and caster sugar in a mixing bowl and beat using an electric hand mixer or
    wooden spoon until the mixture is light and creamy. Add the eggs gradually, beating after
    each addition. Sift in the flour, baking powder and cinnamon and gently fold them into the
    mixture, using a large metal spoon. Scrape the mixture into the tin using a spatula.
4   For the streusel, put the plain flour in a mixing bowl and rub in the chilled butter using your
    fingertips. Add the caster sugar and cinnamon and stir in to make a crumble mixture. Spoon
    the apples over the cake mixture in the tin and top with the streusel.
5   Bake for 55–60 minutes until a skewer inserted into the middle of the cake comes out with no
    cake mixture on it, and the streusel topping is golden brown. Remove the cake from the
    oven and leave to cool in the tin, then turn out on to a serving plate. Serve with custard.

007 Pear & Pecan Upside-Down Cake

PREPARATION TIME 20 minutes **COOKING TIME** 35–40 minutes **SERVES** 8

190g/6½oz butter, softened, plus extra
for greasing
2 tbsp golden syrup
185g/6½oz/1 cup lightly packed dark
muscovado sugar
4 ripe pears, peeled, cored and quartered

100g/3½oz/heaped ½ cup pecan nuts,
coarsely chopped
3 large eggs, lightly beaten
175g/6oz/heaped 1 cup self-raising flour
2 tsp cinnamon

1 Grease and line a 20cm/8in springform cake tin.
2 Put the syrup, 15g/½oz of the butter and 1 tablespoon of the sugar in a saucepan and heat for 5 minutes, stirring, until the sugar has dissolved, then pour into the tin. Place the pear quarters over the toffee sauce and sprinkle the pecans over the top. Leave to cool.
3 Preheat the oven to 180°C/350°F/gas 4. Put the remaining butter and sugar in a mixing bowl and beat using an electric hand mixer or wooden spoon until the mixture is light and creamy. Add the eggs gradually, beating after each addition. Sift in the flour and cinnamon and gently fold them into the mixture, using a large metal spoon. Scrape the mixture on top of the pears using a spatula.
4 Bake for 30–35 minutes until the cake springs back when pressed lightly and a skewer inserted into the middle of the cake comes out clean. Remove the cake from the oven and leave to stand for 10 minutes. Remove the springform sides of the tin and put a serving plate on top of the cake. Holding both plate and tin base securely, tip the cake upside down so that it is inverted on to the plate. Remove the tin base and serve.

008 Blackberry & Apple Upside-Down Cake

PREPARATION TIME 20 minutes **COOKING TIME** 40–45 minutes **SERVES** 8

225g/8oz butter, softened, plus extra
for greasing
3 dessert apples
130g/4½oz/heaped ½ cup light soft
brown sugar
juice of 1 small lemon
200g/7oz/scant 2 cups blackberries

115g/4oz/scant ½ cup caster sugar
4 large eggs, lightly beaten
225g/8oz/1½ cups self-raising flour
2 tsp cinnamon
6 tbsp soured cream
whipped cream, to serve

1 Preheat the oven to 180°C/350°F/gas 4. Grease and line a 20cm/8in springform cake tin.
2 Peel, core and thinly slice 2 of the apples and put in a bowl with 1 tablespoon of the light brown sugar and all the lemon juice, tossing them to make sure they are all coated. Grate the remaining apple. Lay the apple slices and half the blackberries in a pattern on the bottom of the tin.
3 Put the butter, remaining light brown sugar and the caster sugar in a mixing bowl and beat using an electric hand mixer or wooden spoon until the mixture is light and creamy. Add the eggs gradually, beating after each addition. Sift in the flour and cinnamon and gently fold them into the mixture with the grated apple, remaining blackberries and soured cream, using a large metal spoon. Scrape the mixture on top of the fruit using a spatula.
4 Bake for 40–45 minutes until the cake springs back when pressed lightly and a skewer inserted into the middle of the cake comes out clean. Remove the cake from the oven and leave to stand for 10 minutes. Remove the springform sides of the tin and put a serving plate on top of the cake. Holding both plate and tin base securely, tip the cake upside down so that it is inverted on to the plate. Remove the tin base and serve with whipped cream.

009   Baked Apple Cake

PREPARATION TIME 30 minutes   **COOKING TIME** 1 hour 25 minutes–1 hour 40 minutes   **SERVES** 8

225g/8oz butter, softened, plus extra
   for greasing
2 large eating apples
2 tbsp sultanas
2 tbsp golden syrup

225g/8oz/scant 1 cup caster sugar
4 large eggs, lightly beaten
225g/8oz/1½ cups self-raising flour
2 tsp cinnamon
2 tbsp soured cream

1   Preheat the oven to 180°C/350°F/gas 4. Grease and line a 23cm/9in springform cake tin.
2   Wash and core the apples using an apple corer and score a horizontal line around the edge of each apple with a sharp knife to prevent the skins splitting while cooking. Place the apples in an ovenproof dish and fill the centre of each apple with half the sultanas and half the syrup. Add 2 tablespoons water to the dish.
3   Bake for 45–55 minutes until the apples are soft. Turn off the oven and leave the apples to cool, then remove the apple skins to leave a soft apple purée with sultanas.
4   Put the butter and sugar in a mixing bowl and beat using an electric hand mixer or wooden spoon until the mixture is light and creamy. Add the eggs gradually, beating after each addition. Sift in the flour and cinnamon and gently fold them into the mixture with the soured cream and cooled apple purée, using a large metal spoon. Scrape the mixture into the tin using a spatula.
5   Bake for 40–45 minutes until the cake springs back when pressed lightly and a skewer inserted into the middle of the cake comes out clean. Remove the cake from the oven and leave to stand for 5 minutes, then turn out on to a wire rack and leave to cool.

010   Dutch Apple Cake

PREPARATION TIME 20 minutes   **COOKING TIME** 50–55 minutes   **SERVES** 8

4 dessert apples, peeled, cored and
   chopped
1 tbsp vanilla sugar
225g/8oz butter, softened, plus extra
   for greasing
225g/8oz/scant 1 cup caster sugar

4 large eggs, lightly beaten
225g/8oz/1½ cups self-raising flour
1 tsp cinnamon
55g/2oz/½ cup ground almonds
100g/3½oz/⅔ cup flaked almonds
icing sugar, for dusting

1   Put the apples, vanilla sugar and 3 tablespoons water in a saucepan. Cover and simmer for 20 minutes until the apples are soft and have absorbed the water, adding more water if necessary. Set aside to cool.
2   Preheat the oven to 180°C/350°F/gas 4. Grease and line a deep 23cm/9in springform cake tin.
3   Put the butter and sugar in a mixing bowl and beat using an electric hand mixer or wooden spoon until the mixture is light and creamy. Add the eggs gradually, beating after each addition. Sift in the flour and cinnamon and gently fold them into the mixture with the ground almonds, using a large metal spoon.
4   Scrape half of the cake mixture into the tin using a spatula, cover with the apple purée and top with the remaining cake mixture. Sprinkle over the flaked almonds.
5   Bake for 30–35 minutes until the cake springs back when pressed lightly and a skewer inserted into the middle of the cake comes out clean. Remove the cake from the oven and leave to cool in the tin, then turn out on to a serving plate and dust with icing sugar before serving.

011 Spiced Honey & Pear Upside-Down Cake

PREPARATION TIME 20 minutes **COOKING TIME** 40–45 minutes **SERVES** 8

175g/6oz butter, softened, plus extra
  for greasing
4 small pears, peeled, cored and
  thinly sliced
1 tbsp dark soft brown sugar
juice of 1 lemon
175g/6oz/scant ¾ cup caster sugar
3 large eggs, lightly beaten

175g/6oz/heaped 1 cup self-raising flour
2 tsp cinnamon
1 tsp mixed spice
¼ tsp freshly grated nutmeg
100ml/3½fl oz/scant ½ cup
  soured cream
1 tbsp clear honey
whipped cream, to serve

1 Preheat the oven to 190°C/375°F/gas 5. Grease and line a deep 20cm/8in springform cake tin.
2 Put the pear slices in a bowl with the dark brown sugar and lemon juice and toss with your hands to ensure they are all coated. Arrange the pears in a circular pattern on the bottom of the tin.
3 Put the butter and caster sugar in a mixing bowl and beat using an electric hand mixer or wooden spoon until the mixture is light and creamy. Add the eggs gradually, beating after each addition. Sift in the flour and spices and fold in with the soured cream and honey, using a large metal spoon. Scrape the mixture over the pears using a spatula.
4 Bake for 40–45 minutes until the cake springs back when pressed lightly and a skewer inserted into the middle of the cake comes out clean. Remove the cake from the oven and leave to stand for 10 minutes. Remove the springform sides of the tin and put a serving plate on top of the cake. Holding both plate and tin base securely, tip the cake upside down so that it is inverted on to the plate. Remove the tin base and serve with whipped cream.

012 Peach & Amaretto Cake

PREPARATION TIME 20 minutes **COOKING TIME** 40–45 minutes **SERVES** 8

175g/6oz butter, softened, plus extra
  for greasing
175g/6oz/scant ¾ cup caster sugar
3 large eggs, lightly beaten
175g/6oz/heaped 1 cup self-raising flour,
  sifted

55g/2oz/heaped ⅓ cup toasted
  flaked almonds
1 tsp almond extract
2 ripe peaches, stones removed, 1 finely
  chopped and 1 sliced
1 tbsp almond liqueur, such as amaretto
1 tbsp peach or apricot jam

1 Preheat the oven to 180°C/350°F/gas 4. Grease and line a 24 x 12cm/9½ x 4½in loaf tin.
2 Put the butter and sugar in a mixing bowl and beat using an electric hand mixer or wooden spoon until the mixture is light and creamy. Add the eggs gradually, beating after each addition. Add the flour, flaked almonds, almond extract and chopped peach and gently fold them into the mixture, using a large metal spoon. Scrape the mixture into the tin using a spatula. Arrange the peach slices decoratively on top of the cake.
3 Bake for 35–40 minutes until the cake springs back when pressed lightly and a skewer inserted into the middle of the cake comes out clean.
4 Remove the cake from the oven and leave to stand for 5 minutes, then turn out on to a wire rack. Heat the amaretto and jam in a small saucepan until the jam has melted, then brush the glaze over the top of the cake, using a pastry brush. Leave to cool.

013 Summer Berry Meringue Cake

PREPARATION TIME 30 minutes   **COOKING TIME** 50–60 minutes   **SERVES** 8

115g/4oz butter, softened, plus extra
   for greasing
280g/10oz/heaped 1 cup caster sugar
2 large eggs, lightly beaten,
   plus 3 large egg whites
85g/3oz/heaped ½ cup self-raising flour,
   sifted
30g/1oz/heaped ¼ cup ground almonds

1 tsp almond extract
1 tbsp cornflour dissolved in 1 tbsp
   white wine vinegar
200g/7oz/1⅓ cups raspberries
150ml/5fl oz/scant ⅔ cup double cream,
   whipped to stiff peaks
400g/14oz/3½ cups combined strawberries, blackberries and redcurrants

1   Preheat the oven to 140°C/275°F/gas 1. Grease and line a deep 23cm/9in springform cake tin.
2   Put the butter and 115g/4oz/scant ½ cup of the sugar in a mixing bowl and beat using an electric hand mixer or wooden spoon until the mixture is light and creamy. Add the whole eggs gradually, beating after each addition. Add the flour, ground almonds and almond extract and gently fold them into the mixture, using a large metal spoon. Scrape the mixture into the tin using a spatula and set aside while you make the meringue.
3   Put the egg whites in a clean, dry bowl and whisk with an electric hand mixer or a whisk until they form stiff peaks. Whisk in the remaining sugar one-third at a time, incorporating all the sugar before you add more. The meringue should become smooth and glossy. When all the sugar has been added, pour in the cornflour mixture and whisk again. Scatter the raspberries on top of the cake mixture and cover with the meringue.
4   Bake for 50–60 minutes until the meringue is crisp and lightly golden. Remove the cake from the oven and leave to cool in the tin, then turn out on to a serving plate. Just before serving the cake, spoon the cream on top of the meringue and cover with the berries.

014 Sticky Plum Cake

PREPARATION TIME 20 minutes   **COOKING TIME** 50–60 minutes   **SERVES** 8

175g/6oz butter, softened, plus extra
   for greasing
175g/6oz/scant ¾ cup caster sugar
3 large eggs, lightly beaten
6 tbsp soured cream
175g/6oz/heaped 1 cup self-raising flour
2 tsp cinnamon
2 tbsp soft plum jam

6 plums, halved and stones removed
100g/3½oz cream cheese

FOR THE TOPPING
115g/4oz/¾ cup plain flour
85g/3oz chilled butter, chopped
140g/5oz/⅔ cup dark soft brown sugar
1 tsp cinnamon

1   Preheat the oven to 180°C/350°F/gas 4. Grease and line a deep 23cm/9in springform cake tin.
2   Put the butter and the sugar in a mixing bowl and beat using an electric hand mixer or wooden spoon until the mixture is light and creamy. Add the eggs and soured cream gradually, beating after each addition. Sift in the flour and cinnamon and gently fold them into the mixture, using a large metal spoon, then stir in the plum jam. Scrape the mixture into the tin using a spatula. Place the plum halves cut-side down on top of the cake mixture and place small spoonfuls of the cream cheese in between the plums.
3   For the topping, put the flour in a mixing bowl and rub in the butter with your fingertips until the mixture resembles fine breadcrumbs. Stir in the sugar and cinnamon to form a crumble topping, then sprinkle it over the plums.
4   Bake for 50–60 minutes until the cake springs back when pressed lightly and a skewer inserted into the middle of the cake comes out clean. Remove the cake from the oven and leave to cool in the tin, then turn out on to a serving plate.

015 St Clement's Upside-Down Cake

PREPARATION TIME 30 minutes   **COOKING TIME** 1 hour–1 hour 10 minutes   **SERVES** 8

250g/9oz butter, softened, plus extra
  for greasing
1 lemon
1 large orange
55g/2oz/¼ cup light soft brown sugar

115g/4oz/¾ cup pre-cooked polenta
  grains
225g/8oz/scant 1 cup caster sugar
3 large eggs, lightly beaten
115g/4oz/1 cup ground almonds
whipped cream, to serve

1   Grease and line a 20cm/8in springform cake tin.
2   Grate the zest from the lemon and orange and set aside. In a small saucepan, heat the
    brown sugar and 30g/1oz of the butter and simmer until the sugar has dissolved to
    make a caramel syrup. Pour the syrup over the base of the cake tin. Remove the peel
    from the orange and lemon and cut the fruit into thick slices, removing any pips. Place
    the fruit slices in rings on top of the caramel sauce in the tin and leave the caramel to cool.
3   Preheat the oven to 180°C/350°F/gas 4. Simmer the polenta in 500ml/17fl oz/2 cups
    water for 5 minutes until the grains have absorbed all the water and become a thick
    paste. Leave to cool for 5 minutes.
4   Meanwhile, put the remaining butter and the caster sugar in a mixing bowl and beat
    using an electric hand mixer or wooden spoon until the mixture is light and creamy. Add
    the eggs gradually, beating after each addition. Add the orange and lemon zests, ground
    almonds and polenta and fold in, using a large metal spoon. Scrape the mixture over the
    fruit using a spatula.
5   Bake for 50–60 minutes until the cake springs back when pressed lightly and a skewer
    inserted into the middle of the cake comes out clean. Remove the cake from the oven
    and leave to stand for 10 minutes. Remove the springform sides of the tin and put a
    serving plate on top of the cake. Holding both plate and tin base securely, tip the cake
    upside down so that it is inverted on to the plate. Remove the tin base and serve with
    whipped cream.

016 Caramelized Banana Upside-Down Cake

PREPARATION TIME 30 minutes   **COOKING TIME** 1 hour 5 minutes–1 hour 15 minutes   **SERVES** 8

250g/9oz butter, softened, plus extra
   for greasing
2 tbsp dark muscovado sugar
2 tbsp golden syrup
1 tsp cinnamon
3 bananas, peeled and sliced

225g/8oz/1 cup light soft brown sugar
4 large eggs, lightly beaten
225g/8oz/1½ cups self-raising flour, sifted
55g/2oz/heaped ½ cup desiccated
   coconut
2 tbsp coconut milk

1   Grease and line a deep 23cm/9in springform cake tin.
2   Put 30g/1oz of the butter, the muscovado sugar, syrup and cinnamon in a saucepan and simmer gently until the sugar has dissolved to make a caramel sauce. Pour the sauce over the base of the cake tin and arrange the banana slices on top. Set aside to cool.
3   Preheat the oven to 180°C/350°F/gas 4. Put the remaining butter and the light brown sugar in a mixing bowl and beat using an electric hand mixer or wooden spoon until the mixture is light and creamy. Add the eggs gradually, beating after each addition. Add the flour, desiccated coconut and coconut milk and gently fold them into the mixture, using a large metal spoon. Scrape the mixture into the tin using a spatula.
4   Bake for 60–70 minutes until the cake springs back when pressed lightly and a skewer inserted into the middle of the cake comes out clean. Remove the cake from the oven and leave to stand for 10 minutes. Remove the springform sides of the tin and put a serving plate on top of the cake. Holding both plate and tin base securely, tip the cake upside down so that it is inverted on to the plate. Remove the tin base and serve.

017 Mango Upside-Down Cake

PREPARATION TIME 25 minutes   **COOKING TIME** 45–50 minutes   **SERVES** 8

200g/7oz butter, softened, plus extra
   for greasing
55g/2oz/¼ cup dark soft brown sugar
1 tbsp golden syrup
1 large ripe mango, peeled, stone
   removed and flesh cut into thin slices

175g/6oz/¾ cup light soft brown sugar
3 large eggs, lightly beaten
175g/6oz/heaped 1 cup self-raising flour,
   sifted
100g/3½oz/1¼ cups desiccated coconut

1   Preheat the oven to 180°C/350°F/gas 4. Grease and line a deep 23cm/9in springform cake tin.
2   Put 25g/1oz of the butter, the dark brown sugar and syrup in a small saucepan and simmer until the sugar has dissolved to make a caramel sauce. Pour the sauce over the base of the tin. Arrange the mango slices on top of the caramel in patterns. Set aside to cool.
3   Put the remaining butter and the light brown sugar in a mixing bowl and beat using an electric hand mixer or wooden spoon until the mixture is light and creamy. Add the eggs gradually, beating after each addition. Add the flour and coconut and gently fold them into the mixture, using a large metal spoon. Scrape the mixture over the top of the mango using a spatula.
4   Bake for 40–45 minutes until the cake springs back when pressed lightly and a skewer inserted into the middle of the cake comes out clean. Remove the cake from the oven and leave to stand for 10 minutes. Remove the springform sides of the tin and put a serving plate on top of the cake. Holding both plate and tin base securely, tip the cake upside down so that it is inverted on to the plate. Remove the tin base and serve.

018 Toasted Coconut & Caramel Cake

PREPARATION TIME 20 minutes   **COOKING TIME** 35–40 minutes   **SERVES** 8

175g/6oz butter, softened, plus extra
  for greasing
115g/4oz/1¼ cups desiccated coconut
85g/3oz/⅓ cup light soft brown sugar
85g/3oz/⅓ cup light muscovado sugar

3 large eggs, lightly beaten
175g/6oz/heaped 1 cup self-raising flour,
  sifted
3 tbsp toffee sauce
100g/3½oz/⅔ cup icing sugar, sifted

1   Preheat the oven to 190°C/375°F/gas 5. Grease and line a 20cm/8in springform cake tin.
2   Put the desiccated coconut in a dry saucepan and heat until it starts to turn golden brown, stirring all the time to ensure it does not burn. Tip into a dish to cool.
3   Put the butter, light brown sugar and muscovado sugar in a mixing bowl and beat using an electric hand mixer or wooden spoon until the mixture is light and creamy. Add the eggs gradually, beating after each addition. Add the flour, two-thirds of the toasted coconut and 2 tablespoons of the toffee sauce and gently fold them into the mixture, using a large metal spoon. Scrape the mixture into the tin using a spatula.
4   Bake for 30–35 minutes until the cake springs back when pressed lightly and a skewer inserted into the middle of the cake comes out clean. Remove the cake from the oven and leave to stand for 5 minutes, then turn out on to a wire rack and leave to cool.
5   Mix together the icing sugar, remaining toffee sauce and 1 tablespoon water to form a smooth icing and spread this over the top of the cake. Sprinkle the remaining toasted coconut over the cake to decorate.

019 Fig & Vanilla Upside-Down Cake

PREPARATION TIME 30 minutes   **COOKING TIME** 30–35 minutes   **SERVES** 8

butter, for greasing
200g/7oz/¾ cup granulated sugar
seeds from 1 vanilla pod (retain the
  pod for the caramel)
5 figs, thinly sliced

3 large eggs, lightly beaten
125g/4½oz/½ cup caster sugar
125g/4½oz/scant 1 cup plain flour
1 tsp baking powder

1   Preheat the oven to 180°C/350°F/gas 4. Grease and line a 20cm/8in springform cake tin.
2   Put the granulated sugar in a saucepan with 3 tablespoons water and the vanilla pod (but not the seeds) and heat until the sugar has dissolved and turned golden brown. Remove from the heat immediately the caramel starts to colour, otherwise it may burn.
3   Remove and discard the vanilla pod and pour the caramel into the base of the tin. Place the fig slices in patterns on top of the caramel.
4   Put the eggs in a mixing bowl and whisk until they are doubled in size using an electric hand mixer or a whisk, then gradually whisk in the caster sugar. Sift in the flour and baking powder and gently fold them into the mixture with the vanilla seeds, using a large metal spoon. Scrape the mixture on top of the figs using a spatula.
5   Bake for 20–25 minutes until the cake springs back when pressed lightly and a skewer inserted into the middle of the cake comes out clean. Remove the springform sides of the tin and put a serving plate on top of the cake. Holding both plate and tin base securely, tip the cake upside down so that it is inverted on to the plate. Be careful because the hot caramel could spill out and burn you as you turn the tin. Remove the tin base and serve.

020 Tropical Pineapple Cake

PREPARATION TIME 20 minutes   **COOKING TIME** 35–40 minutes   **SERVES** 8

225g/8oz butter, softened, plus extra
   for greasing
225g/8oz/1½ cups self-raising flour,
   sifted, plus extra for dusting
225g/8oz/scant 1 cup caster sugar
4 large eggs, lightly beaten

55g/2oz/heaped ½ cup desiccated
   coconut
6 tinned pineapple rings, finely chopped
200g/7oz/1 cup glacé cherries, halved
1 tsp almond extract

1 Preheat the oven to 180°C/350°F/gas 4. Grease a 23cm/9in ring tin and dust with flour.
2 Put the butter and sugar in a mixing bowl and beat using an electric hand mixer or
   wooden spoon until the mixture is light and creamy. Add the eggs gradually, beating after
   each addition. Add the flour and the remaining ingredients and gently fold them into the
   mixture, using a large metal spoon. Scrape the mixture into the tin using a spatula.
3 Bake for 35–40 minutes until the cake springs back when pressed lightly and a skewer
   inserted into the cake comes out clean. Remove the cake from the oven and leave to
   stand for 5 minutes, then turn out on to a wire rack and leave to cool.

021 Sticky Toffee Nut Upside-Down Cake

PREPARATION TIME 20 minutes   **COOKING TIME** 40–45 minutes   **SERVES** 8

190g/6¾oz butter, softened, plus extra
   for greasing
2 tbsp golden syrup
1 tbsp double cream
85g/3oz/⅓ cup dark soft brown sugar

300g/10½oz/2 cups mixed unsalted
   nuts, one-third chopped finely
85g/3oz/⅓ cup caster sugar
3 large eggs, lightly beaten
175g/6oz/heaped 1 cup self-raising flour,
   sifted

1 Preheat the oven to 180°C/350°F/gas 4. Grease and line a 20cm/8in springform cake tin.
2 In a saucepan, heat 15g/½oz of the butter, the syrup, cream and 1 tablespoon of the dark
   brown sugar gently until the sugar has dissolved to make a thick caramel sauce. Sprinkle
   the whole nuts over the tin base and pour the caramel over the top. Leave until cold.
3 Put the remaining butter and brown sugar with the caster sugar in a mixing bowl and beat
   using an electric hand mixer or wooden spoon until the mixture is light. Add the eggs
   gradually, beating after each addition. Add the flour and chopped nuts and fold them into
   the mixture, using a large metal spoon. Scrape the mixture into the tin using a spatula.
4 Bake for 35–40 minutes until the cake springs back when pressed lightly. Remove the
   springform sides of the tin and put a serving plate on top of the cake. Holding both plate
   and tin base securely, tip the cake upside down so that it is inverted on to the plate.
   Remove the tin base and serve.

022 Cinnamon Macadamia Cake

PREPARATION TIME 20 minutes   **COOKING TIME** 40–45 minutes   **SERVES** 8

225g/8oz butter, softened, plus extra
   for greasing
225g/8oz/1 cup light soft brown sugar
4 large eggs, lightly beaten
225g/8oz/1½ cups self-raising flour

2 tsp cinnamon
1 tsp vanilla extract
200g/7oz/heaped 1 cup macadamia nuts
icing sugar, for dusting

1 Preheat the oven to 180°C/350°F/gas 4. Grease and line a 23cm/9in springform cake tin.
2 Put the butter and sugar in a mixing bowl and beat using an electric hand mixer or wooden
   spoon until the mixture is light and creamy. Add the eggs gradually, beating after each
   addition. Sift in the flour and cinnamon and gently fold them into the mixture with the
   vanilla extract and macadamia nuts, using a large metal spoon. Scrape the mixture into
   the tin using a spatula.
3 Bake for 40–45 minutes until the cake springs back when pressed lightly and a skewer
   inserted into the middle of the cake comes out clean. Remove the cake from the oven
   and leave to stand for 5 minutes, then turn out on to a wire rack and leave to cool. Dust
   with icing sugar before serving.

023 White Chocolate, Apricot & Pistachio Cake

PREPARATION TIME 20 minutes   COOKING TIME 40–45 minutes   SERVES 8

225g/8oz butter, softened, plus extra
  for greasing
225g/8oz/scant 1 cup caster sugar
4 large eggs, lightly beaten
225g/8oz/1½ cups self-raising flour, sifted
100g/3½oz white chocolate, chopped

50g/1¾oz/scant ⅓ cup dried apricots,
  chopped
75g/2½oz/heaped ½ cup pistachio nuts,
  chopped
2 tbsp apricot jam
juice of 1 lemon

1   Preheat the oven to 190°C/375°F/gas 5. Grease and line a 20cm/8in springform cake tin.
2   Put the butter and sugar in a mixing bowl and beat using an electric hand mixer or wooden
    spoon until the mixture is light and creamy. Add the eggs gradually, beating after each
    addition. Add the flour, chocolate, apricots and pistachios and fold them into the mixture,
    using a large metal spoon. Scrape the mixture into the tin using a spatula.
3   Bake for 35–40 minutes until the cake springs back when pressed lightly and a skewer
    inserted into the middle comes out clean. Remove the cake from the oven and leave to
    stand for 5 minutes, then turn out on to a wire rack. Heat the jam and lemon juice in a
    saucepan until the jam melts, then brush the glaze over the top of the cake. Leave to cool.

024 White Chocolate & Peanut Butter Cake

PREPARATION TIME 20 minutes   COOKING TIME 30–35 minutes   SERVES 8

200g/7oz butter, softened, plus extra
  for greasing
250g/9oz/1⅔ cups self-raising flour,
  sifted, plus extra for dusting
2 heaped tbsp smooth peanut butter
225g/8oz/scant 1 cup caster sugar

4 large eggs, lightly beaten
100g/3½oz white chocolate, melted
  and cooled slightly
100g/3½oz/heaped ½ cup plain
  chocolate chips

1   Preheat the oven to 180°C/350°F/gas 4. Grease a 23cm/9in ring tin and dust with flour.
2   Put the butter, peanut butter and sugar in a mixing bowl and beat using an electric hand
    mixer or wooden spoon until the mixture is light and creamy. Add the eggs gradually,
    beating after each addition. Add the flour, melted chocolate and chocolate chips and
    gently fold them into the mixture, using a large metal spoon. Scrape the mixture into the
    tin using a spatula.
3   Bake for 30–35 minutes until the cake springs back when pressed lightly and a skewer
    inserted into the cake comes out clean. Remove the cake from the oven and leave to
    stand for 5 minutes, then turn out on to a wire rack and leave to cool.

025 Flourless Chocolate Cake

PREPARATION TIME 20 minutes   COOKING TIME 30–35 minutes   SERVES 8

100g/3½oz butter, chopped, plus extra
  for greasing
250g/9oz dark chocolate (70% cocoa
  solids), broken into pieces
4 large eggs, separated

175g/6oz/heaped 1 cup icing sugar,
  sifted, plus extra for dusting
1 tsp cinnamon
cocoa powder, for dusting

1   Preheat the oven to 190°C/375°F/gas 5. Grease and line a 23cm/9in springform cake tin.
2   Melt the chocolate and butter together. Leave to cool. Put the egg yolks and icing sugar
    in a bowl and whisk with an electric hand mixer or a whisk until the mixture is light and
    creamy and has doubled in size and the whisk leaves a trail when lifted up. Note that
    the mixture will be quite stiff to start with.
3   Fold the melted chocolate and butter mixture and the cinnamon into the egg yolks and
    sugar, using a large metal spoon. Put the egg whites in a clean, dry bowl and whisk with
    an electric hand mixer or a whisk until they form soft peaks, then fold into the mixture,
    making sure they are incorporated. Scrape the mixture into the tin using a spatula.
4   Bake for 25–30 minutes until the cake has formed a crust but still feels quite soft when
    pressed lightly. Remove the cake from the oven and leave to cool in the tin, then turn out
    on to a serving plate and dust with icing sugar and cocoa.

026 Raspberry & Clotted Cream Cake

PREPARATION TIME 25 minutes   **COOKING TIME** 20–25 minutes   **SERVES** 8

225g/8oz butter, softened, plus extra
  for greasing
225g/8oz/scant 1 cup caster sugar
4 large eggs, lightly beaten
175g/6oz/heaped 1 cup self-raising flour,
  sifted
55g/2oz/½ cup ground almonds

1 tsp almond extract
5 tbsp almond liqueur, such as amaretto
300g/10½oz clotted cream
3 tbsp raspberry jam
400g/14oz/3 cups raspberries
icing sugar, for dusting

1 Preheat the oven to 180°C/350°F/gas 4. Grease and base-line two 20cm/8in sandwich cake tins.

2 Put the butter and sugar in a mixing bowl and beat using an electric hand mixer or wooden spoon until the mixture is light and creamy. Add the eggs gradually, beating after each addition. Add the flour, ground almonds and almond extract and gently fold them into the mixture, using a large metal spoon. Divide the mixture between the tins using a spatula.

3 Bake for 20–25 minutes until the cakes spring back when pressed lightly and a skewer inserted into the middle of each cake comes out clean. Remove the cakes from the oven and leave to stand for 5 minutes, then turn out on to a wire rack and leave to cool.

4 Place one of the cakes on a serving plate, drizzle with half the amaretto and top with half the clotted cream and all the jam. Top with the second cake, drizzle with the remaining amaretto and top with the remaining clotted cream. Arrange the raspberries on top, dust with icing sugar and serve immediately. Any cake not eaten straightaway should be stored in a lidded container in the fridge.

027 Victoria Sandwich

PREPARATION TIME 20 minutes   **COOKING TIME** 20–25 minutes   **SERVES** 8

225g/8oz butter, softened, plus extra
   for greasing
225g/8oz/scant 1 cup caster sugar,
   plus extra for dusting
4 large eggs, lightly beaten

225g/8oz/1½ cups self-raising flour,
   sifted
1 tsp vanilla extract
1 recipe quantity Vanilla Buttercream
   (see page 22)
3 tbsp raspberry jam

1 Preheat the oven to 180°C/350°F/gas 4. Grease and base-line two 20cm/8in sandwich cake tins.
2 Put the butter and sugar in a mixing bowl and beat using an electric hand mixer or wooden spoon until the mixture is light and creamy. Add the eggs gradually, beating after each addition. Add the flour and vanilla extract and gently fold them into the mixture, using a large metal spoon. Divide the mixture between the tins using a spatula.
3 Bake for 20–25 minutes until the cakes spring back when pressed lightly and a skewer inserted into the middle of each cake comes out clean. Remove the cakes from the oven and leave to stand for 5 minutes, then turn out on to a wire rack and leave to cool. Sandwich the cakes with the buttercream and jam and dust the top with caster sugar.

028 All-In-One Vanilla Sponge

PREPARATION TIME 15 minutes   **COOKING TIME** 20–25 minutes   **SERVES** 8

225g/8oz butter, softened, plus extra
   for greasing
225g/8oz/1½ cups self-raising flour
1 tsp baking powder
225g/8oz/scant 1 cup caster sugar
4 large eggs, lightly beaten

1 tsp vanilla extract
2 tbsp plum jam
150ml/5fl oz/scant ⅔ cup whipping
   cream, whipped to stiff peaks
icing sugar, for dusting

1 Preheat the oven to 190°C/375°F/gas 5. Grease and base-line two 20cm/8in sandwich cake tins.
2 Sift the flour and baking powder into a mixing bowl and add the sugar, butter, eggs and vanilla extract. Beat using an electric hand mixer or wooden spoon until everything is incorporated. Divide the mixture between the tins using a spatula.
3 Bake for 20–25 minutes until the cakes spring back when pressed lightly and a skewer inserted into the middle of each cake comes out clean. Remove the cakes from the oven and leave to stand for 5 minutes, then turn out on to a wire rack and leave to cool. Sandwich the cakes with the jam and whipped cream and dust the top with icing sugar.

029 Egg-Free Victoria Sponge

PREPARATION TIME 15 minutes   **COOKING TIME** 35–40 minutes   **SERVES** 8

225g/8oz butter, softened, plus extra
   for greasing
225g/8oz/scant 1 cup caster sugar
350g/12oz/2⅓ cups self-raising flour
½ tsp bicarbonate of soda
250ml/9fl oz/1 cup soured cream

100ml/3½fl oz/scant ½ cup milk
2 tbsp strawberry jam
100ml/3½fl oz/scant ½ cup whipping
   cream, whipped to soft peaks
icing sugar, for dusting

1 Preheat the oven to 180°C/350°F/gas 4. Grease and base-line two 20cm/8in sandwich cake tins.
2 Put the butter and sugar in a mixing bowl and beat using an electric hand mixer or wooden spoon until the mixture is light and creamy. Sift in the flour and bicarbonate of soda and gently fold them into the mixture with the soured cream and milk, using a large metal spoon. Divide the mixture between the tins using a spatula.
3 Bake for 35–40 minutes until the cakes spring back when pressed lightly and a skewer inserted into the middle of each cake comes out clean. Remove the cakes from the oven and leave to stand for 5 minutes, then turn out on to a wire rack and leave to cool. Sandwich the cakes with the jam and whipped cream and dust the top with icing sugar.

030 Lemon Curd Cake

PREPARATION TIME 20 minutes   **COOKING TIME** 20–25 minutes   **SERVES** 8

225g/8oz butter, softened, plus extra
    for greasing
225g/8oz/1 cup light soft brown sugar
4 large eggs, lightly beaten
225g/8oz/1½ cups self-raising flour,
    sifted
finely grated zest of 2 lemons
edible silver balls, to decorate (optional)

FOR THE FILLING
6 tbsp lemon curd
375ml/13fl oz/1½ cups double cream,
    whipped to stiff peaks

FOR THE ICING
200g/7oz/1⅓ cups icing sugar, sifted
1–2 tbsp lemon juice

1   Preheat the oven to 190°C/375°F/gas 5. Grease and base-line two 20cm/8in sandwich cake tins.
2   Put the butter and sugar in a mixing bowl and beat using an electric hand mixer or wooden spoon until the mixture is light and creamy. Add the eggs gradually, beating after each addition. Add the flour and gently fold it and the lemon zest into the mixture, using a large metal spoon. Divide the mixture between the tins using a spatula.
3   Bake for 20–25 minutes until the cakes spring back when pressed lightly and a skewer inserted into the middle of each cake comes out clean. Remove the cakes from the oven and leave to stand for 5 minutes, then turn out on to a wire rack and leave to cool.
4   Cut each cake in half horizontally and sandwich the four layers together using one-third of the lemon curd and one-third of the whipped cream between each layer.
5   For the icing, mix together the icing sugar and lemon juice to make a smooth, thick icing. Spoon over the top of the cake and decorate with edible silver balls, if using. Leave the icing to set before serving.

031 Chocolate & Blackcurrant Cake

PREPARATION TIME 20 minutes   **COOKING TIME** 20–25 minutes   **SERVES** 8

225g/8oz butter, softened, plus extra
    for greasing
225g/8oz/scant 1 cup caster sugar
4 large eggs, lightly beaten
200g/7oz/1⅓ cups plain flour
4 tbsp cocoa powder

100g/3½oz dark chocolate
    (70% cocoa solids), grated
3 tbsp blackcurrant jam
150ml/5fl oz/scant ⅔ cup double cream,
    whipped to stiff peaks
icing sugar, for dusting

1   Preheat the oven to 180°C/350°F/gas 4. Grease and base-line two 20cm/8in sandwich cake tins.
2   Put the butter and sugar in a mixing bowl and beat using an electric hand mixer or wooden spoon until the mixture is light and creamy. Add the eggs gradually, beating after each addition. Sift in the flour and cocoa and gently fold them and the grated chocolate into the mixture, using a large metal spoon. Divide the mixture between the tins using a spatula.
3   Bake for 20–25 minutes until the cakes spring back when pressed lightly and a skewer inserted into the middle of each cake comes out clean. Remove the cakes from the oven and leave to stand for 5 minutes, then turn out on to a wire rack and leave to cool.
4   Sandwich the cakes together with the jam and whipped cream and dust the top with icing sugar.

032 Coffee & Walnut Sandwich

PREPARATION TIME 20 minutes   **COOKING TIME** 20–25 minutes   **SERVES** 8

225g/8oz butter, softened, plus extra
  for greasing
225g/8oz/scant 1 cup caster sugar
4 large eggs, lightly beaten
225g/8oz/1½ cups self-raising flour,
  sifted
100g/3½oz/heaped ½ cup walnut
  halves, 8 reserved for decoration

2 tbsp instant coffee granules
  dissolved in 2 tbsp boiling water
  and cooled
150ml/5fl oz/scant ⅔ cup double cream,
  whipped to stiff peaks
100g/3½oz/⅔ cup fondant icing sugar,
  sifted

1   Preheat the oven to 190°C/375°F/gas 5. Grease and base-line two 20cm/8in sandwich
    cake tins.
2   Put the butter and caster sugar in a mixing bowl and beat using an electric hand mixer
    or wooden spoon until the mixture is light and creamy. Add the eggs gradually, beating
    after each addition. Add the flour, walnut halves and 1 tablespoon of the coffee liquid
    and gently fold them into the mixture, using a large metal spoon. Divide the mixture
    between the tins using a spatula.
3   Bake for 20–25 minutes until the cakes spring back when pressed lightly and a skewer
    inserted into the middle of each cake comes out clean. Remove the cakes from the oven
    and leave to stand for 5 minutes, then turn out on to a wire rack and leave to cool.
4   For the filling, fold 1½ teaspoons of the coffee liquid into the whipped cream and use
    this coffee cream to sandwich the cakes together. For the icing, mix the fondant icing
    sugar with the remaining coffee liquid and 1 tablespoon water to make a thick, smooth
    icing. (You may not need all the water, so add it gradually.) Spoon the coffee fondant
    icing over the cake and decorate with the reserved walnut halves.

033 Polka Dot Chocolate Sandwich

PREPARATION TIME 20 minutes   **COOKING TIME** 20–25 minutes   **SERVES** 8

225g/8oz butter, softened, plus extra
  for greasing
225g/8oz/scant 1 cup caster sugar
4 large eggs, lightly beaten
225g/8oz/1½ cups self-raising flour,
  sifted

100g/3½oz/heaped ½ cup plain
  chocolate chips
1 tsp vanilla extract
1 recipe quantity Chocolate Buttercream
  (see page 22)
55g/2oz/⅓ cup white chocolate buttons,
  to decorate

1   Preheat the oven to 180°C/350°F/gas 4. Grease and base-line two 20cm/8in sandwich
    cake tins.
2   Put the butter and sugar in a mixing bowl and beat using an electric hand mixer or wooden
    spoon until the mixture is light and creamy. Add the eggs gradually, beating after each
    addition. Add the flour, chocolate chips and vanilla extract and gently fold them into the
    mixture, using a large metal spoon. Divide the mixture between the tins using a spatula.
3   Bake for 20–25 minutes until the cakes spring back when pressed lightly and a skewer
    inserted into the middle of each cake comes out clean. Remove the cakes from the oven
    and leave to stand for 5 minutes, then turn out on to a wire rack and leave to cool.
4   Sandwich the cakes together with half the buttercream. Spread the remaining
    buttercream over the top and decorate with the white chocolate buttons.

Chocolate Cherry Cake

PREPARATION TIME 20 minutes   COOKING TIME 20–25 minutes   SERVES 8

225g/8oz butter, softened, plus extra
    for greasing
225g/8oz/scant 1 cup caster sugar
4 large eggs, lightly beaten
200g/7oz/1⅓ cups self-raising flour
7 tbsp cocoa powder

100g/3½oz/½ cup milk chocolate chips
½ recipe quantity Chocolate Buttercream
    (see page 22)
200g/7oz plain chocolate, melted and
    cooled slightly
12 glacé cherries, to decorate

1   Preheat the oven to 190°C/375°F/gas 5. Grease and base-line two 20cm/8in sandwich
    cake tins.
2   Put the butter and sugar in a mixing bowl and beat using an electric hand mixer or
    wooden spoon until the mixture is light and creamy. Add the eggs gradually, beating after
    each addition. Sift in the flour and cocoa and gently fold them into the mixture, using a
    large metal spoon, then fold in the chocolate chips. Divide the mixture between the tins
    using a spatula.
3   Bake for 20–25 minutes until the cakes spring back when pressed lightly and a skewer
    inserted into the middle of each cake comes out clean. Remove the cakes from the oven
    and leave to stand for 5 minutes, then turn out on to a wire rack and leave to cool.
4   Sandwich the cakes together with the buttercream. Pour the melted chocolate over the
    top of the cake and swirl it attractively with a round-bladed knife. Place the cherries
    around the edge of the cake to decorate.

035 Egg-Free Chocolate Cake

PREPARATION TIME 15 minutes   **COOKING TIME** 40–45 minutes   **SERVES** 8

225g/8oz butter, softened, plus extra
  for greasing
225g/8oz/scant 1 cup caster sugar
280g/10oz/scant 2 cups self-raising flour
55g/2oz/⅓ cup cocoa powder
½ tsp bicarbonate of soda
250ml/9fl oz/1 cup soured cream

100g/3½oz/heaped ½ cup milk
  chocolate chips
100ml/3½fl oz/scant ½ cup milk
250ml/9fl oz/1 cup crème fraîche
3 tbsp blackcurrant jam
icing sugar, for dusting

1   Preheat the oven to 180°C/350°F/gas 4. Grease and base-line two 20cm/8in sandwich cake tins.
2   Put the butter and sugar in a mixing bowl and beat using an electric hand mixer or wooden spoon until the mixture is light and creamy. Sift in the flour, cocoa and bicarbonate of soda and gently fold them into the mixture with the soured cream, chocolate chips and milk, using a large metal spoon. Divide the mixture between the tins using a spatula.
3   Bake for 40–45 minutes until the cakes spring back when pressed lightly and a skewer inserted into the middle of each cake comes out clean. Remove the cakes from the oven, turn out on to a wire rack and leave to cool. Sandwich the cakes together with the crème fraîche and jam and dust with icing sugar.

036 Double Chocolate Chip Fudge Cake

PREPARATION TIME 25 minutes   **COOKING TIME** 25–30 minutes   **SERVES** 10

145g/5oz butter, softened, plus extra
  for greasing
175g/6oz/¾ cup light soft brown sugar
55g/2oz/¼ cup dark muscovado sugar
3 large eggs, lightly beaten
150ml/5fl oz/scant ⅔ cup soured cream
200g/7oz/1⅓ cups plain flour
55g/2oz/½ cup cocoa powder
1 tsp bicarbonate of soda
1 tsp baking powder
100g/3½oz/heaped ½ cup white
  chocolate chips

FOR THE FILLING
150g/5½oz/1 cup icing sugar, sifted
100g/3½oz white chocolate, melted and
  cooled slightly
30g/1oz butter, softened
1–2 tbsp milk

FOR THE FROSTING
2 tbsp icing sugar
2 tbsp cocoa powder
200g/7oz plain chocolate, melted and
  cooled slightly
150ml/5fl oz/scant ⅔ cup double cream

1   Preheat the oven to 190°C/375°F/gas 5. Grease and base-line two 20cm/8in sandwich cake tins.
2   Put 115g/4oz of the butter, the light brown sugar and muscovado sugar in a mixing bowl and beat using an electric hand mixer or wooden spoon until the mixture is light and creamy. Add the eggs gradually, beating after each addition, then beat in the soured cream. Sift in the flour, cocoa, bicarbonate of soda and baking powder and gently fold them into the mixture with the chocolate chips, using a large metal spoon. Divide the mixture between the tins using a spatula.
3   Bake for 25–30 minutes until the cakes spring back when pressed lightly and a skewer inserted into the middle of each cake comes out clean. Remove the cakes from the oven and leave to stand for 5 minutes, then turn out on to a wire rack and leave to cool.
4   For the filling, put all the ingredients in a bowl and beat using an electric hand mixer or wooden spoon until light and creamy. Cut each cake in half and sandwich together the four layers with a third of the white chocolate cream between each layer.
5   For the frosting, sift the icing sugar and cocoa into a bowl, add the melted plain chocolate and beat together using an electric hand mixer or wooden spoon. While still beating, pour in the cream and continue beating until you have a thick fudge frosting. Cover the top and sides of the cake with the frosting.

037　Cinnamon Devil's Food Cake

PREPARATION TIME 20 minutes, plus chilling　**COOKING TIME** 50–55 minutes　**SERVES** 8

115g/4oz butter, melted and cooled,
　plus extra for greasing
55g/2oz/⅓ cup cocoa powder
3 tbsp warm milk
225g/8oz/1½ cups plain flour
1 tsp baking powder
1 tsp bicarbonate of soda
225g/8oz/1 cup light soft brown sugar
3 large eggs, separated
200ml/7fl oz/scant 1 cup soured cream

2 tsp cinnamon
chocolate sprinkles, to decorate

FOR THE ICING
200g/7oz/heaped ¾ cup caster sugar
115g/4oz butter, softened
115g/4oz plain chocolate, broken
　into pieces
250ml/9fl oz/1 cup milk
500g/1lb 2oz/3⅓ cups icing sugar, sifted

1　Preheat the oven to 190°C/375°F/gas 5. Grease and line a 20cm/8in springform cake tin.
2　In a mixing bowl, dissolve the cocoa in the warm milk, ensuring there are no lumps. Sift
　in the flour, baking powder and bicarbonate of soda, add the melted butter, light brown
　sugar and egg yolks and beat using an electric hand mixer or wooden spoon until creamy.
3　Put the egg whites in a clean, dry bowl and whisk with an electric hand mixer or a whisk
　until they form stiff peaks. Fold them into the cake mixture with the soured cream and
　cinnamon, using a large metal spoon. Scrape the mixture into the tin using a spatula.
4　Bake for 45–50 minutes until the cake springs back when pressed lightly and a skewer
　inserted into the middle of the cake comes out clean. Remove the cake from the oven
　and leave to stand for 5 minutes, then turn out on to a wire rack and leave to cool.
5　For the icing, put the caster sugar, butter, chocolate and milk into a saucepan and heat
　for 5 minutes, stirring, until the chocolate melts and the sugar dissolves. Bring to the
　boil, then remove from the heat and leave to cool. When cooled, add the icing sugar and
　beat vigorously with an electric hand mixer or wooden spoon until the icing becomes
　thick. This may take up to 15 minutes. Cut the cake in half and sandwich together with
　a third of the icing, then cover the cake with the remaining icing. Decorate with
　chocolate sprinkles and refrigerate until the icing has set before serving.

038　Vanilla Bundt Cake

PREPARATION TIME 20 minutes　**COOKING TIME** 50–55 minutes　**SERVES** 8

250g/9oz butter, softened, plus extra,
　melted, for greasing
400g/14oz/2⅔ cups plain flour,
　plus extra for dusting
400g/14oz/1⅔ cups caster sugar
4 large eggs, lightly beaten

seeds from 2 vanilla pods
　(retain the pods for the icing)
250ml/9fl oz/1 cup milk
2 tsp baking powder
150g/5½oz/1 cup icing sugar, sifted

1　Preheat the oven to 180°C/350°F/gas 4. Grease a 25cm/10in bundt tin using a pastry
　brush and the melted butter, and dust with flour.
2　Put the butter and caster sugar in a mixing bowl and beat using an electric hand mixer
　or wooden spoon until the mixture is light and creamy. Add the eggs gradually, beating
　after each addition.
3　Add the vanilla seeds and milk to the cake mixture, sift in the flour and baking powder
　and beat again until the mixture is smooth and creamy. Scrape the mixture into the tin
　using a spatula.
4　Bake for 45–50 minutes until the cake springs back when pressed lightly and a skewer
　inserted into the middle of the cake comes out clean. Remove the cake from the oven and
　leave to stand for 5 minutes, then turn out on to a wire rack and leave to cool completely.
5　When the cake has cooled, heat the icing sugar, 2 tablespoons water and the vanilla pods
　in a small saucepan, stirring to form a smooth, runny icing. Simmer for 3–5 minutes to
　allow the vanilla flavour to infuse, then remove and discard the pods. Spoon the icing
　over the cake to glaze and leave to set before serving.

039 Mint Choc Chip Bundt Cake

PREPARATION TIME 20 minutes   **COOKING TIME** 25–30 minutes   **SERVES** 8

225g/8oz butter, softened, plus extra,
  melted, for greasing
225g/8oz/1½ cups self-raising flour,
  sifted, plus extra for dusting

225g/8oz/scant 1 cup caster sugar
4 large eggs, lightly beaten
1 tsp vanilla extract
100g/3½oz mint plain chocolate, grated

1 Preheat the oven to 180°C/350°F/gas 4. Grease a 23cm/9in bundt tin using a pastry
   brush and the melted butter, and dust with flour.
2 Put the butter and sugar in a mixing bowl and beat using an electric hand mixer or wooden
   spoon until the mixture is light and creamy. Add the eggs gradually, beating after each
   addition. Add the flour, vanilla extract and mint chocolate and gently fold them into the
   mixture, using a large metal spoon. Scrape the mixture into the tin using a spatula.
3 Bake for 25–30 minutes until the cake springs back when pressed lightly and a skewer
   inserted into the middle of the cake comes out clean. Remove the cake from the oven
   and leave to stand for 5 minutes, then turn out on to a wire rack and leave to cool.

040 Silver Cake

PREPARATION TIME 25 minutes   **COOKING TIME** 30–35 minutes   **SERVES** 8

225g/8oz butter, softened, plus extra for
  greasing
175g/6oz/heaped 1 cup self-raising flour,
  sifted, plus extra for dusting

225g/8oz/scant 1 cup caster sugar
7 egg whites
55g/2oz/½ cup ground almonds

1 Preheat the oven to 180°C/350°F/gas 4. Grease a 23cm/9in ring tin and dust with flour.
2 Put the butter and sugar in a mixing bowl and beat using an electric hand mixer or
   wooden spoon until the mixture is light and creamy. Put the egg whites in a clean, dry
   bowl and whisk with an electric hand mixer or a whisk until they form stiff peaks. Fold
   half of the whisked egg whites into the creamed mixture, using a large metal spoon. Add
   the flour and ground almonds and fold them in gently with the metal spoon, followed by
   the remaining egg whites. Scrape the mixture into the tin using a spatula.
3 Bake for 30–35 minutes until the cake springs back when pressed lightly and a skewer
   inserted into the cake comes out clean. Remove the cake from the oven and leave to
   stand for 5 minutes, then turn out on to a wire rack and leave to cool.

041 Lemon & Poppy Seed Ring Cake

PREPARATION TIME 20 minutes   **COOKING TIME** 30–35 minutes   **SERVES** 8

225g/8oz butter, softened, plus extra
  for greasing
225g/8oz/1½ cups self-raising flour,
  sifted, plus extra for dusting
225g/8oz/scant 1 cup caster sugar

4 large eggs, lightly beaten
2 tbsp poppy seeds
2 tbsp natural yogurt
juice and finely grated zest of 2 lemons
2 tbsp icing sugar

1 Preheat the oven to 180°C/350°F/gas 4. Grease a 23cm/9in ring tin and dust with flour.
2 Put the butter and caster sugar in a mixing bowl and beat using an electric hand mixer or
   wooden spoon until the mixture is light and creamy. Add the eggs gradually, beating after
   each addition. Add the flour, poppy seeds, yogurt and lemon zest and gently fold them into
   the mixture, using a large metal spoon. Scrape the mixture into the tin using a spatula.
3 Bake for 30–35 minutes until the cake springs back when pressed lightly and a skewer
   inserted into the cake comes out clean.
4 Just before the cake comes out of the oven, put the lemon juice and icing sugar in a
   saucepan and heat until the sugar has dissolved, then boil for 1 minute to create a
   syrup. Remove the cake from the oven and pour the syrup over the cake. Leave the cake
   to cool in the tin, then turn out on to a serving plate.

Blueberry Yogurt Bundt Cake

PREPARATION TIME 20 minutes   **COOKING TIME** 45–50 minutes   **SERVES** 8

225g/8oz butter, softened, plus extra, melted, for greasing
225g/8oz/1½ cups self-raising flour, sifted, plus extra for dusting
225g/8oz/scant 1 cup caster sugar
4 large eggs, lightly beaten

finely grated zest of 2 lemons and 1–2 tbsp of the juice
2 tbsp natural yogurt
250g/9oz/heaped 1 cup blueberries
100g/3½oz/⅔ cup icing sugar

1   Preheat the oven to 180°C/350°F/gas 4. Grease a 23cm/9in bundt tin using a pastry brush and the melted butter, and dust with flour.

2   Put the butter and caster sugar in a mixing bowl and beat using an electric hand mixer or wooden spoon until the mixture is light and creamy. Add the eggs gradually, beating after each addition. Add the flour, lemon zest and yogurt and gently fold them into the mixture, using a large metal spoon, then fold in the blueberries. Scrape the mixture into the tin using a spatula.

3   Bake for 45–50 minutes until the cake springs back when pressed lightly and a skewer inserted into the cake comes out clean. Remove the cake from the oven and leave to stand for 5 minutes, then turn out on to a wire rack and leave to cool.

4   Put the icing sugar and lemon juice in a small bowl and stir to make a thick icing. Drizzle over the top of the cake and leave to set before serving.

043 Lemon & Lime Butter Cake

PREPARATION TIME 20 minutes   **COOKING TIME** 30–35 minutes   **SERVES** 8

250g/9oz butter, softened, plus extra
   for greasing
175g/6oz/heaped 1 cup self-raising flour,
   sifted, plus extra for dusting
225g/8oz/scant 1 cup caster sugar

juice and finely grated zest of 1 lemon
4 large eggs, lightly beaten
55g/2oz/½ cup ground almonds
4 tbsp natural yogurt
juice and finely grated zest of 2 limes

1   Preheat the oven to 180°C/350°F/gas 4. Grease a 23cm/9in ring tin and dust with flour.
2   Put 225g/8oz of the butter, the sugar and lemon zest in a mixing bowl and beat using an electric hand mixer or wooden spoon until the mixture is light and creamy. Add the eggs gradually, beating after each addition. Add the flour, ground almonds and yogurt and gently fold them into the mixture, using a large metal spoon. Scrape the mixture into the tin using a spatula.
3   Bake for 30–35 minutes until the cake springs back when pressed lightly and a skewer inserted into the cake comes out clean.
4   Just before the cake comes out of the oven, heat the remaining butter in a saucepan with the lime juice and zest and the lemon juice for 2–3 minutes until the butter has melted, then boil for 1 minute. Remove the cake from the oven and pour the citrus butter over the cake. Leave the cake to cool in the tin, then turn out on to a serving plate.

044 Lemon & Chocolate Cake

PREPARATION TIME 20 minutes   **COOKING TIME** 35–40 minutes   **SERVES** 8

225g/8oz butter, softened, plus extra
   for greasing
225g/8oz/1½ cups self-raising flour,
   sifted, plus extra for dusting
225g/8oz/scant 1 cup caster sugar

4 large eggs, lightly beaten
finely grated zest of 2 lemons
200g/7oz plain chocolate, half finely
   chopped; half melted

1   Preheat the oven to 180°C/350°F/gas 4. Grease a 23cm/9in ring tin and dust with flour.
2   Put the butter and sugar in a mixing bowl and beat using an electric hand mixer or wooden spoon until the mixture is light and creamy. Add the eggs gradually, beating after each addition. Add the flour, lemon zest and chopped chocolate and gently fold them into the mixture, using a large metal spoon. Scrape the mixture into the tin using a spatula.
3   Bake for 35–40 minutes until the cake springs back when pressed lightly and a skewer inserted into the cake comes out clean. Remove the cake from the oven and leave to cool in the tin, then turn out on to a serving plate.
4   When the cake has cooled, drizzle the melted chocolate over the top of the cake, using a fork to form a decorative pattern.

045 Chocolate Cherry Ripple Cake

PREPARATION TIME 20 minutes   **COOKING TIME** 40–50 minutes   **SERVES** 8

225g/8oz butter, softened, plus extra
   for greasing
175g/6oz/heaped 1 cup self-raising flour,
   plus extra for dusting
225g/8oz/1 cup light soft brown sugar
4 large eggs, lightly beaten

55g/2oz/⅓ cup cocoa powder
100g/3½oz plain chocolate, grated
1 tsp almond extract
200g/7oz/heaped 1 cup preserved
   cherries, stones removed
icing sugar, for dusting

1   Preheat the oven to 180°C/350°F/gas 4. Grease a 23cm/9in ring tin and dust with flour.
2   Put the butter and brown sugar in a mixing bowl and beat using an electric hand mixer or wooden spoon until the mixture is light and creamy. Add the eggs gradually, beating after each addition. Sift in the flour and cocoa and gently fold them into the mixture with the grated chocolate and almond extract, using a large metal spoon. Stir in the cherries, folding them lightly through the mixture. Scrape the mixture into the tin using a spatula.
3   Bake for 40–50 minutes until the cake springs back when pressed lightly and a skewer inserted into the cake comes out clean. Remove the cake from the oven and leave to stand for 5 minutes, then turn out on to a wire rack and leave to cool. Dust with icing sugar.

046 Chocolate & Chilli Pound Cake

PREPARATION TIME 20 minutes   **COOKING TIME** 45–50 minutes   **SERVES** 8

250g/9oz butter, softened, plus extra
  for greasing
200g/7oz/¾ cup caster sugar
4 large eggs, lightly beaten
200g/7oz/1⅓ cups self-raising flour
6 tbsp cocoa powder

½ tsp chilli powder
100g/3½oz/heaped ½ cup plain
  chocolate chips
200g/7oz plain chilli chocolate,
  melted and cooled slightly
red sugar sprinkles, to decorate

1 Preheat the oven to 170°C/325°F/gas 3. Grease a deep 23cm/9in springform cake tin.
2 Put the butter and sugar in a mixing bowl and beat using an electric hand mixer or wooden spoon until the mixture is light and creamy. Add the eggs gradually, beating after each addition. Sift in the flour, cocoa and chilli powder and gently fold them into the mixture with the chocolate chips, using a large metal spoon. Scrape the mixture into the tin using a spatula.
3 Bake for 45–50 minutes until the cake springs back when pressed lightly and a skewer inserted into the cake comes out clean. Remove the cake from the oven and leave in the tin to cool, then turn out on to a serving plate. Drizzle the melted chocolate over the top. Decorate with the sprinkles and leave the chocolate to set before serving.

047 Chocolate Marble Ring

PREPARATION TIME 20 minutes   **COOKING TIME** 25–30 minutes   **SERVES** 8

225g/8oz butter, softened, plus extra
  for greasing
225g/8oz/1½ cups self-raising flour,
  sifted, plus extra for dusting
225g/8oz/scant 1 cup caster sugar

4 large eggs, lightly beaten
1 tsp vanilla extract
4 tbsp cocoa powder
100g/3½oz/heaped ½ cup plain
  chocolate chips

1 Preheat the oven to 180°C/350°F/gas 4. Grease a 23cm/9in ring tin and dust with flour.
2 Put the butter and sugar in a mixing bowl and beat using an electric hand mixer or wooden spoon until the mixture is light and creamy. Add the eggs gradually, beating after each addition. Add the flour and gently fold it into the mixture, using a large metal spoon.
3 Divide the cake mixture between 2 bowls. Add the vanilla extract to one bowl and fold it in. Add the cocoa and chocolate chips to the other bowl and fold them in gently.
4 Place large spoonfuls of the cake mixtures alternately into the ring tin, using a spatula to get all of the mixtures out of the bowls. Gently pull a spoon round the centre of the ring so that the different cake mixtures are slightly swirled together.
5 Bake for 25–30 minutes until the cake springs back when pressed lightly and a skewer inserted into the cake comes out clean. Remove the cake from the oven and leave to stand for 5 minutes, then turn out on to a wire rack and leave to cool.

048 German Sand Cake

PREPARATION TIME 20 minutes   **COOKING TIME** 40–45 minutes   **MAKES** 20 slices

200g/7oz butter, melted and cooled,
  plus extra for greasing
75g/2½oz digestive biscuits,
  roughly broken
6 large eggs
225g/8oz/scant 1 cup caster sugar

125g/4½oz/scant 1 cup plain flour
2 tsp baking powder
100g/3½oz/scant ⅔ cup plain
  chocolate chips
6 tbsp natural yogurt
1 tsp vanilla extract

1 Preheat the oven to 180°C/350°F/gas 4. Grease and line a 38 x 25 x 6cm/15 x 10 x 2½in baking tin.
2 Put the broken biscuits in a food processor and pulse to fine crumbs. Alternatively, put them in a plastic bag and crush with a rolling pin. Sprinkle the biscuit crumbs over the base of the tin.
3 Put the eggs and sugar in a mixing bowl and whisk with an electric hand mixer or whisk until doubled in size and very creamy, and the whisk leaves a trail when lifted up. Slowly pour in the melted butter while still whisking. Sift in the flour and baking powder and gently fold them, the chocolate chips, yogurt and vanilla extract into the mixture, using a large metal spoon. Spoon the mixture over the crumb base in the tin using a spatula.
4 Bake for 40–45 minutes until the cake springs back when pressed lightly and a skewer inserted into the middle of the cake comes out clean. Remove the cake from the oven and leave to stand for 5 minutes, then invert on to a wire rack and leave to cool.

049 Coffee Streusel Layer Cake

PREPARATION TIME 25 minutes   **COOKING TIME** 1–1½ hours   **SERVES** 8

115g/4oz butter, softened, plus extra
  for greasing
115g/4oz/scant ½ cup caster sugar
2 large eggs, lightly beaten
175g/6oz/heaped 1 cup self-raising flour,
  sifted
4 tbsp milk
1 tbsp instant coffee granules dissolved
  in 1 tbsp boiling water and cooled

100g/3½oz/⅔ cup icing sugar, sifted
30g/1oz/¼ cup walnut pieces

FOR THE STREUSEL
85g/3oz/⅔ cup walnut pieces
1 level tbsp instant coffee granules
115g/4oz/½ cup soft brown sugar
2 tbsp plain flour
30g/1oz butter, melted and cooled

1 Preheat the oven to 160°C/325°F/gas 3. Grease and line a 20cm/8in loose-bottomed square cake tin.
2 For the streusel, put the walnuts, coffee granules, sugar and flour into a blender and whizz to a fine powder. Pour the melted butter into the blender and mix together. Set aside.
3 Put the softened butter and caster sugar in a mixing bowl and beat using an electric hand mixer or wooden spoon until the mixture is light and creamy. Add the eggs gradually, beating after each addition. Add the flour and milk and gently fold them into the mixture, using a large metal spoon.
4 Scrape half the cake mixture into the cake tin using a spatula and sprinkle over half the streusel, covering the cake mixture completely. Top with the remaining cake mixture and sprinkle over the remaining streusel.
5 Bake for 1–1½ hours until the cake springs back when pressed lightly and a skewer inserted into the middle of the cake comes out clean. Remove the cake from the oven and leave to stand for 5 minutes, then turn out on to a wire rack.
6 Meanwhile, in a bowl stir the coffee liquid and the icing sugar together to form a thick, smooth icing, adding a little more hot water if needed.
7 Drizzle the icing over the top of the cake in lines and sprinkle the walnut pieces over the cake before serving.

050 Orange Sultana Drizzle Cake

PREPARATION TIME 20 minutes **COOKING TIME** 30–35 minutes **SERVES** 8

115g/4oz butter, softened, plus extra
    for greasing
280g/10oz/heaped 1 cup caster sugar
2 large eggs, lightly beaten
225g/8oz/1½ cups self-raising flour,
    sifted

150ml/5fl oz/scant ⅔ cup milk
175g/6oz/heaped ⅔ cup sultanas
55g/2oz/heaped ⅓ cup flaked almonds
juice and finely grated zest of
    1 large orange
juice and finely grated zest of 1 lemon

1   Preheat the oven to 180°C/350°F/gas 4. Grease and line a 23cm/9in loose-bottomed
    square cake tin.
2   Put the butter and 225g/8oz/scant 1 cup of the sugar in a mixing bowl and beat using
    an electric hand mixer or wooden spoon until the mixture is light and creamy. Add the
    eggs gradually, beating after each addition. Add the flour, milk, sultanas, almonds and
    orange and lemon zests and gently fold them into the mixture, using a large metal
    spoon. Scrape the mixture into the tin using a spatula.
3   Bake for 25–30 minutes until the cake springs back when pressed lightly and a skewer
    inserted into the middle of the cake comes out clean. Remove the cake from the oven
    and turn out on to a wire rack.
4   Put the lemon and orange juice and the remaining sugar in a small saucepan and heat
    until the sugar has dissolved, then boil for 1 minute to create a syrup. Spoon the syrup
    over the cake while it is still warm, then leave to cool completely.

051 Cinnamon Drizzle Cake

PREPARATION TIME 20 minutes   **COOKING TIME** 35–40 minutes   **SERVES** 8

175g/6oz butter, softened, plus extra
  for greasing
85g/3oz/⅓ cup caster sugar
85g/3oz/⅓ cup dark muscovado sugar
3 large eggs, lightly beaten

175g/6oz/heaped 1 cup self-raising flour
1 heaped tsp cinnamon
125ml/4fl oz/½ cup maple syrup
1 cinnamon stick

1   Preheat the oven to 180°C/350°F/gas 4. Grease and line a 24 x 12cm/9½ x 4½in loaf tin.
2   Put the butter, caster sugar and muscovado sugar in a mixing bowl and beat using an
    electric hand mixer or wooden spoon until the mixture is light and creamy. Add the eggs
    gradually, beating after each addition. Sift in the flour and cinnamon and gently fold them
    into the mixture, using a large metal spoon. Scrape the mixture into the tin using a spatula.
3   Bake for 35–40 minutes until the cake springs back when pressed lightly and a skewer
    inserted into the middle of the cake comes out clean.
4   Just before the cake comes out of the oven, put the maple syrup, cinnamon stick and
    3 tablespoons water in a small saucepan and heat gently for 5 minutes until the syrup
    smells of cinnamon. Remove the cinnamon stick.
5   Remove the cake from the oven and pour the syrup over the cake. Leave the cake to cool
    in the tin, then turn out on to a serving plate. Place the cinnamon stick on the cake to
    decorate, if wished, but remove it before cutting.

052 Cinnamon Banana Loaf Cake

PREPARATION TIME 20 minutes   **COOKING TIME** 40–45 minutes   **SERVES** 8

115g/4oz butter, softened, plus extra
  for greasing
175g/6oz/¾ cup dark soft brown sugar
3 ripe bananas, peeled and mashed with
  a fork

2 large eggs, lightly beaten
225g/8oz/1½ cups self-raising flour
1 tsp baking powder
1 tsp cinnamon
115g/4oz/scant 1 cup chopped walnuts

1   Preheat the oven to 180°C/350°F/gas 4. Grease and line a 24 x 12cm/9½ x 4½in loaf tin.
2   Put the butter and sugar in a mixing bowl and beat using an electric hand mixer or wooden
    spoon until the mixture is light and creamy. Add the bananas and eggs and beat again.
3   Sift in the flour, baking powder and cinnamon and gently fold them and the walnuts into
    the mixture, using a large metal spoon. Scrape the mixture into the tin using a spatula.
4   Bake for 40–45 minutes until the cake springs back when pressed lightly and a skewer
    inserted into the middle of the cake comes out clean. Remove the cake from the oven
    and leave to stand for 5 minutes, then turn out on to a wire rack and leave to cool.

053　Date & Walnut Loaf Cake

PREPARATION TIME 25 minutes　**COOKING TIME** 45–50 minutes　**SERVES** 8

175g/6oz butter, softened, plus extra
　for greasing
175g/6oz/¾ cup light soft brown sugar
3 large eggs, lightly beaten
175g/6oz/heaped 1 cup self-raising flour,
　sifted

100g/3½oz/heaped ½ cup dates,
　chopped
100g/3½oz/heaped ½ cup walnuts,
　chopped
200ml/7fl oz/¾ cup maple syrup

1　Preheat the oven to 180°C/350°F/gas 4. Grease and line a 24 x 12cm/9½ x 4½in loaf tin.
2　Put the butter and sugar in a mixing bowl and beat using an electric hand mixer or wooden spoon until the mixture is light and creamy. Add the eggs gradually, beating after each addition. Add the flour, dates, walnuts and half the maple syrup and gently fold them into the mixture, using a large metal spoon. Scrape the mixture into the tin using a spatula.
3　Bake for 45–50 minutes until the cake springs back when pressed lightly and a skewer inserted into the middle of the cake comes out clean.
4　Just before the cake comes out of the oven, heat the remaining maple syrup in a small saucepan for a few minutes. Remove the cake from the oven and pour the syrup over the cake. Leave the cake to cool in the tin, then turn out on to a serving plate.

054　Date & Raisin Drizzle Cake

PREPARATION TIME 20 minutes, plus soaking　**COOKING TIME** 1–1¼ hours　**SERVES** 8

150ml/5fl oz/scant ⅔ cup maple syrup
100g/3½oz/½ cup raisins
175g/6oz butter, plus extra for greasing
175g/6oz/¾ cup light soft brown sugar
3 large eggs, lightly beaten

175g/6oz/heaped 1 cup self-raising flour
1 tsp cinnamon
100g/3½oz/heaped ½ cup dates,
　chopped

1　Put the maple syrup in a saucepan with the raisins, bring to the boil, then leave for 1 hour to cool so the raisins soak up some of the syrup.
2　Preheat the oven to 180°C/350°F/gas 4. Grease and line a 24 x 12cm/9½ x 4½in loaf tin.
3　Put the butter and sugar in a mixing bowl and beat using an electric hand mixer or wooden spoon until the mixture is light and creamy. Add the eggs gradually, beating after each addition. Sift in the flour and cinnamon and gently fold them into the mixture with the dates, using a large metal spoon. Strain the raisins, reserving the maple syrup to glaze the cake, and fold the soaked raisins into the mixture. Scrape the mixture into the tin using a spatula.
4　Bake for 1–1¼ hours until the cake springs back when pressed lightly and a skewer inserted into the middle of the cake comes out clean. Remove the cake from the oven and spoon the maple syrup over the top. Leave the cake to cool in the tin, then turn out on to a serving plate.

055 Lavender Drizzle Cake

PREPARATION TIME 20 minutes   **COOKING TIME** 25–30 minutes   **SERVES** 8

225g/8oz butter, softened, plus extra
  for greasing
225g/8oz/scant 1 cup caster sugar
4 large eggs, lightly beaten

225g/8oz/1½ cups self-raising flour,
  sifted
juice and finely grated zest of 2 lemons
1 heaped tbsp icing sugar, sifted
2 tsp culinary lavender

1   Preheat the oven to 190°C/375°F/gas 5. Grease and line a 25cm/10in springform cake tin.
2   Put the butter and caster sugar in a mixing bowl and whisk using an electric hand mixer
    or wooden spoon until the mixture is light and creamy. Add the eggs gradually, beating
    after each addition. Add the flour and lemon zest and gently fold them into the mixture,
    using a large metal spoon. Scrape the mixture into the tin using a spatula.
3   Bake for 25–30 minutes until the cake springs back when pressed lightly and a skewer
    inserted into the middle of the cake comes out clean.
4   Just before the cake comes out of the oven, heat the lemon juice with the icing sugar
    and lavender in a saucepan until the sugar has dissolved, then boil for 1 minute to make
    a syrup. Remove the cake from the oven and pour the syrup over the cake. Leave the
    cake to cool in the tin, then turn out on to a serving plate.

056 Sticky White Chocolate & Marmalade Loaf

PREPARATION TIME 15 minutes   **COOKING TIME** 40–45 minutes   **SERVES** 8

175g/6oz butter, softened, plus extra
  for greasing
175g/6oz/¾ cup light soft brown sugar
3 large eggs, lightly beaten
175g/6oz/heaped 1 cup self-raising flour,
  sifted

3 tbsp thin-shred marmalade
finely grated zest of 1 orange
100g/3½oz white chocolate,
  coarsely chopped

1   Preheat the oven to 180°C/350°F/gas 4. Grease and line a 24 x 12cm/9½ x 4½in loaf tin.
2   Put the butter and sugar in a mixing bowl and beat using an electric hand mixer or
    wooden spoon until the mixture is light and creamy. Add the eggs gradually, beating after
    each addition. Add the flour and gently fold it into the mixture, using a large metal
    spoon, then fold in 2 tablespoons of the marmalade, the orange zest and white
    chocolate. Scrape the mixture into the tin using a spatula.
3   Bake for 35–40 minutes until the cake springs back when pressed lightly and a skewer
    inserted into the middle of the cake comes out clean.
4   Remove the cake from the oven and leave to stand for 5 minutes, then turn out on to a
    wire rack. Heat the remaining marmalade in a small saucepan, then brush it over the
    top of the cake to glaze. Leave to cool.

057 Maple Apple Loaf

PREPARATION TIME 20 minutes **COOKING TIME** 45–50 minutes **SERVES** 8

175g/6oz butter, softened, plus extra
  for greasing
175g/6oz/¾ cup light soft brown sugar
3 large eggs, lightly beaten
175g/6oz/heaped 1 cup self-raising flour,
  sifted
2 tbsp natural yogurt

1 large cooking apple, peeled, cored
  and grated
100g/3½oz/heaped ½ cup
  sultanas
55g/2oz/½ cup walnuts, chopped
2 tbsp maple syrup

1 Preheat the oven to 190°C/375°F/gas 5. Grease and line a 24 x 12cm/9½ x 4½in loaf tin.
2 Put the butter and light brown sugar in a mixing bowl and beat using an electric hand
  mixer or wooden spoon until the mixture is light and creamy. Add the eggs gradually,
  beating after each addition. Add the flour, yogurt, grated apple, sultanas and walnuts
  and gently fold them into the mixture, using a large metal spoon. Scrape the mixture into
  the tin using a spatula.
3 Bake for 45–50 minutes until the cake springs back when pressed lightly and a skewer
  inserted into the middle of the cake comes out clean.
4 Just before the cake comes out of the oven, warm the maple syrup gently in a saucepan.
  Remove the cake from the oven and pour the syrup over the cake. Leave the cake to cool
  in the tin, then turn out on to a serving plate.

058 Carrot Loaf Cake

PREPARATION TIME 20 minutes **COOKING TIME** 50–60 minutes **SERVES** 8

125ml/4fl oz/½ cup vegetable oil,
  plus extra for greasing
2 large eggs, lightly beaten
125ml/4fl oz/½ cup natural yogurt
250g/9oz/1 cup light soft brown sugar
180g/6¼oz/1¼ cups plain flour
1 tsp mixed spice
1 tsp cinnamon

1 tsp bicarbonate of soda
2 large carrots, peeled and grated
½ tsp salt
100g/3½oz/heaped ½ cup pecan nuts,
  roughly chopped
juice and finely grated zest of 1 orange
2 tbsp icing sugar, sifted
crème fraîche or whipped cream, to serve

1 Preheat the oven to 160°C/325°F/gas 3. Grease and line a 24 x 12cm/9½ x 4½in loaf tin.
2 Put the eggs, oil, yogurt and light brown sugar in a mixing bowl and whisk with an
  electric hand mixer or a whisk to combine all the ingredients. Sift in the flour, spices and
  bicarbonate of soda and fold in with the grated carrots, salt, pecans and orange zest,
  using a large metal spoon. Scrape the mixture into the tin using a spatula.
3 Bake for 50–60 minutes until the cake springs back when pressed lightly and a skewer
  inserted into the middle of the cake comes out clean.
4 Just before the cake comes out of the oven, heat the orange juice and icing sugar in a
  small saucepan until the sugar has dissolved, then boil for 1 minute to create a syrup.
  Remove the cake from the oven and pour the syrup over the cake. Leave the cake to cool
  in the tin, then turn out on to a serving plate and serve with crème fraîche or cream.

059 Carrot & Courgette Cake

PREPARATION TIME 25 minutes **COOKING TIME** 1½–1¾ hours **SERVES** 8

185ml/6fl oz/¾ cup vegetable oil, plus extra for greasing
3 large carrots, peeled
100g/3½oz/⅔ cup icing sugar, sifted
3 large eggs, lightly beaten
100ml/3½fl oz/scant ½ cup soured cream
200g/7oz/1 cup lightly packed dark muscovado sugar
150g/5½oz/scant ⅔ cup caster sugar
250g/9oz/1⅔ cups plain flour
1 tsp mixed spice
1 tsp bicarbonate of soda

1 courgette, trimmed and grated
100g/3½oz/heaped ½ cup chopped walnuts
finely grated zest of 1 lemon
finely grated zest of 1 orange
100g/3½oz/heaped 1 cup desiccated coconut

FOR THE ICING
150g/5½oz cream cheese
300g/10½oz/2 cups icing sugar, sifted
55g/2oz butter, softened
1 tbsp lemon juice

1. Preheat the oven to 160°C/325°F/gas 3. Grease and line a deep 23cm/9in springform cake tin.
2. Shred 1 of the carrots into strips using a zester for the candied carrot decoration and put in a saucepan with 100ml/3½fl oz/scant ½ cup water and the icing sugar. Bring to the boil, then drain and set aside to cool.
3. Put the eggs, oil, soured cream, muscovado sugar and caster sugar in a mixing bowl and whisk with an electric hand mixer or a whisk to combine all the ingredients. Sift in the flour, mixed spice and bicarbonate of soda, grate the remaining carrots and add with the courgette, walnuts, lemon and orange zest and coconut and fold them in, using a large metal spoon until mixed well. Scrape the mixture into the cake tin using a spatula.
4. Bake for about 1½–1¾ hours until the cake springs back when pressed lightly and a skewer inserted into the middle of the cake comes out clean. Remove the cake from the oven and leave to stand for 5 minutes, then turn out on to a wire rack and leave to cool.
5. Put the icing ingredients in a bowl and beat together using an electric hand mixer or wooden spoon until light and creamy. Spread the icing over the top of the cake and decorate with the candied carrot.

Farmhouse Fruit Cake

PREPARATION TIME 20 minutes   **COOKING TIME** 45–60 minutes   **SERVES** 8

115g/4oz butter, softened, plus extra
  for greasing
115g/4oz/½ cup light soft brown sugar
3 large eggs, lightly beaten
225g/8oz/1½ cups self-raising flour
1 tsp mixed spice

½ tsp salt
175g/6oz/1 cup mixed dried fruit
30g/1oz/scant ¼ cup glacé cherries,
  halved
85g/3oz/½ cup flaked almonds

1   Preheat the oven to 180°C/350°F/gas 4. Grease and line an 18cm/7in springform cake tin.
2   Put the butter and sugar in a mixing bowl and beat using an electric hand mixer or
    wooden spoon until the mixture is light and creamy. Add the eggs gradually, beating after
    each addition. Sift in the flour and mixed spice and gently fold them into the mixture
    with the salt, mixed dried fruit, cherries and almonds, using a large metal spoon. Scrape
    the mixture into the tin using a spatula.
3   Bake for 45–60 minutes until the cake springs back when pressed lightly and a skewer
    inserted into the middle of the cake comes out clean. Remove the cake from the oven
    and leave to cool in the tin, then turn out on to a serving plate.

061 Dundee Cake

PREPARATION TIME 20 minutes, plus soaking   COOKING TIME 2–2¼ hours   SERVES 8

225g/8oz butter, softened, plus extra for greasing
30g/1oz/¼ cup blanched whole almonds
3 tbsp milk
225g/8oz/scant 1 cup caster sugar
4 large eggs, lightly beaten
280g/10oz/scant 2 cups self-raising flour, sifted
juice and finely grated zest of 1 lemon

finely grated zest of 1 orange and half the juice
400g/14oz/2 cups mixed dried fruit, such as raisins, currants and sultanas
100g/3½oz/½ cup glacé cherries, chopped
100g/3½oz/heaped ½ cup mixed peel
1 tsp almond extract
2 tbsp apricot jam

1   Preheat the oven to 160°C/325°F/gas 3. Grease and line a deep 20cm/8in springform cake tin. Put the almonds in a bowl with the milk and soak for 20 minutes.

2   Put the butter and sugar in a mixing bowl and beat using an electric hand mixer or wooden spoon until the mixture is light and creamy. Add the eggs gradually, beating after each addition. Add the flour, lemon and orange zests, mixed dried fruit, cherries, mixed peel and almond extract and gently fold them into the mixture, using a large metal spoon. Scrape the mixture into the tin using a spatula and arrange the soaked almonds over the top of the cake in a circular pattern.

3   Bake for about 2–2¼ hours until the cake springs back when pressed lightly and a skewer inserted into the middle of the cake comes out clean.

4   Remove the cake from the oven and leave to stand for 5 minutes, then turn out on to a wire rack. Put the lemon and orange juice and jam in a small saucepan over a gentle heat and stir until melted, then brush the apricot glaze over the top of the cake. Leave to cool.

062 Earl Grey Tea Bread

PREPARATION TIME 20 minutes, plus soaking   COOKING TIME 1–1¼ hours   SERVES 8

115g/4oz/heaped ½ cup sultanas
250ml/9fl oz/1 cup black Earl Grey tea
55g/2oz chilled butter, chopped, plus extra for greasing
225g/8oz/1½ cups self-raising flour

1 tsp baking powder
55g/2oz/¼ cup dark soft brown sugar
finely grated zest of 1 lemon
finely grated zest of 1 orange
2 large eggs, lightly beaten

1   Soak the sultanas in the tea for about 3 hours. Preheat the oven to 160°C/325°F/gas 3. Grease and line a 24 x 12cm/9½ x 4½in loaf tin.

2   Sift the flour and baking powder into a mixing bowl. Add the butter and rub it into the flour with your fingertips until the mixture resembles fine breadcrumbs.

3   Stir in the soaked sultanas and tea, the sugar, lemon and orange zests and eggs and beat well with a wooden spoon to combine all the ingredients. Scrape the mixture into the tin using a spatula.

4   Bake for 1–1¼ hours until the tea bread springs back when pressed lightly and a skewer inserted into the middle of the loaf comes out clean. Remove the loaf from the oven and leave to stand for 5 minutes, then turn out on to a wire rack and leave to cool.

063 Cut & Come Again Cake

PREPARATION TIME 25 minutes **COOKING TIME** 1¼–1½ hours **SERVES** 8

115g/4oz chilled butter, chopped, plus extra for greasing
225g/8oz/1½ cups self-raising flour
1 tsp baking powder
1 tsp mixed spice
1 tsp cinnamon
115g/4oz/½ cup light soft brown sugar
200g/7oz/1 cup sultanas

85g/3oz/heaped ⅓ cup dried apricots, chopped
85g/3oz/scant ½ cup glacé cherries, chopped
2 large eggs, lightly beaten
150ml/5fl oz/scant ⅔ cup milk
2 tbsp natural yogurt

1   Preheat the oven to 180°C/350°F/gas 4. Grease and line a 20cm/8in springform cake tin.
2   Sift the flour, baking powder, mixed spice and cinnamon into a mixing bowl and stir well with a wooden spoon. Add the butter and rub it into the flour mixture with your fingertips so that the mixture resembles fine breadcrumbs. Stir in the sugar, sultanas, apricots and cherries, then add the beaten eggs, milk and yogurt and mix well with a large metal spoon. Scrape the mixture into the tin using a spatula.
3   Bake for 1¼–1½ hours until the cake springs back when pressed lightly and a skewer inserted into the middle of the cake comes out clean. Remove the cake from the oven and leave to stand for 5 minutes, then turn out on to a wire rack and leave to cool.

064 Rosewater Bara Brith

PREPARATION TIME 20 minutes, plus soaking **COOKING TIME** 45–50 minutes **SERVES** 8

115g/4oz/heaped ½ cup currants
115g/4oz/heaped ½ cup sultanas
115g/4oz/heaped ½ cup raisins
400ml/14fl oz/1½ cups hot tea
2 tbsp rosewater
butter, for greasing and to serve

55g/2oz/¼ cup glacé cherries, halved
85g/3oz/⅓ cup light muscovado sugar
3 large eggs, lightly beaten
400g/14oz/2⅔ cups self-raising flour
1 tsp mixed spice
1 tsp cinnamon

1   Soak the currants, sultanas and raisins in the hot tea and rosewater in a mixing bowl overnight so that they become plump and absorb some of the liquid.
2   Preheat the oven to 180°C/350°F/gas 4. Grease and line a 23cm/9in loose-bottomed square cake tin.
3   Strain the fruit, retaining the liquid, and put the fruit in a mixing bowl. Stir in the cherries, sugar and eggs and sift in the flour, mixed spice and cinnamon, mixing well with a large metal spoon. Slowly pour in the soaking liquid and mix in well. Scrape the mixture into the tin using a spatula.
4   Bake for 45–50 minutes until the cake springs back when pressed lightly and a skewer inserted into the middle of the cake comes out clean. Remove the cake from the oven and leave to cool in the tin, then turn out on to a serving plate. Serve slices spread with butter.

065 Coffee Battenberg

PREPARATION TIME 40 minutes   **COOKING TIME** 20–25 minutes   **SERVES** 8

250g/9oz butter, softened, plus extra
    for greasing
175g/6oz/scant ¾ cup caster sugar
3 large eggs, lightly beaten
175g/6oz/heaped 1 cup self-raising flour
1 tsp baking powder

1 tbsp cocoa powder
1 tbsp instant coffee granules dissolved
    in 2 tbsp boiling water, then cooled
150g/5½oz/1 cup icing sugar, sifted,
    plus extra for dusting
400g/14oz white marzipan

1   Preheat the oven to 190°F/375°C/gas 5. Grease and line two 24 x 12cm/9½ x 4½in
    loaf tins.
2   Put the 175g/6oz of the butter and the sugar in a mixing bowl and beat using an electric
    hand mixer or wooden spoon until the mixture is light and creamy. Add the eggs gradually,
    beating after each addition. Sift in the flour and baking powder and gently fold them into
    the mixture, using a large metal spoon.
3   Scrape half the mixture into one of the tins using a spatula. Add the cocoa and half the
    coffee liquid to the remaining mixture and scrape that into the other tin.
4   Bake for 20–25 minutes until the cakes spring back when pressed lightly and a skewer
    inserted into the middle of each cake comes out clean. Remove the cakes from the oven
    and leave to stand for 5 minutes, then turn out on to a wire rack and leave to cool.
5   Put the icing sugar, remaining butter and remaining coffee liquid in a bowl and beat
    using an electric hand mixer or wooden spoon to make a smooth buttercream.
6   When the cakes have cooled, cut each cake in half lengthways and trim the four cakes
    with a knife so you have four equal-sized rectangular cakes. Sandwich the cakes
    together with a thin layer of buttercream in alternate colours to make a large rectangle.
    Cover the outside of the cake with a thin layer of buttercream.
7   Sift icing sugar on to a clean work surface and roll the marzipan out to 5mm/¼in thick
    into a rectangle with a width as long as the cake and a length just over four times the
    width of the cake, using a rolling pin. Trim the edges of the marzipan and wrap it around
    the cake, smoothing it down with your hands, making a firm join and pinching the
    corners to neaten them. Place the cake on a serving plate with the join underneath.

066 Strawberry & Vanilla Swiss Roll

PREPARATION TIME 20 minutes **COOKING TIME** 10–12 minutes **SERVES** 8

butter, for greasing
3 large eggs, lightly beaten
100g/3½oz/heaped ⅓ cup caster sugar
125g/4½oz/scant 1 cup self-raising flour,
   sifted
1 tsp vanilla extract

3 tbsp icing sugar, sifted
240ml/8fl oz/scant 1 cup double cream,
   whipped to stiff peaks
3 tbsp strawberry jam
200g/7oz/2 cups strawberries, hulled
   and sliced

1 Preheat the oven to 180°C/350°F/gas 4. Grease and line a 30 x 20cm/12 x 8in Swiss roll tin.
2 Put the eggs and caster sugar in a mixing bowl and whisk together using an electric hand mixer or a whisk until they are creamy and pale yellow and the whisk leaves a trail when lifted up. Add the flour and vanilla extract and fold them in, using a large metal spoon. Scrape the mixture into the tin using a spatula.
3 Bake for 10–12 minutes until the cake springs back when pressed lightly. Remove the cake from the oven and leave for a few minutes.
4 Put a sheet of baking parchment on a clean work surface and dust with the icing sugar. Turn the cake out on to the sugar-covered paper, cover with a damp tea towel and leave to cool for 10 minutes. Remove the tea towel and lining paper and cut away the edges of the cake to neaten it. Roll the cake up from a short end using the sugar-covered paper to help you and leave to cool completely. (The paper will end up rolled inside the cake.)
5 Unroll the cake, spread the cream and jam over and cover with the strawberries. Roll the Swiss roll up, using the paper to help you but this time not rolling it inside the cake, and place on a serving plate. As the Swiss roll contains fresh cream, it should be eaten straightaway or stored in a lidded container in the fridge.

067 Caramel Angel Food Cake

PREPARATION TIME 20 minutes **COOKING TIME** 30–35 minutes **SERVES** 8

butter, for greasing
125g/4½oz/scant 1 cup plain flour
375g/13oz/heaped 2 cups golden
   icing sugar, plus extra for dusting

10 large egg whites
½ tsp cream of tartar
3 tbsp maple syrup,
   plus extra to serve

1 Preheat the oven to 190°C/375°F/gas 5. Grease a 25cm/10in angel food cake tin.
2 Sift the flour and icing sugar together 3 or 4 times until they are very light and airy. Put the egg whites in a clean, dry bowl and whisk with an electric hand mixer or a whisk until they form stiff peaks. Add the cream of tartar and whisk again for 1 minute, then gently fold the egg whites into the flour and sugar mixture, using a large metal spoon. Stir in the maple syrup, then scrape the mixture into the tin using a spatula.
3 Bake for 30–35 minutes until the cake springs back when pressed lightly and a skewer inserted into the middle of the cake comes out clean. Remove the cake from the oven and leave to stand for 5 minutes, then turn out on to a wire rack and leave to cool. Dust the cake with icing sugar and serve slices with extra maple syrup drizzled over.

068 Pistachio Marzipan Ring

PREPARATION TIME 25 minutes, plus rising **COOKING TIME** 25–30 minutes **SERVES** 8

55g/2oz butter, melted and cooled,
  plus extra for greasing and to serve
450g/1lb/3 cups strong white bread
  flour, sifted, plus extra for dusting
1 tsp salt
2 tsp fast action dried yeast

2 tbsp sugar
2 large eggs, beaten
55g/2oz marzipan, grated or finely
  chopped
100g/3½oz/heaped ½ cup pistachio
  nuts, chopped

1 Grease a 23cm/9in ring tin and dust with flour.
2 Put the flour, salt, yeast and sugar in a large mixing bowl and make a well in the middle. Add the beaten eggs, melted butter and 170ml/5½fl oz/⅔ cup warm water and bring together with your hands to form a soft dough.
3 Sift flour on to a clean work surface and turn the dough out. Knead well, then leave to rest for 10 minutes before adding the grated marzipan and chopped pistachios and kneading for a further 5–6 minutes. Put the dough in the tin, cover with a damp tea towel and leave in a warm place to rise for about 1 hour or until the dough has doubled in size. Preheat the oven to 180°C/350°F/gas 4.
4 Bake for 25–30 minutes until the bread is golden. Remove the cake from the oven and tip it out upside down on to a wire rack. Tap it with a knuckle, and, if it sounds hollow, it is ready. (If it does not sound hollow, return it to the oven for 5 minutes longer, then test it again.) Turn right-way up on the rack and leave to cool slightly, then slice and serve warm with butter.

069 Lardy Cake

PREPARATION TIME 30 minutes, plus rising **COOKING TIME** 25–35 minutes **SERVES** 8

115g/4oz butter, half chilled and
  chopped; half melted, plus extra
  for greasing
2 tsp fast action dried yeast
225g/8oz/scant 1 cup caster sugar
125ml/4fl oz/½ cup warm milk

1 pinch saffron stamens
225g/8oz/1½ cups plain flour, sifted,
  plus extra for dusting
1 large egg, lightly beaten
1 tsp cinnamon
150g/5½oz/heaped ⅔ cup currants

1 Grease a 20cm/8in loose-bottomed square cake tin.
2 Put the yeast in a cup with 1 tablespoon of the sugar and the warm milk and saffron and leave for 10 minutes until the mixture is foamy.
3 Put the flour into a large mixing bowl, add the chilled butter and rub it into the flour with your fingertips until the mixture resembles fine breadcrumbs. Add the yeast mixture and beaten egg to the flour and mix in with your hands to form a soft dough. Add a little more flour if the dough is too sticky.
4 Sift flour on to a clean work surface and knead the dough vigorously for 8 minutes. Roll the dough out into a 40 x 20cm/16 x 8in rectangle and brush with a third of the melted butter. Sprinkle over a third of the remaining sugar, cinnamon and currants. Fold the dough in half and seal the sides by pressing tightly with your fingers. Roll the dough into a rectangle again and repeat the rolling and folding twice more so that you have made 3 layers of butter and currants in the dough and finish with a 20cm/8in square of dough.
5 Put the dough in the tin, cover with a damp tea towel and leave in a warm place for about 1 hour until the dough has doubled in size. Preheat the oven to 180°C/350°F/gas 4.
6 Bake for 25–35 minutes until the cake is golden. Remove the cake from the oven and tip it out upside down on to a wire rack. Tap it with a knuckle, and, if it sounds hollow, it is ready. (If it does not sound hollow, return it to the oven for 5 minutes, then try again.) Turn right-way up on the rack and leave to cool completely.

CHAPTER 2

SMALL CAKES

This chapter contains a wide variety of small and dainty cakes, perfect for afternoon teas, parties or lunch boxes. Pretty cake stands and plates laden with small cakes and delicacies can't fail to delight – try Amaretto & Hazelnut Fondant Fancies, Banoffi Choux Buns and Chocolate Éclairs. These are afternoon treats that will delight any guest. Cupcakes and muffins are hugely popular and always disappear quickly, especially when served still warm from the oven. From plain but highly flavoured Peshwari Cupcakes to indulgent Rocky Road Cupcakes, and from Toffee Popcorn Muffins to Triple Chocolate Muffins, there is something to suit all tastes. There are traditional Iced Cherry Cupcakes and more unusual Lemongrass & Soured Cream Mini Loaf Cakes, dainty Orange Syrup Friands and scones in a wide variety of flavours. Most of these recipes can be prepared very quickly, making them perfect for visitors, for children coming home from school or to sell at school bazaars and summer fêtes.

BANOFFI CHOUX BUNS *(SEE PAGE 95)*

070 Lemon & Apricot Muffins

PREPARATION TIME 20 minutes   **COOKING TIME** 25–30 minutes   **MAKES** 10 muffins

250g/9oz/1⅔ cups self-raising flour
2 tsp baking powder
1 tsp bicarbonate of soda
100g/3½oz/heaped ⅓ cup caster sugar
100g/3½oz/½ cup dried apricots, chopped
juice and finely grated zest of 1 lemon

150ml/5fl oz/scant ⅔ cup milk
4 tbsp natural yogurt
100g/3½oz butter, melted and cooled
3 tbsp apricot jam, warmed
2 large eggs, lightly beaten

1   Preheat the oven to 180°C/350°F/gas 4. Put 10 muffin cases in a 12-hole muffin tin.
2   Sift the flour, baking powder and bicarbonate of soda into a mixing bowl, add the sugar
    and stir well with a wooden spoon. Stir in the apricots and lemon zest.
3   In a separate bowl, whisk together the milk, yogurt, melted butter and 2 tablespoons of
    the jam with an electric hand mixer or a whisk. Add the eggs and whisk again. Pour the
    liquid into the bowl containing the dry ingredients and fold in with a large metal spoon.
    Do not overmix: the mixture should be thick and slightly lumpy. Spoon the mixture into
    the muffin cases.
4   Bake for 20–25 minutes until the muffins spring back when pressed lightly and a
    skewer inserted into the middle of a muffin comes out clean. Remove the muffins from
    the oven and turn out on to a wire rack.
5   Heat the remaining jam with the lemon juice in a small saucepan until the jam has
    melted, then brush this syrup over the muffins with a pastry brush. Leave to cool.

071 Cranberry & Orange Muffins

PREPARATION TIME 15 minutes   **COOKING TIME** 15–20 minutes   **MAKES** 10 muffins

250g/9oz/1⅔ cups self-raising flour
1 tsp baking powder
1 tsp bicarbonate of soda
100g/3½oz/heaped ⅓ cup caster sugar
100g/3½oz/¾ cup dried cranberries
juice and finely grated zest of
    1 small orange

150ml/5fl oz/scant ⅔ cup milk
4 tbsp natural yogurt
100g/3½oz butter, melted and cooled
2 large eggs, lightly beaten
2 tbsp icing sugar, sifted

1   Preheat the oven to 180°C/350°F/gas 4. Put 10 muffin cases in a 12-hole muffin tin.
2   Sift the flour, baking powder and bicarbonate of soda into a mixing bowl, add the caster
    sugar, dried cranberries and orange zest and stir well with a wooden spoon.
3   In a separate bowl, whisk together the milk, yogurt and melted butter with an electric
    hand mixer or a whisk, add the eggs and whisk again. Pour the liquid into the bowl
    containing the dry ingredients and fold in with a large metal spoon. Do not overmix:
    the mixture should be thick and slightly lumpy. Spoon the mixture into the muffin cases.
4   Bake for 15–20 minutes until the muffins spring back when pressed lightly and a
    skewer inserted into the middle of a muffin comes out clean.
5   Just before the muffins are cooked, heat the orange juice with the icing sugar in a small
    saucepan, stirring until the sugar has dissolved, then boil for 1 minute to make a syrup.
    Remove the muffins from the oven and drizzle the syrup over them. Leave to cool.

072 Blueberry Muffins

PREPARATION TIME 15 minutes **COOKING TIME** 15–20 minutes **MAKES** 10 muffins

250g/9oz/1²⁄₃ cups self-raising flour
1 tsp baking powder
1 tsp bicarbonate of soda
100g/3½oz/heaped ⅓ cup caster sugar
200g/7oz/heaped 1 cup blueberries
juice and grated zest of 1 large lemon

150ml/5fl oz/scant ²⁄₃ cup milk
4 tbsp soured cream
100g/3½oz butter, melted and cooled
2 large eggs, lightly beaten
150g/5½oz/1 cup icing sugar, sifted

1 Preheat the oven to 180°C/350°F/gas 4. Put 10 muffin cases in a 12-hole muffin tin. Sift the flour, baking powder and bicarbonate of soda into a mixing bowl, add the caster sugar, blueberries and lemon zest and stir well with a wooden spoon.
2 In a separate bowl, whisk together the milk, soured cream and melted butter with an electric hand mixer or a whisk, add the eggs and whisk again. Pour the liquid into the bowl containing the dry ingredients and fold in with a large metal spoon. Do not overmix: the mixture should be thick and slightly lumpy. Spoon the mixture into the muffin cases.
3 Bake for 15–20 minutes until the muffins spring back when pressed lightly. Remove the muffins from the oven, turn out on to a wire rack and leave to cool.
4 Put the icing sugar and 1–2 tablespoons of the lemon juice in a bowl and stir to form a smooth icing. Spoon a little of the icing over each muffin. Leave to set before serving.

073 Banana & Coconut Muffins

PREPARATION TIME 15 minutes **COOKING TIME** 20–25 minutes **MAKES** 10 muffins

115g/4oz butter, softened
55g/2oz/¼ cup dark soft brown sugar
55g/2oz/¼ cup caster sugar
2 large eggs, lightly beaten

1 large, ripe banana, peeled
2 tbsp coconut cream
55g/2oz/heaped ½ cup desiccated coconut
115g/4oz/¾ cup self-raising flour, sifted

1 Preheat the oven to 180°C/350°F/gas 4. Put 10 muffin cases in a 12-hole muffin tin.
2 Put the butter and both sugars in a mixing bowl and beat using an electric hand mixer or wooden spoon until the mixture is creamy. Add the eggs slowly, beating after each addition.
3 Put the banana and coconut cream in a separate bowl and mash them together with a fork, then stir into the cake mixture with the desiccated coconut and flour. Do not overmix: the mixture should be thick and slightly lumpy. Spoon the mixture into the muffin cases.
4 Bake for 20–25 minutes until the muffins spring back when pressed lightly and a skewer inserted into the middle of a muffin comes out clean. Remove the muffins from the oven, turn out on to a wire rack and leave to cool.

074 Coconut & Cardamom Muffins

PREPARATION TIME 15 minutes, plus soaking **COOKING TIME** 15–20 minutes **MAKES** 10 muffins

100g/3½oz/heaped 1 cup desiccated
  coconut
125ml/4fl oz/½ cup coconut milk
250g/9oz/1²⁄₃ cups self-raising flour
1 tsp baking powder
1 tsp bicarbonate of soda
100g/3½oz/heaped ⅓ cup caster sugar

½ tsp ground cardamom
100g/3½oz/heaped ½ cup white
  chocolate chips
100g/3½oz butter, melted
150ml/5fl oz/scant ²⁄₃ cup milk
4 tbsp natural yogurt
2 large eggs, lightly beaten

1 Preheat the oven to 180°C/350°F/gas 4. Put 10 muffin cases in a 12-hole muffin tin. Put the desiccated coconut and coconut milk in a bowl and leave to soak for 20 minutes.
2 Sift the flour, baking powder and bicarbonate of soda into a mixing bowl, add the sugar and stir well. Stir in the coconut, coconut milk, cardamom and white chocolate chips.
3 Put the remaining ingredients in a separate bowl and whisk together using an electric hand mixer or a whisk. Pour the liquid into the bowl containing the dry ingredients and fold in with a large metal spoon. Do not overmix: the mixture should be thick and slightly lumpy. Spoon the mixture into the muffin cases.
4 Bake for 15–20 minutes until the muffins spring back when pressed lightly. Remove the muffins from the oven, turn out on to a wire rack and leave to cool.

075 Pistachio Frangipane Muffins

PREPARATION TIME 20 minutes   **COOKING TIME** 15–20 minutes   **MAKES** 10 muffins

250g/9oz/1⅔ cups self-raising flour
1 tsp baking powder
1 tsp bicarbonate of soda
100g/3½oz/heaped ⅓ cup caster sugar
150ml/5fl oz/scant ⅔ cup milk
4 tbsp natural yogurt
100g/3½oz butter, melted and cooled
2 large eggs

1 tsp vanilla extract
200g/7oz/heaped 1 cup raspberries

FOR THE FRANGIPANE
55g/2oz butter, softened
55g/2oz/¼ cup caster sugar
55g/2oz/½ cup pistachio nuts
1 large egg
2 tbsp plain flour, sifted

1   Preheat the oven to 180°C/350°F/gas 4. Put 10 muffin cases in a 12-hole muffin tin.
2   Sift the flour, baking powder and bicarbonate of soda into a mixing bowl, add the sugar and stir well with a wooden spoon.
3   In a separate bowl, whisk together the milk, yogurt and melted butter with an electric hand mixer or a whisk, add the eggs and the vanilla extract and whisk again. Pour the liquid into the bowl containing the dry ingredients and fold in with a large metal spoon. Do not overmix: the mixture should be thick and slightly lumpy. Fold in the raspberries. Spoon the mixture into the muffin cases.
4   For the frangipane, in a separate bowl, beat together the softened butter and sugar using an electric hand mixer or a wooden spoon. Grind the pistachios to a powder using a mini blender, add to the mixture with the egg and flour and beat again. Place a heaped spoonful of the pistachio frangipane on top of each muffin.
5   Bake for 15–20 minutes until the muffins spring back when pressed lightly and a skewer inserted into the middle of a muffin comes out clean. Remove the muffins from the oven, turn out on to a wire rack and leave to cool.

076 Date & Sesame Muffins

PREPARATION TIME 15 minutes **COOKING TIME** 15–20 minutes **MAKES** 10 muffins

250g/9oz/1⅔ cups self-raising flour
1 tsp baking powder
1 tsp bicarbonate of soda
1 tsp cinnamon
100g/3½oz/heaped ½ cup pitted dates,
   chopped

100g/3½oz/heaped ⅓ cup caster sugar
2 tbsp sesame seeds
150ml/5fl oz/scant ⅔ cup milk
4 tbsp natural yogurt
100g/3½oz butter, melted
2 large eggs, lightly beaten

1 Preheat the oven to 180°C/350°F/gas 4. Put 10 muffin cases in a 12-hole muffin tin.
2 Sift the flour, baking powder, bicarbonate of soda and cinnamon into a mixing bowl, add the chopped dates, sugar and sesame seeds and stir well with a wooden spoon.
3 In a separate bowl, whisk together the milk, yogurt and melted butter with an electric hand mixer or a whisk, add the eggs and whisk again. Pour the liquid into the bowl containing the dry ingredients and fold in with a large metal spoon. Do not overmix: the mixture should be thick and slightly lumpy. Spoon the mixture into the muffin cases.
4 Bake for 15–20 minutes until the muffins spring back when pressed lightly. Remove the muffins from the oven, turn out on to a wire rack and leave to cool.

077 Muesli Muffins

PREPARATION TIME 15 minutes **COOKING TIME** 15–20 minutes **MAKES** 10 muffins

250g/9oz/1⅔ cups self-raising flour
2 tsp baking powder
1 tsp bicarbonate of soda
1 tsp cinnamon
100g/3½oz/heaped ⅓ cup caster sugar
1 small eating apple, peeled, cored
   and grated

55g/2oz/⅓ cup dried apricots, chopped
100g/3½oz/scant 1 cup muesli
150ml/5fl oz/scant ⅔ cup milk
4 tbsp natural yogurt
100g/3½oz butter, melted
2 large eggs
1 tbsp clear honey

1 Preheat the oven to 180°C/350°F/gas 4. Put 10 muffin cases in a 12-hole muffin tin.
2 Sift the flour, baking powder, bicarbonate of soda and cinnamon into a mixing bowl, add the sugar, grated apple, dried apricots and muesli and stir well with a wooden spoon.
3 In a separate bowl, whisk together the milk, yogurt and melted butter with an electric hand mixer or a whisk, add the eggs and honey and whisk again. Pour the liquid into the bowl containing the dry ingredients and fold in with a large metal spoon. Do not overmix: the mixture should be thick and slightly lumpy. Spoon the mixture into the muffin cases.
4 Bake for 15–20 minutes until the muffins spring back when pressed lightly. Remove the muffins from the oven, turn out on to a wire rack and leave to cool.

078 Cranberry & Yogurt Muffins

PREPARATION TIME 15 minutes **COOKING TIME** 15–20 minutes **MAKES** 10 muffins

250g/9oz/1⅔ cups self-raising flour
1 tsp baking powder
1 tsp bicarbonate of soda
1 tsp cinnamon
100g/3½oz/heaped ⅓ cup caster sugar

100g/3½oz/heaped ½ cup dried
   cranberries
150ml/5fl oz/scant ⅔ cup milk
2 tbsp natural yogurt
100g/3½oz butter, melted
2 large eggs, lightly beaten

1 Preheat the oven to 180°C/350°F/gas 4. Put 10 muffin cases in a 12-hole muffin tin.
2 Sift the flour, baking powder, bicarbonate of soda and cinnamon into a mixing bowl, add the caster sugar and dried cranberries and stir well with a wooden spoon.
3 In a separate bowl, whisk together the milk, yogurt and melted butter with an electric hand mixer or a whisk, add the eggs and whisk again. Pour the liquid into the bowl containing the dry ingredients and fold in with a large metal spoon. Do not overmix: the mixture should be thick and slightly lumpy. Spoon the mixture into the muffin cases.
4 Bake for 15–20 minutes until the muffins spring back when pressed lightly. Remove the muffins from the oven, turn out on to a wire rack and leave to cool.

079　Cider Apple Muffins

PREPARATION TIME 20 minutes　**COOKING TIME** 15–20 minutes　**MAKES** 10 muffins

250g/9oz/1⅔ cups self-raising flour
1 tsp baking powder
1 tsp bicarbonate of soda
2 tsp cinnamon
100g/3½oz/heaped ⅓ cup caster sugar
1 eating apple, peeled, cored and grated
55g/2oz/heaped ⅓ cup sultanas

150ml/5fl oz/scant ⅔ cup milk
2 tbsp natural yogurt
100g/3½oz butter, melted and cooled
2 large eggs, lightly beaten
100ml/3½fl oz/scant ½ cup cider
2 tbsp icing sugar

1　Preheat the oven to 180°C/350°F/gas 4. Put 10 muffin cases in a 12-hole muffin tin.
2　Sift the flour, baking powder, bicarbonate of soda and cinnamon into a mixing bowl, add the caster sugar and stir well with a wooden spoon. Stir in the grated apple and sultanas.
3　In a separate bowl, whisk together the milk, yogurt and melted butter with an electric hand mixer or a whisk, add the eggs and whisk again. Pour the liquid into the bowl containing the dry ingredients and fold in with a large metal spoon. Do not overmix: the mixture should be thick and slightly lumpy. Spoon the mixture into the muffin cases.
4　Bake for 15–20 minutes until the muffins spring back when pressed lightly.
5　Just before the muffins are cooked, heat the cider and icing sugar in a saucepan, stirring, make a syrup. Remove the muffins from the oven and drizzle the syrup over. Leave to cool.

080　Spiced Chai Muffins

PREPARATION TIME 20 minutes, plus soaking　**COOKING TIME** 20–25 minutes　**MAKES** 20 muffins

1 chai tea bag
115g/4oz/heaped ½ cup sultanas
225g/8oz butter, softened
225g/8oz/scant 1 cup caster sugar

4 large eggs, lightly beaten
225g/8oz/1½ cups self-raising flour
1 tsp baking powder
2 tsp cinnamon

1　Put the chai tea bag in a bowl with 250ml/9fl oz/1 cup hot water and the sultanas and leave to soak for 1 hour, then remove the tea bag.
2　Preheat the oven to 180°C/350°F/gas 4. Put 20 muffin cases in two 12-hole muffin tins.
3　Put the butter and sugar in a mixing bowl and beat using an electric hand mixer or wooden spoon until the mixture is light and creamy. Add the eggs gradually, beating after each addition. Sift in the flour, baking powder and cinnamon and gently fold them into the mixture, using a large wire whisk. Strain the sultanas and add to the cake mixture, folding in gently. Spoon the mixture into the muffin cases.
4　Bake for 20–25 minutes until the muffins spring back when pressed lightly. Remove the muffins from the oven, turn out on to a wire rack and leave to cool.

081　Triple Chocolate Muffins

PREPARATION TIME 15 minutes　**COOKING TIME** 15–20 minutes　**MAKES** 10 muffins

200g/7oz/scant 1½ cups self-raising flour
4 tbsp cocoa powder
1 tsp baking powder
1 tsp bicarbonate of soda
100g/3½oz/heaped ⅓ cup caster sugar
150ml/5fl oz/scant ⅔ cup milk

4 tbsp natural yogurt
100g/3½oz butter, melted
2 large eggs, lightly beaten
100g/3½oz nougat chocolate, chopped
100g/3½oz/scant ⅔ cup white
　chocolate chips

1　Preheat the oven to 180°C/350°F/gas 4. Put 10 muffin cases in a 12-hole muffin tin. Sift the flour, cocoa, baking powder and bicarbonate of soda into a mixing bowl, add the sugar and stir well with a wooden spoon.
2　In a separate bowl, whisk together the milk, yogurt and melted butter with an electric hand mixer or a whisk, add the eggs and whisk again. Pour the liquid into the bowl containing the dry ingredients and fold in with a large metal spoon. Add the chopped chocolate and white chocolate chips and stir again. Do not overmix: the mixture should be thick and slightly lumpy. Spoon the mixture into the muffin cases.
3　Bake for 15–20 minutes until the muffins spring back when pressed lightly. Remove the muffins from the oven, turn out on to a wire rack and leave to cool.

082 Mocha Walnut Muffins

PREPARATION TIME 30 minutes   **COOKING TIME** 15–20 minutes   **MAKES** 20 muffins

450g/1lb butter, softened
225g/8oz/scant 1 cup caster sugar
4 large eggs, lightly beaten
225g/8oz/1½ cups self-raising flour, sifted
200g/7oz/1 cup walnuts, chopped

1 tbsp instant coffee granules dissolved in 1 tbsp boiling water, then cooled
100g/3½oz/heaped ½ cup plain chocolate chips
450g/1lb/3 cups icing sugar, sifted
225g/8oz cream cheese

1   Preheat the oven to 180°C/350°F/gas 4. Put 20 muffin cases in two 12-hole muffin tins.
2   Put 225g/8oz of the butter and the caster sugar in a mixing bowl and beat using an electric hand mixer or wooden spoon until the mixture is light and creamy. Add the eggs gradually, beating after each addition. Add the flour, half the walnuts, the coffee liquid and chocolate chips and gently fold them into the mixture, using a large metal spoon. Spoon the mixture into the muffin cases.
3   Bake for 15–20 minutes until the muffins spring back when pressed lightly and a skewer inserted into the middle of a muffin comes out clean. Remove the muffins from the oven, turn out on to a wire rack and leave to cool.
4   In a bowl, beat together the icing sugar, cream cheese and remaining butter with an electric hand mixer or a wooden spoon to form a smooth icing. Spoon the icing into an icing bag fitted with a 13mm/½in star nozzle and pipe swirls on top of each muffin, then top with the remaining walnuts. (If you do not have an icing bag, spread the icing over each cake using a round-bladed knife.) Leave the icing to set before serving.

083 Toffee Popcorn Muffins

PREPARATION TIME 25 minutes   **COOKING TIME** 20–25 minutes   **MAKES** 12 muffins

250g/9oz/1⅔ cups self-raising flour
1 tsp baking powder
1 tsp bicarbonate of soda
100g/3½oz/heaped ⅓ cup caster sugar
150ml/5fl oz/scant ⅔ cup milk
150g/5½oz butter, melted and cooled

4 tbsp natural yogurt
2 large eggs, lightly beaten
3 tbsp toffee sauce
4 tbsp dark soft brown sugar
2 tbsp golden syrup
50g/1¾oz/5 cups cooked popcorn

1   Preheat the oven to 180°C/350°F/gas 4. Put 12 muffin cases in a 12-hole muffin tin.
2   Sift the flour, baking powder and bicarbonate of soda into a mixing bowl, add the caster sugar and stir well with a wooden spoon.
3   In a separate bowl, whisk together the milk, 100g/3½oz of the melted butter and the yogurt with an electric hand mixer or a whisk, add the eggs and toffee sauce and whisk again. Pour the liquid into the bowl containing the dry ingredients and fold in with a large metal spoon. Do not overmix: the mixture should be thick and slightly lumpy. Spoon the mixture into the muffin cases.
4   Bake for 15–20 minutes until the muffins spring back when pressed lightly and a skewer inserted into the middle of a muffin comes out clean. Remove the muffins from the oven, turn out on to a wire rack and leave to cool.
5   In a saucepan, heat the remaining melted butter, the dark brown sugar and syrup, stirring until the sugar has all dissolved and you have a smooth, thick caramel. Add the popcorn and stir to make sure it is all covered in the caramel. Leave to cool slightly, then place spoonfuls of the toffee popcorn on top of each muffin.

084 Moroccan Orange & Rosewater Cupcakes

PREPARATION TIME 20 minutes   **COOKING TIME** 15–20 minutes   **MAKES** 20 cakes

225g/8oz butter, softened
225g/8oz/scant 1 cup caster sugar
4 large eggs, lightly beaten
225g/8oz/1½ cups self-raising flour
2 tsp cinnamon
finely grated zest of 1 small orange,
    plus 1–2 tbsp of the juice

3 tbsp rosewater
a few drops of pink food colouring
200g/7oz/1⅓ cups icing sugar
1 recipe quantity Frosted Rose Petals
    (see page 23), to decorate

1   Preheat the oven to 180°C/350°F/gas 4. Put 20 cake cases in two 12-hole bun tins.
2   Put the butter and sugar in a mixing bowl and beat using an electric hand mixer or wooden spoon until the mixture is light and creamy. Add the eggs gradually, beating after each addition. Sift in the flour and cinnamon and gently fold them into the mixture with the orange zest and 2 tablespoons of the rosewater, using a large metal spoon. Spoon the mixture into the muffin cases.
3   Bake for 15–20 minutes until the cakes spring back when pressed lightly and a skewer inserted into the middle of a cake comes out clean. Remove the cakes from the oven, turn out on to a wire rack and leave to cool.
4   Put the orange juice, remaining rosewater, food colouring and icing sugar in a bowl and mix to a smooth icing. Spread each muffin with icing and decorate with the frosted rose petals. Leave the icing to set before serving.

085 Marmalade Cupcakes

PREPARATION TIME 20 minutes   COOKING TIME 20–25 minutes   MAKES 20 cakes

225g/8oz butter, softened
115g/4oz/scant ½ cup caster sugar
115g/4oz/½ cup dark soft brown sugar
4 large eggs, lightly beaten
225g/8oz/1½ cups self-raising flour, sifted

100g/3½oz/heaped ½ cup plain
   chocolate chips
3 tbsp thin-shred marmalade
finely grated zest of 1 orange and 1 tbsp
   of the juice

1   Preheat the oven to 180°C/350°F/gas 4. Put 20 cake cases in two 12-hole bun tins.
2   Put the butter, caster sugar and dark brown sugar in a mixing bowl and beat using an
    electric hand mixer or wooden spoon until the mixture is light and creamy. Add the eggs
    gradually, beating after each addition. Add the flour, chocolate chips, 2 tablespoons of
    the marmalade and the orange zest and gently fold them into the mixture, using a large
    metal spoon. Spoon the mixture into the cake cases.
3   Bake for 15–20 minutes until the cakes spring back when pressed lightly and a skewer
    inserted into the middle of a cake comes out clean. Remove the cakes from the oven and
    turn out on to a wire rack.
4   Heat the remaining marmalade with the orange juice until the marmalade has melted,
    then brush this glaze over the cupcakes with a pastry brush. Leave to cool.

086 Cinnamon & Chocolate Soured Cream Cupcakes

PREPARATION TIME 20 minutes   COOKING TIME 15–20 minutes   MAKES 24 cakes

225g/8oz butter, softened
225g/8oz/scant 1 cup caster sugar
4 large eggs, lightly beaten
225g/8oz/1½ cups self-raising flour
4 tbsp cocoa powder

2 tsp cinnamon
100ml/3½fl oz/scant ½ cup soured
   cream
200g/7oz plain chocolate, finely chopped

1   Preheat the oven to 190°C/375°F/gas 5. Put 24 cake cases in two 12-hole bun tins.
2   Put the butter and sugar in a mixing bowl and beat using an electric hand mixer or
    wooden spoon until the mixture is light and creamy. Add the eggs gradually, beating after
    each addition. Sift in the flour, cocoa and cinnamon and gently fold them into the mixture
    with the soured cream and chopped chocolate, using a large metal spoon. Spoon the
    mixture into the cake cases.
3   Bake for 15–20 minutes until the cakes spring back when pressed lightly and a skewer
    inserted into the middle of a cake comes out clean. Remove the cakes from the oven,
    turn out on to a wire rack and leave to cool.

087 Coffee Cupcakes

PREPARATION TIME 25 minutes   COOKING TIME 15–20 minutes   MAKES 12 cakes

115g/4oz butter, softened
115g/4oz/scant ½ cup caster sugar
2 large eggs, lightly beaten
115g/4oz/¾ cup self-raising flour, sifted

2 tbsp instant coffee granules dissolved
   in 2 tbsp boiling water, then cooled
1 recipe quantity Vanilla Buttercream
   (see page 22)
55g/2oz plain chocolate, grated

1   Preheat the oven to 180°C/350°F/gas 4. Put 12 cake cases in a 12-hole bun tin.
2   Put the butter and sugar in a mixing bowl and beat using an electric hand mixer or
    wooden spoon until the mixture is light and creamy. Add the eggs gradually, beating
    after each addition. Add the flour and half the coffee liquid and gently fold them into
    the mixture, using a large metal spoon. Spoon the mixture into the cake cases.
3   Bake for 15–20 minutes until the cakes spring back when pressed lightly and a skewer
    inserted into the middle of a cake comes out clean. Remove the cakes from the oven,
    turn out on to a wire rack and leave to cool.
4   Mix the remaining coffee liquid into the buttercream and spoon it into an icing bag fitted
    with a 13mm/½in star nozzle. Pipe the buttercream in swirls on top of each cooled cake
    and top with the grated chocolate. (If you do not have an icing bag, spread the icing over
    each cake using a round-bladed knife.) Leave the icing to set before serving.

088   Black & White Chocolate Cupcakes

PREPARATION TIME 30 minutes   **COOKING TIME** 15–20 minutes   **MAKES** 24 cakes

225g/8oz butter, softened
225g/8oz/scant 1 cup caster sugar
4 large eggs, lightly beaten
200g/7oz/1⅓ cups self-raising flour
4 tbsp cocoa powder
100g/3½oz/heaped ½ cup white
  chocolate chips

150g/5½oz plain chocolate, melted and
  cooled slightly
150g/5½oz white chocolate, melted and
  cooled slightly
6 white and 6 plain chocolate truffles,
  halved, to decorate

1   Preheat the oven to 180°C/350°F/gas 4. Put 24 cake cases in two 12-hole bun tins.
2   Put the butter and sugar in a mixing bowl and beat using an electric hand mixer or
   wooden spoon until the mixture is light and creamy. Add the eggs gradually, beating after
   each addition. Sift in the flour and cocoa and gently fold them into the mixture with the
   chocolate chips, using a large metal spoon. Spoon the mixture into the cake cases.
3   Bake for 15–20 minutes until the cakes spring back when pressed lightly and a skewer
   inserted into the middle of a cake comes out clean. Remove the cakes from the oven,
   turn out on to a wire rack and leave to cool.
4   Cover half of the cakes with the melted plain chocolate and top with half a white truffle
   in the centre of each. Cover the remaining cakes with the melted white chocolate and
   top with half a plain chocolate truffle. Leave the chocolate to set before serving.

089   Swirled Cupcakes

PREPARATION TIME 25 minutes   **COOKING TIME** 15–20 minutes   **MAKES** 12 cakes

115g/4oz butter, softened
115g/4oz/scant ½ cup caster sugar
2 large eggs, lightly beaten
85g/3oz/heaped ½ cup self-raising flour
4 tbsp cocoa powder

100g/3½oz/heaped ½ cup chocolate
  chips
a few drops of food colouring (optional)
1 recipe quantity Vanilla Buttercream
  (see page 22)
sugar sprinkles or sweets, to decorate

1   Preheat the oven to 180°C/350°F/gas 4. Put 12 cake cases in a 12-hole bun tin.
2   Put the butter and sugar in a mixing bowl and beat using an electric hand mixer or
   wooden spoon until the mixture is light and creamy. Add the eggs gradually, beating after
   each addition. Sift in the flour and cocoa and gently fold them into the mixture with the
   chocolate chips, using a large metal spoon. Spoon the mixture into the cake cases.
3   Bake for 15–20 minutes until the cakes spring back when pressed lightly and a skewer
   inserted into the middle of a cake comes out clean. Remove the cakes from the oven,
   turn out on to a wire rack and leave to cool.
4   Stir the food colouring, if using, into the buttercream until the colour is uniform, then
   spoon it into an icing bag fitted with a 13mm/½in star nozzle. Pipe the buttercream in
   swirls on top of each cake. Shake the sprinkles over the cake or decorate with sweets of
   your choice. (If you do not have an icing bag, spread the icing over each cake using a
   round-bladed knife.) Leave the icing to set before serving.

090 Coconut & White Chocolate Cupcakes

PREPARATION TIME 25 minutes, plus soaking   **COOKING TIME** 15–20 minutes   **MAKES** 12 cakes

175g/6oz/1½ cups desiccated coconut
2 tbsp coconut milk
115g/4oz butter, softened
115g/4oz/scant ½ cup caster sugar
2 large eggs, lightly beaten
115g/4oz/¾ cup self-raising flour, sifted

55g/2oz/heaped ⅓ cup plain chocolate chips
300g/10½oz white chocolate, melted and cooled slightly
sugar sprinkles, to decorate

1   Preheat the oven to 180°C/350°F/gas 4. Put 12 cake cases in a 12-hole bun tin.
2   Soak 55g/2oz of the desiccated coconut in the coconut milk for 1 hour until soft. Put the butter and sugar in a mixing bowl and beat using an electric hand mixer or wooden spoon until the mixture is light and creamy. Add the eggs gradually, beating after each addition. Add the flour, soaked coconut and chocolate chips and gently fold them into the mixture, using a large metal spoon. Spoon the mixture into the cake cases.
3   Bake for 15–20 minutes until the cakes spring back when pressed lightly and a skewer inserted into the middle of a cake comes out clean. Remove the cakes from the oven, turn out on to a wire rack and leave to cool.
4   Spread half the melted white chocolate over the top of the cakes using a round-bladed knife. Stir the remaining coconut into the rest of the chocolate and place a spoonful of the mixture on top of each cake. Decorate with sugar sprinkles and leave the chocolate to set before serving.

091 Spiced Chocolate Orange Cupcakes

PREPARATION TIME 15 minutes   **COOKING TIME** 15–20 minutes   **MAKES** 24 cakes

225g/8oz butter, softened
225g/8oz/1 cup dark soft brown sugar
4 large eggs, lightly beaten
175g/6oz/heaped 1 cup self-raising flour
4 tbsp cocoa powder
100g/3½oz/heaped ½ cup chocolate chips

1 tsp cinnamon
finely grated zest of 1 orange
200g/7oz plain chocolate, melted and cooled slightly
orange sweets or sugar sprinkles, to decorate

1   Preheat the oven to 180°C/350°F/gas 4. Put 24 cake cases in two 12-hole bun tins.
2   Put the butter and sugar in a mixing bowl and beat using an electric hand mixer or wooden spoon until the mixture is light and creamy. Add the eggs gradually, beating after each addition. Sift in the flour and cocoa and gently fold them into the mixture with the chocolate chips, cinnamon and orange zest, using a large metal spoon. Spoon the mixture into the cake cases.
3   Bake for 15–20 minutes until the cakes spring back when pressed lightly and a skewer inserted into the middle of a cake comes out clean. Remove the cakes from the oven, turn out on to a wire rack and leave to cool. Cover each cake with melted chocolate and decorate with orange sweets or sprinkles. Leave the chocolate to set before serving.

092 Maple Pecan Cupcakes

PREPARATION TIME 30 minutes   **COOKING TIME** 15–20 minutes   **MAKES** 24 cakes

350g/12oz butter, softened
225g/8oz/1 cup light soft brown sugar
4 large eggs, lightly beaten
225g/8oz/1½ cups self-raising flour,
  sifted

5 tbsp maple syrup
100g/3½oz/heaped ½ cup pecan nuts,
  chopped, plus 24 whole pecan nuts,
  to decorate
250g/9oz/1⅔ cups icing sugar, sifted

1   Preheat the oven to 180°C/350°F/gas 4. Put 24 cake cases in two 12-hole bun tins.
2   Put 225g/8oz of the butter and the light brown sugar in a mixing bowl and beat using an
    electric hand mixer or wooden spoon until the mixture is light and creamy. Add the eggs
    gradually, beating after each addition. Add the flour, 2 tablespoons of the maple syrup
    and the chopped pecans and gently fold them into the mixture, using a large metal
    spoon. Spoon the mixture into the muffin cases.
3   Bake for 15–20 minutes until the cakes spring back when pressed lightly and a skewer
    inserted into the middle of a cake comes out clean. Remove the cakes from the oven,
    turn out on to a wire rack and leave to cool.
4   For the buttercream, put the remaining butter and maple syrup with the icing sugar in a
    bowl and beat using an electric hand mixer or wooden spoon until the mixture is light and
    creamy. Spoon the buttercream into an icing bag fitted with a 13mm/½in star nozzle and
    pipe swirls on top of each cooled cake, then top with the whole pecans. (If you do not
    have an icing bag, spread the icing over each cake using a round-bladed knife.) Leave
    the buttercream to set before serving.

093 Buttermilk Cupcakes

PREPARATION TIME 30 minutes   **COOKING TIME** 15–20 minutes   **MAKES** 20 cakes

270g/9½oz butter, softened
350g/12oz/1⅓ cups caster sugar
3 large eggs, lightly beaten
250ml/9fl oz/1 cup plus 2 tbsp
  buttermilk

seeds from 1 vanilla pod
300g/10½oz/2 cups self-raising flour
1 tsp baking powder
400g/14oz/2⅔ cups icing sugar, sifted
chocolate sprinkles, to decorate

1   Preheat the oven to 180°C/350°F/gas 4. Put 20 cake cases in two 12-hole bun tins.
2   Put 175g/6oz of the butter, the caster sugar and eggs in a mixing bowl and whisk using
    an electric hand mixer or a whisk until the mixture is light and creamy. Add 250ml/9fl oz/
    1 cup of the buttermilk and the vanilla seeds and whisk again. Sift in the flour and
    baking powder and gently fold them in, using a large metal spoon. Spoon the mixture
    into the cake cases.
3   Bake for 15–20 minutes until the cakes spring back when pressed lightly and a skewer
    inserted into the middle of a cake comes out clean. Remove the cakes from the oven,
    turn out on to a wire rack and leave to cool.
4   For the buttercream, put the remaining 2 tablespoons of buttermilk, remaining butter and
    the icing sugar in a bowl and beat with an electric hand mixer or wooden spoon until
    you have a light and creamy icing. Spoon the buttercream into an icing bag fitted with a
    13mm/½in star nozzle and pipe swirls on top of each cooled cake, then decorate with
    the chocolate sprinkles. (If you do not have an icing bag, spread the icing over each cake
    using a round-bladed knife.) Leave the buttercream to set before serving.

094 Rocky Road Cupcakes

PREPARATION TIME 20 minutes   **COOKING TIME** 15–20 minutes   **MAKES** 12 cakes

115g/4oz butter, softened
115g/4oz/scant ½ cup caster sugar
2 tbsp crunchy peanut butter
2 large eggs, lightly beaten
85g/3oz/heaped ½ cup self-raising flour
4 tbsp cocoa powder

100g/3½oz/heaped ½ cup plain chocolate chips
100g/3½oz/heaped ½ cup pecan nuts, chopped, 24 reserved for decorating
200g/7oz plain chocolate, melted and cooled slightly
24 mini marshmallows, to decorate

1   Preheat the oven to 180°C/350°F/gas 4. Put 12 cake cases in a 12-hole bun tin.
2   Put the butter, sugar and peanut butter in a mixing bowl and beat using an electric hand mixer or wooden spoon until the mixture is light and creamy. Add the eggs gradually, beating after each addition. Sift in the flour and cocoa and gently fold them into the mixture with the chocolate chips and chopped pecans, using a large metal spoon. Spoon the mixture into the cake cases.
3   Bake for 15–20 minutes until the cakes spring back when pressed lightly and a skewer inserted into the middle of a cake comes out clean. Remove the cakes from the oven, turn out on to a wire rack and leave to cool.
4   Spread some of the melted chocolate over the top of each cake using a knife, retaining a little of the chocolate to drizzle over the topping. Place 2 mini marshmallows and 2 pecans on top of each cake and drizzle with the remaining chocolate. Leave the chocolate to set before serving.

095 Toffee Pop Cupcakes

PREPARATION TIME 20 minutes **COOKING TIME** 15–20 minutes **MAKES** 24 cakes

225g/8oz butter, softened
225g/8oz/1 cup dark soft brown sugar
4 large eggs, lightly beaten
225g/8oz/1½ cups self-raising flour,
   sifted

3 tbsp toffee sauce
24 chocolate-covered soft caramels
200g/7oz/1⅓ cups icing sugar
100g/3½oz white chocolate, chopped,
   to decorate

1 Preheat the oven to 180°C/350°F/gas 4. Put 24 cake cases in two 12-hole bun tins.
2 Put the butter and dark brown sugar in a mixing bowl and beat using an electric hand
   mixer or wooden spoon until the mixture is light and creamy. Add the eggs gradually,
   beating after each addition. Add the flour and 2 tablespoons of the toffee sauce and
   gently fold them into the mixture, using a large metal spoon.
3 Spoon half the mixture into the cake cases and place a chocolate caramel in the middle
   of each, then cover with the remaining mixture, making sure the caramels are covered.
4 Bake for 15–20 minutes until the cakes spring back when pressed lightly and a skewer
   inserted into the middle of a cake comes out clean. Remove the cakes from the oven,
   turn out on to a wire rack and leave to cool.
5 To make the icing, mix the remaining toffee sauce with the icing sugar and 1–2
   tablespoons water in a bowl to form a smooth icing. Spread each cake with icing and
   sprinkle with the chopped white chocolate. Leave the icing to set before serving.

096 Rum & Raisin Cupcakes

PREPARATION TIME 20 minutes   **COOKING TIME** 20–25 minutes   **MAKES** 12 cakes

115g/4oz butter, softened
115g/4oz/scant ½ cup caster sugar
2 large eggs, lightly beaten
115g/4oz/¾ cup self-raising flour, sifted
100g/3½oz rum and raisin fudge,
   chopped into small pieces
chocolate sprinkles, to decorate

FOR THE ICING
80ml/2½fl oz/⅓ cup rum
350g/12oz/2⅓ cups icing sugar
55g/2oz butter, chopped

1   Preheat the oven to 180°C/350°F/gas 4. Put 12 cake cases in a 12-hole bun tin.
2   Put the butter and sugar in a mixing bowl and beat using an electric hand mixer or wooden spoon until light and creamy. Add the eggs, beating after each addition. Add the flour and fudge and fold them in, using a large metal spoon. Spoon the mixture into the cases.
3   Bake for 15–20 minutes until the cakes spring back when pressed lightly and a skewer inserted into the middle of a cake comes out clean. Remove the cakes from the oven, turn out on to a wire rack and leave to cool.
4   Put the icing ingredients in a saucepan and heat until the icing sugar has dissolved and the butter has melted. Beat with a wooden spoon to make a smooth icing. Spread the icing on top of each cake using a round-bladed knife and decorate with the chocolate sprinkles. Leave the icing to set before serving.

097 Macadamia Toffee Cupcakes

PREPARATION TIME 15 minutes   **COOKING TIME** 15–20 minutes   **MAKES** 24 cakes

225g/8oz butter, softened
225g/8oz/scant 1 cup caster sugar
4 large eggs, lightly beaten
225g/8oz/1½ cups self-raising flour,
   sifted

4 tbsp toffee sauce
100g/3½oz/heaped ½ cup macadamia
   nuts, coarsely chopped
200g/7oz/1⅓ cups icing sugar, sifted
chocolate sprinkles, to decorate

1   Preheat the oven to 180°C/350°F/gas 4. Put 24 cake cases in two 12-hole bun tins.
2   Put the butter and caster sugar in a mixing bowl and beat using an electric hand mixer or wooden spoon until the mixture is light and creamy. Add the eggs gradually, beating after each addition. Add the flour, 2 tablespoons of the toffee sauce and the nuts and fold them into the mixture, using a large metal spoon. Spoon the mixture into the cake cases.
3   Bake for 15–20 minutes until the cakes spring back when pressed lightly and a skewer inserted into the middle of a cake comes out clean. Remove the cakes from the oven, turn out on to a wire rack and leave to cool.
4   To make the icing, put the icing sugar, remaining toffee sauce and 1 tablespoon water in a bowl and mix with a spoon to form a smooth toffee icing. If the icing is too stiff, add a further tablespoon of water. Spread the icing over each cake and decorate with chocolate sprinkles. Leave the icing to set before serving.

098 Honey Cupcakes

PREPARATION TIME 20 minutes   **COOKING TIME** 15–20 minutes   **MAKES** 12 cakes

115g/4oz butter, softened
115g/4oz/scant ½ cup caster sugar
2 large eggs, lightly beaten
115g/4oz/¾ cup self-raising flour

1 tsp mixed spice
1 tsp cinnamon
1 tbsp clear honey

1   Preheat the oven to 190°C/375°F/gas 5. Put 12 cake cases in a 12-hole bun tin.
2   Put the butter and sugar in a mixing bowl and beat using an electric hand mixer or wooden spoon until the mixture is light and creamy. Add the eggs gradually, beating after each addition. Sift in the flour, mixed spice and cinnamon and gently fold them into the mixture with the honey, using a large metal spoon. Spoon the mixture into the cake cases.
3   Bake for 15–20 minutes until the cakes spring back when pressed lightly and a skewer inserted into the middle of a cake comes out clean. Remove the cakes from the oven, turn out on to a wire rack and leave to cool.

099 Peshwari Cupcakes

PREPARATION TIME 20 minutes   **COOKING TIME** 15–20 minutes   **MAKES** 24 cakes

55g/2oz/⅓ cup sultanas
55g/2oz/heaped ½ cup desiccated
  coconut
55g/2oz/heaped ⅓ cup pistachio nuts
225g/8oz butter, softened

225g/8oz/scant 1 cup caster sugar
4 large eggs, lightly beaten
250g/9oz/1⅔ cups self-raising flour,
  sifted
2 tbsp coconut cream

1 Preheat the oven to 180°C/350°F/gas 4. Put 24 cake cases in two 12-hole bun tins.
2 Put the sultanas, desiccated coconut and pistachios in a blender and whizz to chop finely.
   Set aside while you prepare the cake mixture.
3 Put the butter and sugar in a mixing bowl and beat using an electric hand mixer or
   wooden spoon until the mixture is light and creamy. Add the eggs gradually, beating after
   each addition. Add the flour, chopped nut and sultana mix and the coconut cream and
   gently fold them into the mixture, using a large metal spoon. Spoon the mixture into the
   cake cases.
4 Bake for 15–20 minutes until the cakes spring back when pressed lightly and a skewer
   inserted into the middle of a cake comes out clean. Remove the cakes from the oven,
   turn out on to a wire rack and leave to cool.

100 Stem Ginger Cream Cupcakes

PREPARATION TIME 20 minutes   **COOKING TIME** 15–20 minutes   **MAKES** 24 cakes

225g/8oz butter, softened
225g/8oz/1 cup light soft brown sugar
4 large eggs, lightly beaten
250g/9oz/1⅔ cups self-raising flour,
   sifted

3 tbsp soured cream
2 tbsp chopped stem ginger in syrup,
   plus extra to decorate (optional)
1 tsp ground ginger
5 tbsp syrup from the stem ginger

1   Preheat the oven to 180°C/350°F/gas 4. Put 24 cake cases in two 12-hole bun tins.
2   Put the butter and sugar in a mixing bowl and beat using an electric hand mixer or
    wooden spoon until the mixture is light and creamy. Add the eggs gradually, beating
    after each addition. Add the flour, soured cream and chopped and ground ginger and
    gently fold them into the mixture, using a large metal spoon. Spoon the mixture into the
    cake cases.
3   Bake for 15–20 minutes until the cakes spring back when pressed lightly and a skewer
    inserted into the middle of a cake comes out clean.
4   Just before the cakes are done, heat the ginger syrup in a saucepan. Remove the cakes
    from the oven and drizzle with the syrup, then turn out on to a wire rack and leave to
    cool. Decorate with a little extra chopped stem ginger, if you wish.

101 Nutmeg & Hazelnut Cupcakes

PREPARATION TIME 20 minutes   **COOKING TIME** 15–20 minutes   **MAKES** 24 cakes

225g/8oz butter, softened
225g/8oz/scant 1 cup caster sugar
4 large eggs, lightly beaten
225g/8oz/1½ cups self-raising flour, sifted

100g/3½oz/heaped ½ cup chopped
   roasted hazelnuts
½ tsp freshly grated nutmeg

1   Preheat the oven to 180°C/350°F/gas 4. Place 24 cake cases in two 12-hole bun tins.
2   Put the butter and sugar in a mixing bowl and beat using an electric hand mixer or
    wooden spoon until the mixture is light and creamy. Add the eggs gradually, beating after
    each addition. Add the flour, hazelnuts and nutmeg and gently fold them into the mixture,
    using a large metal spoon. Spoon the mixture into the cake cases.
3   Bake for 15–20 minutes until the cakes spring back when pressed lightly and a skewer
    inserted into the middle of a cake comes out clean. Remove the cakes from the oven,
    turn out on to a wire rack and leave to cool.

102 Treacle Cupcakes

PREPARATION TIME 20 minutes   **COOKING TIME** 15–20 minutes   **MAKES** 12 cakes

115g/4oz butter, softened
55g/2oz/¼ cup caster sugar
55g/2oz/¼ cup dark muscovado sugar
2 tsp treacle
2 large eggs, lightly beaten

115g/4oz/¾ cup self-raising flour
1 tsp cinnamon
1 tsp mixed spice
55g/2oz/⅓ cup sultanas
55g/2oz cream cheese

1   Preheat the oven to 180°C/350°F/gas 4. Put 12 cake cases in a 12-hole bun tin.
2   Put the butter, caster sugar, muscovado sugar and treacle in a mixing bowl and beat
    using an electric hand mixer or wooden spoon until the mixture is light and creamy. Add
    the eggs gradually, beating after each addition. Sift in the flour, cinnamon and mixed
    spice and gently fold them into the mixture with the sultanas, using a large metal spoon.
3   Put 1 tablespoon of the mixture into each cake case, top with 1 teaspoon of the cream
    cheese and cover with the remaining cake mixture so the cheese is completely covered.
4   Bake for 15–20 minutes until the cakes spring back when pressed lightly and a skewer
    inserted into the middle of a cake comes out clean. Remove the cakes from the oven,
    turn out on to a wire rack and leave to cool.

103 Cherry & Almond Cupcakes

PREPARATION TIME 20 minutes   **COOKING TIME** 15–20 minutes   **MAKES** 24 cakes

225g/8oz butter, softened
225g/8oz/scant 1 cup caster sugar
4 large eggs, lightly beaten
225g/8oz/1½ cups self-raising flour, sifted
200g/7oz/heaped 1 cup preserved
  morello cherries, 12 halved and
  reserved to decorate

3 tbsp natural yogurt
1 tsp almond extract
1 recipe quantity Chocolate Buttercream
  (see page 22)
100g/3½oz white chocolate, melted and
  cooled slightly, to decorate

1   Preheat the oven to 180°C/350°F/gas 4. Put 24 cake cases in two 12-hole bun tins.
2   Put the butter and sugar in a mixing bowl and beat using an electric hand mixer or
    wooden spoon until the mixture is light and creamy. Add the eggs gradually, beating after
    each addition. Add the flour, cherries, yogurt and almond extract and gently fold them
    into the mixture, using a large metal spoon. Spoon the mixture into the cake cases.
3   Bake for 15–20 minutes until the cakes spring back when pressed lightly and a skewer
    inserted into the middle of a cake comes out clean. Remove the cakes from the oven,
    turn out on to a wire rack and leave to cool.
4   Spoon the buttercream into an icing bag fitted with a 13mm/½in star nozzle and pipe
    a star on each cake, then place half a cherry on top. Dip a fork into the melted white
    chocolate and drizzle it over the top of each cake. Leave the chocolate to set before serving.

104 Iced Cherry Cupcakes

PREPARATION TIME 20 minutes   **COOKING TIME** 15–20 minutes   **MAKES** 24 cakes

225g/8oz butter, softened
225g/8oz/scant 1 cup caster sugar
4 large eggs, lightly beaten
225g/8oz/1½ cups self-raising flour, sifted
2 tbsp natural yogurt

100g/3½oz/½ cup glacé cherries,
  chopped, plus 12, halved, to decorate
1 tsp vanilla extract
400g/14oz/2⅔ cups icing sugar

1   Preheat the oven to 180°C/350°F/gas 4. Put 24 cake cases in two 12-hole bun tins.
2   Put the butter and caster sugar in a mixing bowl and beat using an electric hand mixer or
    wooden spoon until the mixture is light and creamy. Add the eggs gradually, beating after
    each addition. Add the flour, yogurt, chopped glacé cherries and vanilla extract and
    gently fold them into the mixture, using a large metal spoon. Spoon the mixture into the
    cake cases.
3   Bake for 15–20 minutes until the cakes spring back when pressed lightly and a skewer
    inserted into the middle of a cake comes out clean. Remove the cakes from the oven,
    turn out on to a wire rack and leave to cool.
4   Mix the icing sugar with 3–4 tablespoons water in a small bowl to form a smooth, thick
    icing and spread it over the tops of the cakes using a round-bladed knife. Place half a
    cherry on each cake. Leave the icing to set before serving.

105 Peaches & Cream Cupcakes

PREPARATION TIME 25 minutes **COOKING TIME** 20–25 minutes **MAKES** 20 cakes

225g/8oz butter, softened
225g/8oz/scant 1 cup caster sugar
4 large eggs, lightly beaten
250g/9oz/1⅔ cups self-raising flour,
    sifted

3 tbsp soured cream
3 tbsp peach jam
2 ripe peaches, stones removed and
    cut into 40 thin slices
1 tbsp lemon juice

1 Preheat the oven to 180°C/350°F/gas 4. Put 20 cake cases in two 12-hole bun tins.
2 Put the butter and sugar in a mixing bowl and beat using an electric hand mixer or
   wooden spoon until the mixture is light and creamy. Add the eggs gradually, beating after
   each addition. Add the flour, soured cream and 2 tablespoons of the jam and gently fold
   them into the mixture, using a large metal spoon. Spoon the mixture into the cake cases
   and place 2 peach slices on top of each cake.
3 Bake for 15–20 minutes until the cakes spring back when pressed lightly and a skewer
   inserted into the middle of a cake comes out clean.
4 Remove the cakes from the oven and turn out on to a wire rack. Heat the remaining jam
   with the lemon juice in a small saucepan until the jam has melted, then brush the peach
   glaze over the top of the cakes with a pastry brush. Leave to cool.

106 Tuttifrutti Cupcakes

PREPARATION TIME 20 minutes   COOKING TIME 15–20 minutes   MAKES 24 cakes

225g/8oz butter, softened
225g/8oz/scant 1 cup caster sugar
4 large eggs, lightly beaten
225g/8oz/1½ cups self-raising flour, sifted
2 tbsp peach jam
55g/2oz/⅓ cup raisins

55g/2oz/⅓ cup sultanas
30g/1oz/¼ cup mixed peel
30g/1oz/scant ¼ cup glacé cherries, chopped
30g/1oz/¼ cup pistachio nuts, chopped
icing sugar, for dusting

1   Preheat the oven to 180°C/350°F/gas 4. Put 24 cake cases in two 12-hole bun tins.
2   Put the butter and sugar in a mixing bowl and beat using an electric hand mixer or wooden spoon until the mixture is light and creamy. Add the eggs gradually, beating after each addition. Add the flour, jam, raisins, sultanas, mixed peel, glacé cherries and pistachios and gently fold them into the mixture, using a large metal spoon. Spoon the mixture into the cake cases.
3   Bake for 15–20 minutes until the cakes spring back when pressed lightly and a skewer inserted into the middle of a cake comes out clean. Remove the cakes from the oven, turn out on to a wire rack and leave to cool. Dust with icing sugar to serve.

107 Jelly Bean Cupcakes

PREPARATION TIME 25 minutes   COOKING TIME 15–20 minutes   MAKES 24 cakes

225g/8oz butter, softened
225g/8oz/scant 1 cup caster sugar
4 large eggs, lightly beaten
225g/8oz/1½ cups self-raising flour, sifted

1 tsp vanilla extract
3 tbsp strawberry jam
400g/14oz/2⅔ cups icing sugar, sifted
jelly beans, to decorate

1   Preheat the oven to 180°C/350°F/gas 4. Put 24 cake cases in two 12-hole bun tins.
2   Put the butter and caster sugar in a mixing bowl and beat using an electric hand mixer or wooden spoon until the mixture is light and creamy. Add the eggs gradually, beating after each addition. Add the flour and gently fold it into the mixture with the vanilla extract and jam, using a large metal spoon. Spoon the mixture into the cake cases.
3   Bake for 15–20 minutes until the cakes spring back when pressed lightly and a skewer inserted into the middle of a cake comes out clean. Remove the cakes from the oven, turn out on to a wire rack and leave to cool.
4   Mix together the icing sugar and 3–4 tablespoons water to form a smooth, thick icing and spread it over each cake using a round-bladed knife. Top each cake with a few jelly beans and leave the icing to set before serving.

108 Turkish Delight Cupcakes

PREPARATION TIME 20 minutes   COOKING TIME 15–20 minutes   MAKES 12 cakes

115g/4oz butter, softened
115g/4oz/scant ½ cup caster sugar
2 large eggs, lightly beaten
140g/5oz/1 cup self-raising flour, sifted
2 tbsp soured cream

150g/5½oz chocolate-covered Turkish Delight, chopped
200g/7oz plain chocolate, melted and cooled slightly

1   Preheat the oven to 180°C/350°F/gas 4. Put 12 cake cases in a 12-hole bun tin.
2   Put the butter and sugar in a mixing bowl and beat using an electric hand mixer or wooden spoon until the mixture is light and creamy. Add the eggs gradually, beating after each addition. Add the flour, soured cream and two-thirds of the Turkish Delight and gently fold them into the mixture, using a large metal spoon. Spoon the mixture into the cake cases.
3   Bake for 15–20 minutes until the cakes spring back when pressed lightly and a skewer inserted into the middle of a cake comes out clean. Remove the cakes from the oven, turn out on to a wire rack and leave to cool.
4   Spread the melted chocolate over the cakes and top each one with a piece of the remaining chopped Turkish Delight.

109 Apple & Hazelnut Mini Loaf Cakes

PREPARATION TIME 15 minutes **COOKING TIME** 20–25 minutes **MAKES** 6 cakes

115g/4oz butter, softened, plus extra
  for greasing
55g/2oz/¼ cup dark muscovado sugar
55g/2oz/¼ cup caster sugar
2 large eggs, lightly beaten

115g/4oz/¾ cup self-raising flour, sifted
1 apple, peeled, cored and grated
55g/2oz/⅓ cup chopped toasted
  hazelnuts
4 tbsp maple syrup

1 Preheat the oven to 190°C/375°F/gas 5. Grease and line six 10 x 5 x 5cm/4 x 2 x 2in mini loaf tins.

2 Put the butter, muscovado sugar and caster sugar in a mixing bowl and beat using an electric hand mixer or wooden spoon until the mixture is light and creamy. Add the eggs gradually, beating after each addition. Add the flour, grated apple, hazelnuts and 2 tablespoons of the maple syrup and gently fold them into the mixture, using a large metal spoon. Divide the mixture between the tins using a spatula.

3 Bake for 20–25 minutes until the cakes spring back when pressed lightly and a skewer inserted into the middle of a cake comes out clean.

4 Just before the cakes come out of the oven, heat the remaining maple syrup with 1 tablespoon water in a small saucepan to form a light syrup. Remove the cakes from the oven and drizzle the syrup over the cakes. Leave the cakes to cool in the tins, then turn out on to a serving plate.

110 Coconut Mini Loaf Cakes

PREPARATION TIME 15 minutes **COOKING TIME** 20–25 minutes **MAKES** 6 cakes

115g/4oz butter, softened, plus extra
  for greasing
175g/6oz/scant ¾ cup caster sugar
2 large eggs, lightly beaten

115g/4oz/¾ cup self-raising flour, sifted
200ml/7fl oz/scant 1 cup coconut cream
55g/2oz/heaped ½ cup desiccated
  coconut

1 Preheat the oven to 180°C/350°F/gas 4. Grease and line six 10 x 5 x 5cm/4 x 2 x 2in mini loaf tins.

2 Put the butter and 115g/4oz of the sugar in a mixing bowl and beat using an electric hand mixer or wooden spoon until the mixture is light and creamy. Add the eggs gradually, beating after each addition. Add the flour, 100ml/3½fl oz/scant ½ cup of the coconut cream and the desiccated coconut and gently fold them into the mixture, using a large metal spoon. Divide the mixture between the tins using a spatula.

3 Bake for 20–25 minutes until the cakes spring back when pressed lightly and a skewer inserted into the middle of a cake comes out clean.

4 Just before the cakes come out of the oven, heat the remaining coconut cream and remaining sugar in a saucepan, stirring to make a syrup until the sugar has completely dissolved. Remove the cakes from the oven and drizzle the syrup over the cakes. Leave the cakes to cool in the tins, then turn out on to a serving plate.

111 Lemongrass & Soured Cream Mini Loaf Cakes

PREPARATION TIME 15 minutes   **COOKING TIME** 20–25 minutes   **MAKES** 6 cakes

200g/7oz/heaped ¾ cup caster sugar
1 lemongrass stalk, very finely sliced
juice and finely grated zest of 1 large
  lemon

115g/4oz butter, softened, plus extra
  for greasing
2 large eggs, lightly beaten
115g/4oz/¾ cup self-raising flour, sifted
2 tbsp soured cream

1   Heat 100g/3½oz/heaped ⅓ cup of the sugar, the lemongrass, lemon juice and zest in a
    saucepan until the sugar has dissolved, then boil for 1 minute to create a syrup. Remove
    from the heat and set aside to cool.
2   Preheat the oven to 180°C/350°F/gas 4. Grease and line six 10 x 5 x 5cm/4 x 2 x 2in
    mini loaf tins.
3   Put the butter and remaining sugar in a mixing bowl and beat using an electric hand
    mixer or wooden spoon until the mixture is light and creamy. Add the eggs gradually,
    beating after each addition. Add the flour and soured cream and gently fold them into the
    mixture, using a large metal spoon. Divide the mixture between the tins using a spatula.
4   Bake for 15–20 minutes until the cakes spring back when pressed lightly and a skewer
    inserted into the middle of each cake comes out clean.
5   Remove the cakes from the oven and pour the lemon syrup over them. Leave the cakes
    to cool in the tins, then turn out on to a serving plate.

112 Star Anise Friands

PREPARATION TIME 20 minutes **COOKING TIME** 25–30 minutes **MAKES** 12 friands

100g/3½oz butter, melted and cooled,
  plus extra for greasing
4 large egg whites
100g/3½oz/⅔ cup plain flour
125g/4½oz/scant 1 cup icing sugar
225g/8oz tinned pineapple, finely diced

finely grated zest of 1 lemon
1 tsp cinnamon
100ml/3½fl oz/scant ½ cup pineapple
  juice from the tin
200g/7oz/heaped ¾ cup caster sugar
2 star anise

1 Preheat the oven to 180°C/350°F/gas 4. Grease twelve 8cm/3in oval friand tins or a 12-hole muffin tin.
2 Put the egg whites in a clean, dry bowl and whisk with an electric hand mixer or a whisk until they form stiff peaks. Sift in the flour and icing sugar, add the melted butter, pineapple, lemon zest and cinnamon and fold in gently, using a large metal spoon. Divide the mixture between the friand tins and place on a baking tray.
3 Bake for 20–25 minutes until the cakes spring back when pressed lightly and a skewer inserted into the middle of a cake comes out clean. Remove the cakes from the oven and leave to stand for 5 minutes, then turn out on to a wire rack and leave to cool.
4 Meanwhile, put the pineapple juice, caster sugar, star anise and 100ml/3½fl oz/scant ½ cup water in a saucepan and simmer to form a light syrup. Serve the warm friands with a drizzle of the star anise syrup over the top.

113 Orange Syrup Friands

PREPARATION TIME 20 minutes **COOKING TIME** 25–30 minutes **MAKES** 12 friands

100g/3½oz butter, melted and cooled,
  plus extra for greasing
4 large egg whites
100g/3½oz/⅔ cup plain flour
125g/4½oz/scant 1 cup icing sugar

1 tsp cinnamon
juice and finely grated zest of 1 orange
juice and finely grated zest of 1 lemon
2 tbsp fine-shred marmalade
200g/7oz/heaped ¾ cup caster sugar

1 Preheat the oven to 180°C/350°F/gas 4. Grease twelve 8cm/3in oval friand tins or a 12-hole muffin tin.
2 Put the egg whites in a clean, dry bowl and whisk with an electric hand mixer or a whisk until they form stiff peaks. Sift in the flour, icing sugar and cinnamon, add the melted butter, orange and lemon zests and marmalade and fold in gently, using a large metal spoon. Divide the mixture between the friand tins and place on a baking tray.
3 Bake for 20–25 minutes until the cakes spring back when pressed lightly and a skewer inserted into the middle of a cake comes out clean. Remove the cakes from the oven and leave to stand for 5 minutes, then turn out on to a wire rack and leave to cool.
4 Meanwhile, put the orange and lemon juice, caster sugar and 3 tablespoons water in a small saucepan and simmer to form a light syrup. Drizzle the orange syrup over the friands.

114 Grandma's Rock Cakes

PREPARATION TIME 10 minutes **COOKING TIME** 15–20 minutes **MAKES** 12 cakes

100g/3½oz chilled lard or butter,
  chopped, plus extra for greasing
225g/8oz/1½ cups self-raising flour,
  sifted

100g/3½oz/heaped ⅓ cup caster sugar
115g/4oz/heaped ½ cup sultanas
1 large egg, lightly beaten
1 tbsp thin-shred marmalade

1 Preheat the oven to 170°C/325°F/gas 3. Grease a 12-hole muffin tin.
2 Put the flour in a mixing bowl. Add the lard or butter and rub it into the flour with your fingertips until the mixture resembles fine breadcrumbs. Add the remaining ingredients and mix well with a wooden spoon to create a crumbly mixture. Bring it together with your fingers into large crumbly pieces. Divide the mixture between the tin holes.
3 Bake for 15–20 minutes until golden brown. Remove the cakes from the oven and leave to cool in the tin, then turn out on to a serving plate.

115 Aunty Betty's Welsh Cakes

PREPARATION TIME 10 minutes   **COOKING TIME** 8–16 minutes   **MAKES** 20 cakes

225g/8oz/1½ cups self-raising flour,
  plus extra for dusting
½ tsp baking powder
¼ tsp ground ginger
1 tsp mixed spice
100g/3½oz chilled butter, chopped,
  plus extra for greasing

85g/3oz/⅓ cup caster sugar, plus extra
  for dusting
55g/2oz/⅓ cup sultanas
55g/2oz/⅓ cup currants
55g/2oz/¼ cup glacé cherries, chopped
1 large egg, lightly beaten
1 tbsp milk (optional)

1   Sift the flour, baking powder, ginger and mixed spice into a mixing bowl. Add the butter and rub it in with your fingertips until the mixture resembles fine breadcrumbs. Add the sugar, sultanas, currants, cherries and egg and bring the mixture together with your hands to form a very firm dough, adding the milk if the mixture is too dry.

2   Sift flour on to a clean work surface and roll the dough out to 1cm/⅜in thick using a rolling pin. Cut out 20 circles using a 7cm/2½in round cutter.

3   Grease a large bakestone, cast-iron griddle or heavy frying pan with a little butter and then put on the hob over a gentle heat. Cook the Welsh cakes in batches for 2 minutes on each side, turning every minute to ensure that the cakes brown nicely but do not burn, and adding more butter to the pan before cooking each batch. When the cakes are cooked, remove from the pan and sprinkle with caster sugar. Serve warm.

116 Maple Drop Scones

PREPARATION TIME 10 minutes   **COOKING TIME** 20 minutes   **MAKES** 24 drop scones

225g/8oz/1½ cups plain flour
1 tsp bicarbonate of soda
1 tsp cream of tartar
1 large egg, beaten

300ml/10½fl oz/scant 1¼ cups milk
2 tbsp maple syrup
butter, for frying

1   Sift the flour, bicarbonate of soda and cream of tartar into a mixing bowl and make a well in the middle. Add the egg, milk and maple syrup and mix with an electric hand blender or a whisk to form a smooth, thick batter.

2   Heat a little butter in a large frying pan and put 6 separate tablespoons of the batter in the pan. Cook for about 3 minutes, then turn over and cook for a further 2 minutes until golden brown. Set aside the cooked pancakes and keep warm while you cook the remainder of the batter in the same way, adding a little more butter to the pan each time.

117 Lemon Madeleines

PREPARATION TIME 15 minutes   **COOKING TIME** 10–12 minutes   **MAKES** 24 madeleines

100g/3½oz butter, melted and cooled,
  plus extra for greasing
100g/3½oz/⅔ cup plain flour, plus extra
  for dusting
3 large eggs

100g/3½oz/heaped ⅓ cup caster sugar
1 tsp baking powder
finely grated zest of 1 lemon
icing sugar, for dusting

1   Preheat the oven to 180°C/350°F/gas 4. Grease two 12-hole madeleine tins very well with some melted butter, using a pastry brush, and dust with flour.

2   Put the eggs and caster sugar in a mixing bowl and whisk using an electric hand mixer or a whisk until the mixture is very light and creamy. Sift in the flour and baking powder, pour in the melted butter and add the lemon zest, then fold them in gently with a large metal spoon. Put spoonfuls of the mixture in the tin holes.

3   Bake for 10–12 minutes until the cakes spring back when pressed lightly and a skewer inserted into the middle of a cake comes out clean. Remove the cakes from the oven and leave to cool in the tins, then turn out on to a serving plate and dust with icing sugar.

118 Chocolate Chip Lamingtons

PREPARATION TIME 30 minutes, plus chilling   COOKING TIME 30–35 minutes   MAKES 15 slices

225g/8oz butter, softened, plus extra
  for greasing
200g/7oz/heaped ¾ cup caster sugar
4 large eggs, lightly beaten
400g/14oz/2⅔ cups self-raising flour
1 tsp bicarbonate of soda
2 tsp cream of tartar
250ml/9fl oz/1 cup milk
100g/3½oz/heaped ½ cup plain
  chocolate chips

FOR THE COATING
1 tbsp butter, melted and cooled
1 tbsp cocoa powder
250g/9oz/1⅔ cups icing sugar
125ml/4fl oz/½ cup milk
175g/6oz/heaped 2 cups desiccated
  coconut

1 Preheat the oven to 180°C/350°F/gas 4. Grease a 25 x 20cm/10 x 8in cake tin.
2 Put the butter and sugar in a mixing bowl and beat using an electric hand mixer or
   wooden spoon until the mixture is light and creamy. Add the eggs gradually, beating after
   each addition. Sift in the flour, bicarbonate of soda and cream of tartar and gently fold
   them into the mixture with the milk and chocolate chips, using a large metal spoon.
   Scrape the mixture into the tin using a spatula.
3 Bake for 30–35 minutes until the cake springs back when pressed and a skewer inserted
   into the middle comes out clean. Remove the cake from the oven and leave to stand for
   5 minutes, then turn out on to a wire rack and leave to cool. Refrigerate for 2 hours.
4 For the coating, put the melted butter, cocoa and icing sugar in a bowl and stir in as
   much of the milk as is needed to make a smooth, thin icing. Put the desiccated coconut
   on a large plate. Cut the cake into 15 rectangles, dunk each one into the icing and then
   cover it completely with coconut. Put the coated cakes on a wire rack to drip, and leave
   until the coating is dry before serving.

119 Amaretto & Pistachio Fondant Fancies

PREPARATION TIME 40 minutes, plus chilling   COOKING TIME 30–35 minutes   MAKES 16 cakes

175g/6oz butter, softened
175g/6oz/scant ¾ cup caster sugar
3 large eggs, lightly beaten
175g/6oz/heaped 1 cup self-raising flour,
  sifted
1 recipe quantity Vanilla Buttercream
  (see page 22)

2 tbsp Pistachio Butter (see page 22)
4 tbsp almond liqueur, such as amaretto
750g/1lb 10oz/5 cups fondant icing
  sugar, sifted
a few drops of food colouring
sweets, to decorate

1 Preheat the oven to 180°C/350°F/gas 4. Grease and line a 20cm/8in loose-bottomed
   square cake tin.
2 Put the butter and caster sugar in a mixing bowl and beat using an electric hand mixer
   or wooden spoon until the mixture is light and creamy. Add the eggs gradually, beating
   after each addition. Add the flour and gently fold it into the mixture, using a large metal
   spoon. Scrape the mixture into the tin using a spatula.
3 Bake for 25–30 minutes until the cake springs back when pressed lightly and a skewer
   inserted into the middle of the cake comes out clean. Remove the cake from the oven
   and leave to stand for 5 minutes, then turn out on to a wire rack and leave to cool.
4 Put the buttercream and pistachio butter in a bowl and mix together. Using a sharp
   knife, cut away the edges of the cake, then slice the cake in half and remove the top layer.
   Drizzle the amaretto over the bottom layer and spread over a thin layer of the pistachio
   buttercream. Place the second cake layer on top and cover the whole cake in the
   remaining pistachio buttercream, smoothing along the sides. Refrigerate for at least 1
   hour to set, as this will make it easier for the fondant icing to stick to the buttercream.
5 Heat the fondant icing sugar in a saucepan with 100ml/3½fl oz/scant ½ cup water and
   the food colouring. (You may not need all the water, so add it gradually until you reach a
   thick consistency.) Cut the cake into 16 squares and place them on a wire rack set over
   a piece of greaseproof paper to catch the icing. Spoon the warm fondant icing over each
   cake, leave to set for a few minutes and then decorate each cake with a sweet. When
   the icing has set completely, cut the cakes away from the rack with a sharp knife and
   place in square cake cases to serve.

120 Crispy Chocolate & Berry Cakes

PREPARATION TIME 15 minutes   COOKING TIME 10 minutes   MAKES 24 cakes

200g/7oz plain chocolate, chopped
200g/7oz white chocolate, half chopped;
   half melted and cooled
4 tbsp golden syrup

85g/3oz butter, chopped
200g/7oz/7 cups cornflakes
300g/10½oz/2 cups combined
   raspberries and blueberries

1   Put 24 cake cases in two 12-hole bun tins.
2   Put the plain and white chopped chocolate, syrup and butter in a large saucepan and
    heat, stirring with a wooden spoon, over a gentle heat until the chocolate and butter
    have melted. Remove from the heat, add the cornflakes and stir well to make sure they
    are coated. Fill each cake case with chocolate cornflakes and top with the fresh berries.
3   Drizzle the melted white chocolate over the cakes and leave to set.

121 Traditional Scones

PREPARATION TIME 15 minutes   COOKING TIME 12–15 minutes   MAKES 10 scones

115g/4oz chilled butter, chopped,
   plus extra for greasing
450g/1lb/3 cups self-raising flour,
   plus extra for dusting
1 tsp baking powder

1 tsp salt
55g/2oz/¼ cup caster sugar, plus extra
   for sprinkling
200ml/7fl oz/scant 1 cup milk, plus
   extra for brushing

1   Preheat the oven to 190°C/375°F/gas 5. Grease a 30cm/12in square baking tray.
2   Sift the flour and baking powder into a mixing bowl, add the salt and butter and rub the
    butter into the flour with your fingertips until the mixture resembles fine breadcrumbs.
    Add the sugar and milk and mix to form a soft dough, adding more milk if necessary.
3   Sift flour on to a clean work surface and roll the dough out to 2.5cm/1in thick using a
    rolling pin. Cut out 10 scones with a 6cm/2½in round cutter, gathering up the trimmings
    and re-rolling as necessary, but handling the dough as little as possible. (Dipping the
    cutter in a small bowl of flour between cutting each scone helps them to rise.)
4   Place the scones on the baking tray so that they are touching each other, which helps
    the scones to rise up straight. Brush the tops of the scones with milk using a pastry
    brush and sprinkle with caster sugar.
5   Bake for 12–15 minutes until the scones are golden brown and sound hollow when you
    pick one up with an oven glove and tap it on the bottom. Remove from the oven and
    transfer to a wire rack with a palette knife to cool a little. Serve warm.

122 Mini Cheese & Poppy Seed Scones

PREPARATION TIME 15 minutes   COOKING TIME 12–15 minutes   MAKES 60 scones

115g/4oz chilled butter, chopped,
   plus extra for greasing
450g/1lb/3 cups self-raising flour,
   plus extra for dusting
1 tsp baking powder
1 tsp salt

1 tbsp caster sugar
115g/4oz Cheddar cheese, grated
2 tbsp poppy seeds
200ml/7fl oz/scant 1 cup milk
1 large egg, beaten

1   Preheat the oven to 190°C/375°F/gas 5. Grease two 30cm/12in square baking trays.
2   Sift the flour and baking powder into a mixing bowl, add the salt and butter and rub the
    butter into the flour with your fingertips until it resembles fine breadcrumbs. Add the sugar,
    cheese, poppy seeds and milk and mix to form a soft dough, adding more milk if needed.
3   Sift flour on to a clean work surface and roll the dough out to 2.5cm/1in thick using a
    rolling pin. Cut out 60 scones with a 2.5cm/1in round cutter, gathering up the trimmings
    and re-rolling as necessary, but handling the dough as little as possible. (Dipping the
    cutter in a small bowl of flour between cutting each scone helps them to rise.)
4   Place the scones a little distance apart on the tray and brush the tops with the beaten egg.
5   Bake for 12–15 minutes until the scones are golden brown and sound hollow when you
    pick one up with an oven glove and tap it on the bottom. Remove from the oven and
    transfer to a wire rack with a palette knife to cool a little. Serve warm.

123 Cherry Scones

PREPARATION TIME 15 minutes   **COOKING TIME** 12–15 minutes   **MAKES** 10 scones

115g/4oz chilled butter, chopped, plus extra for greasing
450g/1lb/3 cups self-raising flour, plus extra for dusting
1 tsp baking powder
1 tsp salt

55g/2oz/¼ cup caster sugar, plus extra for sprinkling
200g/7oz/1 cup glacé cherries, chopped
200ml/7fl oz/scant 1 cup milk, plus extra for brushing

1　Preheat the oven to 190°C/375°F/gas 5. Grease a 30cm/12in square baking tray.

2　Sift the flour and baking powder into a mixing bowl, add the salt and butter and rub the butter into the flour with your fingertips until the mixture resembles fine breadcrumbs. Add the sugar, cherries and milk and mix to form a soft dough, adding a little more milk if the mixture is too dry.

3　Sift flour on to a clean work surface and roll the dough out to 2.5cm/1in thick using a rolling pin. Cut out 10 scones with a 6cm/2½in round cutter, gathering up the trimmings and re-rolling as necessary, but handling the dough as little as possible. (Dipping the cutter in a small bowl of flour between cutting each scone ensures a clean cut of the dough, which helps them to rise.)

4　Place the scones on the baking tray so that they are touching each other, which helps the scones to rise up straight. Brush the tops of the scones with milk using a pastry brush and sprinkle with caster sugar.

5　Bake for 12–15 minutes until the scones are golden brown and sound hollow when you pick one up with an oven glove and tap it on the bottom. Remove from the oven and transfer to a wire rack with a palette knife to cool a little. Serve warm.

124 Wholemeal Scones

PREPARATION TIME 15 minutes **COOKING TIME** 12–15 minutes **MAKES** 10 scones

115g/4oz chilled butter, chopped,
  plus extra for greasing
250g/9oz/1⅔ cups self-raising
  wholemeal flour, plus extra for dusting
200g/7oz/1⅓ cups self-raising flour
1 tsp baking powder

1 tsp salt
55g/2oz/¼ cup caster sugar, plus extra
  for sprinkling
200ml/7fl oz/scant 1 cup milk
1 large egg, beaten

1   Preheat the oven to 190°C/375°F/gas 5. Grease a 30cm/12in square baking tray.
2   Sift both flours and the baking powder into a mixing bowl (tipping in the bran left in the sieve), add the salt and butter and rub the butter into the flour with your fingertips until the mixture resembles fine breadcrumbs. Add the sugar and milk and mix to form a soft dough, adding a little more milk if the mixture is too dry.
3   Sift flour on to a clean work surface and roll the dough out to 2.5cm/1in thick using a rolling pin. Cut out 10 scones with a 6cm/2½in round cutter, gathering up the trimmings and re-rolling as necessary, but handling the dough as little as possible. (Dipping the cutter in a small bowl of flour between cutting each scone ensures a clean cut of the dough, which helps them to rise.)
4   Place the scones on the baking tray so that they are touching each other. This will help the scones to rise up straight. Brush the tops of the scones with the beaten egg using a pastry brush and sprinkle with caster sugar.
5   Bake for 12–15 minutes until the scones are golden brown and sound hollow when you pick one up with an oven glove and tap it on the bottom. Remove from the oven and transfer to a wire rack with a palette knife to cool a little. Serve warm.

125 Lavender Scones

PREPARATION TIME 15 minutes **COOKING TIME** 12–15 minutes **MAKES** 10 scones

115g/4oz chilled butter, chopped,
  plus extra for greasing
450g/1lb/3 cups self-raising flour,
  plus extra for dusting
1 tsp baking powder
1 tsp salt

55g/2oz/¼ cup caster sugar, plus extra
  for sprinkling
1 tsp culinary lavender, ground using
  a pestle and mortar
200ml/7fl oz/scant 1 cup milk,
  plus extra for brushing

1   Preheat the oven to 190°C/375°F/gas 5. Grease a 30cm/12in square baking tray.
2   Sift the flour and baking powder into a mixing bowl, add the salt and butter and rub the butter into the flour with your fingertips until the mixture resembles fine breadcrumbs. Add the sugar, lavender and milk and mix to form a soft dough, adding a little more milk if the mixture is too dry.
3   Sift flour on to a clean work surface and roll the dough out to 2.5cm/1in thick using a rolling pin. Cut out 10 scones with a 6cm/2½in round cutter, gathering up the trimmings and re-rolling as necessary, but handling the dough as little as possible. (Dipping the cutter in a small bowl of flour between cutting each scone ensures a clean cut of the dough, which helps them to rise.)
4   Place the scones on the baking tray so that they are touching each other. This will help the scones to rise up straight. Brush the tops of the scones with milk using a pastry brush and sprinkle with caster sugar.
5   Bake for 12–15 minutes until the scones are golden brown and sound hollow when you pick one up with an oven glove and tap it on the bottom. Remove from the oven and transfer to a wire rack with a palette knife to cool a little. Serve warm.

126 Date & Walnut Scones

PREPARATION TIME 15 minutes   **COOKING TIME** 12–15 minutes   **MAKES** 10 scones

115g/4oz chilled butter, chopped,
   plus extra for greasing
250g/9oz/1⅔ cups self-raising flour,
   plus extra for dusting
200g/7oz/1⅓ cups self-raising
   wholemeal flour
1 tsp baking powder

1 tsp salt
55g/2oz/¼ cup light soft brown sugar
200ml/7fl oz/scant 1 cup milk
55g/2oz/⅓ cup pitted dates, chopped
55g/2oz/scant ½ cup walnuts, chopped
1 large egg, beaten
1 tbsp caster sugar

1   Preheat the oven to 190°C/375°F/gas 5. Grease a 30cm/12in square baking tray.
2   Sift both flours and the baking powder into a mixing bowl (tipping in the bran left in the sieve), add the salt and butter and rub the butter into the flour with your fingertips until the mixture resembles fine breadcrumbs. Add the sugar and milk and mix to form a soft dough, adding a little more milk if the mixture is too dry. Add the chopped dates and nuts.
3   Sift flour on to a clean work surface and roll the dough out to 2.5cm/1in thick using a rolling pin. Cut out 10 scones with a 6cm/2½in round cutter, gathering up the trimmings and re-rolling as necessary, but handling the dough as little as possible. (Dipping the cutter in a small bowl of flour between cutting each scone ensures a clean cut of the dough, which helps them to rise.)
4   Place the scones on the baking tray so that they are touching each other. This will help the scones to rise up straight. Brush the tops of the scones with beaten egg using a pastry brush and sprinkle with caster sugar.
5   Bake for 12–15 minutes until the scones are golden brown and sound hollow when you pick one up with an oven glove and tap it on the bottom. Remove from the oven and transfer to a wire rack with a palette knife to cool a little. Serve warm.

127 Rosewater-Glazed Scones

PREPARATION TIME 15 minutes   **COOKING TIME** 12–15 minutes   **MAKES** 10 scones

115g/4oz chilled butter, chopped,
   plus extra for greasing
450g/1lb/3 cups self-raising flour,
   plus extra for dusting
1 tsp baking powder
1 tsp salt

55g/2oz/¼ cup caster sugar,
   plus extra for sprinkling
200ml/7fl oz/scant 1 cup milk,
   plus extra for brushing
1 tbsp rosewater

1   Preheat the oven to 190°C/375°F/gas 5. Grease a 30cm/12in square baking tray.
2   Sift the flour and baking powder into a mixing bowl, add the salt and butter and rub the butter into the flour with your fingertips until the mixture resembles fine breadcrumbs. Add the sugar and the milk and mix to form a soft dough, adding a little more milk if the mixture is too dry.
3   Sift flour on to a clean work surface and roll the dough out to 2.5cm/1in thick using a rolling pin. Cut out 10 scones with a 6cm/2½in round cutter, gathering up the trimmings and rerolling as necessary, but handling the dough as little as possible. (Dipping the cutter in a small bowl of flour between cutting each scone ensures a clean cut of the dough, which helps them to rise.)
4   Place the scones on the baking tray so that they are touching each other. This will help the scones to rise up straight. Mix the rosewater with a few teaspoons of milk and brush over the tops of the scones. Sprinkle with caster sugar.
5   Bake for 12–15 minutes until the scones are golden brown and sound hollow when you pick one up with an oven glove and tap it on the bottom. Remove from the oven and transfer to a wire rack with a palette knife to cool a little. Serve warm.

128 Raspberry Devonshire Splits

PREPARATION TIME 25 minutes, plus rising **COOKING TIME** 15–20 minutes **MAKES** 15 splits

2 tsp fast action dried yeast
55g/2oz/¼ cup caster sugar
300ml/10½fl oz/scant 1¼ cups
    warm milk
500g/1lb 2oz/scant 3⅓ cups self-raising
    flour, sifted, plus extra for dusting

30g/1oz butter, melted and cooled,
    plus extra for greasing
225g/8oz clotted cream
200g/7oz/heaped 1 cup raspberries
4 tbsp raspberry jam
icing sugar, for dusting

1   Put the yeast, 1 tablespoon of the caster sugar and 2 tablespoons of the warm milk in
    a cup and leave to stand for 10–20 minutes until the mixture has become frothy.
2   Put the flour, yeast mixture, remaining sugar, remaining milk and the melted butter into
    a large mixing bowl and bring the mixture together with your hands.
3   Sift flour on to a clean work surface, turn the mixture out and knead for 10 minutes to
    form a soft dough. Add a little more flour if the dough is too sticky. Return the dough
    to the bowl, cover with cling film and leave in a warm place for about 1 hour until the
    dough has doubled in size. Grease and line two 30cm/12in square baking trays.
4   Tip the dough on to the floured work surface and punch it a few times to knock the air
    out of it, then cut into 15 pieces. Form each piece into a ball and place on the baking
    trays, spaced 2.5cm/1in apart. Cover with a damp tea towel and leave in a warm place
    to rise for about 30 minutes until the buns have doubled in size. Preheat the oven to
    200°C/400°F/gas 6.
5   Bake for 15–20 minutes until the buns are golden brown and sound hollow when you
    pick one up with an oven glove and tap it on the bottom. Remove from the oven and
    transfer to a wire rack with a spatula to cool.
6   Cut each bun in half from top to bottom (but not right through) and fill with clotted
    cream, a few raspberries and 1 teaspoon of the jam. Dust with icing sugar to serve.

129 Iced Raspberry Buns

PREPARATION TIME 25 minutes, plus rising   **COOKING TIME** 15–20 minutes   **MAKES** 24 buns

2 tsp fast action dried yeast
55g/2oz/¼ cup caster sugar
300ml/10½fl oz/scant 1¼ cups
    warm milk
500g/1lb 2oz/3⅓ cups strong white
    flour, sifted, plus extra for dusting

30g/1oz butter, melted and cooled,
    plus extra for greasing
350g/12oz raspberry jam
200g/7oz/1⅓ cups fondant icing sugar
a few drops of pink food colouring

1   Put the yeast, 1 tablespoon of the sugar and 2 tablespoons of the milk in a cup and leave to stand for 10–20 minutes until the mixture has become frothy.
2   Put the flour, yeast mixture, remaining sugar, remaining milk and the melted butter in a large mixing bowl and bring the mixture together with your hands.
3   Sift flour on to a clean work surface, turn the mixture out and knead for 10 minutes to form a soft dough. Add a little more flour if the dough is too sticky. Return the dough to the bowl, cover with cling film and leave in a warm place for about 1 hour until the dough has doubled in size. Grease and line two 30cm/12in square baking trays.
4   Tip the dough on to the floured work surface and punch it a few times to knock the air out of it, then cut into 24 pieces. Form each piece into a sausage shape and place on the baking trays, spaced 2.5cm/1in apart. Cover with a damp tea towel and leave in a warm place to rise for about 30 minutes until the buns have doubled in size. Preheat the oven to 200°C/400°F/gas 6.
5   Bake for 15–20 minutes until the buns are golden brown and sound hollow when you pick one up with an oven glove and tap it on the bottom. Remove from the oven and transfer to a wire rack with a spatula to cool.
6   Push a sharp, thin-bladed knife into each bun from one end, to make a cavity for the jam. Do not push right through the bun, or the jam will come out the other end. Put the raspberry jam into an icing bag and pipe roughly 1 tablespoonful into each hole.
7   Mix the fondant icing sugar with 1–2 tablespoons water and the food colouring to form a smooth, thick icing. Spread the icing over the top of each bun using a round-bladed knife. Leave the icing to set before serving.

130 Glazed Cinnamon Buns

PREPARATION TIME 25 minutes, plus rising   **COOKING TIME** 15–20 minutes   **MAKES** 20 buns

2 tsp fast action dried yeast
90g/3¼oz/⅓ cup caster sugar
300ml/10½fl oz/scant 1¼ cups
    warm milk
500g/1lb 2oz/3⅓ cups strong white
    flour, sifted, plus extra for dusting

200g/7oz/1 cup sultanas
2 tsp cinnamon
30g/1oz butter, melted and cooled,
    plus extra for greasing
1 cinnamon stick

1   Put the yeast, 1 tablespoon of the sugar and 2 tablespoons of the milk in a cup and leave to stand for 10–20 minutes until the mixture has become frothy.
2   Put the flour, yeast mixture, 55g/2oz/¼ cup of the sugar, the remaining milk, sultanas, cinnamon and melted butter into a large mixing bowl and bring together with your hands.
3   Sift flour on to a clean work surface, turn the mixture out and knead for 10 minutes to form a soft dough. Add a little more flour if the dough is too sticky. Return the dough to the bowl, cover with cling film and leave in a warm place for about 1 hour until the dough has doubled in size. Grease and line two 30cm/12in square baking trays.
4   Tip the dough on to the floured work surface and punch it a few times to knock the air out of it, then cut into 20 pieces. Form each piece into a ball and place on the baking trays, spaced 2.5cm/1in apart. Cover with a damp tea towel and leave in a warm place to rise for about 30 minutes until the buns have doubled in size. Preheat the oven to 200°C/400°F/gas 6.
5   Bake for 15–20 minutes until the buns are golden brown and sound hollow when you pick one up with an oven glove and tap it on the bottom. Remove from the oven and turn out on to a wire rack. Heat the remaining sugar, cinnamon stick and 3 tablespoons water in a small saucepan over a gentle heat until the sugar has dissolved, then bring to the boil. Brush the syrup over the buns with a pastry brush. Serve warm.

131 Saffron & Rosewater Buns

PREPARATION TIME 25 minutes **COOKING TIME** 20–25 minutes **MAKES** 20 buns

2 tsp fast action dried yeast
90g/3¼oz/⅓ cup caster sugar
300ml/10½fl oz/scant 1¼ cups
  warm milk
3 tbsp rosewater
1 level tsp saffron stamens

500g/1lb 2oz/3⅓ cups strong white
  flour, sifted, plus extra for dusting
30g/1oz butter, melted and cooled,
  plus extra for greasing
200g/7oz/1 cup sultanas

1 Put the yeast, 1 tablespoon of the sugar, 2 tablespoons of the milk, 1 tablespoon of the rosewater and the saffron in a cup and leave for 10–20 minutes until the mixture is frothy.
2 Put the flour, yeast mixture, 55g/2oz/¼ cup of the sugar, the remaining milk and the melted butter into a large mixing bowl and bring the mixture together with your hands.
3 Sift flour on to a clean work surface, turn the mixture out and knead for 10 minutes to form a soft dough. Add a little more flour if the dough is too sticky. Return the dough to the bowl, cover with cling film and leave in a warm place for about 1 hour until the dough has doubled in size. Grease and line two 30cm/12in square baking trays.
4 Tip the dough on to the floured work surface and punch it a few times to knock the air out of it, then add the sultanas and cut into 20 pieces. Form each piece into a ball and place on the baking trays, spaced 2.5cm/1in apart. Cover with a damp tea towel and leave in a warm place to rise for about 30 minutes until the buns have doubled in size. Preheat the oven to 200°C/400°F/gas 6.
5 Bake for 15–20 minutes until the buns are golden brown and sound hollow when you pick one up with an oven glove and tap it on the bottom. Remove from the oven and turn out on to a wire rack. Heat the remaining rosewater and sugar in a small saucepan over a gentle heat until the sugar has dissolved, then bring to the boil. Brush the syrup over the buns with a pastry brush. Serve warm.

132 Chocolate Éclairs

PREPARATION TIME 25 minutes **COOKING TIME** 30–35 minutes **MAKES** 15 éclairs

115g/4oz butter, chopped, plus extra
  for greasing
140g/5oz/1 cup plain flour, sifted
4 large eggs, lightly beaten

200g/7oz plain chocolate, melted and
  cooled slightly
300ml/10½fl oz/scant 1¼ cups double
  cream, whipped to stiff peaks

1 Preheat the oven to 200°C/400°F/gas 6. Grease and line two 30cm/12in square baking trays.
2 Put the butter and 250ml/9fl oz/1 cup water in a saucepan and heat until the butter has melted. Bring to the boil, then remove from the heat and quickly add the flour all at once. Return the pan to the heat and beat the mixture hard with a wooden spoon until the mixture forms a ball of dough and leaves the sides of the pan clean. Remove from the heat and add the eggs gradually, beating after each addition. When all the eggs have been incorporated, you should have a smooth, soft paste.
3 Spoon the paste into an icing bag fitted with a 2cm/¾in plain nozzle and pipe 15 lines of the choux pastry approximately 10cm/4in in length on the baking trays.
4 Bake for 20–25 minutes until the pastry is golden brown. Remove from the oven and make a small slit at the end of each éclair with a knife to allow the steam to escape, then return to the oven for a further 5 minutes. Remove from the oven and transfer to a wire rack to cool.
5 Spread a little melted chocolate on each éclair and leave to set. When you are ready to serve, spoon the whipped cream into an icing bag and pipe the cream into the hole at the end of each éclair to fill. Serve immediately.

133 Violet Choux Buns

PREPARATION TIME 25 minutes   **COOKING TIME** 30–35 minutes   **MAKES** 15 buns

115g/4oz butter, chopped, plus extra
  for greasing
140g/5oz/1 cup plain flour, sifted
4 large eggs, lightly beaten
200g/7oz/1⅓ cups fondant icing sugar
2 tbsp violet syrup

¼ tsp purple food colouring paste
2 tbsp violet liqueur
300ml/10½fl oz/scant 1¼ cups double
  cream, whipped to stiff peaks
15 purple sugar flowers, to decorate

1   Preheat the oven to 200°C/400°F/gas 6. Grease and line two 30cm/12in square baking trays.
2   Put the butter and 250ml/9fl oz/1 cup water in a saucepan and heat until the butter has melted. Bring to the boil, then remove from the heat and quickly add the flour all at once. Return the pan to the heat and beat the mixture hard with a wooden spoon until the mixture forms a ball of dough and leaves the sides of the pan clean. Remove from the heat and add the eggs gradually, beating after each addition. When all the eggs have been incorporated, you should have a smooth, soft paste.
3   Place 15 tablespoons of the paste in balls about 5cm/2in in diameter on the trays.
4   Bake for 20–25 minutes until the pastry is golden brown. Remove from the oven and make a small slit in each bun with a knife to allow the steam to escape, then return to the oven for a further 5 minutes. Remove from the oven and transfer to a wire rack to cool.
5   Put the sugar, violet syrup and colouring paste in a small bowl and mix to form a thick icing. Spread the fondant icing over each bun using a round-bladed knife and top with a purple sugar flower. Leave the icing to set.
6   When you are ready to serve, stir the violet liqueur gently into the whipped cream. Spoon the violet cream into an icing bag and pipe the cream into the hole at the end of each bun to fill. Serve immediately.

134 Banoffi Choux Buns

PREPARATION TIME 25 minutes   **COOKING TIME** 35–40 minutes   **MAKES** 15 buns

115g/4oz butter, chopped, plus extra
  for greasing
140g/5oz/1 cup plain flour
4 large eggs, lightly beaten
300ml/10½fl oz/scant 1¼ cups
  double cream

100g/3½oz/heaped ⅓ cup dark soft
  brown sugar
3 tbsp maple syrup
2 bananas
100g/3½oz/⅔ cup icing sugar
55g/2oz/heaped ⅓ cup toasted
  flaked almonds

1   Preheat the oven to 200°C/400°F/gas 6. Grease and line two 30cm/12in square baking trays.
2   Put the butter and 250ml/9fl oz/1 cup water in a saucepan and heat until the butter has melted. Bring to the boil, then remove from the heat and quickly add the flour all at once. Return the pan to the heat and beat the mixture hard with a wooden spoon until the mixture forms a ball of dough and leaves the sides of the pan clean. Remove from the heat and add the eggs gradually, beating after each addition. When all the eggs have been incorporated, you should have a smooth, soft paste.
3   Place 15 tablespoons of the paste in balls about 5cm/2in in diameter on the trays.
4   Bake for 20–25 minutes until the pastry is golden brown. Remove from the oven and make a small slit in each bun with a knife to allow the steam to escape, then return to the oven for a further 5 minutes. Remove from the oven and transfer to a wire rack to cool.
5   To prepare the toffee sauce, put 100ml/3½fl oz/scant ½ cup of the double cream in a saucepan with the dark brown sugar and maple syrup and stir over a gentle heat until the sugar has dissolved. Remove from the heat and leave to cool.
6   When you are ready to serve the buns, place the bananas and icing sugar on a large plate and mash using the back of a fork until soft. Whip the remaining cream to stiff peaks using an electric hand mixer or a whisk and gently fold in the mashed banana using a large metal spoon. Slit each bun in half and fill with the banana cream. Spoon the toffee sauce over the top and sprinkle with the flaked almonds. Serve immediately.

CHAPTER 3

DESSERTS

This chapter contains delicious cakes that are suitable for serving
as desserts, and most are prepared in advance, making them
ideal for dinner parties. Wow your guests with a Baked Mocha
Alaska filled with coffee ice cream, banana and chocolate,
topped with a chewy hot meringue; classics such as Sacher
Torte and Black Forest Gateau; luxurious cheesecakes made
with clotted cream and summer berries; and party favourites
Arctic Roulade and gooey Hazelnut Brownies with Chocolate
Sauce. Why not try Gregg Wallace's favourite Sticky Toffee Nut
Cheesecake – a creamy baked cheesecake topped with nuts in
a caramel sauce? From delicate, meringue-shelled cloud cakes,
sumptuously filled with cream and berries, to unusual twists on
traditional favourites, such as Pecan Pie Cake and Key Lime
Mousse Cake, there is a dessert here for every occasion.

135　Lemon & Raspberry Cloud Cake

PREPARATION TIME 40 minutes, plus chilling　**COOKING TIME** 1 hour　**SERVES** 8

butter, for greasing
4 large egg whites
½ tsp cream of tartar
250g/9oz/1 cup caster sugar
3 heaped tbsp lemon curd
juice and finely grated zest of ½ lemon
150g/5½oz cream cheese

2 tbsp lemon liqueur, such as limoncello
400ml/14fl oz/1½ cups double cream,
　whipped to stiff peaks
400g/14oz/3 cups raspberries
100g/3½oz white chocolate made
　into curls, to decorate

1　Preheat the oven to 140°C/275°F/gas 1. Grease and base-line a deep 23cm/9in springform cake tin.
2　Put the egg whites in a clean, dry bowl and whisk with an electric hand mixer or a whisk until they form stiff peaks. Add the cream of tartar and whisk again, then add the sugar a little at a time, whisking until the mixture forms a glossy meringue. Spoon the meringue into the cake tin, making a well in the centre so that the higher sides will contain the filling when cooked.
3　Bake for 1 hour until the meringue is crisp. Remove the meringue from the oven and leave to cool in the tin.
4　Put the lemon curd, lemon juice and zest, cream cheese and limoncello in a mixing bowl and beat to form a smooth lemon cream, using an electric hand mixer or wooden spoon. Add the whipped cream and fold the mixtures gently but thoroughly together, using a large metal spoon. Fold in half the raspberries and spoon the cream into the meringue case.
5　Refrigerate for 1 hour. Remove the meringue from the tin and place on a serving plate. Top with the remaining raspberries and the white chocolate curls.

136　Strawberry Cloud Cake

PREPARATION TIME 40 minutes, plus chilling　**COOKING TIME** 1 hour 10 minutes　**SERVES** 8

butter, for greasing
4 large egg whites
½ tsp cream of tartar
350g/12oz/1⅓ cups caster sugar
1 vanilla pod

400g/14oz/heaped 3 cups strawberries,
　hulled and sliced
1 tbsp powdered gelatine
500ml/17fl oz/2 cups double cream

1　Preheat the oven to 140°C/275°F/gas 1. Grease and base-line a deep 23cm/9in springform cake tin.
2　Put the egg whites in a clean, dry bowl and whisk with an electric hand mixer or a whisk until they form stiff peaks. Add the cream of tartar and whisk again, then add 250g/9oz/ 1 cup of the sugar a little at a time, whisking until the mixture forms a glossy meringue. Spoon the meringue into the cake tin, making a well in the centre so that the higher sides will contain the filling when cooked.
3　Bake for 1 hour until the meringue is crisp. Remove the meringue from the oven and leave to cool in the tin.
4　Slit the vanilla pod in half with a sharp knife and put it in a saucepan with half the strawberries, 100ml/3½fl oz/scant ½ cup water and the remaining sugar. Simmer for 10 minutes until the strawberries are soft. Remove and discard the vanilla pod (scraping out any seeds that have not come out during the cooking process). Pour the mixture into a sieve and press out all the juice from the strawberries using a wooden spoon. Discard the contents of the sieve and return the strawberry juice to the pan.
5　Sprinkle the gelatine over the warm strawberry liquid and stir until the gelatine has dissolved. Leave the syrup to cool completely, then strain the mixture through a fine-mesh sieve.
6　Put 290ml/10fl oz/1¼ cups of the cream in a mixing bowl and whip to stiff peaks, using an electric hand mixer or a whisk. Add the cooled strawberry syrup and whisk again. Spoon the strawberry mousse into the meringue case.
7　Refrigerate for 2 hours. Remove the meringue from the tin and place on a serving plate. Whip the remaining cream to stiff peaks and spread over the top of the mousse. Top with the remaining strawberries.

137 Coconut Cream Cloud Cake

PREPARATION TIME 35 minutes, plus chilling **COOKING TIME** 1 hour 5 minutes **SERVES** 8

butter, for greasing
4 large egg whites and 2 large yolks
½ tsp cream of tartar
250g/9oz/1 cup caster sugar
30g/1oz/heaped ¼ cup desiccated
  coconut

200g/7oz plain chocolate, melted and
  cooled slightly
400ml/14fl oz/1½ cups double cream,
  whipped to soft peaks
2 tbsp coconut cream
2 tbsp coconut rum

1 Preheat the oven to 150°C/300°F/gas 2. Grease and base-line a deep 23cm/9in
   springform cake tin.
2 Put the egg whites in a clean, dry bowl and whisk with an electric hand mixer or a whisk
   until they form stiff peaks. Add the cream of tartar and whisk again, then add the sugar
   a little at a time, whisking until the mixture forms a glossy meringue. Spoon the
   meringue into the cake tin, making a well in the centre so that the higher sides will
   contain the filling when cooked. Make sure that the sides are thickly covered.
3 Bake for 1 hour until the meringue is crisp. Remove the meringue from the oven and
   leave to cool in the tin.
4 Put the desiccated coconut in a dry saucepan and heat until it starts to turn golden
   brown, stirring all the time to ensure it does not burn. Tip into a dish to cool.
5 Put the egg yolks in a mixing bowl, add the melted chocolate and then fold in half the
   whipped cream, the coconut cream and rum, using a large metal spoon. Spoon the
   mixture into the meringue case. Cover with the remaining cream and sprinkle over the
   coconut. Refrigerate for 2 hours, then remove from the tin and place on a serving plate.

138 Sacher Torte

PREPARATION TIME 30 minutes, plus chilling **COOKING TIME** 50–55 minutes **SERVES** 8

175g/6oz butter, softened, plus extra
  for greasing
400g/14oz plain chocolate
175g/6oz/scant ¾ cup caster sugar
8 large eggs, separated

140g/5oz/1 cup plain flour, sifted
3 tbsp brandy
3 tbsp apricot jam
4 tbsp double cream
sugar flowers, to decorate

1 Preheat the oven to 180°C/350°F/gas 4. Grease and line a deep 23cm/9in springform
   cake tin.
2 Melt 175g/6oz of the chocolate and leave to cool. Put the butter and sugar in a mixing
   bowl and beat using an electric hand mixer or wooden spoon until the mixture is light
   and creamy. Stir in the melted chocolate and egg yolks and mix well.
3 Put the egg whites in a clean, dry bowl and whisk with an electric hand mixer or a whisk
   until they form stiff peaks, then fold them gently but thoroughly into the chocolate
   mixture, using a large metal spoon. Add the flour and fold that in too. Scrape the mixture
   into the tin using a spatula.
4 Bake for 45–50 minutes until a crust has formed on top of the torte and a skewer
   inserted into the middle of the torte comes out clean. Remove the torte from the oven
   and leave to stand for 5 minutes, then turn out on to a wire rack and leave to cool.
5 Remove the torte from the tin, cut it in half horizontally and place the bottom layer on
   a serving plate. Drizzle the brandy over the bottom layer and then sandwich the layers
   together with half the jam. Warm the remaining jam in a little saucepan, then spread
   over the sides and top of the torte.
6 Melt the remaining chocolate, add the cream and stir until you have a smooth chocolate
   icing. Spread the icing over the top and sides of the torte, using a round-bladed knife,
   and decorate with the sugar flowers.

139 White Chocolate Sacher Torte

PREPARATION TIME 30 minutes   **COOKING TIME** 50–55 minutes   **SERVES** 8

175g/6oz butter, softened, plus extra
  for greasing
175g/6oz/scant ¾ cup caster sugar
400g/14oz white chocolate, melted and
  cooled slightly
8 large eggs, separated
140g/5oz/1 cup plain flour, sifted
3 tbsp almond liqueur, such as amaretto

3 tbsp apricot jam
225g/8oz plain chocolate, melted and
  cooled slightly
4 tbsp double cream
100g/3½oz white chocolate made
  into curls
sugar flowers, to decorate

1   Preheat the oven to 180°C/350°F/gas 4. Grease and line a deep 23cm/9in springform cake tin.
2   Put the butter and sugar in a mixing bowl and beat using an electric hand mixer or wooden spoon until the mixture is light and creamy. Stir in the melted white chocolate and egg yolks and mix well.
3   Put the egg whites in a clean, dry bowl and whisk with an electric hand mixer or a whisk until they form stiff peaks, then fold them gently but thoroughly into the chocolate mixture, using a large metal spoon. Add the flour and fold that in too. Scrape the mixture into the tin using a spatula.
4   Bake for 45–50 minutes until a crust has formed on top of the torte and a skewer inserted into the middle of the torte comes out clean. Remove the torte from the oven and leave to stand for 5 minutes, then turn out on to a wire rack and leave to cool.
5   Remove the torte from the tin, cut it in half horizontally and place the bottom layer on a serving plate. Drizzle the amaretto over the bottom layer and then sandwich the layers together with half the jam. Warm the remaining jam in a little saucepan, then spread over the sides and top of the torte. Put the melted plain chocolate in a bowl, add the cream and stir until you have a smooth chocolate icing. Spread the icing over the top and sides of the torte, using a round-bladed knife, sprinkle with the white chocolate curls and decorate with sugar flowers.

140 Cinnamon Truffle Torte with Plum Compote

PREPARATION TIME 30 minutes   **COOKING TIME** 40 minutes   **SERVES** 8

100g/3½oz butter, chopped, plus extra
  for greasing
250g/9oz dark chocolate (70% cocoa
  solids), broken into pieces
4 large eggs, separated
175g/6oz/heaped 1 cup icing sugar,
  sifted, plus extra for dusting
1 tsp cinnamon

10 ripe red plums, stones removed,
  flesh cut into chunks
2 cinnamon sticks
100g/3½oz/heaped ⅓ cup caster sugar,
  plus extra if necessary
cocoa powder, for dusting
crème fraîche, to serve

1   Preheat the oven to 180°C/350°F/gas 4. Grease and line a deep 23cm/9in springform cake tin.
2   Melt the butter and chocolate together. Leave to cool.
3   Put the egg yolks and icing sugar in a mixing bowl and beat using an electric hand mixer or wooden spoon until the mixture is light and creamy. Stir in the melted chocolate and butter mixture and the cinnamon.
4   Put the egg whites in a clean, dry bowl and whisk with an electric hand mixer or a whisk until they form soft peaks, then fold them gently but thoroughly into the chocolate mixture, using a large metal spoon. Scrape the mixture into the tin using a spatula.
5   Bake for 25–30 minutes until a crust has formed on top of the torte and a skewer inserted into the middle of the torte comes out clean. Meanwhile, put the plums, 100ml/3½fl oz/scant ½ cup water, the cinnamon sticks and caster sugar in a saucepan and simmer for about 30 minutes, until the plums are soft and the liquid has reduced. Taste the sauce and add a little more sugar if needed. Remove the cinnamon sticks.
6   Remove the torte from the oven and leave to set in the tin. Turn out on to a serving plate and dust with the cocoa and icing sugar before serving with the plum compote and some crème fraîche.

141 Chocolate & Nectarine Torte

PREPARATION TIME 20 minutes   **COOKING TIME** 30–35 minutes   **SERVES** 8

150g/5½oz butter, chopped, plus extra
    for greasing
250g/9oz dark chocolate (70% cocoa
    solids), broken into pieces
4 large eggs, separated
175g/6oz/heaped 1 cup icing sugar,
    sifted, plus extra for dusting

3 ripe nectarines, quartered and stones
    removed
100g/3½oz amaretti biscuits
100g/3½oz marzipan, chopped
200ml/7fl oz/scant 1 cup double cream
2 tbsp almond liqueur, such as amaretto

1   Preheat the oven to 190°C/375°F/gas 5. Grease and line a deep 23cm/9in springform
    cake tin.
2   Melt 100g/3½oz of the butter and all the chocolate together. Put the egg yolks and icing
    sugar in a mixing bowl and beat using an electric hand mixer or wooden spoon until the
    mixture is light and creamy. Stir in the melted chocolate and butter mixture and mix well.
3   Put the egg whites in a clean, dry bowl and whisk with an electric hand mixer or a whisk
    until they form stiff peaks, then fold them gently but thoroughly into the chocolate
    mixture, using a large metal spoon. Scrape the mixture into the tin using a spatula, and
    top with the nectarine quarters, placed skin side down.
4   Put the amaretti biscuits in a plastic bag and crush them with a rolling pin. In a separate
    bowl, mix together the amaretti crumbs with the marzipan. Melt the remaining butter,
    add it to the bowl and mix to form a crumble. Sprinkle the mixture in small lumps over
    the top of the cake.
5   Bake for 25–30 minutes until a crust has formed on the top of the torte and the
    nectarines are soft and juicy. (The torte will still be very gooey under the crust, but this
    will set as it cools to give a truffle-like texture.) Remove the torte from the oven and leave
    to cool in the tin. Put the cream and amaretto in a bowl and whip to stiff peaks, using an
    electric hand mixer or a whisk. Remove the torte from the tin and place on a serving
    plate. Serve with the amaretto cream.

142 Raspberry & Chocolate Torte

PREPARATION TIME 30 minutes   **COOKING TIME** 30–35 minutes   **SERVES** 8

100g/3½oz butter, chopped, plus extra
  for greasing
250g/9oz dark chocolate (70% cocoa
  solids), broken into pieces

4 large eggs, separated
200g/7oz/1⅓ cups icing sugar, sifted
400g/14oz/scant 3 cups raspberries
crème fraîche, to serve

1   Preheat the oven to 180°C/350°F/gas 4. Grease and line a deep 23cm/9in springform
    cake tin.
2   Melt the butter and chocolate together and leave to cool. Put the egg yolks and 175g/6oz/
    heaped 1 cup of the icing sugar in a mixing bowl and beat using an electric hand mixer
    or wooden spoon until the mixture is light and creamy. Stir in the melted chocolate and
    butter mixture and mix well.
3   In a separate bowl, whisk the egg whites until they form soft peaks, using an electric
    hand mixer or a whisk, then fold them gently but thoroughly into the chocolate mixture,
    using a large metal spoon. Sprinkle half the raspberries over the bottom of the cake tin
    and spoon the chocolate mixture over them.
4   Bake for 25–30 minutes until a crust has formed on top of the torte and a skewer
    inserted into the middle of the torte comes out clean. Remove the torte from the oven
    and leave to set in the tin.
5   Using a fork, crush the remaining raspberries with the remaining icing sugar. Remove
    the torte from the tin and place on a serving plate. Serve slices of the torte with a drizzle
    of the crushed raspberries and some crème fraîche.

143 Blueberry Streusel Torte

PREPARATION TIME 20 minutes   **COOKING TIME** 55–60 minutes   **SERVES** 8

250g/9oz butter, softened, plus extra
  for greasing
200g/7oz/heaped ¾ cup caster sugar
5 large eggs
280g/10oz/scant 2 cups self-raising flour

1 tsp cinnamon
300g/10½oz cream cheese
200g/7oz/heaped 1 cup blueberries
55g/2oz/heaped ⅓ cup flaked almonds

1   Preheat the oven to 180°C/350°F/gas 4. Grease and line a 25cm/10in springform
    cake tin.
2   Put 175g/6oz of the butter and 175g/6oz/scant ¾ cup of the sugar in a mixing bowl and
    beat using an electric hand mixer or wooden spoon until the mixture is light and creamy.
    Add 3 of the eggs and beat again. Sift in 175g/6oz/scant 1¼ cups of the flour and the
    cinnamon and fold them in, using a large metal spoon. Scrape the mixture into the tin
    using a spatula.
3   In a separate bowl, beat together the cream cheese, remaining eggs and 1 tablespoon
    of the remaining sugar using an electric hand mixer or wooden spoon, then stir in the
    blueberries. Spoon on top of the cake mixture.
4   Put the remaining flour in a bowl and rub in the remaining butter with your fingertips
    to make large crumble pieces. Mix in the remaining sugar and the flaked almonds and
    sprinkle the crumble topping over the top.
5   Bake for 55–60 minutes until the crumble topping is golden brown, the cream is set and
    a skewer inserted into the middle of the torte comes out clean. Remove the torte from
    the oven and leave to cool in the tin for 10 minutes, then place on a serving plate.

144 Rhubarb & Custard Torte

PREPARATION TIME 30 minutes **COOKING TIME** 35–40 minutes **SERVES** 8

175g/6oz butter, softened, plus extra
 for greasing
600g/1lb 2oz rhubarb, peeled and cut
 into 2.5cm/1in pieces
185g/6½oz/scant ¾ cup caster sugar
juice of 1 lemon
3 large eggs plus 3 large egg yolks
175g/6oz/heaped 1 cup self-raising flour,
 sifted
100ml/3½fl oz/scant ½ cup buttermilk

30g/1oz/scant ¼ cup cornflour
400ml/14fl oz/1½ cups milk
100g/3½oz white chocolate, melted
 and cooled slightly
1 tsp vanilla extract
500ml/17fl oz/2 cups double cream,
 whipped to soft peaks
30g/1oz/scant ¼ cup pistachio nuts,
 finely chopped, to decorate

1 Preheat the oven to 190°C/375°F/gas 5. Grease a 23cm/9in raised-base flan tin and line
   the raised centre of the tin with baking parchment.
2 Put the rhubarb in an ovenproof dish and sprinkle with 1 tablespoon of the sugar and
   the lemon juice. Set aside.
3 Put the butter and remaining sugar in a mixing bowl and beat using an electric hand
   mixer or wooden spoon until the mixture is light and creamy. Add the whole eggs and
   whisk again. Add the flour and buttermilk and fold them into the mixture, using a large
   metal spoon. Scrape the mixture into the tin using a spatula.
4 Put the torte and rhubarb in the oven. Bake for 20–25 minutes until a skewer inserted
   into the middle comes out clean. Remove the torte from the oven, leaving the rhubarb
   for another 5 minutes. Leave the torte to stand for 5 minutes, then invert on to a wire
   rack and leave to cool. Remove the rhubarb from the oven.
5 In a separate bowl, whisk together the cornflour and egg yolks with an electric hand mixer
   or a whisk. The mixture will be stiff at first but it will become lighter as you progress.
6 Put the milk in a saucepan and bring to the boil, then pour it into the egg mixture,
   whisking all the time. Stir in the melted white chocolate and vanilla extract and whisk
   well to combine. Pour the mixture back into the saucepan the milk was heated in, and
   heat gently for a few minutes until the custard thickens, whisking all the time. When it is
   thick, remove from the heat and set aside to cool.
7 When you are ready to serve, fold the cooked rhubarb and half the whipped cream into
   the white chocolate custard, using a large metal spoon. Put the flan case on a serving
   plate and spoon the rhubarb custard into the sunken area. Spoon the remaining cream
   into an icing bag fitted with a 13mm/½in star-shaped nozzle and pipe stars all over the
   rhubarb, then sprinkle with the pistachios.

145 Mango & Passion Fruit Torte

PREPARATION TIME 30 minutes, plus chilling **COOKING TIME** 25–30 minutes **SERVES** 8

115g/4oz butter, softened, plus extra
 for greasing
115g/4oz/scant ½ cup caster sugar
2 large eggs, lightly beaten
115g/4oz/¾ cup self-raising flour, sifted
2 tbsp natural yogurt

200ml/7fl oz/scant 1 cup crème fraîche
400g/14oz cream cheese
2 tbsp icing sugar
pulp and seeds from 4 passion fruit
2 ripe mangoes, peeled, stoned and
 chopped

1 Preheat the oven to 190°C /375°F/gas 5. Grease and line a 20cm/8in springform cake tin.
2 Put the butter and sugar in a mixing bowl and beat using an electric hand mixer or
   wooden spoon until the mixture is light and creamy. Add the eggs and beat again. Add
   the flour and fold it into the mixture with the yogurt, using a large metal spoon. Scrape
   the mixture into the tin using a spatula.
3 Bake for 25–30 minutes until a skewer inserted into the middle of the torte comes out
   clean. Remove the torte from the oven and leave to cool in the tin.
4 In a separate bowl, mix together the crème fraîche, cream cheese, icing sugar and half
   the passion fruit pulp and seeds. Pour the mixture on top of the torte in the cake tin and
   refrigerate for 2 hours. Remove the torte from the tin and place on a serving plate. Top
   with the chopped mango and the remaining pulp and seeds.

146 Torte Di Mascarpone

PREPARATION TIME 30 minutes, plus chilling **COOKING TIME** 30–35 minutes **SERVES** 8

115g/4oz butter, softened, plus extra
 for greasing
115g/4oz/scant ½ cup caster sugar
2 tbsp Pistachio Butter (see page 22)
2 large eggs, lightly beaten
115g/4oz/¾ cup self-raising flour, sifted

3 tbsp almond liqueur, such as amaretto
3 tbsp raspberry jam
500g/1lb 2oz mascarpone cheese
250ml/9fl oz/1 cup crème fraîche
2 tbsp icing sugar, sifted
450g/1lb/3 cups raspberries

1   Preheat the oven to 180°C/350°F/gas 4. Grease and line a 20cm/8in springform cake tin.
2   Put the butter and sugar and 1 tablespoon of the pistachio butter in a mixing bowl and
    beat using an electric hand mixer or wooden spoon until the mixture is light and creamy.
    Add the eggs and beat again. Add the flour and fold in, using a large metal spoon.
    Scrape the mixture into the tin using a spatula.
3   Bake for 30–35 minutes until a skewer inserted into the middle of the torte comes out
    clean. Remove the torte from the oven and leave to stand for 5 minutes, then turn out on
    to a wire rack and leave to cool a little. Spoon over the amaretto and leave to cool
    completely, then spread the jam over the torte. Return the torte to the tin.
4   In a separate bowl, mix together the mascarpone cheese, crème fraîche, remaining
    pistachio butter, icing sugar and a third of the raspberries using an electric hand mixer
    or wooden spoon. Spoon this mixture over the torte in the tin and refrigerate for 2 hours.
    Top the torte with the remaining raspberries and transfer to a serving plate.

147 Black Forest Gateau

PREPARATION TIME 30 minutes, plus chilling **COOKING TIME** 35–40 minutes **SERVES** 8

225g/8oz butter, softened, plus extra
 for greasing
225g/8oz/scant 1 cup caster sugar
4 large eggs, lightly beaten
200g/7oz/1⅓ cups self-raising flour
4 tbsp cocoa powder
4 tbsp cherry liqueur, such as kirsch

3 tbsp black cherry jam
200g/7oz/1½ cups preserved cherries,
 drained and halved
500ml/17fl oz/2 cups double cream,
 whipped to stiff peaks
150g/5½oz plain chocolate, grated
5 glacé cherries, halved, to decorate

1   Preheat the oven to 180°C/350°F/gas 4. Grease and line a 23cm/9in springform cake tin.
2   Put the butter and sugar in a mixing bowl and beat using an electric hand mixer or
    wooden spoon until the mixture is light and creamy. Add the eggs gradually, beating after
    each addition. Sift in the flour and cocoa and gently fold them into the mixture, using a
    large metal spoon. Scrape the mixture into the tin using a spatula.
3   Bake for 35–40 minutes until the cake springs back when pressed lightly and a skewer
    inserted into the middle of the cake comes out clean. Remove the cake from the oven
    and leave to stand for 5 minutes, then turn out on to a wire rack and leave to cool.
4   Cut the cake into 3 layers using a sharp knife. Drizzle the kirsch over the bottom and
    middle layers and place the bottom layer on a serving plate. Spread half the jam and
    preserved cherries on the bottom layer and top with a quarter of the whipped cream.
    Cover with the next cake layer and repeat. When all 3 layers are assembled, cover the
    sides and top of the cake with the remaining whipped cream, retaining a few spoonfuls.
    Sprinkle the grated chocolate over the top and sides of the cake, then spoon the
    remaining cream into an icing bag fitted with a 13mm/½in star nozzle and pipe around
    the top of the cake. Top the cream stars with the glacé cherry halves. Refrigerate for
    1 hour before serving.

148 Coffee Gateau

PREPARATION TIME 20 minutes   **COOKING TIME** 20–25 minutes   **SERVES** 8

225g/8oz butter, softened, plus extra
 for greasing
225g/8oz/scant 1 cup caster sugar
4 large eggs, beaten
225g/8oz/1½ cups self-raising flour,
 sifted
1 tbsp instant coffee granules dissolved
 in 2 tbsp boiling water, then cooled

200g/7oz coffee chocolate, half chopped;
 half made into large curls
100ml/3½fl oz/scant ½ cup coffee
 liqueur
100ml/3½fl oz/scant ½ cup double
 cream, whipped to stiff peaks
200g/7oz/1⅓ cups icing sugar, sifted,
 plus extra for dusting

1   Preheat the oven to 190°C/375°F/gas 5. Grease and base-line two 20cm/8in sandwich
    cake tins.
2   Put the butter and sugar in a mixing bowl and beat using an electric hand mixer or
    wooden spoon until the mixture is light and creamy. Add the eggs gradually, beating after
    each addition. Add the flour and gently fold it into the mixture with half the coffee liquid
    and the chopped coffee chocolate, using a large metal spoon. Divide the mixture
    between the tins using a spatula.
3   Bake for 20–25 minutes until the cakes spring back when pressed lightly and a skewer
    inserted into the middle of each cake comes out clean. Remove the cakes from the oven
    and leave to stand for 5 minutes, then turn out on to a wire rack and leave to cool.
4   Drizzle half the coffee liqueur over the top of each cake using a spoon. Fold the
    remaining liqueur into the whipped cream and use this to sandwich the cakes together.
    Place the cake on a serving plate.
5   Put the icing sugar in a bowl, add the remaining coffee liquid and 1–2 tablespoons water
    (gradually) and mix to form a thick icing. Spoon the icing over the top of the cake,
    decorate with the coffee chocolate curls and dust with icing sugar.

149 Strawberry Caramel Gateau

PREPARATION TIME 30 minutes   **COOKING TIME** 30–35 minutes   **SERVES** 8

600ml/21fl oz/scant 2½ cups double
 cream
4 tbsp light muscovado sugar
2 tbsp golden syrup
280g/10oz butter, softened, plus extra
 for greasing
225g/8oz/scant 1 cup caster sugar

4 large eggs, lightly beaten
225g/8oz/1½ cups self-raising flour
1 tsp baking powder
400g/14oz/heaped 3 cups strawberries,
 hulled and thinly sliced
icing sugar, for dusting

1 Put 200ml/7fl oz/scant 1 cup of the double cream in a saucepan with the muscovado sugar, syrup and 55g/2oz of the butter and simmer for about 5 minutes until the sugar has dissolved to make a caramel sauce. Set aside to cool.

2 Preheat the oven to 180°C/350°F/gas 4. Grease and base-line two 20cm/8in sandwich cake tins.

3 Put the remaining butter and the caster sugar in a mixing bowl and beat using an electric hand mixer or wooden spoon until the mixture is light and creamy. Add the eggs gradually, beating after each addition. Sift in the flour and baking powder and gently fold them into the mixture, using a large metal spoon. Divide the mixture between the tins using a spatula.

4 Bake for 25–30 minutes until the cakes spring back when pressed lightly and a skewer inserted into the middle of each cake comes out clean. Remove the cakes from the oven and leave to stand for 5 minutes, then turn out on to a wire rack and leave to cool.

5 Put the remaining cream in a bowl and whisk to stiff peaks using an electric hand mixer or a whisk. Cut each cake in half horizontally and place the bottom layer on a serving plate. Spread a third of the cream over the bottom layer, cover with a third of the strawberries and drizzle over some of the caramel sauce. Repeat with the remaining layers and dust the top layer with icing sugar. Serve with the rest of the caramel sauce on the side.

150 White Chocolate Gateau

PREPARATION TIME 30 minutes, plus chilling   **COOKING TIME** 30–35 minutes   **SERVES** 8

225g/8oz butter, softened, plus extra
 for greasing
225g/8oz/scant 1 cup caster sugar
4 large eggs, lightly beaten
225g/8oz/1½ cups self-raising flour,
 sifted
4 tbsp soured cream
100g/3½oz/heaped ½ cup white
 chocolate chips

100g/3½oz/1¼ cups desiccated coconut
4 tbsp toffee liqueur
1 recipe quantity Coffee Buttercream
 (see page 22)
300ml/10½fl oz/scant 1¼ cups double
 cream, whipped to stiff peaks
100g/3½oz white chocolate made into
 curls, to decorate

1 Preheat the oven to 180°C/350°F/gas 4. Grease and base-line two 20cm/8in sandwich cake tins.

2 Put the butter and sugar in a mixing bowl and beat using an electric hand mixer or wooden spoon until the mixture is light and creamy. Add the eggs and beat again. Add the flour, soured cream and white chocolate chips and fold them in, using a large metal spoon. Divide the mixture between the tins using a spatula.

3 Bake for 25–30 minutes until the cakes spring back when pressed lightly and a skewer inserted into the middle of each cake comes out clean. Remove the cakes from the oven and leave to stand for 5 minutes, then turn out on to a wire rack and leave to cool.

4 Put the desiccated coconut in a dry saucepan and heat gently for about 5 minutes until it starts to turn golden brown, stirring all the time to ensure it does not burn. Tip into a dish to cool.

5 Drizzle half the toffee liqueur over each cake and sandwich them together with the buttercream. Place the cake on a serving plate. Cover the sides and top of the cake with the whipped cream and sprinkle the toasted coconut all over it. Top with the white chocolate curls and refrigerate for 1 hour before serving.

151　Pear & Blackberry Crumble Cake

PREPARATION TIME 20 minutes　**COOKING TIME** 40–45 minutes　**SERVES** 8

225g/8oz butter, softened, plus extra
　for greasing
3 large pears, peeled, cored and chopped
3 tbsp light soft brown sugar
200g/7oz/heaped ¾ cup caster sugar

3 large eggs, lightly beaten
225g/8oz/1½ cups self-raising flour
1 tsp cinnamon
250g/9oz/scant 2 cups blackberries
55g/2oz/½ cup ground almonds

1　Preheat the oven to 180°C/350°F/gas 4. Grease and line a deep 23cm/9in springform cake tin.

2　Put the pears, light brown sugar and 100ml/3½fl oz/scant ½ cup water in a saucepan and simmer for 15 minutes until the pears are soft. Drain off any remaining water and set the pears aside.

3　Put 175g/6oz of the butter and 175g/6oz/scant ¾ cup of the caster sugar in a mixing bowl and beat using an electric hand mixer or wooden spoon until the mixture is light and creamy. Add the eggs gradually, beating after each addition. Sift in 175g/6oz/scant 1¼ cups of the flour and the cinnamon and gently fold them into the mixture, using a large metal spoon. Scrape the mixture into the tin using a spatula, then cover with the pears and blackberries.

4　Put the remaining flour and the ground almonds in a bowl and rub in the remaining butter with your fingertips to make large crumble pieces. Mix in the remaining caster sugar with your fingers. Sprinkle the crumble topping over the fruit.

5　Bake for 25–30 minutes until the crumble topping is golden brown. Remove the cake from the oven and leave to stand for 5 minutes, then turn out on to a serving plate and serve while still warm.

152　Pineapple Upside-Down Cake

PREPARATION TIME 25 minutes　**COOKING TIME** 30–35 minutes　**SERVES** 8

280g/10oz butter, softened, plus extra
　for greasing
3 tbsp golden syrup
8 canned pineapple rings in juice,
　drained
8 glacé cherries

225g/8oz/scant 1 cup caster sugar
4 large eggs, lightly beaten
225g/8oz/1½ cups self-raising flour
1 tsp cinnamon
2 tbsp milk
custard or cream, to serve

1　Preheat the oven to 190°C/375°F/gas 5. Grease and line a 23cm/9in springform cake tin.

2　Put the syrup and 55g/2oz of the butter in a small saucepan and heat gently for about 5 minutes, stirring, until the butter has melted. Pour the mixture into the bottom of the tin. Arrange the pineapple rings on top of the mixture with a cherry in the middle of each one. Set aside.

3　Put the butter and sugar in a mixing bowl and beat using an electric hand mixer or wooden spoon until the mixture is light and creamy. Add the eggs gradually, beating after each addition. Sift in the flour and cinnamon and fold them into the mixture with the milk, using a large metal spoon. Scrape the mixture on top of the pineapple using a spatula.

4　Bake for 25–30 minutes until the cake springs back when pressed lightly and a skewer inserted into the middle of the cake comes out clean. Remove the cake from the oven and leave to stand for 5 minutes. Remove the springform sides of the tin and put a serving plate on top of the cake. Holding both plate and tin base securely, tip the cake upside down so that it is inverted on to the plate. Remove the tin base and serve warm with custard or cream.

153 Pecan Pie Cake

PREPARATION TIME 20 minutes **COOKING TIME** 50–60 minutes **SERVES** 8

225g/8oz butter, softened, plus extra
  for greasing
175g/6oz/¾ cup light soft brown sugar
3 large eggs, lightly beaten
175g/6oz/heaped 1 cup self-raising flour,
  sifted

juice and finely grated zest of 1 large
  lemon
100g/3½oz/scant 1 cup pecan halves
55g/2oz/¼ cup dark muscovado sugar
2 tbsp golden syrup
custard or cream, to serve

1 Preheat the oven to 150°C/300°F/gas 2. Grease and line a deep 23cm/9in springform cake tin.

2 Put 175g/6oz of the butter and the light brown sugar in a mixing bowl and beat using an electric hand mixer or wooden spoon until the mixture is light and creamy. Add the eggs gradually, beating after each addition. Add the flour and gently fold it into the mixture with the lemon zest, using a large metal spoon. Scrape the mixture into the tin using a spatula and arrange the pecan halves in a circular pattern on top of the cake.

3 Bake for 50–60 minutes until the cake springs back when pressed lightly and a skewer inserted into the middle of the cake comes out clean.

4 Just before the cake is cooked, put the remaining butter, the lemon juice, muscovado sugar and syrup in a saucepan and heat gently, stirring, until the sugar has dissolved, then boil for 1 minute to create a syrup. Remove the cake from the oven and pour the syrup over the cake. Leave the cake to cool in the tin, then turn out on to a serving plate. Serve warm or cold with custard or cream.

154 Soured Cream & Rhubarb Upside-Down Cake

PREPARATION TIME 30 minutes   **COOKING TIME** 45–50 minutes   **SERVES** 8

225g/8oz butter, softened, plus extra
   for greasing
400g/14oz rhubarb, peeled and cut into
   2.5cm/1in pieces
juice and finely grated zest of 1 lemon
1 tbsp caster sugar
225g/8oz/1 cup dark soft brown sugar

4 large eggs, lightly beaten
225g/8oz/1½ cups self-raising flour,
   sifted
145ml/4¾fl oz/scant ⅔ cup soured
   cream
100g/3½oz/heaped ½ cup sultanas
clotted cream or crème fraîche, to serve

1   Preheat the oven to 180°C/350°F/gas 4. Grease and line a deep 23cm/9in springform cake tin.
2   Put the rhubarb, lemon juice and caster sugar in a saucepan with enough water to cover the fruit. Simmer for about 5 minutes until the rhubarb is soft but still retains its shape. Drain and arrange in circles over the base of the cake tin.
3   Put the butter and dark brown sugar in a mixing bowl and beat using an electric hand mixer or wooden spoon until the mixture is light and creamy. Add the eggs gradually, beating after each addition. Add the flour and gently fold it into the mixture with the soured cream, sultanas and lemon zest, using a large metal spoon. Spoon the mixture over the rhubarb.
4   Bake for 40–45 minutes until the cake springs back when pressed lightly and a skewer inserted into the middle of the cake comes out clean. Remove the cake from the oven and leave to stand for 10 minutes. Remove the springform sides of the tin and put a serving plate on top of the cake. Holding both plate and tin base securely, tip the cake upside down so that it is inverted on to the plate. Remove the tin base and serve warm with clotted cream or crème fraîche.

155 Buttered Rum Cake

PREPARATION TIME 25 minutes   **COOKING TIME** 25–30 minutes   **SERVES** 8

150g/5½oz butter, melted and cooled,
   plus extra for greasing
4 large eggs, separated
100g/3½oz/⅔ cup icing sugar, sifted
100g/3½oz/⅔ cup plain flour, sifted

100g/3½oz/scant 1 cup ground hazelnuts
100g/3½oz/scant 1 cup ground almonds
125ml/4fl oz/½ cup rum
3 tbsp dark muscovado sugar
fresh berries and crème fraîche, to serve

1   Preheat the oven to 190°C/375°F/gas 5. Grease and line a deep 23cm/9in springform cake tin.
2   Put the egg yolks and icing sugar in a mixing bowl and beat using an electric hand mixer or wooden spoon until the mixture is light and creamy. Add the flour, 100g/3½oz of the melted butter and the ground nuts and mix well.
3   Put the egg whites in a clean, dry bowl and whisk with an electric hand mixer or a whisk until they form stiff peaks, then gently fold them into the cake mixture, using a large metal spoon. Scrape the mixture into the tin using a spatula.
4   Bake for 25–30 minutes until the cake springs back when pressed lightly and a skewer inserted into the middle of the cake comes out clean.
5   Just before the cake is cooked, heat the rum with the remaining melted butter and muscovado sugar in a small saucepan until the sugar has dissolved, then boil for 1 minute to create a syrup. Remove the cake from the oven and pour the syrup over the cake. Leave the cake to cool in the tin, then turn out on to a serving plate. Serve with fresh berries and crème fraîche.

156 Warm Apple & Cinnamon Yogurt Cake

PREPARATION TIME 25 minutes **COOKING TIME** 50–60 minutes **SERVES** 8

200g/7oz butter, softened, plus extra
  for greasing
3 dessert apples, peeled, cored and
  thinly sliced
115g/4oz/½ cup dark muscovado sugar
juice of ½ lemon

115g/4oz/scant ½ cup caster sugar
3 large eggs, lightly beaten
200g/7oz/1⅓ cups self-raising flour
2 tsp cinnamon
200ml/7fl oz/scant 1 cup Greek yogurt
  with honey

1 Preheat the oven to 180°C/350°F/gas 4. Grease and line a 20cm/8in springform cake tin.
2 Put the sliced apples in a bowl with 1 tablespoon of the muscovado sugar and the lemon juice and stir well to coat. Place the apples in circles on the bottom of the tin, overlapping them so that the base is completely covered.
3 Put the butter, caster sugar and remaining muscovado sugar in a mixing bowl and beat using an electric hand mixer or wooden spoon until the mixture is light and creamy. Add the eggs gradually, beating after each addition. Sift in the flour and cinnamon and gently fold them into the mixture with the yogurt, using a large metal spoon. Gently spoon the cake mixture on top of the apples.
4 Bake for 50–60 minutes until the cake springs back when pressed lightly and a skewer inserted into the middle of the cake comes out clean. (If the top of the cake starts to brown too much, cover it with a piece of baking parchment.) Remove the cake from the oven and leave to stand for 5 minutes, then invert on to a serving plate and serve warm.

157 Vin Santo & Raspberry Trifle Cake

PREPARATION TIME 40 minutes, plus chilling **COOKING TIME** 35–40 minutes **SERVES** 8

175g/6oz butter, softened, plus extra
  for greasing
175g/6oz/scant ¾ cup caster sugar
3 large eggs, lightly beaten
175g/6oz/heaped 1 cup self-raising flour,
  sifted
100g/3½oz/scant 1 cup ground almonds
2 tbsp natural yogurt
1 tsp almond extract

240ml/8fl oz/scant 1 cup vin santo
  or other dessert wine
1 tbsp powdered gelatine
200ml/7fl oz/scant 1 cup ready-made
  custard
200g/7oz/heaped 1 cup raspberries
200ml/7fl oz/scant 1 cup double cream,
  whipped to stiff peaks
icing sugar, for dusting

1 Preheat the oven to 180°C/350°F/gas 4. Grease and line a deep 23cm/9in springform cake tin.
2 Put the butter and sugar in a mixing bowl and beat using an electric hand mixer or wooden spoon until the mixture is light and creamy. Add the eggs gradually, beating after each addition. Add the flour and gently fold it into the mixture with the ground almonds, yogurt and almond extract, using a large metal spoon. Scrape the mixture into the tin using a spatula.
3 Bake for 30–35 minutes until the cake springs back when pressed lightly and a skewer inserted into the middle of the cake comes out clean. Remove the cake from the oven and leave to stand for 5 minutes, then turn out on to a wire rack and leave to cool.
4 Meanwhile, pour 125ml/4¼fl oz/½ cup of the vin santo into a saucepan and heat gently for about 5 minutes. Remove from the heat, sprinkle over the gelatine and stir until it has dissolved. Set aside to cool, then strain through a fine-mesh sieve.
5 Cut the cake in half horizontally, using a sharp knife. Drizzle the remaining vin santo over the cut sides of the cake using a spoon. Return the bottom layer of cake to the tin with the springform side clipped back in place. Fold the custard, gelatine mixture and raspberries gently into the whipped cream, using a large metal spoon. Pour the custard cream into the cake tin and top with the second cake layer. Refrigerate for 2 hours, then gently transfer to a serving plate and dust with icing sugar.

158 Key Lime Mousse Cake

PREPARATION TIME 35 minutes, plus chilling **COOKING TIME** 35–40 minutes **SERVES** 8

175g/6oz butter, softened, plus extra
   for greasing
400g/14oz/1⅔ cups caster sugar
3 large eggs, lightly beaten
175g/6oz/heaped 1 cup self-raising flour
1 tsp baking powder
400ml/14fl oz/1½ cups double cream

250g/9oz mascarpone cheese
juice and finely grated zest of 5 limes
juice of 1 small orange
1 tbsp powdered gelatine
a few drops of green food colouring
   (optional)
icing sugar, for dusting

1. Preheat the oven to 160°C/325°F/gas 3. Grease and line a deep 23cm/9in springform cake tin.
2. Put the butter and 175g/6oz/scant ¾ cup of the sugar in a mixing bowl and beat using an electric hand mixer or wooden spoon until the mixture is light and creamy. Add the eggs gradually, beating after each addition. Sift in the flour and baking powder and gently fold them into the mixture, using a large metal spoon. Scrape the mixture into the tin using a spatula.
3. Bake for 30–35 minutes until the cake springs back when pressed lightly and a skewer inserted into the middle of the cake comes out clean. Remove the cake from the oven and leave to stand for 5 minutes, then turn out on to a wire rack and leave to cool.
4. In a separate bowl, beat the remaining sugar with the cream, mascarpone cheese, lime juice and zest and orange juice to a smooth cream using an electric hand mixer or wooden spoon.
5. Put 2 tablespoons water in a bowl on top of a saucepan half-full of simmering water. Sprinkle the gelatine over the water and stir until the gelatine has dissolved. Do not overheat, otherwise the gelatine will lose its setting qualty. Stir the gelatine mixture into the lime cream with the food colouring, if using. Beat again.
6. Cut the cake in half horizontally, using a sharp knife. Return the bottom layer of the cake to the tin with the side clipped back in place. Pour the lime mousse over the cake, then top with the second layer. Refrigerate for 2 hours, then gently transfer to a serving plate and dust with icing sugar.

159 Blackcurrant & Cassis Cake

PREPARATION TIME 30 minutes   **COOKING TIME** 35–45 minutes   **SERVES** 8

200g/7oz/heaped 1 cup fresh or thawed
   frozen blackcurrants
55g/2oz/¼ cup light soft brown sugar
175g/6oz butter, softened, plus extra
   for greasing
175g/6oz/scant ¾ cup caster sugar
3 large eggs, lightly beaten
140g/5oz/1 cup self-raising flour

55g/2oz/heaped ¼ cup cocoa powder
100g/3½oz plain chocolate, grated
250g/9oz mascarpone cheese
200ml/7fl oz/scant 1 cup crème fraîche
2 tbsp icing sugar, sifted, plus extra
   for dusting
4 tbsp blackcurrant liqueur,
   such as cassis

1   Put the blackcurrants, light brown sugar and 100ml/3½fl oz/scant ½ cup water in a saucepan and simmer for 5–10 minutes until the fruit is soft. Strain and set aside to cool.

2   Preheat the oven to 180°C/350°F/gas 4. Grease and line a deep 23cm/9in springform cake tin.

3   Put the butter and caster sugar in a mixing bowl and beat using an electric hand mixer or wooden spoon until the mixture is light and creamy. Add the eggs gradually, beating after each addition. Sift in the flour and cocoa and gently fold them into the mixture with the grated chocolate, using a large metal spoon. Scrape the mixture into the tin using a spatula.

4   Bake for 30–35 minutes until the cake springs back when pressed lightly and a skewer inserted into the middle of the cake comes out clean. Remove the cake from the oven and leave to stand for 5 minutes, then turn out on to a wire rack and leave to cool.

5   In a bowl, mix together the mascarpone cheese, crème fraîche and icing sugar and gently fold in the poached blackcurrants to create purple swirls of fruit. Cut the cake in half horizontally, using a sharp knife, and drizzle the cassis over the 2 cut sides of the cake. Place the bottom layer on a serving plate, cover with the blackcurrant cream and top with the remaining cake half. Dust with icing sugar before serving.

160 Tiramisu Cake

PREPARATION TIME 30 minutes, plus chilling   **COOKING TIME** 30–35 minutes   **SERVES** 8

175g/6oz butter, softened, plus extra
   for greasing
175g/6oz/scant ¾ cup caster sugar
3 large eggs, lightly beaten
150g/5½oz/1 cup self-raising flour
4 tbsp cocoa powder, plus extra
   for dusting
250g/9oz mascarpone cheese

200ml/7fl oz/scant 1 cup crème fraîche
3 tbsp icing sugar, sifted, plus extra
   for dusting
100g/3½oz nougat chocolate, coarsely
   chopped
2 tbsp instant coffee granules dissolved
   in 3 tbsp boiling water, then cooled
5 tbsp almond liqueur, such as amaretto

1   Preheat the oven to 180°C/350°F/gas 4. Grease and line a deep 23cm/9in springform cake tin.

2   Put the butter and sugar in a mixing bowl and beat using an electric hand mixer or wooden spoon until the mixture is light and creamy. Add the eggs gradually, beating after each addition. Sift in the flour and cocoa and gently fold them into the mixture, using a large metal spoon. Scrape the mixture into the tin using a spatula.

3   Bake for 30–35 minutes until the cake springs back when pressed lightly and a skewer inserted into the middle of the cake comes out clean. Remove the cake from the oven and leave to stand for 5 minutes, then turn out on to a wire rack and leave to cool.

4   Meanwhile, put the mascarpone cheese, crème fraîche and icing sugar in a bowl and beat using an electric hand mixer or a wooden spoon. Stir in the nougat chocolate. Set aside

5   Combine the coffee liquid and amaretto. Cut the cake in half horizontally, using a sharp knife, and spoon the coffee mixture over both cut sides of the cake. Return the bottom layer of the cake to the tin with the springform side clipped back in place. Spoon the mascarpone cheese mixture over the base of the cake and smooth with a spatula, then top with the second layer. Refrigerate for 2 hours, then gently turn out on to a serving plate. Dust with icing sugar and cocoa before serving.

161 Plum & White Chocolate Flan

PREPARATION TIME 30 minutes   COOKING TIME 55–60 minutes   SERVES 8

175g/6oz butter, softened, plus extra
  for greasing
8 plums, halved and stoned
2 tbsp clear honey
2 tsp cinnamon
175g/6oz/scant ¾ cup caster sugar
3 large eggs, lightly beaten

175g/6oz/heaped 1 cup self-raising flour
1 tsp baking powder
100g/3½oz white chocolate, grated
3 tbsp plum jam
juice of 1 lemon
200ml/7fl oz/scant 1 cup double cream,
  whipped to stiff peaks

1 Preheat the oven to 190°C/375°F/gas 5. Grease a 23cm/9in raised-base flan tin and line
   the raised centre of the tin with baking parchment.
2 Put the plums in an ovenproof dish and bake with the honey, cinnamon and 2 tablespoons
   water for 30 minutes until the plums are soft but still hold their shape. Remove from the
   oven and leave to cool completely.
3 Put the butter and sugar in a mixing bowl and beat using an electric hand mixer or
   wooden spoon until the mixture is light and creamy. Add the eggs gradually, beating after
   each addition. Sift in the flour and baking powder and gently fold them into the mixture
   with the grated chocolate, using a large metal spoon. Scrape the mixture into the tin
   using a spatula.
4 Bake for 20–25 minutes until the cake springs back when pressed lightly and a skewer
   inserted into the middle of the cake comes out clean. Remove the cake from the oven
   and leave to stand for 5 minutes, then turn out on to a wire rack and leave to cool.
5 Put the jam and lemon juice in a small saucepan and heat gently until the jam has
   melted. Put the flan on a serving plate. Fill the centre of the flan with the whipped cream
   and top with the plums. Brush the glaze over the plums using a pastry brush and serve.

162 Apple & Pine Nut Crumble Tart

PREPARATION TIME 30 minutes   COOKING TIME 45–50 minutes   SERVES 8

85g/3oz chilled butter, chopped,
  plus extra for greasing
115g/4oz/¾ cup plain flour, sifted,
  plus extra for dusting
1 recipe quantity Shortcrust Pastry
  (see page 23)
4 large cooking apples, peeled, cored
  and thinly sliced

juice of 1 lemon
2 tbsp dark soft brown sugar
200g/7oz mascarpone cheese
55g/2oz/¼ cup caster sugar
55g/2oz/heaped ⅓ cup pine nuts
icing sugar, for dusting

1 Preheat the oven to 180°C/350°F/gas 4. Grease a 23cm/9in round loose-bottomed flan tin.
2 Sift flour on to a clean work surface and roll the pastry out to 1cm/⅜in thick using a rolling
   pin. Line the tin with the pastry and trim the edge neatly using a knife.
3 Toss the apple slices in the lemon juice and dark brown sugar and spoon into the pastry
   case. Dot small spoonfuls of the mascarpone cheese over the apples.
4 Put the flour and butter in a mixing bowl and rub the butter into the flour with your
   fingertips until the mixture resembles fine breadcrumbs, then mix in the caster sugar and
   pine nuts to form a crumble topping. Sprinkle over the apples.
5 Bake for 45–50 minutes until the apples are cooked and the topping is golden brown.
   Remove the tart from the oven and leave to cool in the tin, then turn out on to a serving
   plate. Dust with icing sugar to serve.

163 Glazed Summer Fruit Flan

PREPARATION TIME 30 minutes **COOKING TIME** 25–30 minutes **SERVES** 8

175g/6oz butter, softened, plus extra
  for greasing
175g/6oz/scant ¾ cup caster sugar
3 large eggs, lightly beaten
175g/6oz/heaped 1 cup self-raising flour
1 tsp baking powder
1 tsp vanilla extract
2 tbsp strawberry jam

juice of 1 lime
200ml/7fl oz/scant 1 cup double cream,
  whipped to stiff peaks
2 ripe peaches or nectarines, stoned
  and sliced
400g/14oz/scant 3 cups combined
  raspberries and strawberries,
  destalked and hulled

1 Preheat the oven to 180°C/350°F/gas 4. Grease a 23cm/9in raised-base flan tin and line
the raised centre of the tin with baking parchment.

2 Put the butter and sugar in a mixing bowl and beat using an electric hand mixer or
wooden spoon until the mixture is light and creamy. Add the eggs gradually, beating after
each addition. Sift in the flour and baking powder and gently fold them into the mixture
with the vanilla extract, using a large metal spoon. Scrape the mixture into the tin using
a spatula.

3 Bake for 20–25 minutes until the cake springs back when pressed lightly and a skewer
inserted into the middle of the cake comes out clean. Remove the cake from the oven
and leave to stand for 5 minutes, then turn out on to a wire rack and leave to cool.

4 Heat the jam and lime juice in a small saucepan until the jam has melted, then leave to
cool. Place the flan on a serving plate, fill the centre with the whipped cream and top
with the peaches or nectarines and the raspberries and strawberries. Brush over the
strawberry glaze with a pastry brush and serve immediately.

164 Chocolate Chip Cheesecake

PREPARATION TIME 30 minutes, plus chilling   **COOKING TIME** 50–60 minutes   **SERVES** 8

125g/4½oz butter, melted and cooled,
    plus extra for greasing
300g/10½oz chocolate-covered digestive
    biscuits, roughly broken
600g/1lb 5oz cream cheese

3 large eggs and 1 large egg yolk
150g/5½oz/scant ⅔ cup caster sugar
90ml/3fl oz/scant ½ cup double cream
seeds from 2 vanilla pods
100g/3½oz/½ cup plain chocolate chips

1   Preheat the oven to 150°C/300°F/gas 2. Grease and base-line a 25cm/10in springform cake tin. Wrap the sides and base of the tin with cling film so that it is watertight.
2   Put the broken biscuits in a food processor and pulse to fine crumbs. Alternatively, put them in a plastic bag and crush with a rolling pin. Mix the biscuit crumbs and melted butter together and press tightly into the base of the tin using the back of a spoon.
3   Put the cream cheese, whole eggs and egg yolk, sugar, cream and vanilla seeds into a blender and whizz until you have a smooth cream. Add the chocolate chips, then pour the mixture on top of the biscuit base.
4   Half fill a roasting tin with water and place the cheesecake in the tin. Transfer the cheesecake in the bain marie into the oven.
5   Bake for 50–60 minutes until the cheesecake is firm. Remove the cheesecake from the oven and from the bain marie and leave to cool in the tin, then refrigerate for 1 hour. Remove from the tin and place on a serving plate.

165 New York Soured Cream Cheesecake

PREPARATION TIME 30 minutes, plus chilling   **COOKING TIME** 1 hour–1 hour 10 minutes   **SERVES** 8

125g/4½oz butter, melted and cooled,
    plus extra for greasing
300g/10½oz digestive biscuits,
    roughly broken
seeds from 1 vanilla pod
600g/1lb 5oz cream cheese

250ml/9fl oz/1 cup condensed milk
3 large eggs and 1 large egg yolk
150g/5½oz/scant ⅔ cup caster sugar
290ml/10fl oz/heaped 1 cup soured
    cream
2 tbsp icing sugar, sifted

1   Preheat the oven to 150°C/300°F/gas 2. Grease and base-line a 23cm/9in springform cake tin. Wrap the sides and base of the tin with cling film so that it is watertight.
2   Put the broken biscuits in a food processor and pulse to fine crumbs. (Alternatively, put them in a plastic bag and crush with a rolling pin.) Add the biscuit crumbs to the melted butter and mix together, then press the mixture firmly into the base of the tin using the back of a spoon.
3   Put the vanilla seeds, cream cheese, condensed milk, whole eggs and egg yolk, caster sugar and 100ml/3½fl oz/scant ½ cup of the soured cream into a blender and whizz until you have a smooth cream. Pour the cheesecake filling on top of the base.
4   Half fill a roasting tin with water and place the cheesecake in the tin. Transfer the cheesecake in the bain marie into the oven.
5   Bake for 50–60 minutes until the cheesecake is firm. In a separate bowl, beat the remaining soured cream with the icing sugar until smooth, using a wooden spoon. Pour over the cheesecake and return to the oven for 10 minutes. Remove the cheesecake from the oven and from the bain marie and leave to cool in the tin, then refrigerate for 1 hour. Remove from the tin and place on a serving plate.

166 Banoffi Cheesecake

PREPARATION TIME 20 minutes, plus chilling **SERVES** 8

125g/4½oz butter, melted and cooled,
  plus extra for greasing
300g/10½oz digestive biscuits,
  roughly broken
2 bananas, peeled and sliced
4 tbsp toffee sauce

500g/1lb 2oz mascarpone cheese
250ml/9fl oz/1 cup crème fraîche
2 heaped tbsp icing sugar, sifted
100g/3½oz plain chocolate made
  into curls, to decorate

1   Grease and base-line a 20cm/8in springform cake tin.
2   Put the broken biscuits in a food processor and pulse to fine crumbs. (Alternatively, put them in a plastic bag and crush with a rolling pin.) Add the biscuit crumbs to the melted butter and mix together, then press the mixture firmly into the base of the tin using the back of a spoon.
3   Place the banana slices on the biscuit crumbs and top with the toffee sauce.
4   In a bowl, beat together the mascarpone cheese, crème fraîche and icing sugar with an electric hand mixer or a wooden spoon. Scrape the mixture into the tin using a spatula. Top with the chocolate curls and refrigerate for at least 2 hours. Remove from the tin and place on a serving plate.

167 Gregg's Sticky Toffee Nut Cheesecake

PREPARATION TIME 30 minutes, plus chilling   **COOKING TIME** 55–65 minutes   **SERVES** 8

140g/5oz butter, melted and cooled,
  plus extra for greasing
300g/10½oz digestive biscuits,
  roughly broken
100g/3½oz/1 cup ground almonds
400g/14oz cream cheese
150g/5½oz/scant ⅔ cup caster sugar
2 large eggs and 1 egg yolk
100ml/3½fl oz/scant ½ cup double
  cream

1 tsp vanilla extract
1 tbsp Pistachio or Hazelnut Butter
  (see page 22)

FOR THE TOPPING
1 tbsp light muscovado sugar
15g/½oz butter, softened
1 rounded tbsp golden syrup
350g/12oz/2½ cups mixed unsalted nuts

1   Preheat the oven to 150°C/300°F/gas 2. Grease and base-line a deep 23cm/9in springform cake tin. Wrap the sides and base of the tin with cling film so it is watertight.
2   Put the broken biscuits in a food processor and pulse to fine crumbs. (Alternatively, put them in a plastic bag and crush with a rolling pin.) Add the biscuit crumbs and ground almonds to the melted butter and mix together, then press the mixture firmly into the base of the tin using the back of a spoon.
3   Put the cream cheese, sugar, eggs and egg yolk, cream, vanilla extract and nut butter in a blender and whizz until you have a smooth cream. Pour the mixture over the biscuit base.
4   Half fill a roasting tin with water and place the cheesecake in the tin. Transfer the cheesecake in the bain marie into the oven.
5   Bake for 50–60 minutes until the cheesecake is firm. Remove the cheesecake from the oven and from the bain marie and leave to cool in the tin, then refrigerate for 1 hour. Remove from the tin and place on a serving plate.
6   For the topping, put the sugar, butter and syrup in a saucepan and heat gently for about 5 minutes, stirring, until the sugar has dissolved. Add the nuts and stir to coat, then spoon the nut mixture on top of the cheesecake to serve.

168 Blueberry & Lemon Cheesecake

PREPARATION TIME 40 minutes, plus chilling   **COOKING TIME** 1 hour 5 minutes–1 hour 20 minutes
SERVES 8

30g/1oz chilled butter, chopped,
   plus extra for greasing
140g/5oz/1 cup self-raising flour
1 tsp baking powder
125g/4½oz/½ cup caster sugar
4 large eggs
1 tbsp milk (optional)

450g/1lb cream cheese
100ml/3½fl oz/scant ½ cup double cream
juice and finely grated zest of 2 lemons
400g/14oz/2½ cups blueberries
2 tbsp light soft brown sugar
icing sugar, for dusting

1   Preheat the oven to 180°C/350°F/gas 4. Grease and line a deep 23cm/9in springform
    cake tin. Wrap the sides and base of the tin with cling film so that it is watertight.
2   Sift the flour and baking powder into a mixing bowl, add the butter and rub it in with
    your fingertips until the mixture resembles fine breadcrumbs. Add 2 tablespoons of the
    caster sugar and 1 of the eggs and mix to form a soft dough with your fingers, adding
    the milk if the dough is too dry. Press the dough over the base of the tin and cover with
    baking parchment and ceramic baking beans or dried pulses.
3   Bake blind for 10–15 minutes until the base (when you lift up the paper and beans) has
    a slight crust but is still pale. Remove the base from the oven, carefully lift out the beans
    on the paper and leave the base to cool.
4   Put the cream cheese, remaining caster sugar, cream, remaining eggs and the juice and
    zest of 1 of the lemons in a blender and whizz to form a smooth cream. Pour the mixture
    into the cake tin and scatter half the blueberries over the top. (They will sink in.)
5   Half fill a roasting tin with water and place the cheesecake in the tin. Transfer the
    cheesecake in the bain marie into the oven.
6   Bake for 50–60 minutes until the cheesecake is firm. Remove the cheesecake from the
    oven and from the bain marie and leave to cool in the tin, then refrigerate for 1 hour.
7   Put the remaining blueberries, remaining lemon juice and zest, 100ml/3½fl oz/scant
    ½ cup water and the light brown sugar in a saucepan and heat until the fruit is very
    soft. Blitz with a hand blender to form a sauce. Remove the cheesecake from the tin and
    place on a serving plate. Dust with icing sugar and serve with the sauce.

169   Cherry Cheesecake

PREPARATION TIME 20 minutes, plus chilling   **COOKING TIME** 3–5 minutes   **SERVES** 8

125g/4½oz butter, melted and cooled,
  plus extra for greasing
300g/10½oz plain chocolate-coated
  digestive biscuits, roughly broken
250g/9oz/2 cups preserved or fresh
  cherries, stones removed

3 tbsp cherry jam
500g/1lb 2oz mascarpone cheese
500ml/17fl oz/2 cups crème fraîche
finely grated zest of 2 lemons plus the
  juice of 1 lemon
2 heaped tbsp icing sugar

1   Grease and base-line a 20cm/8in springform cake tin.
2   Put the broken biscuits in a food processor and pulse to fine crumbs. (Alternatively, put
    them in a plastic bag and crush with a rolling pin.) Add the biscuit crumbs to the melted
    butter and mix together, then press the mixture firmly into the base of the tin using the
    back of a spoon.
3   Put the cherries and jam in a saucepan and heat gently for 3–5 minutes, then set aside
    to cool. Put the mascarpone cheese, crème fraîche, lemon juice and zest and icing sugar
    in a large bowl and beat using an electric hand mixer or wooden spoon until the mixture
    is light and creamy. Scrape the mixture on top of the biscuit base using a spatula. Cover
    with the cooled cherries and refrigerate for 2 hours, then remove from the tin and place
    on a serving plate.

170   Peach Melba Cheesecake

PREPARATION TIME 40 minutes, plus chilling   **COOKING TIME** 1 hour–1 hour 15 minutes   **SERVES** 8

30g/1oz chilled butter, chopped,
  plus extra for greasing
140g/5oz/1 cup self-raising flour
1 tsp baking powder
270g/9½oz/heaped 1 cup caster sugar
5 large eggs, 1 lightly beaten
1 tbsp milk
2 tbsp peach jam
2 ripe peaches, stones removed and
  thinly sliced

seeds from 1 vanilla pod (retain the pod
  for the fruit sauce)
600g/1lb 5oz cream cheese
100ml/3½fl oz/scant ½ cup double
  cream
225g/8oz clotted cream
400g/14oz/heaped 3 cups strawberries,
  hulled and sliced
400g/14oz/scant 3 cups raspberries

1   Preheat the oven to 180°C/350°F/gas 4. Grease and base-line a deep 23cm/9in
    springform cake tin. Wrap the sides and base of the tin with cling film so it is watertight.
2   Sift the flour and baking powder into a mixing bowl, add the butter and rub it in with
    your fingertips until the mixture resembles fine breadcrumbs. Add 2 tablespoons of the
    caster sugar and the beaten egg and mix to form a soft dough with your hands, adding
    the milk if the dough is too dry. Press the dough over the base of the tin and cover with
    baking parchment and ceramic baking beans or dried pulses.
3   Bake blind for 10–15 minutes until the base (when you lift up the paper and beans) has
    a slight crust but is still pale. Remove the base from the oven, carefully lift out the beans
    on the paper and leave the base to cool.
4   Spread the jam over the base and top with the peach slices. Put the vanilla seeds, cream
    cheese, 140g/4½oz/heaped ½ cup of the caster sugar, double cream, clotted cream and
    whole eggs in a blender and whizz to form a smooth cream.
5   Half fill a roasting tin with water and place the cheesecake in the tin. Transfer the
    cheesecake in the bain marie into the oven.
6   Bake for 50–60 minutes until the cheesecake is firm. Remove the cheesecake from the
    oven and from the bain marie and leave to cool in the tin, then refrigerate for 1 hour.
7   Meanwhile, put 200g/7oz of the strawberries, 100g/3½oz of the raspberries, remaining
    sugar, vanilla pod and 100ml/3½fl oz/scant ½ cup water in a saucepan and heat until
    the fruit is very soft. Tip the mixture into a sieve and press out all the juice from the fruit
    and pod using the back of a spoon. Discard the contents of the sieve. Leave the sauce to
    cool. Remove from the tin and place on a serving plate. Cover with the remaining berries
    and serve with the summer berry sauce drizzled over.

171 Coffee Cheesecake

PREPARATION TIME 30 minutes, plus chilling   **COOKING TIME** 20–25 minutes   **SERVES** 8

115g/4oz butter, softened, plus extra
  for greasing
115g/4oz/½ cup light soft brown sugar
2 large eggs, lightly beaten
115g/4oz/¾ cup self-raising flour, sifted
1 tbsp instant coffee granules dissolved
  in 2 tbsp boiling water, then cooled

500g/1lb 2oz mascarpone cheese
500ml/17fl oz/2 cups crème fraiche
3 heaped tbsp icing sugar, sifted
200g/7oz plain chocolate, finely grated
4 tbsp coffee liqueur
100g/3½oz white chocolate made into
  curls, to decorate

1 Preheat the oven to 190°C/375°F/gas 5. Grease and base-line a deep 23cm/9in springform cake tin.
2 Put the butter and light brown sugar in a mixing bowl and beat using an electric hand mixer or wooden spoon until the mixture is light and creamy. Add the eggs gradually, beating after each addition. Add the flour and gently fold it into the mixture with half the coffee liquid, using a large metal spoon. Scrape the mixture into the tin using a spatula.
3 Bake for 20–25 minutes until the cake springs back when pressed lightly and a skewer inserted into the middle of the cake comes out clean. Remove the cake from the oven and leave to cool completely.
4 Put the mascarpone cheese, crème fraîche, icing sugar and the remaining coffee liquid in a mixing bowl and beat using an electric hand mixer or wooden spoon until the mixture is light and creamy. Fold in half the grated chocolate. Drizzle the coffee liqueur over the sponge cake and top with the coffee cream, smoothing over the top with a spatula. Scatter the white chocolate curls and remaining grated chocolate over the top to decorate. Refrigerate for at least 2 hours, then remove the cheesecake from the tin and place on a serving plate.

172 Poppy Seed & Lemon Cheesecake

PREPARATION TIME 30 minutes, plus chilling   **COOKING TIME** 50–60 minutes   **SERVES** 8

125g/4½oz butter, melted and cooled,
  plus extra for greasing
300g/10½oz digestive biscuits,
  roughly broken
3 tbsp lemon curd
600g/1lb 5oz cream cheese
250ml/9fl oz/1 cup condensed milk

150g/5½oz/scant ⅔ cup caster sugar
3 large eggs, lightly beaten
100ml/3½fl oz/scant ½ cup double
  cream
juice and finely grated zest of 2 lemons
2 tbsp poppy seeds

1 Preheat the oven to 180°C/350°F/gas 4. Grease and base-line a deep 23cm/9in springform cake tin. Wrap the sides and base of the tin with cling film so it is watertight.
2 Put the broken biscuits in a food processor and pulse to fine crumbs. (Alternatively, put them in a plastic bag and crush with a rolling pin.) Add the biscuit crumbs to the melted butter and mix together, then press the mixture firmly into the base of the tin using the back of a spoon. Spoon the lemon curd over the top.
3 Put the remaining ingredients in a blender and whizz until you have a smooth cream. Pour the mixture over the biscuit base.
4 Half fill a roasting tin with water and place the cheesecake in the tin. Transfer the cheesecake in the bain marie into the oven.
5 Bake for 50–60 minutes until the cheesecake is firm. Remove the cheesecake from the oven and from the bain marie and leave to cool in the tin, then refrigerate for 1 hour. Remove from the tin and place on a serving plate.

173 Summer Berry Cheesecake

PREPARATION TIME 30 minutes, plus chilling   **COOKING TIME** 50–60 minutes   **SERVES** 8

125g/4½oz butter, melted and cooled,
  plus extra for greasing
300g/10½oz digestive biscuits,
  roughly broken
seeds from 1 vanilla pod (retain the pod
  for the fruit sauce)
600g/1lb 5oz cream cheese

3 large eggs and 1 large egg yolk
235g/8½oz/scant 1 cup caster sugar
225g/8oz clotted cream
2 tbsp strawberry jam
600g/1lb 5oz/5 cups strawberries
200g/7oz/1½ cups raspberries

1   Preheat the oven to 180°C/350°F/gas 4. Grease and base-line a deep 23cm/9in springform cake tin. Wrap the sides and base of the tin with cling film so that it is watertight.
2   Put the broken biscuits in a food processor and pulse to fine crumbs. (Alternatively, put them in a plastic bag and crush with a rolling pin.) Add the biscuit crumbs to the melted butter and mix together, then press the mixture firmly into the base of the tin using the back of a spoon.
3   Put the vanilla seeds, cream cheese, eggs and egg yolk, 140g/4½oz/heaped ½ cup of the sugar, the clotted cream and jam into a blender and whizz to form a smooth cream. Scape the mixture over the biscuit base using a spatula.
4   Half fill a roasting tin with water and place the cheesecake in the tin. Transfer the cheesecake in the bain marie into the oven.
5   Bake for 50–60 minutes until the cheesecake is firm. Remove the cheesecake from the oven and from the bain marie and leave to cool in the tin, then refrigerate for 1 hour.
6   Meanwhile, put 200g/7oz of the strawberries in a saucepan with 100ml/3½fl oz/scant ½ cup water, the remaining sugar and the vanilla pod and simmer for 10 minutes until the fruit is soft. Strain the mixture through a fine-mesh sieve, pressing all the juice out of the strawberries. Discard the contents of the sieve. Remove the cheesecake from the tin and place on a serving plate. Arrange the remaining strawberries and the raspberries on top of the cheesecake and pour the strawberry sauce over the top.

174 Mango Cheesecake

PREPARATION TIME 30 minutes, plus chilling   **COOKING TIME** 55–65 minutes   **SERVES** 8

125g/4½oz butter, melted and cooled,
  plus extra for greasing
300g/10½oz ginger biscuits, roughly
  broken
400g/14oz cream cheese
150g/5½oz/scant ⅔ cup caster sugar
2 large eggs and 1 large egg yolk

100ml/3½fl oz/scant ½ cup double
  cream
juice and finely grated zest of 2 limes
½ tsp freshly grated nutmeg
2 large fresh mangoes, peeled, stoned
  and thinly sliced
2 tbsp tropical fruit jam

1   Preheat the oven to 150°C/300°F/gas 2. Grease and base-line a deep 23cm/9in springform cake tin. Wrap the sides and base of the tin with cling film so it is watertight.
2   Put the broken biscuits in a food processor and pulse to fine crumbs. (Alternatively, put them in a plastic bag and crush with a rolling pin.) Add the biscuit crumbs to the melted butter and mix together, then press the mixture firmly into the base of the tin using the back of a spoon.
3   Put the cream cheese, sugar, whole eggs and egg yolk, cream, lime zest and nutmeg in a blender and whizz to form a smooth cream. Pour on top of the biscuit base.
4   Half fill a roasting tin with water and place the cheesecake in the tin. Transfer the cheesecake in the bain marie into the oven.
5   Bake for 50–60 minutes until the cheesecake is firm. Remove the cheesecake from the oven and the bain marie and leave to cool in the tin, then refrigerate for 1 hour. Remove from the tin and place on a serving plate. Arrange the mango slices on top in circles. Put the jam and lime juice in a small saucepan and heat gently, stirring, until the jam has melted. Brush the liquid over the mango slices with a pastry brush.

175 Redcurrant & Rosewater Cheesecake

PREPARATION TIME 20 minutes, plus chilling   **COOKING TIME** 3–5 minutes   **SERVES** 8

125g/4½oz butter, melted and cooled,
   plus extra for greasing
300g/10½oz digestive biscuits,
   roughly broken
250g/9oz mascarpone cheese
400g/14oz cream cheese
250ml/9fl oz/1 cup crème fraîche
3 heaped tbsp icing sugar, sifted

3 tbsp rosewater
finely grated zest of 1 lemon
200g/7oz/heaped 1 cup redcurrants
200g/7oz/heaped 1 cup raspberries
100ml/3½fl oz/scant ½ cup dessert wine
3 tbsp redcurrant jelly
1 tbsp powdered gelatine

1   Grease and base-line a deep 23cm/9in springform cake tin.

2   Put the broken biscuits in a food processor and pulse to fine crumbs. (Alternatively, put them in a plastic bag and crush with a rolling pin.) Add the biscuit crumbs to the melted butter and mix together, then press the mixture firmly into the base of the tin using the back of a spoon.

3   Put the mascarpone cheese, cream cheese, crème fraîche, icing sugar, 1 tablespoon of the rosewater and the lemon zest in a mixing bowl and beat using an electric hand mixer or wooden spoon until the mixture is light and creamy. Scrape the mixture over the biscuit base, smoothing the top with a spatula. Place the redcurrants and raspberries on top of the cheesecake.

4   Put the dessert wine, redcurrant jelly and remaining rosewater in a small saucepan and heat gently until the jelly dissolves. Sprinkle the gelatine over the warm jelly mixture and stir for 3–5 minutes until the gelatine has dissolved. Leave the jelly to cool, then strain through a fine-mesh sieve and pour over the fruit. Refrigerate for at least 2 hours, then remove from the tin and place on a serving plate.

176 Kiwi Fruit & Lemon Cheesecake

PREPARATION TIME 20 minutes, plus chilling   **COOKING TIME** 3–5 minutes   **SERVES** 8

125g/4½oz butter, melted and cooled,
   plus extra for greasing
300g/10½oz digestive biscuits,
   roughly broken
250g/9oz mascarpone cheese
300g/10½oz cream cheese

250ml/9fl oz/1 cup crème fraîche
juice and finely grated zest of 2 lemons
2 heaped tbsp icing sugar, sifted
1 kiwi fruit, peeled and thinly sliced
2 tsp powdered gelatine

1   Grease and base-line a deep 23cm/9in springform cake tin.

2   Put the broken biscuits in a food processor and pulse to fine crumbs. (Alternatively, put them in a plastic bag and crush with a rolling pin.) Add the biscuit crumbs to the melted butter and mix together, then press the mixture firmly into the base of the tin using the back of a spoon.

3   Put the mascarpone cheese, cream cheese, crème fraîche, lemon zest and icing sugar in a mixing bowl and beat using an electric hand mixer or wooden spoon until the mixture is light and creamy. Scrape the mixture into the tin using a spatula and cover with the sliced kiwi fruit.

4   Put the lemon juice and 3 tablespoons water in a small saucepan and heat gently. Remove from the heat, sprinkle over the gelatine and stir until the gelatine has dissolved. Leave the mixture to cool for 20 minutes, then strain through a fine-mesh sieve and pour over the top of the cheesecake. Refrigerate for at least 2 hours, then remove from the tin and place on a serving plate.

177 Raspberry & Lemon Roulade

PREPARATION TIME 30 minutes **COOKING TIME** 12–15 minutes **SERVES** 8

butter, for greasing
4 large eggs
115g/4oz/scant ½ cup caster sugar
115g/4oz/¾ cup plain flour, sifted
finely grated zest of 2 lemons
icing sugar, for dusting

4 tbsp almond liqueur, such as amaretto
500ml/17fl oz/2 cups double cream,
 whipped to stiff peaks
4 tbsp lemon curd
300g/10½oz/2 cups raspberries

1 Preheat the oven to 190°C/375°F/gas 5. Grease and line a 30 x 20cm/12 x 8in Swiss roll tin.
2 Put the eggs and caster sugar in a mixing bowl and whisk together using an electric hand mixer or a whisk until the mixture is creamy and pale yellow and the whisk leaves a trail when lifted up. Add the flour and gently fold it into the mixture with the lemon zest, using a large metal spoon. Scrape the mixture into the tin using a spatula.
3 Bake for 12–15 minutes until the cake springs back when pressed lightly. Remove the cake from the oven and leave for a few minutes.
4 Put a sheet of baking parchment on a clean work surface and dust with icing sugar. Turn the cake out on to the sugar-covered paper, cover with a damp tea towel and leave to cool for 10 minutes. Remove the tea towel and lining paper and cut away the edges of the cake to neaten it. Roll the cake up from a short end using the sugar-covered paper to help you and leave to cool completely. (The paper will end up rolled inside the cake.)
5 When the cake has cooled, unroll it gently, but don't worry if it cracks, because the cream will hold it together when it is rolled up again. Drizzle over the amaretto using a spoon. Spread over the cream and lemon curd and cover with the raspberries. Roll the roulade up, using the paper to help you but this time not rolling it inside the cake, and lift on to a serving plate. Dust with icing sugar before serving. As the roulade contains fresh cream, it should be eaten straight away or stored in a lidded container in the fridge.

178 Arctic Roulade

PREPARATION TIME 30 minutes **COOKING TIME** 10–12 minutes **SERVES** 8

butter, for greasing
3 large eggs
85g/3oz/⅓ cup caster sugar
85g/3oz/heaped ½ cup self-raising flour,
 sifted

1 tsp vanilla extract
icing sugar, for dusting
3 tbsp raspberry jam
500ml/17fl oz/2 cups strawberry
 ice cream, softened

1 Preheat the oven to 200°C/400°/gas 6. Grease and line a 30 x 20cm/12 x 8in Swiss roll tin.
2 Put the eggs and caster sugar in a mixing bowl and whisk together using an electric hand mixer or a whisk until the mixture is creamy and pale yellow and the whisk leaves a trail when lifted up. Add the flour and vanilla extract and fold them in, using a large metal spoon. Scrape the mixture into the tin using a spatula.
3 Bake for 10–12 minutes until the cake springs back when pressed lightly. Remove the cake from the oven and leave for a few minutes.
4 Put a sheet of baking parchment on a clean work surface and dust with icing sugar. Turn the cake out on to the sugar-covered paper and cut away the edges of the cake to neaten. Roll the cake up from a short end using the sugar-covered paper to help you and leave to cool completely. (The paper will end up rolled inside the cake.)
5 When the cake has cooled, unroll it gently, but don't worry if it cracks, because the ice cream will hold it together when it is rolled up again. Spread over the jam and cover with the ice cream. Roll the roulade up, using the paper to help you but this time not rolling it inside the cake, and lift on to a serving plate. Serve immediately. Any remaining roulade should be wrapped and stored in the freezer.

179 Chestnut Cream Roulade

PREPARATION TIME 30 minutes   **COOKING TIME** 18–25 minutes   **SERVES** 8

butter, for greasing
5 heaped tbsp cocoa powder, sifted,
   plus extra for dusting
150ml/5fl oz/scant ⅔ cup milk
5 large eggs, separated
140g/4½oz/heaped ½ cup caster sugar
55g/2oz/⅓ cup icing sugar, sifted, plus
   extra for dusting

4 tbsp coffee liqueur
200g/7oz chestnut purée
200ml/7fl oz/scant 1 cup crème fraiche
100g/3½oz coffee chocolate, melted
   and cooled slightly
500ml/17fl oz/2 cups double cream,
   whipped to stiff peaks

1   Preheat the oven to 190°C/375°F/gas 5. Grease and line a 37 x 27cm/14½ x 10½in Swiss roll tin.

2   Heat the cocoa and milk in a saucepan for 3–5 minutes until the cocoa has dissolved. Put the egg yolks and caster sugar in a mixing bowl and whisk together using an electric hand mixer or a whisk until the mixture is creamy and pale yellow and the whisk leaves a trail when lifted up. Stir in the cocoa mixture.

3   Put the egg whites in a clean, dry bowl and whisk with an electric hand mixer or a whisk until they form stiff peaks, then fold into the cake mixture, using a large metal spoon. Scrape the mixture into the tin using a spatula.

4   Bake for 15–20 minutes until the cake springs back when pressed lightly. Remove the cake from the oven and leave for a few minutes.

5   Put a sheet of baking parchment on a clean work surface and dust with icing sugar and cocoa. Turn the cake out on to the sugar- and cocoa-covered paper, cover with a damp tea towel and leave to cool for 10 minutes. Remove the tea towel and lining paper and drizzle the coffee liqueur over the cake using a spoon. Cut away the edges of the cake to neaten it. Roll up the cake from a short end using the sugar- and cocoa-covered paper to help you and leave to cool completely. (The paper will end up rolled inside the cake.)

6   In a mixing bowl, mix the chestnut purée, crème fraiche and icing sugar together using a whisk, then fold in the melted chocolate and half the double cream.

7   When the cake has cooled, unroll it gently, but don't worry if it cracks, because the cream will hold it together when it is rolled up again. Spread the chocolate filling over the cake, then top with the remaining cream and roll up the roulade, using the paper to help you but this time not rolling it inside the cake, and lift on to a serving plate. As the roulade contains fresh cream, it should be eaten straight away or stored in a lidded container in the fridge.

180 Baked Mocha Alaska

PREPARATION TIME 25 minutes   **COOKING TIME** 25–30 minutes   **SERVES** 8

115g/4oz butter, softened, plus extra
for greasing
280g/10oz/heaped 1 cup caster sugar
2 large eggs and 4 large egg whites
85g/3oz/⅔ cup self-raising flour
4 tbsp cocoa powder
1 tbsp instant coffee granules dissolved
in 1 tbsp boiling water, then cooled

100ml/3½fl oz/scant ½ cup coffee
liqueur
500ml/17fl oz/2 cups good-quality
coffee ice cream
1 banana, peeled and thinly sliced
55g/2oz plain chocolate, grated

1   Preheat the oven to 190°C/375°F/gas 5. Grease and line a 20cm/8in springform cake tin.
2   Put the butter and 115g/4oz/scant ½ cup of the sugar in a mixing bowl and beat using
    an electric hand mixer or wooden spoon until the mixture is light and creamy. Add the
    whole eggs one at a time, beating after each addition. Sift in the flour and cocoa and
    gently fold them into the mixture with the coffee liquid, using a large metal spoon.
    Scrape the mixture into the tin using a spatula.
3   Bake for 20–25 minutes until the cake springs back when pressed lightly and a skewer
    inserted into the middle of the cake comes out clean. Remove the cake from the oven
    and leave to stand for 5 minutes, then turn out on to a wire rack and leave to cool.
4   When you are ready to serve the Alaska, preheat the oven to 240°C/475°F/gas 9. Put
    the egg whites in a clean, dry bowl and whisk with an electric hand mixer or a whisk
    until they form stiff peaks. Slowly pour in the remaining sugar, whisking all the time,
    until the meringue is thick and glossy.
5   Place the cake in the centre of a shallow ovenproof dish that is larger than the cake.
    Pour over the coffee liqueur. Top the cake with the ice cream in scoops and the banana
    and sprinkle over the grated chocolate. Cover with the meringue, making sure that the
    cake and filling are all covered, and swirl the surface into peaks using a spatula. Bake
    the Alaska for 3–4 minutes until the meringue is lightly golden. Remove the Alaska
    from the oven and serve immediately.

181 Baked Lemon Alaska

PREPARATION TIME 25 minutes   COOKING TIME 25–30 minutes   SERVES 8

115g/4oz butter, softened, plus extra
  for greasing
280g/10oz/heaped 1 cup caster sugar
2 large eggs and 4 large egg whites
115g/4oz/heaped ½ cup self-raising
  flour, sifted

juice and finely grated zest of 2 lemons
3 tbsp icing sugar, sifted
500ml/17fl oz/2 cups good-quality
  lemon sorbet
3 tbsp lemon curd

1   Preheat the oven to 190°C/375°F/gas 5. Grease and line a 20cm/8in springform cake tin.
2   Put the butter and 115g/4oz/scant ½ cup of the caster sugar in a mixing bowl and beat using an electric hand mixer or wooden spoon until the mixture is light and creamy. Add the whole eggs one at a time, beating after each addition. Add the flour and gently fold it into the mixture with the lemon zest, using a large metal spoon. Scrape the mixture into the tin using a spatula.
3   Bake for 20–25 minutes until the cake springs back when pressed lightly and a skewer inserted into the middle of the cake comes out clean. Shortly before the cake is cooked, heat the lemon juice with the icing sugar in a small saucepan until the sugar has dissolved, then boil for 1 minute. Remove the cake from the oven and pour over the lemon syrup. Leave to stand for 5 minutes, then turn out on to a wire rack and leave to cool.
4   When you are ready to serve the Alaska, preheat the oven to 240°C/475°F/gas 9. Put the egg whites in a clean, dry bowl and whisk with an electric hand mixer or a whisk until they form stiff peaks. Slowly pour in the remaining caster sugar, whisking all the time, until the meringue is thick and glossy.
5   Place the lemon cake in the centre of a shallow ovenproof dish that is larger than the cake. Top the cake with the lemon sorbet in scoops and spoon over the lemon curd. Cover with the meringue, ensuring that the cake and filling are all covered, and smooth the surface into swirled peaks using a spatula.
6   Bake the Alaska for 3–4 minutes until the meringue is lightly golden. Remove the Alaska from the oven and serve immediately.

182 Hazelnut Brownies with Chocolate Sauce

PREPARATION TIME 20 minutes   COOKING TIME 45–50 minutes   SERVES 8

250g/9oz butter, chopped, plus extra
  for greasing
400g/14oz plain chocolate,
  350g/11oz broken into pieces;
  50g/2oz chopped
250g/9oz/1 cup caster sugar
250g/9oz/1 cup light soft brown sugar
5 large eggs
1 tsp vanilla extract
200g/7oz/1⅓ cups plain flour, sifted

100g/3½oz/½ cup chopped toasted
  hazelnuts
400g/14oz/heaped 2 cups raspberries

FOR THE SAUCE
150g/5½oz plain chocolate,
  broken into pieces
30g/1oz butter
2 tbsp golden syrup
100ml/3½fl oz/scant ½ cup
  double cream

1   Preheat the oven to 190°C/375°F/gas 5. Grease and line a 30 x 23 x 6cm/12 x 9 x 2½in baking tin.
2   Melt the butter and broken chocolate together and leave to cool.
3   Put the caster sugar, light brown sugar, eggs and vanilla extract in a mixing bowl and whisk using an electric hand mixer or a whisk until the mixture has almost doubled in size. While still whisking, gently pour in the melted chocolate and butter mixture until it is all incorporated. Add the flour and fold it in with the nuts and the chopped chocolate. Pour the cake mixture into the tin.
4   Bake for 35–40 minutes until the brownie has formed a crust and a skewer inserted into the middle of the cake comes out clean. Remove the brownie from the oven and leave to cool in the tin before cutting into 16 slices.
5   Meanwhile, in a saucepan heat the sauce ingredients, stirring, until the chocolate and butter have melted to form a smooth chocolate sauce. Serve the brownies with the sauce and raspberries.

183 Bakewell Puff

PREPARATION TIME 20 minutes   **COOKING TIME** 25–30 minutes   **SERVES** 6–8

175g/6oz butter, softened, plus extra
  for greasing
85g/3oz/heaped ½ cup plain flour,
  sifted, plus extra for dusting
500g/1lb 2oz block puff pastry
2 tbsp raspberry jam

175g/6oz/scant ¾ cup caster sugar
85g/3oz/¾ cup ground almonds
2 large egg yolks
55g/2oz/heaped ⅓ cup flaked almonds
icing sugar, for dusting

1   Preheat the oven to 180°C/350°F/gas 4. Lightly grease a 30cm/12in square baking tray.
2   Sift flour on to a clean work surface and roll the pastry out into a 40 x 20cm/16 x 8in
    rectangle, 5mm/¼in thick, using a rolling pin. Place the pastry on the tray.
3   Score a line 2cm/¾in in from the edge of the pastry all the way round the rectangle with
    a sharp knife, taking care not to cut through the pastry. Spread the jam over the pastry,
    keeping inside the scored lines.
4   Put the butter and sugar in a mixing bowl and beat using an electric hand mixer or
    wooden spoon until the mixture is light and creamy. Add the ground almonds, egg yolks
    and flour and beat again. Spread the almond topping over the jam and sprinkle with the
    flaked almonds.
5   Bake for 25–30 minutes until the topping is golden brown and the pastry is cooked.
    Remove the buns from the oven and leave to cool on the tray, then dust with icing sugar
    to serve.

184 Toffee Choux Buns with Caramel Sauce

PREPARATION TIME 25 minutes   **COOKING TIME** 35–40 minutes   **MAKES** 16 buns

115g/4oz butter, chopped, plus extra
  for greasing
140g/5oz/1 cup plain flour, sifted
4 large eggs, beaten

4 tbsp maple syrup
1 tbsp dark soft brown sugar
400ml/14fl oz/1½ cups double cream
2 tbsp toffee or Irish cream liqueur

1   Preheat the oven to 200°C/400°/gas 6. Grease and line two 30cm/12in square
    baking trays.
2   Put the butter and 250ml/9fl oz/1 cup water in a saucepan and heat until the butter has
    melted. Bring to the boil, then remove from the heat and quickly add the flour all at once.
    Return the pan to the heat and beat the mixture hard with a wooden spoon until it forms
    a ball of dough and leaves the sides of the pan clean.
3   Remove from the heat and add the eggs gradually, beating after each addition. When
    all the eggs have been incorporated, you should have a smooth, soft paste. Place
    16 tablespoons of the paste in balls about 5cm/2in in diameter on the trays.
4   Bake for 20–25 minutes until the pastry is golden brown. Remove the buns from the
    oven and make a small slit in each one with a knife to allow the steam to escape. Return
    to the oven for a further 5 minutes to crisp. Remove and leave to cool on a wire rack.
5   Heat the maple syrup, dark brown sugar and 150ml/5fl oz/scant ⅔ cup of the cream in
    a saucepan, stirring, until the sugar has dissolved and you have a runny toffee sauce.
    Set aside to cool.
6   Put the remaining cream in a bowl and whip to stiff peaks using an electric hand mixer
    or a whisk, then fold in the liqueur. Fill the buns with the cream and serve with the
    toffee sauce drizzled over them.

185 Raspberry & Almond Choux Ring

PREPARATION TIME 25 minutes   **COOKING TIME** 50 minutes   **SERVES** 6

115g/4oz butter, chopped, plus extra
  for greasing
140g/5oz/1 cup plain flour, sifted
4 large eggs, beaten
55g/2oz/heaped ⅓ cup flaked almonds
2 tsp almond extract

2 tbsp icing sugar, sifted, plus extra
  for dusting
400ml/14fl oz/1½ cups double cream,
  whipped to stiff peaks
200g/7oz/heaped 1 cup raspberries

1   Preheat the oven to 200°C/400°/gas 6. Grease and line a 30cm/12in square baking tray.
2   Put the butter and 250ml/9fl oz/1 cup water in a saucepan and heat until the butter has
    melted. Bring to the boil, then remove from the heat and quickly add the flour all at once.
    Return the pan to the heat and beat the mixture hard with a wooden spoon until it forms
    a ball of dough and leaves the sides of the pan clean.
3   Remove from the heat and add the eggs gradually, beating after each addition. When all
    the eggs have been incorporated, you should have a smooth, soft paste. Spoon the paste
    into an icing bag fitted with a 2cm/¾in plain nozzle and pipe a 20cm/8in ring of small
    balls on the baking tray. Sprinkle with the flaked almonds.
4   Bake for 15 minutes, then turn the temperature down to 180°C/350°F/gas 4 and bake
    for 30 minutes until the pastry is golden brown. Remove the ring from the oven and
    make a small slit in it with a knife to allow the steam to escape. Leave to cool.
5   Fold the almond extract and icing sugar into the whipped cream. Cut the ring in half
    horizontally and fill with the almond cream and raspberries. Top with the other half of
    the choux ring and dust with icing sugar.

CHAPTER 4

BISCUITS, COOKIES & SLICES

Delicious biscuits, cookies and slices of all shapes and sizes fill this chapter, and with many of them taking less than 20 minutes to bake, they are ready in no time. Traditional favourites include Orange Butter Cookies, Garibaldi Biscuits and Coconut Macaroons. New twists on old favourites are Lavender Shortbread, Rose & Violet Cream Biscuits and Chocolate & Cinnamon Streusel Cookies. Delicate meringues, such as Mini Chocolate Meringue Kisses and sumptuous Pistachio & Chestnut Meringues, just melt in the mouth. Tray bakes perfect for fêtes and fayres include flapjacks, gingerbreads, brownies and blondies and fruit slices topped with apples, peaches and cream, gooseberries or raspberries. If nuts are your favourite, try the Peanut Cookies, Pine Nut Biscuits, Macadamia Chocolate Cookies or Attwood Cookies, scented with almond extract and rich with white chocolate and sour cherries. With over 80 quick and easy recipes to choose from, there is something for everyone.

ATTWOOD COOKIES *(SEE PAGE 133)*

186 Malted Chocolate Cookies

PREPARATION TIME 20 minutes   **COOKING TIME** 12–15 minutes   **MAKES** 15 cookies

115g/4oz butter, softened, plus extra
  for greasing
55g/2oz/¼ cup light soft brown sugar
1 medium egg, lightly beaten
175g/6oz/heaped 1 cup plain flour

4 tbsp cocoa powder
30g/1oz/¼ cup malted milk powder
100g/3½oz/heaped ½ cup plain
  chocolate chips

1   Preheat the oven to 180°C/350°F/gas 4. Grease two 30cm/12in square baking trays.
2   Put the butter and sugar in a mixing bowl and beat using an electric hand mixer or
    wooden spoon until the mixture is light and creamy. Beat in the egg. Sift in the flour,
    cocoa and malted milk powder and add the chocolate chips. Mix together with your
    hands to form a soft dough.
3   Divide the dough into 15 walnut-sized balls and place on the baking trays, leaving about
    5cm/2in between them for spreading. Press each cookie down slightly using your fingers.
4   Bake for 12–15 minutes until just firm. Remove the cookies from the oven and leave to
    cool on the trays for a few minutes, then transfer to a wire rack with a palette knife to cool.

187 Chocolate Praline Cookies

PREPARATION TIME 20 minutes   **COOKING TIME** 10–12 minutes   **MAKES** 18 cookies

115g/4oz butter, softened, plus extra
  for greasing
140g/4½oz/heaped ½ cup caster sugar
1 heaped tbsp Hazelnut Butter
  (see page 22)
1 medium egg, lightly beaten

210g/7½oz/1⅓ cups plain flour
4 tbsp cocoa powder
1 tsp bicarbonate of soda
200g/7oz plain chocolate, half chopped;
  half melted and cooled slightly

1   Preheat the oven to 180°C/350°F/gas 4. Grease two 30cm/12in square baking trays.
2   Put the butter, sugar and hazelnut butter in a mixing bowl and beat using an electric
    hand mixer or wooden spoon until the mixture is light and creamy. Beat in the egg. Sift
    in the flour, cocoa and bicarbonate of soda and add the chopped chocolate. Mix together
    with your hands to form a soft, fairly sticky dough. Add a little more flour if it is too sticky.
3   Divide the dough into 18 walnut-sized balls and place on the baking trays, leaving about
    5cm/2in between them for spreading. Press each cookie down slightly using your fingers.
4   Bake for 10–12 minutes until just firm. Remove the cookies from the oven and leave to
    cool on the trays for a few minutes, then transfer to a wire rack with a palette knife to cool.
    Drizzle the melted chocolate over the cookies in thin lines to decorate them, using a fork.

188 Tollhouse Cookies

PREPARATION TIME 15 minutes   **COOKING TIME** 14–18 minutes   **MAKES** 20 cookies

125g/4½oz butter, chopped, plus extra
  for greasing
350g/12oz/2⅓ cups plain flour
½ tsp bicarbonate of soda
2 tsp cinnamon
100g/3½oz/heaped ⅓ cup caster sugar
100g/3½oz/heaped ⅓ cup light soft
  brown sugar

1 tbsp golden syrup
1 large egg, lightly beaten
100g/3½oz/heaped ½ cup plain
  chocolate chips
100g/3½oz/heaped ½ cup walnuts,
  chopped

1   Preheat the oven to 180°C/350°F/gas 4. Grease two 30cm/12in square baking trays.
2   Sift the flour, bicarbonate of soda and cinnamon into a mixing bowl and add the caster
    sugar and light brown sugar. Mix together with a wooden spoon. Put the butter and
    syrup in a saucepan and heat gently until the butter melts. Cool slightly, then beat into
    the dry ingredients with the egg, chocolate chips and walnuts to form a soft dough.
3   Divide the dough into 20 walnut-sized balls and place on the baking trays, leaving about
    5cm/2in between them for spreading. Press each cookie down slightly using your fingers.
4   Bake for 12–15 minutes until golden brown and just firm. Remove the cookies from the
    oven and leave to cool on the trays for a few minutes, then transfer to a wire rack to cool.

189 Chocolate Coconut Cookies

PREPARATION TIME 15 minutes   COOKING TIME 14–18 minutes   MAKES 24 cookies

125g/4½oz butter, chopped, plus extra
   for greasing
280g/10oz/scant 2 cups self-raising flour
55g/2oz/heaped ¼ cup cocoa powder
85g/3oz/1 cup desiccated coconut
200g/7oz/heaped ¾ cup caster sugar

1 tbsp golden syrup
1 large egg, beaten
115g/3½oz chocolate-coated coconut
   bars, chopped into small pieces
1 tbsp milk (optional)

1   Preheat the oven to 180°C/350°F/gas 4. Grease two 30cm/12in square baking trays.
2   Sift the flour and cocoa into a mixing bowl and add the coconut. Heat the butter, sugar and syrup gently in a saucepan until the butter has melted, then pour over the dry ingredients and mix in. Leave the mixture to cool slightly. Mix in the egg and stir in the chocolate-coated coconut pieces to form a soft dough, adding the milk if the mixture is too dry.
3   Divide the dough into 24 walnut-sized balls and place on the baking trays, leaving about 5cm/2in between them for spreading. Press each cookie down slightly using your fingers.
4   Bake for 12–15 minutes until just firm. Remove the cookies from the oven and leave to cool on the trays for a few minutes, then transfer to a wire rack with a palette knife to cool.

190 All-American Chocolate Chunk Cookies

PREPARATION TIME 20 minutes, plus chilling   COOKING TIME 10–12 minutes   MAKES 12 cookies

200g/7oz/scant 1 cup light brown sugar
100g/3½oz/heaped ⅓ cup caster sugar
1 tsp vanilla extract
175g/6oz butter, melted, plus for greasing
1 large egg and 1 large egg yolk

300g/10½oz/2 cups plain flour,
   plus extra for dusting
½ tsp bicarbonate of soda
300g/10½oz milk chocolate, chopped
100g/3½oz/½ cup sultanas

1   Put the light brown sugar, caster sugar, vanilla extract and melted butter in a mixing bowl and beat using an electric hand mixer or wooden spoon until the mixture is light and creamy. Beat in the egg and egg yolk. Sift in the flour and bicarbonate of soda and add the chocolate and sultanas. Mix together with your hands to form a soft dough.
2   Sift flour on to a clean work surface and roll the dough into a 7.5cm/3in diameter cylinder. Wrap the cylinder in cling film and refrigerate for 1 hour.
3   Preheat the oven to 180°C/350°F/gas 4. Grease two 30cm/12in square baking trays. Cut the dough into 12 slices and place on the baking trays, leaving 5cm/2in gaps.
4   Bake for 10–12 minutes until golden brown. Remove from the oven and leave to cool on the trays for a few minutes, then transfer to a wire rack with a palette knife to cool.

191 Chocolate & Cinnamon Streusel Cookies

PREPARATION TIME 20 minutes   COOKING TIME 10–12 minutes   MAKES 10 cookies

150g/5½oz butter, softened, plus extra
   for greasing
100g/3½oz/heaped ⅓ cup caster sugar
1 large egg, lightly beaten
150g/5½oz/1 cup plain flour
½ tsp bicarbonate of soda
4 tbsp cocoa powder
1 tsp vanilla extract

100g/3½oz/heaped ½ cup white
   chocolate chips

FOR THE STREUSEL
55g/2oz/⅓ cup plain flour
3 tbsp caster sugar
45g/1½oz chilled butter, chopped
1 tsp cinnamon

1   Preheat the oven to 190°C/375°F/gas 5. Grease two 30cm/12in square baking trays.
2   Put the streusel ingredients in a bowl and rub with your fingertips to form breadcrumbs.
3   Put the butter and sugar in a mixing bowl and beat using an electric hand mixer or wooden spoon until the mixture is light. Add the egg and beat again. Sift in the flour, bicarbonate of soda and cocoa and add the vanilla extract and chocolate chips. Mix to a soft dough.
4   Divide the dough into 10 walnut-sized balls and place on the baking trays, leaving 5cm/2in gaps. Press each cookie down flat with a fork and top with a little of the streusel topping.
5   Bake for 10–12 minutes until just firm. Remove from the oven and leave to cool on the trays for a few minutes, then transfer to a wire rack with a palette knife to cool.

192 Chocolate, Peanut & Walnut Cookies

PREPARATION TIME 20 minutes   **COOKING TIME** 10–12 minutes   **MAKES** 15 cookies

125g/4½oz butter, softened, plus extra
   for greasing
70g/2½oz/⅓ cup light soft brown sugar
70g/2½oz/scant ⅓ cup caster sugar
1 large egg, lightly beaten
200g/7oz/1⅓ cups plain flour

1 tsp bicarbonate of soda
2 tbsp crunchy peanut butter
200g/7oz plain chocolate, half chopped;
   half melted and cooled slightly
100g/3½oz/heaped ½ cup chopped
   walnuts

1   Preheat the oven to 190°C/375°F/gas 5. Grease two 30cm/12in square baking trays.

2   Put the butter, light brown sugar and caster sugar in a mixing bowl and beat using an electric hand mixer or wooden spoon until the mixture is light and creamy. Beat in the egg. Sift in the flour and bicarbonate of soda and add the peanut butter, chopped chocolate and walnuts. Mix together with your hands to form a soft, fairly sticky dough, making sure the chocolate and nuts are evenly distributed. Add a little more flour if the dough is too sticky.

3   Divide the dough into 15 walnut-sized balls and place on the baking trays, leaving about 5cm/2in between them to allow for spreading.

4   Bake for 10–12 minutes until golden brown and just firm. Remove the cookies from the oven and leave to cool on the trays for a few minutes, then transfer to a wire rack with a palette knife to cool. Drizzle the melted chocolate over them, using a fork to make decorative lines. Alternatively, put the chocolate in an icing bag fitted with a 3mm/⅛in plain nozzle and pipe lines across the cookies.

193 Chocolate Cornflake Crunch Cookies

PREPARATION TIME 15 minutes   **COOKING TIME** 12–15 minutes   **MAKES** 15 cookies

115g/4oz butter, softened, plus extra
  for greasing
115g/4oz/½ cup soft light brown sugar
1 large egg yolk
100g/3½oz/⅔ cup plain flour

4 tbsp cocoa powder
1 tsp baking powder
100g/3½oz/heaped ½ cup
  plain chocolate chips
55g/2oz/scant 2 cups cornflakes

1 Preheat the oven to 190°C/375°F/gas 5. Grease two 30cm/12in square baking trays.
2 Put the butter and sugar in a mixing bowl and beat using an electric hand mixer or wooden spoon until the mixture is light and creamy. Beat in the egg yolk. Sift in the flour, cocoa and baking powder and add the chocolate chips and cornflakes. Mix together with your hands to form a soft dough.
3 Divide the dough into 15 walnut-sized balls and place on the baking trays, leaving about 5cm/2in between them to allow for spreading. Press each cookie down slightly using your fingers or a fork.
4 Bake for 12–15 minutes until just firm. Remove the cookies from the oven and leave to cool on the trays for a few minutes, then transfer to a wire rack with a palette knife to cool.

194 Vicarage Cookies

PREPARATION TIME 15 minutes   **COOKING TIME** 12–15 minutes   **MAKES** 15 cookies

115g/4oz butter, softened, plus extra
  for greasing
200g/7oz/heaped ¾ cup caster sugar
1 large egg, lightly beaten
1 tbsp golden syrup
200g/7oz/1⅓ cups self-raising flour

1 tsp baking powder
150g/5½oz/scant 2 cups porridge oats
2 wholewheat breakfast biscuits, crushed
100g/3½oz/heaped ½ cup white
  chocolate chips

1 Preheat the oven to 180°C/350°F/gas 4. Grease two 30cm/12in square baking trays.
2 Put the butter and sugar in a mixing bowl and beat using an electric hand mixer or wooden spoon until the mixture is light and creamy. Beat in the egg and syrup. Sift in the flour and baking powder and add the oats, crushed biscuits and chocolate chips. Mix together with your hands to form a soft dough, adding a little extra flour if the dough is too sticky.
3 Divide the dough into 15 walnut-sized balls and place on the baking trays, leaving about 5cm/2in between them to allow for spreading. Press each cookie down slightly using your fingers or a fork.
4 Bake for 12–15 minutes until golden brown and just firm. Remove the cookies from the oven and leave to cool on the trays for a few minutes, then transfer to a wire rack with a palette knife to cool.

195 Attwood Cookies

PREPARATION TIME 15 minutes   **COOKING TIME** 10–12 minutes   **MAKES** 20 cookies

175g/6oz butter, melted and cooled,
  plus extra for greasing
1 large egg
115g/4oz/scant ½ cup caster sugar
1 tsp almond extract
300g/10½oz/2 cups plain flour, sifted

200g/7oz white chocolate, chopped
55g/2oz/heaped ⅓ cup flaked almonds,
  plus extra for sprinkling
75g/2½oz/heaped ⅓ cup dried sour
  cherries

1 Preheat the oven to 180°C/350°F/gas 4. Grease two 30cm/12in square baking trays.
2 Put the egg and sugar in a mixing bowl and beat using an electric hand mixer or wooden spoon until the mixture is light and creamy. Beat in the almond extract and melted butter. Add the flour, chopped chocolate, flaked almonds and dried cherries and mix together with your hands to form a soft dough.
3 Place 20 large spoonfuls of the cookie mixture on the baking trays, leaving about 5cm/2in between them to allow for spreading. Sprinkle over the extra flaked almonds.
4 Bake for 10–12 minutes until golden brown and just firm. Remove the cookies from the oven and leave to cool on the trays for a few minutes, then transfer to a wire rack to cool.

196 Banana Chip Cookies

PREPARATION TIME 15 minutes **COOKING TIME** 10–12 minutes **MAKES** 15 cookies

85g/3oz butter, softened, plus extra
   for greasing
125g/4½oz/½ cup caster sugar
1 large egg, lightly beaten
125g/4½oz/scant 1 cup plain flour

1 tsp baking powder
55g/2oz/½ cup dried banana chips,
   chopped
1 tbsp banana milkshake powder

1   Preheat the oven to 180°C/350°F/gas 4. Grease two 30cm/12in square baking trays.
2   Put the butter and sugar in a mixing bowl and beat using an electric hand mixer or wooden spoon until the mixture is light and creamy. Beat in the egg. Sift in the flour and baking powder and add the banana chips and milkshake powder. Mix together with your hands to form a soft dough.
3   Divide the dough into 15 walnut-sized balls and place on the baking trays, leaving about 5cm/2in between them to allow for spreading. Press each cookie down slightly using your fingers or a fork.
4   Bake for 10–12 minutes until golden brown and just firm. Remove the cookies from the oven and leave to cool on the trays for a few minutes, then transfer to a wire rack with a palette knife to cool.

197 Cherry & Hazelnut Cookies

PREPARATION TIME 20 minutes, plus chilling **COOKING TIME** 12–15 minutes **MAKES** 20 cookies

115g/4oz butter, softened, plus extra
   for greasing
55g/2oz/¼ cup caster sugar
175g/6oz/heaped 1 cup plain flour,
   sifted, plus extra for dusting

55g/2oz/¼ cup glacé cherries, chopped
1 tbsp milk (optional)
55g/2oz/⅓ cup toasted hazelnuts,
   chopped

1   Put the butter and sugar in a mixing bowl and beat using an electric hand mixer or wooden spoon until the mixture is light and creamy. Add the flour and cherries and mix together with your hands to form a soft dough, adding the milk if the mixture is too dry.
2   Sift flour on to a clean work surface and roll the dough into a 5cm/2in diameter cylinder. Put the chopped hazelnuts on a sheet of foil or baking parchment and roll the dough in the nuts, covering it completely. Wrap the cylinder in cling film and refrigerate for 1 hour.
3   Preheat the oven to 180°C/350°F/gas 4. Grease two 30cm/12in square baking trays. Cut the dough into 20 slices and place on the baking trays.
4   Bake for 12–15 minutes until golden brown and just firm. Remove the cookies from the oven and leave to cool on the trays for a few minutes, then transfer to a wire rack with a palette knife to cool.

198 Sour Cherry Drops

PREPARATION TIME 20 minutes **COOKING TIME** 15–20 minutes **MAKES** 18 cookies

115g/4oz butter, softened, plus extra
   for greasing
115g/4oz/scant ½ cup caster sugar
2 large eggs, separated

225g/8oz/1½ cups plain flour, sifted
115g/4oz/¾ cup dried sour cherries
1 tsp almond extract

1   Preheat the oven to 180°C/350°F/gas 4. Grease two 30cm/12in square baking trays.
2   Put the butter, sugar and egg yolks in a mixing bowl and beat using an electric hand mixer or wooden spoon until the mixture is light and creamy. Beat in the flour, dried sour cherries and almond extract.
3   Put the egg whites in a clean, dry bowl and whisk with an electric hand mixer or a whisk until they form stiff peaks then fold gently into the mixture, using a large metal spoon.
4   Place 18 tablespoons of the mixture on the baking trays, leaving about 5cm/2in between them to allow for spreading.
5   Bake for 15–20 minutes until golden brown and just firm. Remove the cookies from the oven and leave to cool on the trays for a few minutes, then transfer to a wire rack with a palette knife to cool.

199 Spiced Syrup Oat Cookies

PREPARATION TIME 15 minutes   **COOKING TIME** 12–15 minutes   **MAKES** 18 cookies

115g/4oz butter, softened, plus extra
   for greasing
115g/4oz/scant ½ cup caster sugar
1 large egg, lightly beaten
2 tbsp golden syrup

115g/4oz/¾ cup plain flour
1 tsp baking powder
1 tsp mixed spice
1 tsp cinnamon
115g/4oz/heaped 1 cup porridge oats

1   Preheat the oven to 180°C/350°F/gas 4. Grease two 30cm/12in square baking trays.
2   Put the butter and sugar in a mixing bowl and beat using an electric hand mixer or wooden spoon until the mixture is light and creamy. Beat in the egg and syrup. Sift in the flour, baking powder, mixed spice and cinnamon and add the oats. Mix together with your hands to form a soft dough.
3   Divide the dough into 18 walnut-sized balls and place on the baking trays, leaving about 5cm/2in between them to allow for spreading. Press each cookie down slightly using your fingers or a fork.
4   Bake for 12–15 minutes until golden brown and just firm. Remove the cookies from the oven and leave to cool on the trays for a few minutes, then transfer to a wire rack with a palette knife to cool.

200 Peanut Caramel Cookies

PREPARATION TIME 15 minutes   **COOKING TIME** 14–18 minutes   **MAKES** 15 cookies

100g/3½oz butter, chopped, plus extra
for greasing
350g/12oz/2⅓ cups self-raising flour
1 tsp bicarbonate of soda
200g/7oz/heaped ¾ cup caster sugar

1 tbsp golden syrup
1 large egg, lightly beaten
2 tbsp caramel sauce
2 tbsp crunchy peanut butter
55g/2oz/scant ½ cup salted peanuts

1 Preheat the oven to 180°C/350°F/gas 4. Grease two 30cm/12in square baking trays.
2 Sift the flour and bicarbonate of soda into a mixing bowl, add the sugar and mix with a wooden spoon. Put the butter and syrup in a saucepan and heat gently for 2–3 minutes until the butter has melted. Cool slightly, then beat into the dry ingredients with the egg, caramel sauce, peanut butter and peanuts to form a soft dough.
3 Divide the dough into 15 walnut-sized pieces and place on the baking trays, leaving about 5cm/2in between them to allow for spreading. Press each cookie down slightly using your fingers or a fork.
4 Bake for 12–15 minutes until golden brown and just firm. Remove the cookies from the oven and leave to cool on the trays for a few minutes, then transfer to a wire rack to cool.

201 Peanut Cookies

PREPARATION TIME 15 minutes   **COOKING TIME** 12–15 minutes   **MAKES** 18 cookies

125g/4½oz butter, chopped, plus extra
for greasing
350g/12oz/2⅓ cups plain flour
1 tsp bicarbonate of soda
a pinch salt

200g/7oz/heaped ¾ cup caster sugar
2 tbsp golden syrup
1 large egg, lightly beaten
2 tbsp smooth peanut butter
100g/3½oz unsalted peanuts

1 Preheat the oven to 190°C/375°F/gas 5. Grease two 30cm/12in square baking trays.
2 Sift the flour and bicarbonate of soda into a mixing bowl, add the salt and sugar and mix well with a wooden spoon. Put the butter and syrup in a saucepan and heat gently for 2–3 minutes until the butter has melted. Cool slightly, then beat into the dry ingredients with the egg, peanut butter and peanuts to form a soft dough.
3 Divide the dough into 18 walnut-sized balls and place on the baking trays, leaving about 5cm/2in between them to allow for spreading. Press each cookie down slightly using your fingers or a fork.
4 Bake for 10–12 minutes until golden brown and just firm. Remove the cookies from the oven and leave to cool on the trays for a few minutes, then transfer to a wire rack with a palette knife to cool.

202 Macadamia Chocolate Cookies

PREPARATION TIME 15 minutes   **COOKING TIME** 12–15 minutes   **MAKES** 18 cookies

115g/4oz butter, softened, plus extra
for greasing
55g/2oz/¼ cup caster sugar
1 large egg, lightly beaten
2 tbsp golden syrup
200g/7oz/1⅓ cups plain flour

1 tsp bicarbonate of soda
100g/3½oz/heaped ½ cup plain
chocolate chips
100g/3½oz/scant 1 cup macadamia
nut halves

1 Preheat the oven to 180°C/350°F/gas 4. Grease two 30cm/12in square baking trays.
2 Put the butter and sugar in a mixing bowl and beat using an electric hand mixer or wooden spoon until the mixture is light and creamy. Beat in the egg and syrup. Sift in the flour and bicarbonate of soda and add the chocolate chips and nuts. Mix together with your hands to form a soft dough.
3 Divide the dough into 18 walnut-sized balls and place on the baking trays, leaving about 5cm/2in between them to allow for spreading. Press each cookie down slightly using your fingers or a fork.
4 Bake for 12–15 minutes until golden brown and just firm. Remove the cookies from the oven and leave to cool on the trays for a few minutes, then transfer to a wire rack to cool.

203 Honey & Almond Crunch Cookies

PREPARATION TIME 15 minutes **COOKING TIME** 12–15 minutes **MAKES** 20 cookies

115g/4oz butter, softened, plus extra
   for greasing
55g/2oz/¼ cup caster sugar
1 large egg, lightly beaten
1 tbsp clear honey

200g/7oz/1⅓ cups plain flour
1 tsp baking powder
55g/2oz/heaped ⅓ cup flaked almonds
30g/1oz/1 cup cornflakes

1 Preheat the oven to 180°C/350°F/gas 4. Grease two 30cm/12in square baking trays.
2 Put the butter and sugar in a mixing bowl and beat using an electric hand mixer or wooden spoon until the mixture is light and creamy. Beat in the egg and honey. Sift in the flour and baking powder and add the almonds and cornflakes. Mix to form a soft dough.
3 Divide the dough into 20 walnut-sized balls and place on the baking trays, leaving about 5cm/2in between them. Press each cookie down using your fingers or a fork.
4 Bake for 12–15 minutes until golden brown and just firm. Remove from the oven and leave to cool on the trays for a few minutes, then transfer to a wire rack to cool.

204 Coffee Kisses

PREPARATION TIME 20 minutes **COOKING TIME** 10–12 minutes **MAKES** 15 cookies

225g/8oz butter, softened, plus extra
   for greasing
250g/9oz/1⅔ cups icing sugar, sifted
200g/7oz/1⅓ cups plain flour

4 tbsp cocoa powder
1½ tbsp instant coffee granules
   dissolved in 2 tbsp boiling water,
   then cooled

1 Preheat the oven to 180°C/350°F/gas 4. Grease two 30cm/12in square baking trays.
2 Put 175g/6oz of the butter and 55g/2oz/⅓ cup of the icing sugar in a mixing bowl and beat using an electric hand mixer or wooden spoon until the mixture is light and creamy. Sift in the flour and cocoa, add 1 tablespoon of the coffee liquid and mix again.
3 Spoon the mixture into an icing bag fitted with a 13mm/½in star nozzle and pipe thirty 3cm/1¼in stars on the baking trays, leaving about 5cm/2in between them for spreading.
4 Bake for 10–12 minutes until just firm. Remove the cookies from the oven and leave to cool on the trays for a few minutes, then transfer to a wire rack with a palette knife to cool.
5 For the filling, put the remaining icing sugar, butter and coffee liquid in a bowl and beat using an electric hand mixer or a wooden spoon until the mixture is light and creamy. Sandwich pairs of the biscuits together with the coffee cream and place in cake cases.

205 Mocha Cookies

PREPARATION TIME 20 minutes **COOKING TIME** 10–12 minutes **MAKES** 14 cookies

175g/6oz butter, softened, plus extra
   for greasing
85g/3oz/⅓ cup dark soft brown sugar
1 large egg, lightly beaten
1 tbsp instant coffee granules, dissolved
   in 1 tbsp boiling water, then cooled

200g/7oz/1⅓ cups plain flour
1 tsp baking powder
4 tbsp cocoa powder
100g/3½oz coffee chocolate, chopped
100g/3½oz/⅔ cup icing sugar, sifted
chocolate sprinkles, to decorate

1 Preheat the oven to 180°C/350°F/gas 4. Grease two 30cm/12in square baking trays.
2 Put the butter and dark brown sugar in a mixing bowl and beat using an electric hand mixer or wooden spoon until the mixture is light and creamy. Beat in the egg and half of the coffee liquid. Sift in the flour, baking powder and cocoa and add the coffee chocolate. Mix together with your hands to form a soft dough.
3 Divide the dough into 14 walnut-sized balls and place on the baking trays, leaving about 5cm/2in between them. Press each cookie down slightly using your fingers or a fork.
4 Bake for 10–12 minutes until just firm. Remove the cookies from the oven and leave to cool on the trays for a few minutes, then transfer to a wire rack with a palette knife to cool.
5 Put the icing sugar into a bowl, add the remaining coffee liquid and mix together to make a runny icing, adding a little water if it is too thick. Drizzle the icing over the cookies, using a fork to form decorative patterns. Shake the chocolate sprinkles over the icing while it is still wet, then leave to set.

206 Fudge Cookies

PREPARATION TIME 20 minutes   **COOKING TIME** 10–12 minutes   **MAKES** 20 cookies

175g/6oz butter, softened, plus extra
 for greasing
115g/4oz/scant ½ cup caster sugar
100g/3½oz cream cheese

225g/8oz/1½ cups self-raising flour, sifted
100g/3½oz plain chocolate, chopped
100g/3½oz vanilla fudge, chopped into
 small pieces

1 Preheat the oven to 190°C/375°F/gas 5. Grease two 30cm/12in square baking trays.
2 Put the butter, sugar and cream cheese in a mixing bowl, add the flour and beat using
   an electric hand mixer or wooden spoon until the mixture is light and creamy. Fold in the
   chocolate and fudge, making sure the pieces are evenly distributed.
3 Place 20 tablespoons of the mixture on the baking trays, leaving about 5cm/2in between
   them to allow for spreading.
4 Bake for 10–12 minutes until golden brown and just firm. Remove the cookies from the
   oven and leave to cool on the trays for a few minutes, then transfer to a wire rack with
   a palette knife to cool. (Trim away any of the fudge pieces around the edge of the cookies
   that have oozed during cooking.)

207 Sugar-Coated Chocolate Bean Cookies

PREPARATION TIME 20 minutes   **COOKING TIME** 12–18 minutes   **MAKES** 18 cookies

125g/4½oz butter, chopped, plus extra
 for greasing
350g/12oz/2⅓ cups plain flour
1 tsp bicarbonate of soda
a pinch salt

200g/7oz/heaped ¾ cup caster sugar
2 tbsp golden syrup
1 large egg, lightly beaten
1 tbsp milk
115g/4oz sugar-coated chocolate beans

1 Preheat the oven to 180°C/350°F/gas 4. Grease two 30cm/12in square baking trays.
2 Sift the flour, bicarbonate of soda and salt into a mixing bowl with the sugar. Put the
   butter and syrup in a saucepan and heat gently for 2–3 minutes until the butter has
   melted. Cool slightly, then beat into the dry ingredients with the egg and milk, using
   a wooden spoon, to form a soft dough, then gently stir in half the chocolate beans.
3 Divide the dough into 18 walnut-sized pieces and place on the baking trays, leaving
   about 10cm/4in between them to allow for spreading. Press each cookie down slightly
   using your fingers or a fork. Top with the remaining chocolate beans.
4 Bake for 10–15 minutes until golden brown and just firm. Remove the cookies from the
   oven and leave to cool on the trays for a few minutes, then transfer to a wire rack with
   a palette knife to cool.

208 Honeycomb Cookies

PREPARATION TIME 20 minutes   **COOKING TIME** 12–15 minutes   **MAKES** 15 cookies

55g/2oz butter, softened, plus extra
 for greasing
2 tbsp caster sugar
1 large egg, lightly beaten
2 tbsp golden syrup

225g/8oz/1½ cups plain flour
1 tsp bicarbonate of soda
1 tsp salt
85g/3oz chocolate-covered honeycomb,
 coarsely chopped

1 Preheat the oven to 180°C/350°F/gas 4. Grease two 30cm/12in square baking trays.
2 Put the butter and sugar in a mixing bowl and beat using an electric hand mixer or
   wooden spoon until the mixture is light and creamy. Beat in the egg and syrup. Sift in
   the flour, bicarbonate of soda and salt and add the honeycomb, making sure the pieces
   are evenly distributed. Mix together with your hands to form a soft dough.
3 Divide the dough into 15 walnut-sized pieces and place on the baking trays, leaving
   about 5cm/2in between them to allow for spreading. Press each cookie down slightly
   using your fingers or a fork.
4 Bake for 12–15 minutes until golden brown and just firm. Remove the cookies from the
   oven and leave to cool on the trays for a few minutes, then transfer to a wire rack with
   a palette knife to cool.

209 Chewy Ginger Cookies

PREPARATION TIME 15 minutes   **COOKING TIME** 14–18 minutes   **MAKES** 20 cookies

125g/4½oz butter, chopped, plus extra
  for greasing
350g/12oz/2⅓ cups self-raising flour
½ tsp bicarbonate of soda
1 tsp ground ginger
a pinch salt
200g/7oz/heaped ¾ cup caster sugar

finely grated zest of 1 orange
1 tbsp golden syrup
1 large egg, lightly beaten
 4 pieces stem ginger preserved in
  syrup, drained and finely chopped
1 tbsp of the stem ginger syrup

1   Preheat the oven to 180°C/350°F/gas 4. Grease two 30cm/12in square baking trays.
2   Sift the flour, bicarbonate of soda and ground ginger into a mixing bowl and add the salt,
    sugar and orange zest. Mix together with a wooden spoon. Put the butter and syrup in
    a saucepan and heat gently for 2–3 minutes until the butter has melted. Cool slightly,
    then beat into the dry ingredients with the egg, stem ginger and ginger syrup to form
    a soft dough.
3   Divide the dough into 20 walnut-sized pieces and place on the baking trays, leaving
    about 5cm/2in between them to allow for spreading. Press each cookie down slightly
    using your fingers or a fork.
4   Bake for 12–15 minutes until golden brown and just firm. Remove the cookies from the
    oven and leave to cool on the trays for a few minutes, then transfer to a wire rack with
    a palette knife to cool.

210　Cinnamon Snaps

PREPARATION TIME 15 minutes　**COOKING TIME** 14–18 minutes　**MAKES** 20 cookies

125g/4½oz butter, chopped, plus extra
　for greasing
200g/7oz/heaped ¾ cup caster sugar
350g/12oz/2⅓ cups plain flour
a pinch salt

½ tsp bicarbonate of soda
2 tsp cinnamon
1 tbsp golden syrup
1 large egg, lightly beaten

1　Preheat the oven to 180°C/350°F/gas 4. Grease two 30cm/12in square baking trays.
2　Put the sugar in a mixing bowl and sift in the flour, salt, bicarbonate of soda and cinnamon. Mix together with a wooden spoon. Put the butter and syrup in a saucepan and heat gently for 2–3 minutes until the butter has melted. Cool slightly, then beat into the dry ingredients with the egg to form a soft dough.
3　Divide the dough into 20 walnut-sized pieces and place on the baking trays, leaving about 5cm/2in between them to allow for spreading. Press each cookie down slightly using your fingers or a fork.
4　Bake for 12–15 minutes until golden brown and just firm. Remove the cookies from the oven and leave to cool on the trays for a few minutes, then transfer to a wire rack to cool.

211　Golden Citrus Cookies

PREPARATION TIME 15 minutes　**COOKING TIME** 14–18 minutes　**MAKES** 20 cookies

125g/4½oz butter, chopped, plus extra
　for greasing
200g/7oz/heaped ¾ cup caster sugar
finely grated zest of 1 lemon
finely grated zest of 1 orange
350g/12oz/2⅓ cups self-raising flour

a pinch salt
½ tsp bicarbonate of soda
1 tbsp golden syrup
1 large egg, lightly beaten
2 tbsp mixed peel

1　Preheat the oven to 180°C/350°F/gas 4. Grease two 30cm/12in square baking trays.
2　Put the sugar and lemon and orange zests in a mixing bowl and sift in the flour, salt and bicarbonate of soda. Mix together with a wooden spoon. Put the butter and syrup in a saucepan and heat gently for 2–3 minutes until the butter has melted. Cool slightly, then beat into the dry ingredients with the egg and mixed peel to form a soft dough.
3　Divide the dough into 20 walnut-sized pieces and place on the baking trays, leaving about 5cm/2in between them to allow for spreading. Press each cookie down slightly using your fingers or a fork.
4　Bake for 12–15 minutes until golden brown and just firm. Remove the cookies from the oven and leave to cool on the trays for a few minutes, then transfer to a wire rack to cool.

212　Date, Orange & Walnut Cookies

PREPARATION TIME 20 minutes, plus chilling　**COOKING TIME** 12–15 minutes　**MAKES** 18 cookies

115g/4oz butter, softened, plus extra
　for greasing
55g/2oz/¼ cup light soft brown sugar
175g/6oz/heaped 1 cup plain flour, sifted
　plus extra for dusting

55g/2oz/½ cup walnut pieces, chopped
55g/2oz/⅓ cup pitted dates, chopped
finely grated zest of 1 large orange
1 tsp vanilla extract
1 tbsp milk (optional)

1　Put the butter and sugar in a mixing bowl and beat using an electric hand mixer or wooden spoon until the mixture is light and creamy. Add the flour, walnuts, dates, zest and vanilla extract and mix together with your hands to form a soft dough, adding the milk if the mixture is too dry. Wrap in cling film and refrigerate for 1 hour.
2　Preheat the oven to 180°C/350°F/gas 4. Grease two 30cm/12in square baking trays.
3　Sift flour on to a clean work surface and roll the dough out to about 1cm/⅜in thick using a rolling pin. Cut out 18 rectangles using a 2.5 x 7.5cm/1 x 3in cutter, gathering up the trimmings and re-rolling as necessary. Place the cookies on the baking trays.
4　Bake for 12–15 minutes until golden brown and just firm. Remove the cookies from the oven and leave to cool on the trays for a few minutes, then transfer to a wire rack with a palette knife to cool.

213 Glazed Orange Cookies

PREPARATION TIME 20 minutes, plus chilling   **COOKING TIME** 12–15 minutes   **MAKES** 15 cookies

115g/4oz butter, softened, plus extra
  for greasing
55g/2oz/¼ cup caster sugar
175g/6oz/heaped 1 cup plain flour,
  plus extra for dusting
1 tsp cinnamon

finely grated zest of 1 orange, plus
  2 tbsp of the juice
1 tbsp milk (optional)
4 heaped tbsp icing sugar, sifted
a few drops of orange food colouring
chocolate sprinkles, to decorate

1   Put the butter and caster sugar in a mixing bowl and beat using an electric hand mixer or wooden spoon until the mixture is light and creamy. Sift in the flour and cinnamon and add the orange zest. Mix together with your hands to form a soft dough, adding the milk if the mixture is too dry. Wrap in cling film and refrigerate for 1 hour.
2   Preheat the oven to 180°C/350°F/gas 4. Grease two 30cm/12in square baking trays.
3   Sift flour on to a clean work surface and roll the dough out to about 1cm/⅜in thick using a rolling pin. Cut out 15 rounds using a 7.5cm/3in round cutter, gathering up the trimmings and re-rolling as necessary. Place the cookies on the baking trays.
4   Bake for 12–15 minutes until golden brown and just firm. Remove the cookies from the oven and leave to cool on the trays for a few minutes, then transfer to a wire rack to cool.
5   Put the icing sugar, orange juice and food colouring in a bowl and mix to form a thick icing. Drizzle the icing over the cookies in lines using a fork and decorate with chocolate sprinkles. Leave the icing to set before serving.

214 Lemon & Sultana Cookies

PREPARATION TIME 20 minutes, plus chilling   **COOKING TIME** 12–15 minutes   **MAKES** 16 cookies

115g/4oz butter, softened, plus extra
  for greasing
55g/2oz/¼ cup caster sugar
55g/2oz/⅓ cup sultanas

175g/6oz/heaped 1 cup plain flour,
  sifted, plus extra for dusting
finely grated zest of 1 lemon
1 tbsp milk (optional)

1   Put the butter and sugar in a mixing bowl and beat using an electric hand mixer or wooden spoon until the mixture is light and creamy. Add the sultanas, flour and lemon zest and mix together with your hands to form a soft dough, adding the milk if the mixture is too dry. Wrap in cling film and refrigerate for 1 hour.
2   Preheat the oven to 180°C/350°F/gas 4. Grease two 30cm/12in square baking trays.
3   Sift flour on to a clean work surface and roll the dough out to about 1cm/⅜in thick using a rolling pin. Cut out 16 cookies using a 7.5cm/3in round cutter, gathering up the trimmings and re-rolling as necessary. Place the cookies on the baking trays.
4   Bake for 12–15 minutes until golden brown and just firm. Remove the cookies from the oven and leave to cool on the trays for a few minutes, then transfer to a wire rack to cool.

215 Orange Butter Cookies

PREPARATION TIME 20 minutes, plus chilling   **COOKING TIME** 12–15 minutes   **MAKES** 12 cookies

115g/4oz butter, softened, plus extra
  for greasing
55g/2oz/¼ cup caster sugar

175g/6oz/heaped 1 cup plain flour,
  sifted plus extra for dusting
finely grated zest of 1 large orange
1 tbsp milk (optional)

1   Put the butter and sugar in a mixing bowl and beat using an electric hand mixer or wooden spoon until the mixture is light and creamy. Add the flour and zest and mix to form a soft dough, adding the milk if the mixture is too dry. Wrap in cling film and refrigerate for 1 hour.
2   Preheat the oven to 180°C/350°F/gas 4. Grease two 30cm/12in square baking trays.
3   Sift flour on to a clean work surface and roll the dough out to about 1cm/⅜in thick using a rolling pin. Cut out 12 rounds using a 7.5cm/3in round cutter, gathering up the trimmings and re-rolling as necessary. Place the cookies on the baking trays and prick with a fork.
4   Bake for 12–15 minutes until golden brown and just firm. Remove the cookies from the oven and leave to cool on the trays for a few minutes, then transfer to a wire rack with a palette knife to cool.

Margarita Cookies

PREPARATION TIME 20 minutes, plus chilling   **COOKING TIME** 12–15 minutes   **MAKES** 18 cookies

115g/4oz butter, softened, plus extra
  for greasing
55g/2oz/¼ cup caster sugar
175g/6oz/heaped 1 cup plain flour,
  sifted, plus extra for dusting

finely grated zest of 2 limes, plus
  1–2 tbsp of the juice
1 tbsp tequila
4 heaped tbsp icing sugar, sifted
a few drops of green food colouring
1 tsp coarse-ground sea salt

1 Put the butter and sugar in a mixing bowl and beat using an electric hand mixer or
   wooden spoon until the mixture is light and creamy. Add the flour and lime zest and mix
   together with your hands to form a soft dough, adding 1 tablespoon of the lime juice if
   the mixture is too dry. Wrap in cling film and refrigerate for 1 hour.
2 Preheat the oven to 180°C/350°F/gas 4. Grease two 30cm/12in square baking trays.
3 Sift flour on to a clean work surface and roll the dough out to about 1cm/⅜in thick using
   a rolling pin. Cut out 18 rounds using a 5cm/2in round cutter, gathering up the
   trimmings and re-rolling as necessary. Place the cookies on the baking trays.
4 Bake for 12–15 minutes until golden brown and just firm. Remove the cookies from the
   oven and leave to cool on the trays for a few minutes, then transfer to a wire rack to cool.
5 In a bowl, mix together the tequila, icing sugar, food colouring and 1 tablespoon of the
   lime juice to make a runny icing. Drizzle the icing over the cookies in lines using a fork,
   then sprinkle with the sea salt. Leave the icing to set before serving.

217   Orange & Cardamom Cookies

PREPARATION TIME 20 minutes   **COOKING TIME** 12–15 minutes   **MAKES** 18 cookies

115g/4oz butter, softened, plus extra
   for greasing
55g/2oz/¼ cup caster sugar
1 large egg, lightly beaten
2 tbsp golden syrup

200g/7oz/1⅓ cups plain flour
1 tsp bicarbonate of soda
1 tsp ground cardamom
finely grated zest of 1 orange

1   Preheat the oven to 180°C/350°F/gas 4. Grease two 30cm/12in square baking trays.
2   Put the butter and sugar in a mixing bowl and beat using an electric hand mixer or wooden
    spoon until the mixture is light. Beat in the egg and syrup. Sift in the flour, bicarbonate of
    soda and ground cardamom and add the orange zest. Mix to form a soft dough.
3   Divide the dough into 18 walnut-sized balls and place on the baking trays, leaving about
    5cm/2in between them. Press each cookie down slightly using your fingers or a fork.
4   Bake for 12–15 minutes until golden brown and just firm. Remove the cookies from the
    oven and leave to cool on the trays for a few minutes, then transfer to a wire rack to cool.

218   Garibaldi Biscuits

PREPARATION TIME 20 minutes   **COOKING TIME** 15–18 minutes   **MAKES** 16 biscuits

55g/2oz chilled butter, chopped,
   plus extra for greasing
115g/4oz/heaped ½ cup sultanas
finely grated zest of 1 lemon
115g/4oz/¾ cup plain flour, plus extra
   for dusting

1 tsp cinnamon
3 tbsp milk
55g/2oz/¼ cup light soft brown sugar
1 medium egg, beaten
caster sugar, for sprinkling

1   Preheat the oven to 190°C/375°F/gas 5. Grease two 30cm/12in square baking trays.
2   Put the sultanas and lemon zest in a blender or food processor and chop finely. Set aside.
    Sift the flour and cinnamon into a mixing bowl. Rub the butter into the flour with your
    fingertips until the mixture resembles fine breadcrumbs. Add the milk and light brown
    sugar and mix to form a stiff dough.
3   Sift flour on to a clean work surface and roll the dough out into a rectangle 5mm/¼in
    thick using a rolling pin. Cut the rectangle in half and sprinkle one half with the chopped
    fruit mixture. Place the other half on top and press down with the rolling pin.
4   Roll the dough sandwich out to about 1cm/⅜in thick and then cut into sixteen 5 x 10cm/
    2 x 4in rectangles with a sharp knife or a rectangular cutter. Place on the baking trays and
    brush with the beaten egg using a pastry brush, then sprinkle with a little caster sugar.
5   Bake for 15–18 minutes until golden brown and just firm. Remove the biscuits from the
    oven and leave to cool on the trays for a few minutes, then transfer to a wire rack to cool.

219   Orange & Strawberry Biscuits

PREPARATION TIME 20 minutes   **COOKING TIME** 15–18 minutes   **MAKES** 12 biscuits

115g/4oz butter, plus extra for greasing
55g/2oz/¼ cup caster sugar
225g/8oz/1½ cups plain flour
1 tsp bicarbonate of soda
1 tbsp golden syrup

1 large egg, lightly beaten
55g/2oz dried strawberry pieces
100g/3½oz/heaped ½ cup white
   chocolate chips
finely grated zest of 1 orange

1   Preheat the oven to 180°C/350°F/gas 4. Grease two 30cm/12in square baking trays.
2   Put the sugar in a mixing bowl and sift in the flour and bicarbonate of soda. Mix
    together with a wooden spoon. Put the butter and syrup in a saucepan and heat gently
    for 2–3 minutes until the butter has melted. Cool slightly, then beat into the dry ingredients
    with the egg, strawberry pieces, chocolate chips and orange zest to form a soft dough.
3   Divide the dough into 12 walnut-sized pieces and place on the baking trays, leaving
    about 5cm/2in between them to allow for spreading. Press each biscuit down slightly
    using your fingers or a fork.
4   Bake for 12–15 minutes until golden brown and just firm. Remove the biscuits from the
    oven and leave to cool on the trays for a few minutes, then transfer to a wire rack to cool.

220 Chocolate Chip Hearts

PREPARATION TIME 20 minutes, plus chilling   **COOKING TIME** 12–15 minutes   **MAKES** 15 biscuits

115g/4oz butter, softened, plus extra
   for greasing
55g/2oz/¼ cup caster sugar
100g/3½oz/heaped ½ cup chocolate chips

175g/6oz/heaped 1 cup plain flour,
   sifted, plus extra for dusting
1 tbsp milk (optional)

1   Put the butter and sugar in a mixing bowl and beat using an electric hand mixer or wooden spoon until the mixture is light and creamy. Add the chocolate chips and flour and mix together with your hands to form a soft dough, adding the milk if the mixture is too dry. Wrap in cling film and refrigerate for 1 hour.
2   Preheat the oven to 180°C/350°F/gas 4. Grease two 30cm/12in square baking trays.
3   Sift flour on to a clean work surface and roll the dough out to about 1cm/⅜in thick using a rolling pin. Cut out 15 heart shapes using a 10cm/4in heart cutter or a cardboard template and a knife. Place the biscuits on the baking trays using a palette knife.
4   Bake for 12–15 minutes until golden brown and just firm. Remove the biscuits from the oven and leave to cool on the trays for a few minutes, then transfer to a wire rack to cool.

221 Triple Chocolate Chunk Biscuits

PREPARATION TIME 15 minutes   **COOKING TIME** 14–18 minutes   **MAKES** 20 biscuits

125g/4½oz butter, chopped, plus extra
   for greasing
250g/9oz/1⅔ cups self-raising flour
100g/3½oz/⅔ cup cocoa powder
a pinch salt
1 tsp bicarbonate of soda

200g/7oz/heaped ¾ cup caster sugar
1 tbsp golden syrup
1 large egg, lightly beaten
100g/3½oz white chocolate, chopped
100g/3½oz plain chocolate, chopped

1   Preheat the oven to 180°C/350°F/gas 4. Grease two 30cm/12in square baking trays.
2   Sift the flour, cocoa, salt and bicarbonate of soda into a mixing bowl and mix in the sugar. Heat the butter with the syrup until the butter has melted, cool slightly and then stir into the dry ingredients. Beat in the egg and chocolate pieces to form a soft dough.
3   Divide the dough into 20 walnut-sized pieces and place on the baking trays, leaving about 5cm/2in between them. Press each biscuit down slightly using your fingers.
4   Bake for 12–15 minutes until firm. Remove the biscuits from the oven and leave to cool on the trays for a few minutes, then transfer to a wire rack with a palette knife to cool.

222 Coffee Japonaise Cakes

PREPARATION TIME 15 minutes   **COOKING TIME** 25–30 minutes   **MAKES** 8 macaroons

125g/4½oz butter, softened, plus extra
   for greasing
3 egg whites
½ tsp cream of tartar
225g/8oz/scant 1 cup caster sugar

115g/4oz/¾ cup pistachio nuts
350g/12oz/2⅓ cups icing sugar, sifted
1 tbsp instant coffee granules dissolved
   in 1 tbsp boiling water, then cooled

1   Preheat the oven to 180°C/350°F/gas 4. Grease and line two 30cm/12in square baking trays.
2   Put the egg whites and cream of tartar in a clean, dry bowl and whisk with an electric hand mixer or a whisk until they form stiff peaks. Gradually add the caster sugar while still whisking until it has all been whisked in. Grind the pistachios using a pestle and mortar, then gently fold in half of them, using a large metal spoon. Spoon the mixture into an icing bag with a 13mm/½in plain nozzle and pipe sixteen 5cm/2in rounds of meringue on to the trays. (If you do not have an icing bag, make small mounds using 2 teaspoons.)
3   Bake for 25–30 minutes until crisp, then remove from the oven and cool on the trays.
4   Put the butter, icing sugar and coffee liquid in a bowl and beat using an electric hand mixer or wooden spoon until they form a light coffee buttercream. Sandwich pairs of the meringues together with some of the buttercream. Spread a thin layer of buttercream around the sides of each pair and roll in the remaining ground pistachios. Place in cake cases to serve.

223 Toasted Hazelnut Biscuits

PREPARATION TIME 20 minutes, plus chilling   **COOKING TIME** 12–15 minutes   **MAKES** 15 biscuits

115g/4oz butter, softened, plus extra
   for greasing
55g/2oz/¼ cup caster sugar
175g/6oz/heaped 1 cup plain flour,
   sifted, plus extra for dusting

55g/2oz/heaped ⅓ cup toasted
   hazelnuts, chopped
1 tbsp milk (optional)

1   Put the butter and sugar in a mixing bowl and beat using an electric hand mixer or
    wooden spoon until the mixture is light and creamy. Add the flour and toasted hazelnuts,
    then mix together with your hands to form a soft dough, adding the milk if the mixture is
    too dry. Wrap in cling film and refrigerate for 1 hour.
2   Preheat the oven to 180°C/350°F/gas 4. Grease two 30cm/12in square baking trays.
3   Sift flour on to a clean work surface and roll the dough out to about 1cm/⅜in thick using
    a rolling pin. Cut out 15 heart shapes using a 10cm/4in heart cutter or a cardboard
    template and a knife, gathering up the trimmings and re-rolling as necessary. Place the
    biscuits on the baking trays using a palette knife.
4   Bake for 12–15 minutes until golden brown and just firm. Remove the biscuits from the
    oven and leave to cool on the trays for a few minutes, then transfer to a wire rack with
    a palette knife to cool.

224 Anzac Biscuits

PREPARATION TIME 15 minutes   **COOKING TIME** 12–15 minutes   **MAKES** 12 biscuits

115g/4oz butter, chopped, plus extra
for greasing
100g/3½oz/heaped ⅓ cup light soft
brown sugar
100g/3½oz/heaped 1 cup desiccated
coconut

100g/3½oz/1 cup porridge oats
125g/4½oz/scant 1 cup plain flour
1 level tsp bicarbonate of soda
3 tbsp golden syrup

1   Preheat the oven to 180°C/350°F/gas 4. Grease two 30cm/12in square baking trays.
2   Put the sugar, coconut and oats in a mixing bowl, sift in the flour and bicarbonate of
    soda and mix together with a wooden spoon. Put the butter and syrup in a saucepan
    and heat gently for 2–3 minutes until the butter has melted. Cool slightly, then beat into
    the dry ingredients with 1 tablespoon water.
3   Place 12 tablespoons of the biscuit mixture on the baking trays, leaving about 5cm/2in
    between each spoonful to allow for spreading.
4   Bake for 10–12 minutes until golden brown and just firm. Remove the biscuits from the
    oven and leave to cool on the trays for a few minutes, then transfer to a wire rack with a
    palette knife to cool.

225 Pine Nut Biscuits

PREPARATION TIME 20 minutes   **COOKING TIME** 12–15 minutes   **MAKES** 18 biscuits

115g/4oz butter, softened, plus extra
for greasing
55g/2oz/¼ cup caster sugar

175g/6oz/heaped 1 cup plain flour,
sifted, plus extra for dusting
1 tbsp golden syrup
55g/2oz/⅓ cup pine nuts

1   Preheat the oven to 190°C/375°F/gas 5. Grease two 30cm/12in square baking trays.
2   Put the butter and sugar in a mixing bowl and beat using an electric hand mixer or
    wooden spoon until the mixture is light and creamy. Add the flour, syrup and pine nuts
    and mix together with your hands to form a soft dough.
3   Divide the dough into 18 walnut-sized balls and place on the baking trays, leaving about
    5cm/2in between them to allow for spreading. Press each biscuit down slightly using
    your fingers or a fork.
4   Bake for 12–15 minutes until golden brown and just firm. Remove the biscuits from the
    oven and leave to cool on the trays for a few minutes, then transfer to a wire rack with a
    palette knife to cool.

226 Rose & Pistachio Thins

PREPARATION TIME 20 minutes, plus chilling   **COOKING TIME** 12–15 minutes   **MAKES** 20 biscuits

100g/3½oz butter, softened, plus extra
for greasing
100g/3½oz/heaped ⅓ cup caster sugar
1 medium egg, lightly beaten
1 tbsp milk

1 tbsp rosewater
200g/7oz/1⅓ cups plain flour,
plus extra for dusting
1 tsp baking powder
30g/1oz pistachio nuts, finely chopped

1   Put the butter and sugar in a mixing bowl and beat using an electric hand mixer or
    wooden spoon until the mixture is light and creamy. Beat in the egg, milk and rosewater.
    Sift in the flour and baking powder and add the pistachios. Mix together with your hands
    to form a soft dough, adding a little extra flour if the dough is too sticky.
2   Sift flour on to a clean work surface and roll the dough into a 5cm/2in cylinder. Wrap the
    cylinder in cling film and refrigerate for 1 hour.
3   Preheat the oven to 190°C/375°F/gas 5. Grease two 30cm/12in square baking trays.
    Cut the dough into 20 slices and place on the baking trays.
4   Bake for 12–15 minutes until golden brown and just firm. Remove the biscuits from the
    oven and leave to cool on the trays for a few minutes, then transfer to a wire rack with a
    palette knife to cool.

227 Rose & Violet Cream Biscuits

PREPARATION TIME 25 minutes   **COOKING TIME** 10–12 minutes   **MAKES** 10 biscuits

140g/5oz butter, softened, plus extra
for greasing
225g/8oz/scant 1 cup caster sugar
1 large egg, lightly beaten
1 tsp vanilla extract
225g/8oz/1½ cups plain flour
1 tsp baking powder
5 tbsp cocoa powder
100g/3½oz/heaped ½ cup plain
chocolate chips

FOR THE BUTTERCREAM
140g/5oz butter, softened
285g/10oz/scant 2 cups icing sugar,
sifted
2 tbsp milk
1 tbsp rose syrup
a few drops of pink and purple food
colouring
1 tbsp violet syrup or liqueur

1   Preheat the oven to 180°C/350°F/gas 4. Grease two 30cm/12in square baking trays.
2   Put the butter and caster sugar in a mixing bowl and beat using an electric hand mixer
    or wooden spoon until the mixture is light and creamy. Beat in the egg and vanilla extract.
    Sift in the flour, baking powder and cocoa and add the chocolate chips. Mix together
    with your hands to form a soft dough.
3   Divide the dough into 20 walnut-sized balls and place on the baking trays, leaving about
    5cm/2in between them to allow for spreading. Press each biscuit down slightly using
    your fingers or a fork.
4   Bake for 10–12 minutes until just firm. Remove the biscuits from the oven and leave to
    cool on the trays for a few minutes, then transfer to a wire rack with a palette knife to cool.
5   To make the buttercream, put the butter, icing sugar and 1 tablespoon of the milk in a
    bowl and beat using an electric hand mixer or wooden spoon for 5 minutes until light
    and creamy, adding the remaining milk if it is too stiff. Divide the buttercream between
    2 bowls. Add the rose syrup and pink food colouring to 1 bowl and the violet syrup and
    purple food colouring to the other bowl. Stir both creams well with a spoon to mix in the
    flavourings and colourings. Sandwich the cookies together in pairs, some with the rose
    buttercream and some with the violet.

228 Toffee Pecan Shortbread

PREPARATION TIME 20 minutes, plus chilling   **COOKING TIME** 12–15 minutes   **MAKES** 12 shortbread

115g/4oz butter, softened, plus extra
   for greasing
55g/2oz/¼ cup light soft brown sugar
1 tbsp toffee sauce

175g/6oz/heaped 1 cup plain flour,
   sifted, plus extra for dusting
55g/2oz/heaped ⅓ cup pecan nuts,
   coarsely chopped

1   Put the butter, sugar and toffee sauce in a mixing bowl and beat using an electric hand mixer or wooden spoon until the mixture is light and creamy. Add the flour and pecans and mix together with your hands to form a soft dough. Wrap in cling film and refrigerate for 1 hour.
2   Preheat the oven to 180°C/350°F/gas 4. Grease two 30cm/12in square baking trays.
3   Sift flour on to a clean work surface and roll the dough out to about 1cm/⅜in thick using a rolling pin. Cut out 12 circles using a 7.5cm/3in fluted round cutter, gathering up the trimmings and re-rolling as necessary. Place the shortbread on the baking trays.
4   Bake for 12–15 minutes until golden brown and just firm. Remove the shortbread from the oven and leave to cool on the trays for a few minutes, then transfer to a wire rack to cool.

229 Lavender Shortbread

PREPARATION TIME 20 minutes, plus chilling   **COOKING TIME** 12–15 minutes   **MAKES** 12 shortbread

115g/4oz butter, softened, plus extra
   for greasing
2 tbsp Lavender Sugar (see page 23)
2 tbsp caster sugar, plus extra for dusting

175g/6oz/heaped 1 cup plain flour,
   sifted, plus extra for dusting
1 tbsp milk (optional)

1   Put the butter, lavender sugar and caster sugar in a mixing bowl and beat using an electric hand mixer or wooden spoon until the mixture is light and creamy. Add the flour and mix together with your hands to form a soft dough, adding the milk if the mixture is too dry. Wrap in cling film and refrigerate for 1 hour.
2   Preheat the oven to 180°C/350°F/gas 4. Grease two 30cm/12in square baking trays.
3   Sift flour on to a clean work surface and roll the dough out to about 1cm/⅜in thick using a rolling pin. Cut out 12 heart shapes using a 10cm/4in heart cutter, gathering up the trimmings and re-rolling as necessary. Place the shortbread on the baking trays.
4   Bake for 12–15 minutes until golden brown. Remove from the oven, dust with caster sugar and cool on the trays for a few minutes, then transfer to a wire rack, removing any excess caster sugar.

230 Vanilla Shortbread

PREPARATION TIME 20 minutes, plus chilling   **COOKING TIME** 12–15 minutes   **MAKES** 12 shortbread

115g/4oz butter, softened, plus extra
   for greasing
55g/2oz/¼ cup caster sugar
1 tsp vanilla extract

175g/6oz/heaped 1 cup plain flour,
   sifted, plus extra for dusting
1 tbsp milk (optional)

1   Put the butter, sugar and vanilla extract in a mixing bowl and beat using an electric hand mixer or wooden spoon until the mixture is light and creamy. Add the flour and mix together with your hands to form a soft dough, adding the milk if the mixture is too dry. Wrap in cling film and refrigerate for 1 hour.
2   Preheat the oven to 180°C/350°F/gas 4. Grease two 30cm/12in square baking trays.
3   Sift flour on to a clean work surface and roll the dough out to about 1cm/⅜in thick using a rolling pin. Cut out 12 rounds using a 7.5cm/3in round cutter, gathering up the trimmings and re-rolling as necessary. Place the shortbread on the baking trays and prick each one twice in the middle with a fork.
4   Bake for 12–15 minutes until golden brown and just firm. Remove the shortbread from the oven and leave to cool on the trays for a few minutes, then transfer to a wire rack to cool.

231 Honey Shortbread

PREPARATION TIME 20 minutes, plus chilling   **COOKING TIME** 12–15 minutes   **MAKES** 18 shortbread

115g/4oz butter, softened, plus extra
  for greasing
55g/2oz/¼ cup caster sugar
1 tbsp clear honey

175g/6oz/heaped 1 cup plain flour,
  sifted, plus extra for dusting
1 tbsp milk (optional)

1 Put the butter, sugar and honey in a mixing bowl and beat using an electric hand mixer or wooden spoon until the mixture is light and creamy. Add the flour and mix together with your hands to form a soft dough, adding the milk if the mixture is too dry. Wrap in cling film and refrigerate for 1 hour.

2 Preheat the oven to 190°C/375°F/gas 5. Grease two 30cm/12in square baking trays.

3 Sift flour on to a clean work surface and roll the dough out to about 1cm/⅜in thick using a rolling pin. Cut out 18 rounds using a 6cm/2½in round cutter, gathering up the trimmings and re-rolling as necessary. Place the shortbread on the baking trays.

4 Bake for 12–15 minutes until golden brown and just firm. Remove the shortbread from the oven and leave to cool on the trays for a few minutes, then transfer to a wire rack with a palette knife to cool.

232 Lemon & Apricot Shortbread

PREPARATION TIME 20 minutes, plus chilling   **COOKING TIME** 12–15 minutes   **MAKES** 18 shortbread

115g/4oz butter, softened, plus extra
  for greasing
55g/2oz/¼ cup caster sugar
175g/6oz/heaped 1 cup plain flour,
  sifted, plus extra for dusting

55g/2oz/⅓ cup chopped dried apricots
finely grated zest of 1 large lemon
1 tbsp milk (optional)

1 Put the butter and sugar in a mixing bowl and beat using an electric hand mixer or wooden spoon until the mixture is light and creamy. Add the flour, apricots and lemon zest and mix together with your hands to form a soft dough, adding the milk if the mixture is too dry. Wrap in cling film and refrigerate for 1 hour.

2 Preheat the oven to 190°C/375°F/gas 5. Grease two 30cm/12in square baking trays.

3 Sift flour on to a clean work surface and roll the dough out to about 1cm/⅜in thick using a rolling pin. Cut out 18 rounds using a 6cm/2½in round cutter, gathering up the trimmings and re-rolling as necessary. Place the shortbread on the baking trays.

4 Bake for 12–15 minutes until golden brown and just firm. Remove the shortbread from the oven and leave to cool on the trays for a few minutes, then transfer to a wire rack with a palette knife to cool.

233 Cinnamon Viennese Whirls

PREPARATION TIME 25 minutes   **COOKING TIME** 10–15 minutes   **MAKES** 12 biscuits

175g/6oz butter, softened
55g/2oz/⅓ cup icing sugar, sifted
175g/6oz/heaped 1 cup plain flour

1 tsp cinnamon
4 tbsp plum or cherry jam
icing sugar, for dusting

1 Preheat the oven to 180°C/350°C/gas 4. Put 12 cake cases into a 12-hole bun tin.

2 Put the butter and sugar in a mixing bowl and beat using an electric hand mixer or wooden spoon until the mixture is light and creamy. Sift in the flour and cinnamon and mix again.

3 Spoon the mixture into an icing bag fitted with a 15mm/⅝in star nozzle. Pipe a swirl of mixture into each cake case. Press an indent into the centre of each whirl and fill with 1 teaspoon of the jam.

4 Bake for 10–15 minutes until golden brown and just firm. Remove the biscuits from the oven and leave to cool on the trays for a few minutes, then transfer to a wire rack with a palette knife to cool. Dust with icing sugar before serving.

234 Poppy Seed Snaps

PREPARATION TIME 20 minutes   **COOKING TIME** 10–13 minutes   **MAKES** 12 biscuits

55g/2oz butter, chopped, plus extra
   for greasing
150g/5½oz/scant ⅔ cup caster sugar

1 tbsp golden syrup
40g/1½oz/¼ cup plain flour, sifted
2 tbsp poppy seeds

1　Preheat the oven to 190°C/375°F/gas 5. Grease two 30cm/12in square baking trays.
2　Put the butter in a saucepan with the sugar and syrup and heat gently for 2–3 minutes, stirring, until the butter has melted and the sugar has dissolved. Remove the pan from the heat and stir in the flour and poppy seeds. Place 12 tablespoons of the mixture on the baking trays, leaving about 10cm/4in between them to allow for spreading.
3　Bake for 8–10 minutes until golden brown and just firm. Remove the biscuits from the oven and leave to cool for 2 minutes on the trays, then, working quickly, wrap each biscuit around a thin rolling pin to curl it. Alternatively, use a normal-size rolling pin or a drinking glass for a looser curl. If the biscuits set too quickly, return them to the oven for 1 minute to soften, then curl them again.

235 Walnut & Cinnamon Palmiers

PREPARATION TIME 20 minutes   **COOKING TIME** 10–15 minutes   **MAKES** 25 pastries

55g/2oz butter, melted and cooled,
   plus extra for greasing
flour, for dusting
500g/1lb 2oz block puff pastry
100g/3½oz/heaped ⅓ cup dark soft
   brown sugar

100g/3½oz/heaped ½ cup walnuts,
   finely chopped
1 tbsp cinnamon
1 tbsp milk
1 heaped tbsp caster sugar

1　Preheat the oven to 180°C/350°F/gas 4. Grease two 30cm/12in square baking trays.
2　Sift flour on to a clean work surface and roll out the puff pastry into a 40 x 20cm/ 16 x 8in rectangle, 5mm/¼in thick. In a bowl, mix together the dark brown sugar, walnuts and cinnamon.
3　Brush the pastry with the melted butter and sprinkle over half of the walnut mixture. Fold the dough in half lengthways with the walnuts on the inside and roll out again into a rectangle. Brush with butter and sprinkle over the remaining walnut mixture.
4　Fold the two long sides into the middle so that they meet at the centre of the rectangle, and press down with a rolling pin. Brush with butter. Fold in half lengthways so that you have a long, thin piece of dough. Cut crossways into 25 slices about 1cm/⅜in wide and place apart on the baking trays, opening the pastry shapes slightly to form heart shapes. Brush with the milk and sprinkle with the caster sugar.
5　Bake for 10–15 minutes until the pastry has cooked and is golden. Remove the pastries from the oven and leave to cool on the trays for a few minutes, then transfer to a wire rack with a palette knife to cool.

236 Almond Tuiles

PREPARATION TIME 20 minutes   **COOKING TIME** 8–10 minutes   **MAKES** 12 biscuits

55g/2oz butter, melted and cooled,
   plus extra for greasing
55g/2oz/⅓ cup plain flour

55g/2oz/⅓ cup icing sugar
2 medium egg whites
55g/2oz/heaped ⅓ cup flaked almonds

1　Preheat the oven to 190°C/375°F/gas 5. Grease two 30cm/12in square baking trays.
2　Sift the flour and icing sugar into a mixing bowl. Mix in the melted butter and egg whites and mix together with an electric hand mixer or a whisk until the mixture is light and creamy. Place 12 dessertspoons of the mixture on to the trays about 2.5cm/1in apart. Sprinkle each biscuit with flaked almonds.
3　Bake for 8–10 minutes until golden brown. Remove the biscuits from the oven and leave to cool for a few minutes, then, working carefully and speedily, curl each biscuit around a rolling pin to give them a curled shape. If the biscuits set too quickly, return them to the oven for 1 minute to soften, then curl them again.

237 Apricot & Pistachio Florentines

PREPARATION TIME 20 minutes **COOKING TIME** 10–12 minutes **MAKES** 12 florentines

85g/3oz butter, chopped, plus extra
  for greasing
4 tbsp milk
100g/3½oz/⅔ cup icing sugar, sifted
45g/1½oz/⅓ cup plain flour, sifted
45g/1½oz/¼ cup glacé cherries, chopped
85g/3oz/1 cup flaked almonds

45g/1½oz/heaped ¼ cup pistachio nuts,
  chopped
30g/1oz/¼ cup dried apricots, chopped
1 tsp cinnamon
150g/5½oz plain chocolate, melted and
  cooled slightly

1   Preheat the oven to 190°C/375°F/gas 5. Grease and line two 30cm/12in square
    baking trays.
2   Put the butter, milk and icing sugar in a saucepan and heat gently until the butter has
    melted. Add all the remaining ingredients, except the melted chocolate, and mix well
    with a wooden spoon. Leave to cool completely.
3   Place 12 dessertspoons of the mixture on the baking trays, leaving about 2.5cm/1in
    between them to allow for spreading. Press each florentine down with the back of a
    spoon so they are of an even thickness.
4   Bake for 8–10 minutes until lightly browned. Remove the florentines from the oven and
    leave to cool on the trays.
5   Cover the underside of each florentine with the melted chocolate, using a round-bladed
    knife to spread it. Leave to set slightly, and then make wavy lines through the chocolate
    with a fork. Leave the chocolate to set before serving.

238 Coconut Macaroons

PREPARATION TIME 10 minutes   **COOKING TIME** 12–15 minutes   **MAKES** 15 macaroons

butter, for greasing
200g/7oz/2½ cups desiccated coconut
200ml/7fl oz/scant 1 cup
   condensed milk

1 tsp vanilla extract
1 tsp almond extract
150g/5½oz/1 cup self-raising flour,
   sifted

1   Preheat the oven to 180°C/350°F/gas 4. Grease and line two 30cm/12in square
   baking trays.
2   Put all the ingredients in a mixing bowl and stir well with a wooden spoon. Using
   2 teaspoons, place 15 walnut-sized mounds of the coconut mixture on to the trays,
   leaving about 2.5cm/1in between them to allow for spreading.
3   Bake for 12–15 minutes until lightly golden brown and just firm. Remove the macaroons
   from the oven and transfer to a wire rack with a palette knife to cool.

239 Pistachio Macaroons

PREPARATION TIME 20 minutes   **COOKING TIME** 15–20 minutes   **MAKES** 12 macaroons

butter, for greasing
55g/2oz/heaped ¼ cup pistachio nuts,
   12 reserved for decoration

2 large egg whites
100g/3½oz/scant 1 cup ground almonds
200g/7oz/heaped ¾ cup caster sugar

1 Preheat the oven to 170°C/325°F/gas 3. Grease and line two 30cm/12in square baking trays.
2 Place the pistachios in a food processor or blender and chop very finely. Put the egg whites in a clean, dry bowl and whisk with an electric hand mixer or a whisk until they form soft peaks. Add the pistachios, ground almonds and sugar and fold them in well.
3 Divide the mixture into 12 walnut-sized balls and place on the baking trays, leaving about 5cm/2in between them to allow for spreading. Flatten each ball with your fingers and place a whole pistachio in the centre of each one for decoration.
4 Bake for 15–20 minutes until golden brown and just firm. Remove the macaroons from the oven and transfer to a wire rack with a palette knife to cool.

240 Orange Flower Water & Cinnamon Meringues

PREPARATION TIME 25 minutes   **COOKING TIME** 1–1¼ hours   **MAKES** 20 meringues

butter, for greasing
3 large egg whites
175g/6oz/scant ¾ cup caster sugar
2 tsp cinnamon

finely grated zest of 1 orange
1 tbsp orange flower water
250ml/9fl oz/1 cup double cream,
   whipped to stiff peaks

1 Preheat the oven to 140°C/275°F/gas 1. Grease and line two 30cm/12in square baking trays.
2 Put the egg whites and sugar in a heatproof bowl over a saucepan of simmering water. It is important that the bottom of the bowl does not touch the water. Using an electric hand mixer, whisk the egg whites and sugar over the heat for 5 minutes until they form stiff peaks. Remove the bowl from the heat, add the cinnamon and orange zest and continue whisking for a further 5 minutes until the meringue is very stiff.
3 Spoon the meringue into an icing bag fitted with a 13mm/½in star nozzle and pipe forty 4cm/1½in meringues on to the baking trays. If you do not have an icing bag, make small mounds of meringue using 2 teaspoons.
4 Bake for about 1–1¼ hours until dried and crisp. Remove the meringues from the oven and leave to cool on the trays. Fold the orange flower water into the whipped cream with a large metal spoon and sandwich pairs of the meringues together with the cream. Place the meringues in cake cases and serve immediately.

241 Almond Meringue Biscuits

PREPARATION TIME 10 minutes   **COOKING TIME** 1–1¼ hours   **MAKES** 15 biscuits

butter, for greasing
3 large egg whites
175g/6oz/scant ¾ cup caster sugar

100g/3½oz/scant 1 cup ground almonds
1 tsp almond extract
30g/1oz/¼ cup flaked almonds

1 Preheat the oven to 150°C/300°F/gas 2. Grease and line two 30cm/12in square baking trays.
2 Put the egg whites and sugar in a heatproof bowl over a saucepan of simmering water. It is important that the bottom of the bowl does not touch the water. Using an electric hand mixer, whisk the egg whites and sugar over the heat for 5 minutes until they form stiff peaks. Remove the bowl from the heat and continue whisking for a further 5 minutes. Using a spatula, gently fold in the ground almonds and almond extract.
3 Place 15 spoonfuls of the meringue to form small mounds about 5cm/2in in diameter on the baking trays and sprinkle over the flaked almonds.
4 Bake for about 1–1¼ hours until crisp. Remove the biscuits from the oven and leave to cool on the trays for a few minutes, then transfer to a wire rack with a palette knife to cool.

242 Coffee Meringues

PREPARATION TIME 20 minutes **COOKING TIME** 1–1¼ hours **MAKES** 20 meringues

butter, for greasing
3 large egg whites
175g/6oz/scant ¾ cup caster sugar

1 tbsp instant coffee granules dissolved
  in 1 tbsp boiling water, then cooled
250ml/9fl oz/1 cup double cream,
  whipped to stiff peaks

1 Preheat the oven to 140°C/275°F/gas 1. Grease and line two 30cm/12in square
baking trays.
2 Put the egg whites and sugar in a heatproof bowl over a pan of simmering water. It is
important that the bottom of the bowl does not touch the water. Using an electric hand
whisk, whisk the egg whites and sugar over the heat for 5 minutes until they form stiff
peaks. Remove the bowl from the heat and whisk for a further 5 minutes until the
meringue is very stiff. Gently whisk in half of the coffee liquid.
3 Spoon the meringue into an icing bag fitted with a 13mm/½in plain nozzle and pipe
forty 4cm/1½in meringues on to the baking trays. (If you do not have an icing bag,
make small mounds of meringue using 2 teaspoons.)
4 Bake for about 1–1¼ hours until dried and crisp. Remove the meringues from the oven
and leave to cool on the trays.
5 Fold the remaining coffee liquid into the whipped cream with a large metal spoon and
sandwich pairs of the meringues together with the cream. Place the meringues in cake
cases to serve.

243 Mini Chocolate Meringue Kisses

PREPARATION TIME 20 minutes **COOKING TIME** 1–1¼ hours **MAKES** 40 meringues

butter, for greasing
3 large egg whites
175g/6oz/scant ¾ cup caster sugar

150g/5½oz milk chocolate, half grated;
  half melted and cooled slightly

1 Preheat the oven to 140°C/275°F/gas 1. Grease and line two 30cm/12in square baking trays.
2 Put the egg whites and sugar in a heatproof bowl over a pan of simmering water. It is important that the bottom of the bowl does not touch the water. Using an electric hand whisk, whisk the egg whites and sugar over the heat for 5 minutes until they form stiff peaks. Remove the bowl from the heat and whisk for a further 5 minutes until the meringue is very stiff. Gently fold in the grated chocolate.
3 Spoon the meringue into an icing bag fitted with a 13mm/½in star nozzle and pipe forty 4cm/1½in meringues on to the baking trays, or make mounds using 2 teaspoons.
4 Bake for about 1–1¼ hours until dried and crisp. Remove the merinues from the oven and leave to cool on the trays. Drizzle the melted chocolate over the meringues in thin lines.

244 Cassis Cream Meringues

PREPARATION TIME 20 minutes **COOKING TIME** 1–1¼ hours **MAKES** 20 meringues

butter, for greasing
3 large egg whites
175g/6oz/scant ¾ cup caster sugar
3 tbsp cassis

a few drops of purple food colouring
250ml/9fl oz/1 cup double cream,
  whipped to stiff peaks

1 Preheat the oven to 140°C/275°F/gas 1. Grease and line two 30cm/12in square baking trays.
2 Put the egg whites and sugar in a heatproof bowl over a pan of simmering water. It is important that the bottom of the bowl does not touch the water. Using an electric hand whisk, whisk the egg whites and sugar over the heat for 5 minutes until they form stiff peaks. Remove the bowl from the heat, add the cassis and purple food colouring and continue whisking for a further 5 minutes until the meringue is very stiff.
3 Spoon the meringue into an icing bag fitted with a 13mm/½in plain nozzle and pipe forty 4cm/1½in meringues on to the baking trays, or make mounds using 2 teaspoons.
4 Bake for about 1–1¼ hours until dried and crisp. Remove the meringues from the oven and leave to cool on the trays. Fold the remaining cassis into the whipped cream and sandwich pairs of the meringues together with the cream. Place the meringues in cake cases to serve.

245 Violet Meringues

PREPARATION TIME 20 minutes **COOKING TIME** 1–1¼ hours **MAKES** 20 meringues

butter, for greasing
3 large egg whites
175g/6oz/scant ¾ cup caster sugar
1 tbsp violet liqueur or violet syrup

a few drops of purple food colouring
1 tbsp rose syrup
250ml/9fl oz/1 cup double cream,
  whipped to stiff peaks

1 Preheat the oven to 140°C/275°F/gas 1. Grease and line two 30cm/12in square baking trays.
2 Put the egg whites and sugar in a heatproof bowl over a pan of simmering water. It is important that the bottom of the bowl does not touch the water. Using an electric hand whisk, whisk the egg whites and sugar over the heat for 5 minutes until they form stiff peaks. Remove the bowl from the heat and whisk for a further 5 minutes until the meringue is very stiff. Gently whisk in the violet liqueur or syrup and the food colouring.
3 Spoon the meringue into an icing bag fitted with a 13mm/½in star nozzle and pipe forty 4cm/1½in meringues on to the baking trays, or make mounds using 2 teaspoons.
4 Bake for about 1–1¼ hours until dried and crisp. Remove the meringues from the oven and leave to cool on the trays. Fold the rose syrup into the whipped cream and sandwich pairs of meringues together with the cream. Place the meringues in cake cases to serve.

246 Pistachio & Chestnut Meringues

PREPARATION TIME 30 minutes   **COOKING TIME** 1 hour   **MAKES** 10 meringues

butter, for greasing
2 large egg whites
115g/4oz/scant ½ cup caster sugar
100g/3½oz/⅔ cup pistachio nuts

4 tbsp tinned unsweetened
  chestnut purée
2 tbsp icing sugar, sifted
5 glacé chestnuts, finely chopped
whipped cream, to serve

1   Preheat the oven to 140°C/275°F/gas 1. Grease and line two 30cm/12in square baking trays.
2   Put the egg whites in a clean, dry bowl and whisk with an electric hand mixer or a whisk until they form soft peaks, then whisk in the caster sugar until the mixture is glossy. Spoon ten 3cm/1¼in mounds of meringue on to the trays.
3   Bake for about 1 hour until the shells are crisp and the insides are still gooey.
4   Meanwhile, grind the pistachios using a pestle and mortar, then mix well with the chestnut purée, icing sugar and glacé chestnuts in a bowl, using an electric hand mixer or wooden spoon. Spoon the mixture into an icing bag fitted with a 13mm/½in plain nozzle.
5   Remove the meringues from the oven and carefully pipe the nut mixture into them from the underside while they are still warm. Leave to cool before serving with whipped cream.

247 Caramel Chocolate Brownies

PREPARATION TIME 20 minutes   **COOKING TIME** 35–45 minutes   **MAKES** 16 brownies

250g/9oz butter, plus extra for greasing
400g/14oz plain chocolate, broken
  into pieces
250g/9oz/1 cup caster sugar
250g/9oz/1 cup light soft brown sugar

5 large eggs
1 tsp vanilla extract
200g/7oz/1⅓ cups plain flour, sifted
200g/7oz caramel-filled chocolate bar,
  cut into squares

1   Preheat the oven to 190°C/375°F/gas 5. Grease and line a 30 x 23 x 6cm/12 x 9 x 2½in baking tin.
2   Melt the butter and 350g/12oz of the plain chocolate together. Leave to cool. Chop the remaining plain chocolate and set aside.
3   Put both sugars, eggs and vanilla extract in a mixing bowl and whisk using an electric hand mixer or a whisk until the mixture is very light and has doubled in size.
4   While still whisking, slowly pour in the melted chocolate and butter mixture. Fold in the flour, chopped chocolate and the caramel chocolate squares, using a metal spoon. Pour the cake mixture into the tin.
5   Bake for 30–40 minutes until the brownie has formed a crust and a skewer inserted into the middle of the brownie comes out clean. Remove the brownie from the oven and leave to cool in the tin before cutting into 16 slices.

248 White Chocolate Blondies

PREPARATION TIME 20 minutes   **COOKING TIME** 30–40 minutes   **MAKES** 16 blondies

115g/4oz butter, melted and cooled,
  plus extra for greasing
115g/4oz/scant ½ cup caster sugar
2 large eggs, lightly beaten
1 tsp vanilla extract

150g/5½oz/1 cup plain flour
1 tsp baking powder
100g/3½oz/heaped ½ cup white
  chocolate chips
55g/2oz/⅓ cup macadamia nuts, halved

1   Preheat the oven to 180°C/350°F/gas 4. Grease and line a 30 x 23 x 6cm/12 x 9 x 2½in baking tin.
2   Put the melted butter and sugar in a bowl and beat using an electric hand mixer or wooden spoon until the mixture is light and creamy. Add the eggs and vanilla extract and beat again. Sift in the flour and baking powder and fold in with the chocolate chips and nuts, using a large metal spoon. Pour the cake mixture into the tin.
3   Bake for 30–40 minutes until the blondie has formed a crust and a skewer inserted into the middle of the blondie comes out clean. Remove the blondie from the oven and leave to cool in the tin before cutting into 16 slices.

249 Triple Chocolate Mocha Brownies

PREPARATION TIME 20 minutes   **COOKING TIME** 35–45 minutes   **MAKES** 16 brownies

250g/9oz butter, chopped, plus extra
    for greasing
400g/14oz plain chocolate, broken
    into pieces
250g/9oz/1 cup caster sugar
250g/9oz/1 cup light soft brown sugar

5 large eggs
1 tbsp instant coffee granules dissolved
    in 1 tbsp boiling water, then cooled
200g/7oz/1⅓ cups plain flour, sifted
100g/3½oz/⅔ cup white chocolate chips
100g/3½oz/⅔ cup milk chocolate chips

1   Preheat the oven to 190°C/375°F/gas 5. Grease and line a 30 x 23 x 6cm/12 x 9 x 2½in
    baking tin.
2   Melt the butter and 350g/12oz of the plain chocolate together and leave to cool.
    Chop the remaining plain chocolate and set aside.
3   Put the caster sugar, light brown sugar, eggs and coffee liquid in a mixing bowl and
    whisk using an electric hand mixer or a whisk until the mixture is very light and has
    doubled in size.
4   While still whisking, slowly pour in the melted chocolate and butter mixture. Add the
    flour, chopped chocolate and the white and milk chocolate chips, and fold together. Pour
    the cake mixture into the tin.
5   Bake for 30–40 minutes until the brownie has formed a crust and a skewer inserted into
    the middle of the brownie comes out clean. Remove the brownie from the oven and
    leave to cool in the tin before cutting into 16 slices.

250 Nutty Chocolate Brownies

PREPARATION TIME 20 minutes   **COOKING TIME** 35–45 minutes   **MAKES** 16 brownies

250g/9oz butter, chopped, plus extra
   for greasing
400g/14oz plain chocolate, broken
   into pieces
250g/9oz/1 cup caster sugar
250g/9oz/1 cup light soft brown sugar
5 large eggs
1 tsp vanilla extract

200g/7oz/1⅓ cups plain flour, sifted
200g/7oz/heaped 1 cup walnuts,
   chopped
200g/7oz/heaped 1 cup pecan nuts,
   chopped
100g/3½oz/heaped ½ cup pistachio
   nuts, chopped

1 Preheat the oven to 190°C/375°F/gas 5. Grease and line a 30 x 23 x 6cm/12 x 9 x 2½in baking tin.

2 Melt the butter and 350g/12oz of the chocolate together and leave to cool. Chop the remaining chocolate and set aside.

3 Put the caster sugar, light brown sugar, eggs and vanilla extract in a mixing bowl and whisk using an electric hand mixer or a whisk until the mixture is very light and has doubled in size.

4 While still whisking, slowly pour in the melted chocolate and butter mixture. Add the flour, chopped chocolate, walnuts, pecans and pistachios and fold them together, using a large metal spoon. Pour the cake mixture into the tin.

5 Bake for 30–40 minutes until the brownie has formed a crust and a skewer inserted into the middle of the brownie comes out clean. Remove the brownie from the oven and leave to cool in the tin before cutting into 16 slices.

251 Soured Cream Gingerbread

PREPARATION TIME 30 minutes   **COOKING TIME** 1–1¼ hours   **SERVES** 10

250g/9oz butter, chopped, plus extra
   for greasing
500g/1lb 2oz/3⅓ cups plain flour,
   plus extra for dusting
1 tsp salt
1 tsp ground ginger
1 tsp cinnamon
1 tsp mixed spice
1 tsp baking powder
1 tsp bicarbonate of soda
finely grated zest of 1 lemon and
   1 tbsp of the juice

175g/6oz treacle
200g/7oz golden syrup
200g/7oz/scant 1 cup dark soft
   brown sugar
145ml/4¾fl oz/scant ⅔ cup soured
   cream
2 large eggs, lightly beaten
100g/3½oz stem ginger preserved in
   syrup, drained and chopped
150g/5½oz cream cheese
400g/14oz/2⅔ cups icing sugar, sifted

1 Preheat the oven to 180°C/350°F/gas 4. Grease a 23cm/9in ring tin and dust with flour.

2 Sift the flour, salt, spices, baking powder and bicarbonate of soda into a mixing bowl, add the lemon zest and stir with a wooden spoon. Put 170g/6oz of the butter in a saucepan with the treacle, syrup and dark brown sugar and heat gently until the butter has melted and the sugar dissolved. Cool slightly, then beat into the dry ingredients with the soured cream, eggs and stem ginger. Scrape the mixture into the tin using a spatula.

3 Bake for about 1–1¼ hours until the cake springs back when pressed lightly and a skewer inserted into the cake comes out clean. Remove the cake from the oven and leave to stand for 5 minutes, then turn out on to a wire rack.

4 Put the cream cheese, icing sugar, remaining butter and the lemon juice in a mixing bowl and beat using an electric hand mixer or wooden spoon to form a smooth, thick icing. Spread over the cake using a round-bladed knife and leave to set before serving.

252 Apple & Pecan Gingerbread

PREPARATION TIME 20 minutes   **COOKING TIME** 1–1¼ hours   **MAKES** 20 slices

175g/6oz butter, chopped, plus extra
   for greasing
500g/1lb 2oz/3⅓ cups plain flour
1 tsp salt
1 tsp ground ginger
1 tsp cinnamon
1 tsp mixed spice
1 tsp baking powder
1 tsp bicarbonate of soda
140g/5oz treacle
200g/7oz/scant 1 cup dark soft
   brown sugar

200g/7oz golden syrup
300ml/10½fl oz/scant 1¼ cups milk
2 tbsp natural yogurt
2 large eggs, lightly beaten
100g/3½oz/½ cup sultanas
6 pieces of stem ginger preserved in
   syrup, drained and finely chopped
3 large cooking apples, peeled, cored
   and thinly sliced
100g/3½oz/¾ cup pecan nuts
3 tbsp of the stem ginger syrup

1   Preheat the oven to 180°C/350°F/gas 4. Grease and line a 40 x 20 x 6cm/16 x 8 x 2½in baking tin.

2   Sift the flour, salt, spices, baking powder and bicarbonate of soda into a mixing bowl and stir with a wooden spoon. Put the butter, treacle, sugar and syrup in a saucepan and heat gently until the butter has melted and the sugar has dissolved. Leave to cool slightly, then beat into the dry ingredients with the milk, yogurt, eggs, sultanas and stem ginger. Scrape the mixture into the tin using a spatula.

3   Place some of the apple slices in 2 rows overlapping at one end of the tin. Place a row of pecans next to the apples and then repeat with rows of apple slices and pecans until the cake is covered.

4   Bake for about 1–1¼ hours until the cake springs back when pressed lightly and a skewer inserted into the middle of the cake comes out clean.

5   Remove the cake from the oven and leave to stand for 5 minutes, then turn out on to a wire rack. Heat the ginger syrup in a small saucepan, then brush the glaze over the top of the cake with a pastry brush. Leave to cool.

253 Vanilla Flapjacks

PREPARATION TIME 15 minutes   **COOKING TIME** 25–30 minutes   **MAKES** 12 flapjacks

115g/4oz butter, chopped, plus extra
  for greasing
3 tbsp golden syrup

85g/3oz/scant ⅓ cup caster sugar
250g/9oz/2½ cups porridge oats
1 tsp vanilla extract

1   Preheat the oven to 180°C/350°F/gas 4. Grease an 18 x 18 x 5cm/7 x 7 x 2in baking tin.
2   In a saucepan, gently heat the butter, syrup and sugar for 5 minutes until the butter melts
   and the sugar dissolves. Remove from the heat and stir in the porridge oats and vanilla
   extract. Scrape the oat mixture into the tin and spread it out with the back of a spoon.
3   Bake for 20–25 minutes until golden brown. Remove the flapjack from the oven and
   leave to cool in the tin, then cut into 12 slices.

254 Sultana Flapjacks

PREPARATION TIME 15 minutes   **COOKING TIME** 25–30 minutes   **MAKES** 12 flapjacks

115g/4oz butter, chopped, plus extra
  for greasing
3 tbsp golden syrup
85g/3oz/scant ⅓ cup caster sugar

250g/9oz/2½ cups porridge oats
55g/2oz/scant ⅓ cup sultanas
finely grated zest of 1 large lemon
1 tsp vanilla extract

1   Preheat the oven to 180°C/350°F/gas 4. Grease an 18 x 18 x 5cm/7 x 7 x 2in baking tin.
2   In a saucepan, gently heat the butter, syrup and sugar for 5 minutes until the butter melts
   and the sugar dissolves. Remove from the heat and stir in the porridge oats, sultanas,
   lemon zest and vanilla extract. Scrape the oat mixture into the tin and spread it out with
   the back of a spoon.
3   Bake for 20–25 minutes until golden brown. Remove the flapjack from the oven and
   leave to cool in the tin, then cut into 12 slices.

255 Nutty Flapjacks

PREPARATION TIME 15 minutes   **COOKING TIME** 30–35 minutes   **MAKES** 12 flapjacks

130g/4½oz butter, chopped, plus extra
  for greasing
4 tbsp golden syrup
85g/3oz/⅓ cup light soft brown sugar
250g/9oz/2½ cups porridge oats

200g/7oz/1⅓ cups unsalted mixed nuts
1 tsp vanilla extract
1 tbsp crunchy peanut butter
55g/2oz/⅓ cup icing sugar, sifted
1 tbsp milk

1   Preheat the oven to 180°C/350°F/gas 4. Grease an 18 x 18 x 5cm/7 x 7 x 2in baking tin.
2   In a saucepan, gently heat 115g/4oz of the butter, 3 tablespoons of the syrup and the
   light brown sugar for 5 minutes until the butter has melted and the sugar has dissolved.
   Remove from the heat and stir in the porridge oats, nuts and vanilla extract. Scrape the
   oat mixture into the tin and spread it out with the back of a spoon.
3   Bake for 20–25 minutes until golden brown. Remove the flapjack from the oven and
   leave to cool in the tin.
4   Heat the peanut butter, icing sugar, milk and remaining butter and syrup in a saucepan
   for a few minutes until the butter has melted and you have a smooth toffee icing. Spoon
   over the top of the flapjack, still in the tin, and leave to cool, then cut into 12 slices.

256 Chocolate Flapjacks

PREPARATION TIME 15 minutes **COOKING TIME** 25–30 minutes **MAKES** 12 flapjacks

115g/4oz butter, chopped, plus extra for greasing	250g/9oz/2½ cups porridge oats
3 tbsp golden syrup	1 tsp vanilla extract
85g/3oz/⅓ cup light soft brown sugar	100g/3½oz/⅔ cup white chocolate chips
	100g/3½oz/⅔ cup plain chocolate chips

1   Preheat the oven to 180°C/350°F/gas 4. Grease an 18 x 18 x 5cm/7 x 7 x 2in baking tin.
2   In a saucepan, gently heat the butter, syrup and sugar for 5 minutes until the butter melts and the sugar dissolves. Remove from the heat and leave to cool a little, then stir in the porridge oats, vanilla extract and 40g/1½oz each of both types of chocolate chips. Scrape the oat mixture into the tin and spread it out with the back of a spoon. Sprinkle the remaining chocolate chips over the top of the flapjack.
3   Bake for 20–25 minutes until golden brown. Remove the flapjack from the oven and leave to cool in the tin, then cut into 12 slices.

257 Cream Slice

PREPARATION TIME 20 minutes   **COOKING TIME** 15–20 minutes   **MAKES** 8 slices

butter, for greasing	4 tbsp blackcurrant jam
flour, for dusting	375ml/13fl oz/1½ cups double cream, whipped to stiff peaks
500g/1lb 2oz block puff pastry	icing sugar, for dusting
1 medium egg, beaten	
2 tbsp caster sugar	

1   Preheat the oven to 190°C/375°F/gas 5. Lightly grease a 30cm/12in square baking tray.
2   Sift flour on to a clean work surface and roll the pastry out to a 30 x 20cm/12 x 8in rectangle, 5mm/¼in thick, using a rolling pin. Using a sharp knife, trim the edges of the pastry so that the rectangle has straight sides and then cut lengthways down the middle of the pastry to give 2 sheets.
3   Using the rolling pin to help, lift both pieces of pastry on to the baking tray, leaving about 2.5cm/1in between them. Using a pastry brush, brush the tops of the pastry pieces with some of the beaten egg, then sprinkle with the caster sugar.
4   Bake for 15–20 minutes until golden brown and crisp. Remove the slices from the oven and leave to cool on the tray, then cut each slice crossways into 8 equal slices. Spread the jam over half the pastry slices and cover with a layer of whipped cream. Top each one with a second pastry slice and dust with icing sugar to serve.

258 Sticky Pecan Slice

PREPARATION TIME 20 minutes   **COOKING TIME** 35–45 minutes   **MAKES** 12 slices

55g/2oz butter, chopped, plus extra for greasing	85g/3oz/1 cup fresh breadcrumbs, made from day-old bread
flour, for dusting	300g/10½oz/2 cups pecan nuts, coarsely chopped
1 recipe quantity Shortcrust Pastry (see page 23)	juice and finely grated zest of 1 lemon
	350g/12oz golden syrup

1   Preheat the oven to 180°C/350°F/gas 4. Lightly grease and line a 30 x 20cm/12 x 8in cake tin.
2   Sift flour on to a clean work surface and roll the pastry out to 5mm/¼in thick using a rolling pin. Line the cake tin with the pastry, making sure it comes up the sides of the tin as this will hold the pecan filling in. Trim the edges of the pastry with a sharp knife.
3   Put the breadcrumbs, pecans and lemon zest in a mixing bowl. Put the butter, lemon juice and syrup in a saucepan and heat gently until the butter has melted, then pour the lemon syrup over the breadcrumb mixture. Leave to cool for a few minutes, then spoon the mixture into the pastry case.
4   Bake for 30–40 minutes until the pastry is golden brown and the filling is set. Remove the slice from the oven and leave to cool in the tin before cutting into 12 slices.

259 Plum & Cinnamon Slice

PREPARATION TIME 20 minutes   **COOKING TIME** 25–30 minutes   **MAKES** 8 slices

butter, for greasing
flour, for dusting
500g/1lb 2oz block puff pastry
4 tbsp ground almonds
1 tbsp icing sugar
1 tbsp vegetable oil

100g/3½oz marzipan, chilled in the
  freezer for 30 minutes and then grated
1 tsp cinnamon
10 plums, halved and stoned
55g/2oz/⅓ cup flaked almonds
2 tbsp clear honey
milk, for glazing

1   Preheat the oven to 190°C/375°F/gas 5. Grease a 30cm/12in square baking tray.
2   Sift flour on to a clean work surface and roll the pastry out to a 30 x 20cm/12 x 8in
    rectangle 5mm/¼in thick using a rolling pin. Transfer the pastry to the baking tray using
    the rolling pin to help lift it, and score a line 2cm/¾in from the edge of the pastry all the
    way around with a knife. Do not cut all the way through the pastry.
3   Put the ground almonds, icing sugar and oil into a blender and whizz to form a smooth
    paste. Spread the almond paste inside the scored lines and sprinkle with the grated
    marzipan and cinnamon. Place the plum halves on top in rows, cut side down, sprinkle
    with the flaked almonds and drizzle with the honey. Brush the edges of the pastry with
    milk using a pastry brush.
4   Bake for 25–30 minutes until the pastry is golden brown and the plums are tender
    when pierced with a knife. Remove the slice from the oven and leave to cool in the tin,
    then cut into 8 slices.

260 Bakewell Slice

PREPARATION TIME 20 minutes   **COOKING TIME** 25–30 minutes   **MAKES** 16 slices

175g/6oz butter, softened, plus extra
for greasing
85g/3oz/heaped ½ cup plain flour,
sifted, plus extra for dusting
1 recipe Shortcrust Pastry (see page 23)

4 tbsp raspberry jam
140g/4½oz/heaped ½ cup caster sugar
175g/6oz/1½ cups ground almonds
3 egg yolks
55g/2oz/½ cup flaked almonds

1   Preheat the oven to 180°C/350°F/gas 4. Lightly grease and line a 30 x 20cm/12 x 8in Swiss roll tin.
2   Sift flour on to a clean work surface and roll the pastry out to 5mm/¼in thick using a rolling pin. Line the tin with the pastry and trim the edges with a sharp knife. Spread the jam over the pastry base.
3   Put the butter and sugar in a mixing bowl and beat using an electric hand mixer or wooden spoon until the mixture is light and creamy. Add the ground almonds, egg yolks and flour and beat again. Spread the topping over the jam and sprinkle over the flaked almonds.
4   Bake for 25–30 minutes until golden brown. Remove the slice from the oven and leave to cool in the tin, then cut into 16 slices.

261 Mincemeat & Apple Slice

PREPARATION TIME 20 minutes   **COOKING TIME** 1 hour–1 hour 10 minutes   **MAKES** 10 slices

225g/8oz butter, softened, plus extra
for greasing
225g/8oz/scant 1 cup caster sugar
4 large eggs, lightly beaten
225g/8oz/1½ cups self-raising flour
2 tsp cinnamon

2 dessert apples, peeled, cored
and grated
400g/14oz mincemeat
55g/2oz/⅓ cup flaked almonds
icing sugar, for dusting

1   Preheat the oven to 180°C/350°F/gas 4. Grease and line a 20cm/8in loose-bottomed square cake tin.
2   Put the butter and sugar in a mixing bowl and beat using an electric hand mixer or wooden spoon until the mixture is light. Beat in the eggs. Sift in the flour and cinnamon and fold them into the mixture with the grated apple and mincemeat, using a large metal spoon. Scape the mixture into the tin using a spatula. Sprinkle the top with the flaked almonds.
3   Bake for 1 hour–1 hour 10 minutes until golden brown and firm to touch. If the nuts start to brown too much, cover with a sheet of baking parchment. Remove the slice from the oven and leave to stand for 5 minutes, then turn out on to a wire rack and leave to cool. Dust with icing sugar and cut into 10 slices.

262 All-In-One Gooseberry Crumble Slice

PREPARATION TIME 30 minutes   **COOKING TIME** 30–35 minutes   **MAKES** 16 slices

350g/12oz butter, softened, plus extra
for greasing
225g/8oz/1 cup light soft brown sugar
4 large eggs, lightly beaten
225g/8oz/1½ cups self-raising flour, sifted
1 tsp vanilla extract

400g/14oz cooked/preserved gooseberries
200g/7oz cream cheese
100ml/3½fl oz/scant ½ cup double cream
140g/5oz/1 cup plain flour, sifted
115g/4oz/1 cup ground almonds
2 tbsp caster sugar

1   Preheat the oven to 180°C/350°F/gas 4. Grease and line a 40 x 20 x 6cm/16 x 8 x 2½in baking tin.
2   Beat 225g/8oz of the butter, brown sugar, eggs, self-raising flour and vanilla extract with an electric hand mixer or wooden spoon. Scrape into the tin. Scatter the gooseberries on top.
3   In a separate bowl, beat the cream cheese and cream with an electric hand mixer or a wooden spoon until there are no lumps, then spoon the mixture over the gooseberries.
4   Put the plain flour and ground almonds in a bowl and rub in the remaining butter to make large crumble pieces. Mix in the caster sugar. Sprinkle the topping over the cake.
5   Bake for 30–35 minutes until the crumble topping is golden brown and the cream cheese layer has set. Remove from the oven and leave to cool in the tin, then cut into 16 slices.

263 Raspberry Frangipane Slice

PREPARATION TIME 30 minutes **COOKING TIME** 30–35 minutes **MAKES** 16 slices

350g/12oz butter, softened, plus extra
  for greasing
280g/10oz/heaped 1 cup caster sugar
4 large eggs, lightly beaten
225g/8oz/1½ cups self-raising flour, sifted
400g/7oz/2¾ cups raspberries

200g/7oz cream cheese
55g/2oz amaretti biscuits
85g/3oz/¾ cup ground almonds
1 tsp almond extract
55g/2oz/⅓ cup plain flour, sifted
30g/1oz marzipan, finely chopped

1 Preheat the oven to 180°C/350°F/gas 4. Grease and line a 40 x 20 x 6cm/16 x 8 x 2½in baking tin.
2 Put 225g/8oz of the butter and 225g/8oz/scant 1 cup of the caster sugar in a mixing bowl and beat using an electric hand mixer or wooden spoon until the mixture is light and creamy. Add the eggs gradually, beating after each addition. Add the self-raising flour and gently fold it in, using a large metal spoon. Scrape the mixture into the tin using a spatula. Scatter the raspberries over the top and place teaspoons of cream cheese among them.
3 In a separate bowl, beat the remaining butter and sugar as before. Put the amaretti biscuits in a plastic bag and crush them with a rolling pin, then add to the creamed mixture with the remaining ingredients. Cover the cake with teaspoons of the almond topping.
4 Bake for 30–35 minutes until the topping is golden brown and the cake is firm to touch. Remove the slice from the oven and leave to cool in the tin, then cut into 16 slices.

264 Peach Streusel Slice

PREPARATION TIME 30 minutes **COOKING TIME** 30–35 minutes **MAKES** 16 slices

350g/12oz butter, softened, plus extra
  for greasing
280g/10oz/heaped 1 cup caster sugar
4 large eggs, lightly beaten
350g/12oz/2⅓ cups self-raising flour,
  sifted

4 ripe peaches, stones removed and
  flesh sliced
200g/7oz cream cheese
1 tsp vanilla extract
100ml/3½fl oz/scant ½ cup double cream
85g/3oz/¾ cup ground almonds

1 Preheat the oven to 180°C/350°F/gas 4. Grease and line a 40 x 20 x 6cm/16 x 8 x 2½in baking tin.
2 Follow step 2 in recipe 263, using 225g/8oz of the flour. Place the peach slices on top of the mixture instead of the raspberries and cream cheese.
3 In a separate bowl, beat the cream cheese, vanilla extract and cream with an electric hand mixer or wooden spoon until smooth, then spoon the mixture over the peach slices.
4 In a separate bowl, beat the remaining butter and sugar as before. Fold in the remaining flour and the ground almonds. Cover the cake with teaspoons of the almond topping.
5 Bake for 30–35 minutes until the crumble topping is golden brown and the cake is firm. Remove the slice from the oven and leave to cool in the tin, then cut into 16 slices.

265 Soured Cream & Apple Slice

PREPARATION TIME 30 minutes **COOKING TIME** 45–50 minutes **MAKES** 16 slices

6 eating apples, peeled, cored and sliced
1 tbsp light soft brown sugar
2 tsp cinnamon
350g/12oz butter, softened, plus extra
  for greasing
280g/10oz/heaped 1 cup caster sugar

4 large eggs, lightly beaten
225g/8oz/1½ cups self-raising flour
100ml/3½fl oz/scant ½ cup soured cream
85g/3oz/¾ cup ground almonds
55g/2oz/heaped ⅓ cup flaked almonds
55g/2oz/⅓ cup plain flour

1 Simmer the apple slices with 150ml/5fl oz/scant ⅔ cup water, the light brown sugar and 1 teaspoon of the cinnamon for about 20 minutes until the apples are soft. Leave to cool.
2 Preheat the oven to 180°C/350°F/gas 4. Grease and line a 40 x 20 x 6cm/16 x 8 x 2½in baking tin. Follow step 2 in recipe 263. Place the cooked apples on top of the mixture instead of the raspberries and cream cheese, and spoon the soured cream over the apples.
3 In a separate bowl, beat the remaining butter and sugar as before. Mix in the remaining ingredients. Top the cake with the crumble. Bake for 45–50 minutes. Serve as above.

266 Millionaire's Shortbread

PREPARATION TIME 30 minutes, plus chilling   **COOKING TIME** 20–25 minutes   **MAKES** 18 slices

280g/10oz butter, softened, plus extra
  for greasing
85g/3oz/⅓ cup caster sugar
225g/8oz/1½ cups plain flour, sifted
55g/2oz/heaped ½ cup desiccated
  coconut
70g/2½oz/⅓ cup light soft brown sugar
175ml/5½fl oz/⅔ cup condensed milk

a little purple or pink food colouring paste
100g/3½oz white chocolate, melted and
  cooled slightly
2 tsp vegetable oil
100g/3½oz plain chocolate, melted and
  cooled slightly
2 tbsp bought crystallized violets,
  to decorate (optional)

1   Preheat the oven to 190°C/375°F/gas 5. Grease and line a 25 x 20cm/10 x 8in cake tin.
2   Put 185g/6½oz of the butter and the caster sugar in a mixing bowl and beat using an electric hand mixer or wooden spoon until the mixture is light and creamy. Add the flour and coconut, then bring the mixture together with your hands to form a soft dough. Press the dough into the tin with your hands, covering the base evenly.
3   Bake for 12–15 minutes until golden brown. Remove the shortbread from the oven and leave to cool in the tin.
4   In a saucepan, simmer the remaining butter, the brown sugar and condensed milk for 8–10 minutes until the sugar has dissolved, then bring the mixture to the boil and remove from the heat. Pour over the shortbread and leave until cold, then refrigerate for 1 hour.
5   Add a little colouring paste to the white chocolate and stir well with a spoon until the chocolate is an even pink or purple colour. Add 1 teaspoon of the vegetable oil each to both the coloured and plain chocolate and mix well. Place spoonfuls of the coloured and plain chocolate alternately on top of the caramel. Using a fork, swirl the chocolates together so that the whole surface of the caramel is covered with chocolate and you have a pretty, feathered pattern. Sprinkle the crystallized violets over the top, if using, and set aside for 1 hour until the chocolate has set, then cut into 18 slices.

267 Chocolate Peppermint Slice

PREPARATION TIME 20 minutes, plus chilling   **COOKING TIME** 3 to 5 minutes   **MAKES** 18 slices

185g/6½oz butter, chopped, plus extra
  for greasing
400g/14oz chocolate-covered digestive
  biscuits, roughly broken
3 tbsp golden syrup
4 tbsp cocoa powder
100g/3½oz/heaped 1 cup desiccated
  coconut
200g/7oz plain chocolate, broken into
  pieces

PEPPERMINT LAYER
200g/7oz/1⅓ cups icing sugar, sifted
2 tbsp butter
2 tbsp milk
a few drops of peppermint essence
green food colouring

1   Grease and line a 30 x 20cm/12 x 8in Swiss roll tin.
2   Put the broken biscuits in a food processor and pulse to fine crumbs. Alternatively, put them in a plastic bag and crush with a rolling pin. Heat 150g/5½oz of the butter, the syrup and cocoa in a large saucepan for 3–5 minutes until the butter has melted and the sugar has dissolved. Add the biscuit crumbs and coconut and stir well with a wooden spoon to make sure that all the crumbs are coated in the butter mixture. Press the biscuit mixture into the tin and refrigerate for 30 minutes.
3   In a separate bowl, beat the peppermint layer ingredients using an electric hand mixer or wooden spoon to make a smooth cream. Remove the tin from the fridge and spread the mint cream over the biscuit base. Refrigerate again for 30 minutes.
4   When the mint layer has set, melt the chocolate and remaining butter together and stir to form a smooth icing. Leave to cool a little, then spread over the mint layer and leave to set before cutting into 18 slices.

CHAPTER 5

CELEBRATION CAKES & COOKIES

This chapter contains some simple but stunning ideas for

creating cakes and biscuits for special occasions, whether a

children's birthday party, Christmas, Easter or even a wedding.

While looking impressive, the cakes and cookies in this chapter

are also very easy to prepare, using a few simple ideas such as

fresh flower centrepieces, ribbons and edible glitter. Delight your

Christmas visitors with a slice of traditional Iced Christmas Cake,

flavoured with amaretto or brandy. Celebrate Valentine's Day

with Valentine Ribbon Hearts for your friends and family or a

Chocolate Heart Gateau for your loved one. There are decorated

cupcakes to welcome a baby and to celebrate a retirement,

18th Birthday Cupcakes and St Patrick's Day Cupcakes, spooky

cakes and cookies for Halloween and Bonfire Night Treacle

Cookies to munch while watching fireworks. With a Giant

Birthday Cookie, Cinnamon Orange Stollen and delicious Easter

Egg Cupcakes, this chapter contains something for every occasion.

WELCOME BABY CUPCAKES *(SEE PAGE 177)*

268 1st Birthday Cake

PREPARATION TIME 40 minutes **COOKING TIME** 35–40 minutes **SERVES** 10

350g/12oz butter, softened, plus extra
   for greasing
350g/12oz/1⅓ cups caster sugar
6 large eggs, lightly beaten
350g/12oz/2⅓ cups self-raising flour,
   sifted

1 tsp vanilla extract
2 recipe quantities Vanilla Buttercream
   (see page 22)
a few drops of green food colouring
sugar sprinkles, to decorate

1   Preheat the oven to 180°C/350°F/gas 4. Grease and line a 40 x 20 x 6cm/16 x 8 x 2½in baking tin.
2   Put the butter and sugar in a mixing bowl and beat using an electric hand mixer or wooden spoon until the mixture is light and creamy. Add the eggs gradually, beating after each addition. Add the flour and vanilla extract and gently fold them into the mixture, using a large metal spoon. Scrape the mixture into the tin using a spatula.
3   Bake for 35–40 minutes until the cake springs back when pressed lightly and a skewer inserted into the middle of the cake comes out clean. Remove the cake from the oven and leave to stand for 5 minutes, then turn out on to a wire rack and leave to cool.
4   Using the full width and length of the cake, cut out a large number '1' using a sharp knife. (Keep the cut-out bits and either cut into squares ready to ice another day or use in a trifle.) Transfer the cake to a large, foil-covered board the size of the cake tin.
5   Reserve a quarter of the buttercream in a separate bowl and carefully cover the cake with the remainder, making sure the sides and top are all covered. Decorate the top of the cake with the sprinkles. Stir the food colouring into the remaining buttercream until the colour is uniform. Spoon the icing into an icing bag fitted with a 13mm/½in star nozzle and pipe small stars around the outline of the top and the bottom of the cake. Leave the icing to set before serving.

269 18th Birthday Cupcakes

PREPARATION TIME 40 minutes **COOKING TIME** 15–20 minutes **MAKES** 24 cakes

225g/8oz butter, softened
225g/8oz/scant 1 cup caster sugar
4 large eggs, lightly beaten
225g/8oz/1½ cups self-raising flour, sifted
2 tbsp natural yogurt
finely grated zest of 2 lemons
2 tbsp lemon curd
food colouring paste of your choice

55g/2oz ready-to-roll icing
icing sugar, for dusting
2 recipe quantities Vanilla Buttercream
   (see page 22)

TO DECORATE
sugar sprinkles
edible glitter

1   Preheat the oven to 180°C/350°F/gas 4. Put 24 cake cases in two 12-hole bun tins.
2   Put the butter and caster sugar in a mixing bowl and beat using an electric hand mixer or wooden spoon until the mixture is light and creamy. Add the eggs gradually, beating after each addition. Add the flour, yogurt, lemon zest and lemon curd and gently fold them into the mixture, using a large metal spoon. Spoon the mixture into the cake cases.
3   Bake for 15–20 minutes until the cakes spring back when pressed lightly and a skewer inserted into the middle of a cake comes out clean. Remove the cakes from the oven, turn out on to a wire rack and leave to cool.
4   Dip a cocktail stick into the food colouring paste and wipe it on the ready-to-roll icing, then knead the icing until the colour is uniformly even. Repeat, if necessary, to achieve the desired depth of colour. Sift icing sugar on to a clean work surface and roll out the icing to 5mm/¼in thick using a rolling pin. Cut out the numbers '1' and '8', each slightly smaller than the size of the surface of the cupcakes, using number cutters or cardboard templates and a knife.
5   Spoon the buttercream into an icing bag fitted with a 13mm/½in plain nozzle and pipe a swirl on top of each cupcake. Cover each cake with sprinkles and place on a tiered cake stand. Place the '1' and '8' on 2 of the cupcakes in the centre of your display and dust all the cakes with edible glitter.

270 21st Birthday Cake

PREPARATION TIME 1 hour   COOKING TIME 25–30 minutes   SERVES 10

225g/8oz butter, softened, plus extra
  for greasing
225g/8oz/scant 1 cup caster sugar
4 large eggs, lightly beaten
225g/8oz/1½ cups self-raising flour,
  sifted
1 tbsp instant coffee granules dissolved
  in 1 tbsp boiling water, then cooled
100g/3½oz plain chocolate, grated
1 recipe quantity Vanilla Buttercream
  (see page 22)

icing sugar, for dusting
450g/1lb ready-to-roll icing
a few drops of chosen food colouring
½ quantity Royal Icing (see page 22)

TO DECORATE
3.5cm/1½in high floral foam dome on
  a plastic base with self-adhesive pad
flowers to match your icing colour
1.5m x 3cm/5ft x 1¼in wide ribbon
long wooden cocktail stick or lollipop stick

1   Preheat the oven to 180°C/350°F/gas 4. Grease and base-line two 20cm/8in sandwich
    cake tins.
2   Put the butter and sugar in a mixing bowl and beat using an electric hand mixer or wooden
    spoon until the mixture is light and creamy. Add the eggs gradually, beating after each
    addition. Add the flour, coffee liquid and grated chocolate and gently fold them into the
    mixture, using a large metal spoon. Divide the mixture between the tins using a spatula.
3   Bake for 25–30 minutes until the cakes spring back when pressed lightly. Remove from
    the oven and leave to stand for 5 minutes, then turn out on to a wire rack to cool.
4   Sandwich the cakes together with a third of the buttercream and cover the top and sides
    of the cake with the remainder.
5   Sift icing sugar on to a clean work surface and roll out the ready-to-roll icing to 5mm/¼in
    thick using a rolling pin. Lift the icing on top of the cake, using the rolling pin to help,
    and smooth down with your hands to ensure there are no creases. Trim the icing around
    the bottom of the cake with a sharp knife. Add the food colouring to the royal icing and
    stir until the colour is uniform. Spoon it into an icing bag fitted with a 13mm/½in star
    nozzle and pipe stars around the base and the edge of the top of the cake.
6   Just before you wish to serve the cake, soak the foam in water. Cut the flowers so that
    they have 2.5cm/1in stems and press them into the foam. Place the foam on top of the
    cake, sticking it down with the self-adhesive pad. Wrap the ribbon around the cake and
    tie in a bow. Write a 21st birthday message on a small piece of card, secure it on a long
    wooden cocktail stick or lollipop stick and poke it into the centre of the flowers.

271 Gingerbread Man Cupcakes

PREPARATION TIME 40 minutes   COOKING TIME 15–20 minutes   MAKES 12 cakes

115g/4oz butter, softened
115g/4oz/scant ½ cup caster sugar
2 large eggs, lightly beaten
115g/4oz/¾ cup self-raising flour
1 tsp ground ginger
1 tsp cinnamon
55g/2oz plain chocolate, melted and
  cooled slightly

36 sugar-coated chocolate beans
12 small gingerbread men, either made
  following the recipe on page 211, but
  using a smaller cutter, or bought
1 recipe quantity Vanilla Buttercream
  (see page 22)
sugar sprinkles, to decorate

1   Preheat the oven to 180°C/350°F/gas 4. Put 12 cake cases in a 12-hole bun tin.
2   Put the butter and sugar in a mixing bowl and beat using an electric hand mixer or wooden
    spoon until the mixture is light and creamy. Add the eggs gradually, beating after each
    addition. Sift in the flour, ginger and cinnamon and gently fold them into the mixture,
    using a large metal spoon. Spoon the mixture into the cake cases.
3   Bake for 15–20 minutes until the cakes spring back when pressed lightly and a skewer
    inserted into the middle of a cake comes out clean. Remove the cakes from the oven,
    turn out on to a wire rack and leave to cool.
4   Use the melted chocolate to attach 3 chocolate beans to each gingerbread man as
    buttons. Leave the chocolate to set. Spoon the buttercream into an icing bag fitted with a
    13mm/½in star nozzle and pipe a swirl of icing on top of each cake. Stand a gingerbread
    man upright in the centre of each cake so that his feet are fixed into the icing. Shake a
    few sprinkles over the icing to decorate.

272 Chocolate Box Cake

PREPARATION TIME 40 minutes   **COOKING TIME** 25–30 minutes   **SERVES** 10

225g/8oz butter, softened, plus extra
 for greasing
225g/8oz/scant 1 cup caster sugar
4 large eggs, lightly beaten
200g/7oz/1⅓ cups self-raising flour
4 tbsp cocoa powder

½ recipe quantity Chocolate Buttercream
 (see page 22)
1 recipe quantity Chocolate Ganache
 (see page 22)
30 assorted chocolates, wrapped or
 unrapped
1.5m x 5cm/5ft x 2in wide ribbon

1   Preheat the oven to 180°C/350°F/gas 4. Grease and base-line two 20cm/8in sandwich
    cake tins.
2   Put the butter and sugar in a mixing bowl and beat using an electric hand mixer or wooden
    spoon until the mixture is light and creamy. Add the eggs gradually, beating after each
    addition. Sift in the flour and cocoa and gently fold them into the mixture, using a large
    metal spoon. Divide the mixture between the tins using a spatula.
3   Bake for 25–30 minutes until the cakes spring back when pressed lightly and a skewer
    inserted into the middle of each cake comes out clean. Remove the cakes from the oven
    and leave to stand for 5 minutes, then turn out on to a wire rack and leave to cool.
4   Sandwich the cakes together with the buttercream and then cover the top and sides with
    the ganache. Arrange the chocolates on the cake, making sure they cover the whole top,
    and mixing different colours and shapes. Leave the icing to set completely.
5   Wrap the ribbon around the cake and tie it neatly in a bow. Remove the ribbon before
    cutting the cake into slices to serve.

273 Birthday Present Cake

PREPARATION TIME 1 hour   **COOKING TIME** 35–40 minutes   **SERVES** 10

225g/8oz butter, softened, plus extra
 for greasing
225g/8oz/scant 1 cup caster sugar
4 large eggs, lightly beaten
225g/8oz/1½ cups self-raising flour,
 sifted
finely grated zest of 2 lemons
2 tbsp natural yogurt

1 recipe quantity Vanilla Buttercream
 (see page 22)
3 tbsp lemon curd
icing sugar, for dusting
450g/1lb ready-to-roll icing
1.5m x 3cm/5ft x 1¼in wide
 coloured ribbon
edible glitter, for dusting

1   Preheat the oven to 180°C/350°F/gas 4. Grease and line a 20cm/8in loose-bottomed
    square cake tin.
2   Put the butter and sugar in a mixing bowl and beat using an electric hand mixer or wooden
    spoon until the mixture is light and creamy. Add the eggs gradually, beating after each
    addition. Add the flour, lemon zest and yogurt and gently fold them into the mixture,
    using a large metal spoon. Scrape the mixture into the tin using a spatula.
3   Bake for 35–40 minutes until the cake springs back when pressed lightly and a skewer
    inserted into the middle of the cake comes out clean. Remove the cake from the oven
    and leave to stand for 5 minutes, then turn out on to a wire rack and leave to cool.
4   Cut the cake in half horizontally using a sharp knife and sandwich the halves together
    with a third of the buttercream and the lemon curd. Cover the top and sides of the cake
    with the remaining buttercream, saving 1 tablespoonful to fix the ribbons to the cake.
5   Sift icing sugar on to a clean work surface and, using a rolling pin, roll out the icing to
    5mm/¼in thick. Using the rolling pin to help, lift the icing on top of the cake and
    smooth down with your hands to ensure there are no creases. Trim the icing around the
    bottom of the cake with a sharp knife so that you have a neat parcel shape.
6   Cut 2 lengths of the ribbon each long enough to reach over the cake and place on top of
    the cake, crossing in the centre. Fix the ribbons to the bottom of each side of the cake
    with a small amount of buttercream. Tie the remaining ribbon in a bow and fix in the
    centre of the ribbon cross with another dab of buttercream. Dust the cake with edible
    glitter. When you are ready to cut the cake, remove the ribbons.

274 Strawberry Ice Cream Birthday Cake

PREPARATION TIME 40 minutes, plus freezing/chilling   **COOKING TIME** 25–30 minutes   **SERVES** 10

1 litre/35fl oz/4 cups strawberry ice
  cream, softened
350g/12oz butter, softened, plus extra
  for greasing
350g/12oz/1⅓ cups caster sugar
6 large eggs, lightly beaten

350g/12oz/2⅓ cups self-raising flour, sifted
1 tsp vanilla extract
200g/7oz white chocolate, melted and
  cooled slightly
5 strawberries, halved
10 white chocolate truffles

1   Line two 20cm/8in sandwich cake tins with cling film, letting the film come over the top. Divide the ice cream between the tins and freeze for 1 hour. Lift the ice cream out of the tins, using the film, cover with another layer of cling film and return to the freezer.
2   Preheat the oven to 180°C/350°F/gas 4. Wash both tins, then grease and base-line both washed tins and a third tin of the same size.
3   Put the butter and sugar in a mixing bowl and beat using an electric hand mixer or wooden spoon until the mixture is light and creamy. Add the eggs gradually, beating after each addition. Add the flour and vanilla extract and gently fold them into the mixture, using a large metal spoon. Divide the mixture between the tins using a spatula.
4   Bake for 25–30 minutes until the cakes spring back when pressed lightly and a skewer inserted into the middle of each cake comes out clean. Remove the cakes from the oven and leave to stand for 5 minutes, then turn out on to a wire rack and leave to cool.
5   Cover one of the cakes with the melted chocolate and top with the strawberries and truffles.
6   Remove the ice cream layers from the freezer 10 minutes before you are ready to serve the cake so that they soften a little. Stack up the cake and ice-cream layers, finishing with the decorated cake layer. Add candles, if wished, and serve immediately.

275 Rose & Violet Birthday Cake

PREPARATION TIME 40 minutes   **COOKING TIME** 25–30 minutes   **SERVES** 10

225g/8oz butter, softened, plus extra
   for greasing
225g/8oz/scant 1 cup caster sugar
4 large eggs, lightly beaten
200g/7oz/1⅓ cups self-raising flour
4 tbsp cocoa powder
a few drops of pink food colouring

2 tbsp rose syrup or rosewater
½ recipe quantity Vanilla Buttercream
   (see page 22)
2 tbsp rose or raspberry jam
1 recipe quantity Chocolate Ganache
   (see page 22)
10 rose and violet cream chocolates

1   Preheat the oven to 180°C/350°F/gas 4. Grease and base-line two 20cm/8in sandwich cake tins.

2   Put the butter and sugar in a mixing bowl and beat using an electric hand mixer or wooden spoon until the mixture is light and creamy. Add the eggs gradually, beating after each addition. Sift in the flour and cocoa and gently fold them into the mixture, using a large metal spoon. Divide the mixture between the tins using a spatula.

3   Bake for 25–30 minutes until the cakes spring back when pressed lightly and a skewer inserted into the middle of each cake comes out clean. Remove the cakes from the oven and leave to stand for 5 minutes, then turn out on to a wire rack and leave to cool.

4   Stir the food colouring and rose syrup into the buttercream until the colour is uniform. Sandwich the cakes together with the jam, then the buttercream. Cover the top and sides of the cake with the ganache and place the rose and violet chocolates alternately around the top of the cake. Leave to set before serving.

276 Strawberry Windmill Cake

PREPARATION TIME 30 minutes   **COOKING TIME** 25–30 minutes   **SERVES** 8

225g/8oz butter, softened, plus extra
   for greasing
225g/8oz/scant 1 cup caster sugar
4 large eggs, lightly beaten
200g/7oz/1⅓ cups self-raising flour
4 tbsp cocoa powder
3 tbsp almond liqueur, such as amaretto

600ml/21fl oz/scant 2½ cups double
   cream, whipped to stiff peaks
400g/14oz/2⅔ cups strawberries,
   hulled and halved
3 tbsp strawberry jam
icing sugar, for dusting

1   Preheat the oven to 180°C/350°F/gas 4. Grease and base-line two 20cm/8in sandwich cake tins.

2   Put the butter and caster sugar in a mixing bowl and beat using an electric hand mixer or wooden spoon until the mixture is light and creamy. Add the eggs gradually, beating after each addition. Sift in the flour and cocoa and gently fold them into the mixture, using a large metal spoon. Divide the mixture between the tins using a spatula.

3   Bake for 25–30 minutes until the cakes spring back when pressed lightly and a skewer inserted into the middle of each cake comes out clean. Remove the cakes from the oven and leave to stand for 5 minutes, then turn out on to a wire rack and leave to cool.

4   Cut each cake in half horizontally with a sharp knife. Drizzle 1 tablespoon of the amaretto over one cake layer and cover with a third of the cream. Top with a third of the strawberries and 1 tablespoon of the jam. Repeat with the next 2 cake layers. Cut the top layer of cake into 6 equal segments and place on top of the cake at 45-degree angles as though like windmill sails, adjusting the strawberries so that they lie in between the sails. Dust with icing sugar to serve.

277 Chocolate Coconut Birthday Cake

PREPARATION TIME 30 minutes   COOKING TIME 25–30 minutes   SERVES 8

225g/8oz butter, plus extra for greasing
225g/8oz/1½ cups self-raising flour,
  sifted, plus extra for dusting
225g/8oz/scant 1 cup caster sugar
4 large eggs, lightly beaten
250g/9oz/3 cups desiccated coconut

100g/3½oz/heaped ½ cup milk
  chocolate chips
2 tsp cinnamon
300g/10½oz white chocolate, melted
  and cooled slightly
sugar-coated chocolate beans, to decorate

1 Preheat the oven to 180°C/350°F/gas 4. Grease a 23cm/9in ring tin and dust with flour.
2 Put the butter and sugar in a mixing bowl and beat using an electric hand mixer or wooden spoon until the mixture is light. Add the eggs gradually, beating after each addition. Add the flour, 100g/3½oz/1 cup of the coconut, the chocolate chips and cinnamon and fold into the mixture, using a large metal spoon. Scrape the mixture into the tin using a spatula.
3 Bake for 25–30 minutes until the cake springs back when pressed lightly. Remove from the oven and leave to stand for 5 minutes, then turn out on to a wire rack to cool.
4 Cover the top of the cake with half the melted chocolate. Mix the remaining chocolate and coconut and spoon over the top of the cake. Decorate with the chocolate beans.

278 Strawberry & Truffle Chocolate Celebration Cake

PREPARATION TIME 40 minutes   COOKING TIME 25–30 minutes   SERVES 10

225g/8oz butter, softened, plus extra
  for greasing
225g/8oz/scant 1 cup caster sugar
4 large eggs, lightly beaten
200g/7oz/1⅓ cups self-raising flour
4 tbsp cocoa powder

½ recipe quantity Chocolate Buttercream
  (see page 22)
200g/7oz plain chocolate, melted and
  cooled slightly
10 strawberries
10 chocolate truffles

1 Preheat the oven to 180°C/350°F/gas 4. Grease and base-line two 20cm/8in sandwich cake tins.
2 Put the butter and sugar in a mixing bowl and beat using an electric hand mixer or wooden spoon until the mixture is light and creamy. Add the eggs gradually, beating after each addition. Sift in the flour and cocoa and gently fold them into the mixture, using a large metal spoon. Divide the mixture between the tins using a spatula.
3 Bake for 25–30 minutes until the cakes spring back when pressed lightly. Remove the cakes from the oven and leave to stand for 5 minutes, then turn out on to a wire rack to cool.
4 Sandwich the cakes together with the buttercream. Cover the top of the cake with the melted chocolate and arrange the strawberries and truffles alternately around the edge.

279 Giant Birthday Cookie

PREPARATION TIME 30 minutes   COOKING TIME 25–30 minutes   SERVES 10

250g/9oz butter, plus extra for greasing
400g/14oz/1⅔ cups caster sugar
2 large eggs, lightly beaten
2 tsp vanilla extract
550g/1lb 4oz/3⅔ cups plain flour

1 tsp baking powder
100g/3½oz/heaped ½ cup plain
  chocolate chips
½ quantity Royal Icing (see page 22)
sweets and edible silver balls, to decorate

1 Preheat the oven to 180°C/350°F/gas 4. Grease a 30cm/12in fluted square flan tin.
2 Put the butter and sugar in a mixing bowl and beat using an electric hand mixer or wooden spoon until the mixture is light and creamy. Beat in the eggs and vanilla extract. Sift in the flour and baking powder and add the chocolate chips. Mix together with your hands to form a soft dough and press it into the tin evenly with the back of a spoon.
3 Bake for 25–30 minutes until golden brown and just firm. Remove from the oven and leave to cool in the tin, then transfer to a serving plate. Put a third of the royal icing in an icing bag fitted with a 3mm/⅛in plain nozzle and write a message in the centre of the cookie. Put the remaining icing in a bag with a 5mm/¼in star nozzle and pipe stars around the edge. Press the sweets and silver balls into the icing to decorate. Pipe small stars around the message and press a sweet into each. Leave the icing to set before serving.

280 Flowerpot Cakes

PREPARATION TIME 40 minutes   **COOKING TIME** 15–20 minutes   **MAKES** 16 cakes

115g/4oz butter, softened
115g/4oz/scant ½ cup caster sugar
2 large eggs, lightly beaten
115g/4oz/¾ cup self-raising flour, sifted
1 tsp vanilla extract

a few drops of green food colouring
1 recipe quantity Vanilla Buttercream
(see page 22)
16 large sugar flowers
16 sugar leaves

1   Preheat the oven to 180°C/350°F/gas 4. Wash sixteen 3cm/1¼in brand-new terracotta flowerpots and leave to dry, then put a cake case in each one, using your fingers to fold and smooth the paper down so that it fits around the sides of the pots.

2   Put the butter and sugar in a mixing bowl and beat using an electric hand mixer or wooden spoon until the mixture is light and creamy. Add the eggs gradually, beating after each addition. Add the flour and vanilla extract and gently fold them into the mixture, using a large metal spoon. Spoon the mixture into the cake cases using a teaspoon.

3   Place the flowerpots on a baking tray and bake for 15–20 minutes until the cakes spring back when pressed lightly and a skewer inserted into the middle of a cake comes out clean. Remove the cakes from the oven and transfer to a wire rack to cool.

4   Stir the food colouring into the buttercream until the colour is uniform. Spoon it into an icing bag fitted with a 5mm/¼in star nozzle. Pipe a swirl of buttercream on top of each cake. If you do not have an icing bag, spread a thick layer of icing over each cake using a round-bladed knife.) Top each cake with a sugar flower and leaf.

281 Gift Tag Cookies

PREPARATION TIME 30 minutes, plus chilling   COOKING TIME 12–15 minutes   MAKES 10 cookies

115g/4oz butter, softened, plus extra
  for greasing
55g/2oz/¼ cup caster sugar
175g/6oz/heaped 1 cup plain flour,
  sifted, plus extra for dusting
1 tbsp milk (optional)
300g/10½oz/2 cups icing sugar, sifted

TO DECORATE
edible gel writing pen
sugar-coated chocolate beans or
  small sweets, to decorate
2m x 3mm/6ft 6in x ⅛in wide ribbon

1 Put the butter and sugar in a mixing bowl and beat using an electric hand mixer or wooden spoon until the mixture is light. Add the flour and mix with your hands to form a soft dough, adding the milk if the mixture is too dry. Wrap in cling film and refrigerate for 1 hour.
2 Preheat the oven to 180°C/350°F/gas 4. Grease two 30cm/12in square baking trays.
3 Sift flour on to a clean work surface and roll the dough out to about 1cm/⅜in thick using a rolling pin. Cut out 5 large rectangles and 5 large rounds using cutters or a knife, gathering up the trimmings and re-rolling as necessary. Place the cookies on the baking trays and, using a skewer or a cocktail stick, make a 5mm/¼in hole near one edge of each cookie. This will have ribbon threaded through it to attach the gift tag to your present.
4 Bake for 12–15 minutes until golden brown and just firm. Remove the cookies from the oven and leave to cool on the trays for a few minutes, then transfer to a wire rack to cool.
5 In a bowl, mix the icing sugar with 2–3 tablespoons water to make a smooth icing and spread it over the cookies. Use the skewer or cocktail stick to reopen the holes if they closed during baking or if they fill with icing. Leave the icing to set, then write names on the gift tags with the gel pen and decorate around the edge of each tag with chocolate beans. Cut the ribbon into 20cm/8in lengths, thread one length through the hole on each cookie and attach to your present.

282 Fresh Flower Cake

PREPARATION TIME 40 minutes   COOKING TIME 25–30 minutes   SERVES 10

225g/8oz butter, softened, plus extra
  for greasing
225g/8oz/scant 1 cup caster sugar
4 large eggs, lightly beaten
200g/7oz/1⅓ cups self-raising flour
4 tbsp cocoa powder
1 recipe quantity Chocolate Buttercream
  (see page 22)

1 recipe quantity Chocolate Ganache
  (see page 22)

TO DECORATE
chocolate truffles and chocolate
  buttons
3.5cm/1½in high floral foam dome on a
  plastic base with self-adhesive pad
fresh flowers of your choice

1 Preheat the oven to 180°C/350°F/gas 4. Grease and base-line two 20cm/8in sandwich cake tins.
2 Put the butter and caster sugar in a mixing bowl and beat using an electric hand mixer or wooden spoon until the mixture is light and creamy. Add the eggs gradually, beating after each addition. Sift in the flour and cocoa and gently fold them into the mixture, using a large metal spoon. Divide the mixture between the tins using a spatula.
3 Bake for 25–30 minutes until the cakes spring back when pressed lightly and a skewer inserted into the middle of each cake comes out clean. Remove the cakes from the oven and leave to stand for 5 minutes, then turn out on to a wire rack and leave to cool.
4 Sandwich the cakes together with half of the buttercream and then cover the top and sides of the cake with the ganache, working gently with a palette knife to smooth it evenly.
5 Gently lift the cake on to a serving plate or cake stand. Spoon the remaining buttercream into an icing bag fitted with a 13mm/½in star nozzle and pipe around the edge of the top and around the base of the cake. Press chocolate buttons all around the edge of the buttercream where it sandwiches the cakes together. Use the remaining buttons and the truffles to decorate the top, leaving the centre free for the flowers. Leave the icing to set.
6 When you are ready to display the cake, soak the floral foam in water for a few minutes. Cut the flower stems down to 2.5cm/1in long and press them into the foam, covering the entire dome to the top with flowers. Remove the backing paper on the self-adhesive pad on the base of the plastic tray and stick the dome in the centre of the top of the cake.

283 Feather Cake

PREPARATION TIME 40 minutes   **COOKING TIME** 25–30 minutes   **SERVES** 8

225g/8oz butter, plus extra for greasing
225g/8oz/scant 1 cup caster sugar
4 large eggs, lightly beaten
225g/8oz/1½ cups self-raising flour
4 tbsp cocoa powder
3 tbsp natural yogurt

90g/3¼oz/½ cup plain chocolate chips
½ recipe quantity Coffee Buttercream
(see page 22)
1 recipe quantity Chocolate Ganache
(see page 22)
jelly beans and clean feathers, to decorate

1   Preheat the oven to 180°C/350°F/gas 4. Grease and base-line two 20cm/8in sandwich cake tins.
2   Put the butter and sugar in a mixing bowl and beat using an electric hand mixer or wooden spoon until the mixture is light. Add the eggs gradually, beating after each addition. Sift in the flour and cocoa and gently fold them into the mixture with the yogurt and chocolate chips, using a large metal spoon. Divide the mixture between the tins using a spatula.
3   Bake for 25–30 minutes until the cakes spring back when pressed lightly. Remove from the oven and leave to stand for 5 minutes, then turn out on to a wire rack to cool.
4   Sandwich the cakes together with the buttercream and cover the top and sides of the cake with the ganache. Arrange the jelly beans in a pattern around the edge of the top of the cake. Leave the ganache to set. Poke the feathers into the centre of the cake to decorate.

284 Children's Party Cupcakes

PREPARATION TIME 30 minutes   **COOKING TIME** 15–20 minutes   **MAKES** 24 cakes

225g/8oz butter, softened
225g/8oz/scant 1 cup caster sugar
4 large eggs, lightly beaten
225g/8oz/1½ cups self-raising flour
4 tbsp cocoa powder
3 tbsp natural yogurt

100g/3½oz/heaped ½ cup milk
chocolate chips
a few drops of food colouring of choice
2 recipe quantities Vanilla Buttercream
(see page 22)
sweets and edible glitter, to decorate

1   Preheat the oven to 180°C/350°F/gas 4. Put 24 cake cases in two 12-hole bun tins.
2   Put the butter and sugar in a mixing bowl and beat using an electric hand mixer or wooden spoon until the mixture is light and creamy. Add the eggs gradually, beating after each addition. Sift in the flour and cocoa and gently fold them into the mixture with the yogurt and chocolate chips, using a large metal spoon. Spoon the mixture into the cake cases.
3   Bake for 15–20 minutes until the cakes spring back when pressed lightly. Remove the cakes from the oven, turn out on to a wire rack and leave to cool.
4   Stir the food colouring into the buttercream until the colour is uniform. Spoon the buttercream into an icing bag fitted with a 13mm/½in star nozzle and pipe swirls on top of each cake, then add a sweet and a sprinkle of edible glitter.

285 Chocolate Brownie Birthday Stack

PREPARATION TIME 40 minutes   **COOKING TIME** 35–45 minutes   **SERVES** 16

250g/9oz butter, plus extra for greasing
350g/12½oz plain chocolate
250g/9oz/1 cup caster sugar
250g/9oz/1 cup light soft brown sugar
5 large eggs

1 tsp vanilla extract
200g/7oz/1⅓ cups plain flour, sifted
200g/7oz white chocolate, melted and
cooled slightly
sweets, to decorate

1   Preheat the oven to 190°C/375°F/gas 5. Grease a 30 x 23 x 6cm/12 x 9 x 2½in baking tin.
2   Melt the butter and plain chocolate together and leave to cool. Put both sugars, the eggs and vanilla extract in a bowl and whisk using an electric hand mixer or a whisk until the mixture is very light and has doubled in size. While still whisking, slowly pour in the melted chocolate and butter mixture. Fold in the flour, using a large metal spoon, then scrape the mixture into the tin using a spatula.
3   Bake for 30–40 minutes until the brownie has formed a crust and a skewer inserted into the middle comes out clean. Remove from the oven, leave to cool in the tin, then cut into 16 slices. Stack the slices on a plate, drizzle with white chocolate and decorate with sweets.

286 Christening Cake

PREPARATION TIME 1 hour   COOKING TIME 25–30 minutes   SERVES 10

225g/8oz butter, softened, plus extra
   for greasing
225g/8oz/scant 1 cup caster sugar
4 large eggs, lightly beaten
225g/8oz/1½ cups self-raising flour, sifted
1 tsp vanilla extract
1 recipe quantity Vanilla Buttercream
   (see page 22)
2 tbsp raspberry jam
icing sugar, for dusting

450g/1lb ready-to-roll icing
a few drops of pink or blue food colouring
½ quantity Royal Icing (see page 22)

TO DECORATE
 3.5cm/1½in high floral foam dome on
   a plastic base with self-adhesive pad
pink or blue/purple flowers
1.5m x 3cm/5ft x 1¼in wide pink or
   blue ribbon

1   Preheat the oven to 180°C/350°F/gas 4. Grease and base-line two 20cm/8in sandwich cake tins.
2   Put the butter and sugar in a mixing bowl and beat using an electric hand mixer or wooden spoon until the mixture is light and creamy. Add the eggs gradually, beating after each addition. Add the flour and vanilla extract and gently fold them into the mixture, using a large metal spoon. Divide the mixture between the tins using a spatula.
3   Bake for 25–30 minutes until the cakes spring back when pressed lightly and a skewer inserted into the middle of each cake comes out clean. Remove the cakes from the oven and leave to stand for 5 minutes, then turn out on to a wire rack and leave to cool.
4   Sandwich the cakes together with a third of the buttercream and the jam and use the remainder to cover the top and sides. Sift icing sugar on to a clean work surface and roll out the ready-to-roll icing to 5mm/¼in thick using a rolling pin. Lift the icing on top of the cake, using the rolling pin to help, and smooth down with your hands to ensure there are no creases. Trim the icing around the bottom of the cake with a sharp knife.
5   Stir the relevant food colouring into the royal icing until the colour is uniform, then spoon it into an icing bag fitted with a 13mm/½in star nozzle. Pipe pink or blue stars around the base and the edge of the top of the cake.
6   When you are ready to display the cake, soak the floral foam in water for a few minutes. Cut the flower stems down to 2.5cm/1in long and press them into the foam, covering the entire dome to the top with flowers. Remove the backing paper on the self-adhesive pad on the base of the plastic tray and stick the dome in the centre of the top of the cake. On a 7.5 x 4cm/3 x 1½in piece of card, neatly write the name of the child being christened. Using a craft knife or small sharp scissors, cut a slit on each side of the card, wide enough to thread the ribbon through, with the ribbon lying behind the name. Tie the ribbon around the sides of the cake so that the child's name is at the front.

287 Welcome Baby Cupcakes

PREPARATION TIME 40 minutes   COOKING TIME 15–20 minutes   MAKES 24 cakes

225g/8oz butter, softened
225g/8oz/scant 1 cup caster sugar
4 large eggs, lightly beaten
225g/8oz/1½ cups self-raising flour,
   sifted
2 tbsp natural yogurt
1 tsp vanilla extract

a few drops each of pink or blue
   food colouring
2 recipe quantities Vanilla Buttercream
   (see page 22)

TO DECORATE
edible glitter
baby-themed cake decorations (optional)

1   Preheat the oven to 180°C/350°F/gas 4. Put 24 cake cases in two 12-hole bun tins.
2   Put the butter and sugar in a mixing bowl and beat using an electric hand mixer or wooden spoon until the mixture is light and creamy. Add the eggs gradually, beating after each addition. Add the flour, yogurt and vanilla extract and gently fold them into the mixture, using a large metal spoon. Spoon the mixture into the cake cases.
3   Bake for 15–20 minutes until the cakes spring back when pressed lightly. Remove the cakes from the oven, turn out on to a wire rack and leave to cool.
4   Stir the relevant food colouring into the buttercream until the colour is uniform. Spoon the buttercream into an icing bag fitted with a 13mm/½in plain nozzle and pipe a swirl of icing on top of each cake. Decorate with edible glitter and baby decorations, if wished.

288 Country Wedding Cake

PREPARATION TIME 2½ hours **COOKING TIME** 45 minutes **SERVES** 60–70 (small slices)

680g/1lb 8oz butter, softened, plus extra
  for greasing
680g/1lb 8oz/2¾ cups caster sugar
12 large eggs, lightly beaten
680g/1lb 8oz/4½ cups self-raising flour,
  sifted
juice and finely grated zest of 8 lemons
4 tbsp icing sugar, sifted, plus extra
  for dusting
3 recipe quantities Vanilla Buttercream
  (see page 22)
8 tbsp lemon curd

1.3kg/3lb ready-to-roll icing
2 recipe quantities Royal Icing
  (see page 22)

TO DECORATE
silver dragees and white chocolate truffles
3.5cm/1½in high floral foam dome on a
  plastic base with self-adhesive pad
white and cream flowers of choice
6m x 3mm/19ft 6in x ⅛in wide ribbons
  in cream, silver and white
edible glitter

1 Preheat the oven to 180°C/350°F/gas 4. Grease and line a 17cm/7in, 20cm/8in and 23cm/9in springform cake tin.

2 Put the butter and sugar in a very large mixing bowl and beat using an electric hand mixer or wooden spoon until the mixture is light and creamy. Add the eggs gradually, beating after each addition. Add the flour and lemon zest and gently fold them into the mixture, using a large metal spoon. Divide the mixture between the tins proportionally.

3 Bake the cakes for about 25, 35 and 45 minutes respectively, until each cake springs back when pressed lightly and a skewer inserted into the middle of each cake comes out clean. (Note that if you are not using a fan oven, cakes on the bottom shelf may take longer to cook than the given times.)

4 Just before the cakes come out of the oven, heat the lemon juice with the icing sugar in a saucepan until the icing sugar has dissolved, then boil for 1 minute to create a syrup. Remove the cakes from the oven and pour the syrup over them in proportional amounts. Leave the cakes to cool, then turn out on to a wire rack.

5 Cut each cake in half horizontally using a sharp knife and sandwich together with some of the buttercream and all the lemon curd. Use nearly all the remaining buttercream to cover each cake with a thin coat, reserving just a little for step 7.

6 Put the largest cake on a 30cm/12in round cake board. Divide the ready-to-roll icing into thirds, then take some icing from one ball and add it to another, giving you 3 balls of increasing size. Sift icing sugar on to a clean work surface and roll out the largest ball to 5mm/¼in thick using a rolling pin. Lift the icing over the largest cake using the rolling pin to help you. Using your hands, smooth down the top and sides of the icing, making sure there are no creases. Trim the bottom edges of the icing with a sharp knife. Repeat with the other 2 cakes and their icing.

7 Stack the cakes in size order, handling them as gently as possible to minimize fingerprints and using the reserved buttercream to secure them.

8 Spoon the royal icing into a large icing bag fitted with a 13mm/½in star nozzle (you may have to do this in batches) and pipe stars of icing around the base of the cake and to cover the joins between each cake. Pipe a row of stars around the edge of the top cake. Decorate the icing stars with the silver dragees and white chocolate truffles, making sure they are evenly spaced. Leave the icing to set.

9 When you are ready to display the cake, soak the floral foam in water for a few minutes. Cut the flower stems down to 2.5cm/1in long and press them into the foam, covering the entire dome to the top with flowers. Cut the 3 ribbons into quarters and drape the 12 lengths over the top of the cake and down the sides to give 24 ribbons equally spaced around the cake. Remove the backing paper on the self-adhesive pad on the base of the plastic tray and stick the flower dome in the centre of the top of the cake, where the ribbons cross. Dust the cake with edible glitter before serving.

289 Birthday Rose Muffins

PREPARATION TIME 20 minutes   **COOKING TIME** 15–20 minutes   **MAKES** 10 muffins

280g/10oz/scant 2 cups plain flour
2 tsp baking powder
1 tsp bicarbonate of soda
115g/4oz/scant ½ cup caster sugar
250ml/9fl oz/1 cup milk
125ml/4fl oz/½ cup crème fraîche

115g/4oz butter, melted and cooled
2 large eggs, lightly beaten
3 tbsp rose syrup or rosewater
200g/7oz/1⅓ cups icing sugar, sifted
30 small sugar roses, to decorate

1   Preheat the oven to 180°C/350°F/gas 4. Put 10 muffin cases in a 12-hole muffin tin.
2   Sift the flour, baking powder and bicarbonate of soda into a mixing bowl, add the caster sugar and stir well with a wooden spoon.
3   In a separate bowl, whisk together the milk, crème fraîche and melted butter with an electric hand mixer or a whisk, add the eggs and 1 tablespoon of the rose syrup and whisk again. Pour the liquid into the bowl containing the dry ingredients and fold in with a large metal spoon. Do not overmix: the mixture should be thick and slightly lumpy. Spoon the mixture into the muffin cases.
4   Bake for 15–20 minutes until the muffins spring back when pressed lightly and a skewer inserted into the middle of a muffin comes out clean. Remove the muffins from the oven, turn out on to a wire rack and leave to cool.
5   In a bowl, mix the remaining rose syrup with the icing sugar to form a smooth icing, adding a little water if it is too stiff. Spread some of the icing over each muffin using a round-bladed knife and top the muffins with 3 sugar roses, adding candles if wished.

290 Wedding Cupcakes

PREPARATION TIME 1 hour, plus soaking   **COOKING TIME** 15–20 minutes   **MAKES** 48 cakes

200g/7oz/heaped 1 cup sultanas
200ml/7fl oz/scant 1 cup almond
   liqueur, such as amaretto
450g/1lb butter, softened
450g/1lb/1¾ cups caster sugar
8 large eggs, lightly beaten
450g/1lb/3 cups self-raising flour

2 tsp baking powder
1 tbsp almond extract
200g/7oz/1⅓ cups flaked almonds
4 recipe quantities Vanilla Buttercream
   (see page 22)
48 silver sugar almonds and
   edible glitter, to decorate

1   Soak the sultanas in the amaretto overnight. Preheat the oven to 180°C/350°F/gas 4.
    Put 48 cake cases in four 12-hole bun tins.
2   Put the butter and sugar in a mixing bowl and beat using an electric hand mixer or wooden
    spoon until the mixture is light. Add the eggs gradually, beating after each addition. Sift in
    the flour and baking powder and gently fold them into the mixture with the almond extract,
    flaked almonds and fruit, using a large metal spoon. Spoon the mixture into the cake cases.
3   Bake for 15–20 minutes until the cakes spring back when pressed lightly. Remove the
    cakes from the oven, turn out on to a wire rack and leave to cool.
4   Spoon the buttercream into a large icing bag fitted with a 13mm/½in star nozzle (you
    may have to do this in batches) and pipe a large swirl of icing on each cake. Place a
    silver sugar almond in the centre of each cake and sprinkle with edible glitter.

291 Golden Wedding Anniversary Cake

PREPARATION TIME 1 hour   **COOKING TIME** 25–30 minutes   **SERVES** 8–10

225g/8oz butter, plus extra for greasing
225g/8oz/scant 1 cup caster sugar
4 large eggs, lightly beaten
225g/8oz/1½ cups self-raising flour, sifted
finely grated zest of 2 lemons
1 recipe quantity Vanilla Buttercream
   (see page 22)
3 tbsp lemon curd
icing sugar, for dusting
450g/1lb ready-to-roll icing

a few drops of yellow food colouring
½ quantity Royal Icing (see page 22)

TO DECORATE
60g/2oz marzipan
2 small sheets edible gold leaf
3.5cm/1½in high floral foam dome on a
   plastic base with self-adhesive pad
yellow and golden flowers
1.5m x 3cm/5ft x 1¼in wide gold ribbon

1   Preheat the oven to 180°C/350°F/gas 4. Grease and base-line two 20cm/8in sandwich
    cake tins.
2   Put the butter and sugar in a mixing bowl and beat using an electric hand mixer or wooden
    spoon until the mixture is light and creamy. Add the eggs gradually, beating after each
    addition. Add the flour and lemon zest and gently fold them into the mixture, using a
    large metal spoon. Divide the mixture between the tins using a spatula.
3   Bake for 25–30 minutes until the cakes spring back when pressed lightly. Remove from
    the oven, turn out on to a wire rack and leave to cool. Sandwich together with a third of
    the buttercream and the lemon curd. Cover the cake with the remaining buttercream.
4   Sift icing sugar on to a clean work surface and roll out the ready-to-roll icing to 5mm/¼in
    thick using a rolling pin. Lift the icing on top of the cake, using the rolling pin to help,
    and smooth down with your hands to make sure there are no creases. Trim the icing
    around the bottom of the cake with a sharp knife.
5   Stir the food colouring into the royal icing until the colour is uniform, then spoon it into an
    icing bag with a 13mm/½in star nozzle and pipe stars around the base and top of the cake.
6   Roll out the marzipan to 5mm/¼in thick with the rolling pin on the dusted work surface.
    Crumble the gold leaf sheets on top and roll again to press them into the marzipan. Cut
    out the numbers '5' and '0' using large number cutters or a sharp knife. Using a pastry
    brush, lightly brush a very small amount of water on to the top cake where you want to
    place the numbers, which should be offset to one side, then press them into place.
7   When you are ready to display the cake, soak the floral foam in water for a few minutes.
    Cut the flower stems down to 2.5cm/1in long and press them into the foam, covering
    the entire dome to the top with flowers. Remove the backing paper on the self-adhesive
    pad on the base of the plastic tray and stick the flower dome behind the numbers on the
    top cake. Wrap the golden ribbon around the cake and tie in a bow.

292 Valentine Ribbon Hearts

PREPARATION TIME 25 minutes, plus chilling   **COOKING TIME** 12–15 minutes   **MAKES** 12 cookies

115g/4oz butter, softened, plus extra
   for greasing
55g/2oz/¼ cup caster sugar

175g/6oz/heaped 1 cup plain flour,
   sifted, plus extra for dusting
1 tbsp milk (optional)
3m x 3mm/10ft x ⅛in wide ribbon

1   Put the butter and sugar in a mixing bowl and beat using an electric hand mixer or wooden spoon until the mixture is light and creamy. Add the flour and mix together with your hands to form a soft dough, adding the milk if the mixture is too dry. Wrap in cling film and refrigerate for 1 hour.

2   Preheat the oven to 180°C/350°F/gas 4. Grease two 30cm/12in square baking trays.

3   Sift flour on to a clean work surface and roll the dough out to about 1cm/⅜in thick using a rolling pin. Cut out 12 heart shapes using a large heart cutter or a cardboard template and a knife, gathering up the trimmings and re-rolling as necessary. Place the cookies on the baking trays and, using a skewer or cocktail stick, make two 5mm/¼in holes at the top of the cookies on either side of the centre of the heart.

4   Bake for 12–15 minutes until golden brown and just firm. Remove the cookies from the oven and use the skewer or cocktail stick to reopen any holes that have closed during cooking while the cookies are still warm. Leave to cool on the trays for a few minutes, then transfer to a wire rack using a palettte knife to cool. Cut the ribbon into twelve 25cm/10in lengths. Thread a ribbon through each hole and tie in a bow at the front of each cookie.

293 Chocolate Heart Gateau

PREPARATION TIME 30 minutes   **COOKING TIME** 25–30 minutes   **SERVES** 10–12

350g/12oz butter, softened, plus extra
  for greasing
350g/12oz/1⅓ cups caster sugar
6 large eggs, lightly beaten
280g/10oz/scant 2 cups self-raising flour
55g/2oz/⅓ cup cocoa powder

300ml/10½fl oz/1¼ cups double cream,
  whipped to stiff peaks
2 tbsp strawberry jam
400g/14oz/2⅔ cups strawberries, hulled
  and sliced
200g/7oz plain chocolate, melted and
  cooled slightly

1   Preheat the oven to 180°C/350°F/gas 4. Grease and base-line two 30cm/12in heart-shaped cake tins.
2   Put the butter and sugar in a mixing bowl and beat using an electric hand mixer or wooden spoon until the mixture is light and creamy. Add the eggs gradually, beating after each addition. Sift in the flour and cocoa and gently fold them into the mixture, using a large metal spoon. Divide the mixture between the tins using a spatula.
3   Bake for 25–30 minutes until the cakes spring back when pressed lightly and a skewer inserted into the middle of each cake comes out clean. Remove the cakes from the oven and leave to stand for 5 minutes, then turn out on to a wire rack and leave to cool.
4   Place one of the cakes on a serving plate or board. Cover the top of the cake with the whipped cream, jam and strawberry slices, retaining about 30 slices for decoration. Place the second cake on top and cover with the melted chocolate. Arrange the reserved strawberry slices around the edge of the cake. Leave the chocolate to set before serving.

294 Valentine Cupcakes

PREPARATION TIME 40 minutes   **COOKING TIME** 15–20 minutes   **MAKES** 24 cakes

225g/8oz butter, softened
225g/8oz/scant 1 cup caster sugar
4 large eggs, lightly beaten
225g/8oz/1½ cups self-raising flour
4 tbsp cocoa powder
3 tbsp natural yogurt
24 chocolate-covered soft caramels

1 recipe quantity Chocolate Ganache
  (see page 22)

TO DECORATE
heart-shaped sugar sprinkles
edible silver balls

1   Preheat the oven to 180°C/350°F/gas 4. Put 24 cake cases in two 12-hole bun tins.
2   Put the butter and sugar in a mixing bowl and beat using an electric hand mixer or wooden spoon until the mixture is light and creamy. Add the eggs gradually, beating after each addition. Sift in the flour and cocoa and gently fold them into the mixture with the yogurt, using a large metal spoon.
3   Put a spoonful of cake mixture into each cake case. Place a chocolate-covered caramel in the centre of each cake and top with a further spoonful of cake mixture, so that the caramel is completely covered.
4   Bake for 15–20 minutes until the cakes spring back when pressed lightly and a skewer inserted into the middle of a cake comes out clean. Remove the cakes from the oven, turn out on to a wire rack and leave to cool.
5   Cover each cake with ganache and sprinkle over the heart-shaped sprinkles and silver balls to decorate. Leave the icing to set before serving.

295 St Patrick's Day Cupcakes

PREPARATION TIME 40 minutes **COOKING TIME** 15–20 minutes **MAKES** 12 cakes

115g/4oz butter, softened
115g/4oz/scant ½ cup caster sugar
2 large eggs, lightly beaten
115g/4oz/¾ cup self-raising flour, sifted
1 recipe quantity Vanilla Buttercream
(see page 22)

TO DECORATE
55g/2oz/heaped ½ cup desiccated
coconut
a few drops of green food colouring
orange-coloured sugar-coated chocolate
beans or orange sweets
12 mini Irish flags on cocktail sticks

1 Preheat the oven to 180°C/350°F/gas 4. Put 12 cake cases in a 12-hole bun tin.
2 Put the butter and sugar in a mixing bowl and beat using an electric hand mixer or wooden spoon until the mixture is light and creamy. Add the eggs gradually, beating after each addition. Add the flour and gently fold it into the mixture, using a large metal spoon. Spoon the mixture into the cake cases.
3 Bake for 15–20 minutes until the cakes spring back when pressed lightly and a skewer inserted into the middle of a cake comes out clean. Remove the cakes from the oven, turn out on to a wire rack and leave to cool.
4 Cover each cake with buttercream using a round-bladed knife. Mix the desiccated coconut with the green food colouring so that the coconut is uniformly coloured green, then sprinkle some of the coconut over each cake. Top with the orange chocolate beans and fix a mini Irish flag in the centre of each cake.

296 Easter Egg Cupcakes

PREPARATION TIME 40 minutes **COOKING TIME** 15–20 minutes **MAKES** 24 cakes

225g/8oz butter
225g/8oz/scant 1 cup caster sugar
4 large eggs, lightly beaten
225g/8oz/1½ cups self-raising flour
4 tbsp cocoa powder
3 tbsp natural yogurt

100g/3½oz Easter egg or milk chocolate,
broken into small pieces
a few drops of yellow food colouring
2 recipe quantities Vanilla Buttercream
(see page 22)
sugar or chocolate eggs, to decorate

1 Preheat the oven to 180°C/350°F/gas 4. Put 24 cake cases in two 12-hole bun tins.
2 Put the butter and sugar in a mixing bowl and beat using an electric hand mixer or wooden spoon until the mixture is light and creamy. Add the eggs gradually, beating after each addition. Sift in the flour and cocoa and gently fold them into the mixture with the yogurt and Easter egg pieces or chocolate, using a large metal spoon. Spoon the mixture into the cake cases.
3 Bake for 15–20 minutes until the cakes spring back when pressed lightly and a skewer inserted into the middle of a cake comes out clean. Remove the cakes from the oven, turn out on to a wire rack and leave to cool.
4 Stir the food colouring into the buttercream until the colour is uniform. Spoon the buttercream into an icing bag fitted with a 13mm/½in star nozzle and pipe swirls on top of the cakes. Decorate each cake with a few sugar or chocolate eggs.

297 Simnel Cake

PREPARATION TIME 45 minutes   COOKING TIME 1¾–2 hours   SERVES 10

175g/6oz butter, softened, plus extra
   for greasing
175g/6oz/¾ cup light soft brown sugar
3 large eggs, lightly beaten, plus
   1 large egg yolk (optional)
225g/8oz/1½ cups plain flour
1 tsp baking powder
2 tsp cinnamon
1 tsp mixed spice
400g/14oz/2 cups sultanas
100g/3½oz/½ cup glacé cherries, halved

100g/3½oz/½ cup mixed peel
finely grated zest of 1 orange
finely grated zest of 1 lemon
icing sugar, for dusting
450g/1lb marzipan
3 tbsp apricot jam

TO DECORATE
sugar flowers
1.5m x 3cm/5ft x 1¼in wide
   yellow ribbon

1   Preheat the oven to 160°C/325°F/gas 3. Grease and line a deep 20cm/8in springform cake tin.
2   Put the butter and light brown sugar in a mixing bowl and beat using an electric hand mixer or wooden spoon until the mixture is light and creamy. Add the whole eggs gradually, beating after each addition. Sift in the flour, baking powder, cinnamon and mixed spice and gently fold them into the mixture with the sultanas, cherries, mixed peel and orange and lemon zests. Spoon half the cake mixture into the tin.
3   Sift icing sugar on to a clean work surface and cut the marzipan in half. Roll out one half to 5mm/¼in thick using a rolling pin and cut out a circle of marzipan the size of the cake tin, saving the trimmings for later. Place the marzipan on top of the cake mixture in the tin and cover with the remaining cake mixture.
4   Bake for about 1¾–2 hours until a skewer inserted into the middle of the cake comes out clean. Remove the cake from the oven and leave to cool in the tin.
5   Roll out the remaining marzipan as before and cut out a second circle the size of your cake tin. Retain the trimmings again. Warm the jam in a small saucepan, then remove the cake from the tin, brush the top with some of the jam and cover with the marzipan.
6   Roll the marzipan trimmings into 11 small balls to represent the 11 apostles and place around the edge of the cake, securing with a little more of the jam. If wished, brush the top of the marzipan lightly with a little of the egg yolk, using a pastry brush, and place under a hot grill for a few minutes until the marzipan starts to brown. Fix the sugar flowers between the balls with the remaining jam and tie the ribbon around the cake.

298 Glazed Easter Cookies

PREPARATION TIME 25 minutes, plus chilling   COOKING TIME 12–15 minutes   MAKES 12 cookies

115g/4oz butter, softened, plus extra
   for greasing
55g/2oz/¼ cup caster sugar
175g/6oz/heaped 1 cup plain flour,
   sifted, plus extra for dusting
55g/2oz marzipan, chilled then grated
55g/2oz/⅓ cup sultanas

1 tsp almond extract
200g/7oz/1⅓ cups icing sugar, sifted
a few drops of yellow food colouring

TO DECORATE
sugar flowers
edible silver balls

1   Put the butter and caster sugar in a mixing bowl and beat using an electric hand mixer or wooden spoon until the mixture is light and creamy. Add the flour, grated marzipan, sultanas and almond extract and mix together with your hands to form a soft dough. Wrap in cling film and refrigerate for 1 hour.
2   Preheat the oven to 180°C/350°F/gas 4. Grease two 30cm/12in square baking trays.
3   Sift flour on to a clean work surface and roll the dough out to about 1cm/⅜in thick, using a rolling pin. Cut out 12 rounds using a 7.5cm/3in round cutter, gathering up the trimmings and re-rolling as necessary. Place the cookies on the baking trays.
4   Bake for 12–15 minutes until golden brown and just firm. Remove the cookies from the oven and leave to cool on the trays for a few minutes, then transfer to a wire rack with a palette knife to cool.
5   Mix the icing sugar with 1–2 tablespoons water and the food colouring to make a runny icing. Spoon the icing over the cookies and decorate with the sugar flowers and silver balls.

299 Mother's Day Rose Petal Sponge

PREPARATION TIME 35 minutes   **COOKING TIME** 25–30 minutes   **SERVES** 10

225g/8oz butter, softened, plus extra
   for greasing
225g/8oz/scant 1 cup caster sugar
4 large eggs, lightly beaten
225g/8oz/1½ cups self-raising flour
1 tsp baking powder
1 tsp vanilla extract
115g/4oz/scant 1 cup pistachio nuts,
   finely chopped

1 recipe quantity Rose Petal Paste
   (see page 23)
250ml/9fl oz/1 cup double cream,
   whipped to stiff peaks
115g/4oz/¾ cup icing sugar, sifted
1–2 tbsp rose syrup or rosewater
1 recipe quantity Frosted Rose Petals
   (see page 23), to decorate

1   Preheat the oven to 180°C/350°F/gas 4. Grease and base-line two 20cm/8in sandwich
    cake tins.
2   Put the butter and sugar in a mixing bowl and beat using an electric hand mixer or wooden
    spoon until the mixture is light and creamy. Add the eggs gradually, beating after each
    addition. Sift in the flour and baking powder and gently fold them into the mixture with
    the vanilla extract and two-thirds of the pistachios, using a large metal spoon. Divide the
    mixture between the tins using a spatula.
3   Bake for 25–30 minutes until the cakes spring back when pressed lightly and a skewer
    inserted into the middle of each cake comes out clean. Remove the cakes from the oven
    and leave to stand for 5 minutes, then turn out on to a wire rack and leave to cool.
4   Fold the rose petal paste into the whipped cream, using a large metal spoon and use to
    sandwich the cakes together. Mix the icing sugar with the rose syrup to form a smooth
    icing and spread over the top of the cake. Sprinkle over the remaining chopped
    pistachios and decorate with the frosted rose petals.

300 Father's Day Biscuits

PREPARATION TIME 25 minutes, plus chilling   **COOKING TIME** 12–15 minutes   **MAKES** 10 biscuits

115g/4oz butter, softened, plus extra
   for greasing
55g/2oz/¼ cup caster sugar
175g/6oz/heaped 1 cup plain flour,
   sifted, plus extra for dusting
1 tbsp milk (optional)

200g/7oz/1⅓ cups icing sugar, sifted
a few drops of blue food colouring

TO DECORATE
flat, fizzy fruit-liquorice strips
sugar-coated chocolate beans

1   Put the butter and caster sugar in a mixing bowl and beat using an electric hand mixer or wooden spoon until the mixture is light and creamy. Add the flour and mix together with your hands to form a soft dough, adding the milk if the mixture is too dry. Wrap in cling film and refrigerate for 1 hour.
2   Preheat the oven to 180°C/350°F/gas 4. Grease two 30cm/12in square baking trays.
3   Sift flour on to a clean work surface and roll the dough out to about 1cm/⅜in thick using a rolling pin. Cut out 10 tie shapes of your choice (bow ties, thin ties or fat ties), gathering up the trimmings and re-rolling as necessary. Place the biscuits on the baking trays.
4   Bake for 12–15 minutes until golden brown and just firm. Remove the biscuits from the oven and leave to cool on the trays for a few minutes, then transfer to a wire rack with a palette knife to cool.
5   Mix the icing sugar with the food colouring and 1–2 tablespoons water to form a smooth icing and spread some over each biscuit. Decorate with the liquorice strips to make striped ties and the chocolate beans to make spotted ties. Leave the icing to set.

301 Bonfire Night Treacle Cookies

PREPARATION TIME 15 minutes   **COOKING TIME** 14–18 minutes   **MAKES** 18 cookies

125g/4½oz butter, softened, plus extra
   for greasing
350g/12oz/2⅓ cups self-raising flour
a pinch salt
½ tsp bicarbonate of soda
1 tsp ground ginger

1 tsp cinnamon
200g/7oz/heaped ¾ cup caster sugar
1 tbsp golden syrup
1 tbsp treacle
1 large egg, beaten

1   Preheat the oven to 180°C/350°F/gas 4. Grease two 30cm/12in square baking trays.
2   Sift the flour, salt, bicarbonate of soda, ginger and cinnamon into a mixing bowl, add the sugar and stir with a wooden spoon. Put the butter, syrup and treacle in a saucepan and heat gently until the butter has melted. Cool slightly, then stir into the dry ingredients. Beat in the egg to make a soft dough.
3   Divide the dough into 18 walnut-sized pieces and place on the baking trays, leaving about 5cm/2in between them to allow for spreading.
4   Bake for 12–15 minutes until golden brown and just firm. Remove the cookies from the oven and leave to cool on the trays for a few minutes, then transfer to a wire rack with a palette knife to cool.

302 Halloween Cupcakes

PREPARATION TIME 40 minutes **COOKING TIME** 15–20 minutes **MAKES** 12 cakes

115g/4oz butter, softened
115g/4oz/scant ½ cup caster sugar
2 large eggs, lightly beaten
115g/4oz/¾ cup self-raising flour, sifted
a few drops each of green and orange
   food colourings

1 recipe quantity Vanilla Buttercream
   (see page 22)
Halloween sweets and chocolates,
   to decorate

1   Preheat the oven to 180°C/350°F/gas 4. Put 12 cake cases in a 12-hole bun tin.
2   Put the butter and sugar in a mixing bowl and beat using an electric hand mixer or wooden
    spoon until the mixture is light and creamy. Add the eggs gradually, beating after each
    addition. Add the flour and gently fold it into the mixture, using a large metal spoon.
3   Divide the cake mixture between 2 bowls and colour one green and one orange using a
    few drops of the food colourings. Spoon the orange cake mixture into half the cake cases
    and the green cake mixture into the other half.
4   Bake for 15–20 minutes until the cakes spring back when pressed lightly and a skewer
    inserted into the middle of a cake comes out clean. Remove the cakes from the oven,
    turn out on to a wire rack and leave to cool.
5   Remove the cake cases from each cake and turn upside down. Divide the buttercream
    between 2 bowls and colour one green and one orange using more of the food colourings.
    Spread orange icing over the green cakes and green icing over the orange cakes and top
    each cake with some Halloween sweets and chocolates.

303 Halloween Ghost Cookies

PREPARATION TIME 25 minutes, plus chilling **COOKING TIME** 12–15 minutes **MAKES** 10 cookies

115g/4oz butter, softened, plus extra
   for greasing
55g/2oz/¼ cup caster sugar
175g/6oz/heaped 1 cup plain flour,
   plus extra for dusting

1 tsp cinnamon
1 tbsp milk (optional)
200g/7oz/1⅓ cups icing sugar, sifted
20 plain chocolate chips, to decorate

1   Put the butter and caster sugar in a mixing bowl and beat using an electric hand mixer
    or wooden spoon until the mixture is light and creamy. Sift in the flour and cinnamon
    and mix together with your hands to form a soft dough, adding the milk if the mixture is
    too dry. Wrap in cling film and refrigerate for 1 hour.
2   Preheat the oven to 180°C/350°F/gas 4. Grease two 30cm/12in square baking trays.
3   Sift flour on to a clean work surface and roll the dough out to about 1cm/⅜in thick using
    a rolling pin. Cut out 10 ghost shapes using a cutter or a cardboard template and a
    knife, gathering up the trimmings and re-rolling as necessary. Place the cookies on the
    baking trays.
4   Bake for 12–15 minutes until golden brown and just firm. Remove the cookies from the
    oven and leave to cool on the trays for a few minutes, then transfer to a wire rack with a
    palette knife to cool.
5   Mix the icing sugar with 1–2 tablespoons water to make a runny icing. Using a round-
    bladed knife, cover each cookie in icing and decorate with 2 chocolate chips for eyes.
    Leave the icing to set before serving.

304 Iced Christmas Cake

PREPARATION TIME 50 minutes, plus soaking   COOKING TIME 2½–3 hours   SERVES 15

1kg/2lb 4oz/5½ cups mixed fruit
  (sultanas, raisins, currants)
200g/7oz/1 cup glacé cherries, halved
125ml/4fl oz/½ cup almond liqueur,
  such as amaretto, plus extra for
  feeding the cake
225g/8oz butter, softened, plus extra
  for greasing
175g/6oz/1 cup lightly packed dark
  muscovado sugar
55g/2oz/¼ cup caster sugar
4 large eggs, lightly beaten
55g/2oz/⅓ cup self-raising flour
175g/6oz/heaped 1 cup plain flour

1 tsp cinnamon
1 tsp mixed spice
¼ tsp freshly grated nutmeg
200g/7oz/1½ cups mixed unsalted nuts,
  roughly chopped
finely grated zest of 2 lemons
1 tbsp treacle
icing sugar, for dusting
450g/1lb marzipan
2 tbsp apricot jam
1 recipe quantity Royal Icing
  (see page 22)
Christmas figures and edible glitter,
  to decorate

1   Soak the mixed fruit and glacé cherries in the amaretto overnight.
2   Preheat the oven to 150°C/300°F/gas 2. Grease and line a 23cm/9in loose-bottomed square cake tin. Wrap the sides in a double layer of brown paper and tie with string.
3   Put the butter, muscovado sugar and caster sugar in a mixing bowl and beat using an electric hand mixer or wooden spoon until the mixture is light and creamy. Add the eggs gradually, beating after each addition. Sift in the self-raising and plain flours and spices and gently fold them into the mixture with the nuts, lemon zest, treacle, soaked fruits and amaretto, using a large metal spoon. Scrape the mixture into the tin using a spatula.
4   Bake for about 2½–3 hours until a skewer comes out clean with no cake mixture on it. (If the top of the cake starts to brown too much, cover it with a piece of baking parchment.) Remove the cake from the oven and leave to cool in the tin, then turn out.
5   Wrap the cake in greaseproof paper and cling film and store in a sealed tin. Open it once a week, prick the surface with a skewer and pour over 1–2 tablespoons of the amaretto. The more weeks you do this for, the richer the cake will become. One month is ideal.
6   Sift icing sugar on to a clean work surface and roll out the marzipan to 5mm/¼in thick using a rolling pin. Heat the jam in a small saucepan and brush it over the cake, then cover with the marzipan, flattening down the top and sides with your hands. Cover the marzipan with royal icing forked into 'snow' and position the Christmas figures in the centre. Dust the cake with edible glitter and leave the icing to set before serving.

305 Candy Cane Cake

PREPARATION TIME 50 minutes   COOKING TIME 2½–3 hours   SERVES 15

225g/8oz butter, softened, plus extra
  for greasing
250g/9oz/1 cup caster sugar
4 large eggs, lightly beaten
225g/8oz/1½ cups self-raising flour
1 tsp cinnamon
400g/14oz/2 cups sultanas
200g/7oz/1 cup glacé cherries, halved

2 tbsp orange liqueur, such as Cointreau
1 tbsp golden syrup
450g/1lb marzipan
2 tbsp apricot jam
1 recipe quantity Royal Icing
  (see page 22)
8 candy canes
1.5m x 5cm/5ft x 2in wide red ribbon

1   Preheat the oven to 150°C/300°F/gas 2. Grease and line a deep 20cm/8in springform cake tin. Wrap the sides in a double layer of brown paper and tie with string.
2   Put the butter and sugar in a mixing bowl and beat using an electric hand mixer or wooden spoon until the mixture is light and creamy. Add the eggs gradually, beating after each addition. Sift in the flour and cinnamon and gently fold them into the mixture with the sultanas, cherries, Cointreau and syrup, using a large metal spoon. Scrape the mixture into the tin using a spatula.
3   Bake for 2½–3 hours until a skewer comes out clean with no cake mixture on it. Remove the cake from the oven and leave to cool in the tin, then turn out.
4   Apply the marzipan and royal icing to the cake following step 6 in recipe 304. Arrange the candy canes around the side of the cake and fix them in place by wrapping the ribbon around the cake and tying it in a bow at the front.

306 Yule Log

PREPARATION TIME 30 minutes   **COOKING TIME** 10–12 minutes   **SERVES** 8

butter, for greasing
3 large eggs
85g/3oz/⅓ cup caster sugar
85g/3oz/heaped ½ cup self-raising flour
1 tsp baking powder

55g/2oz plain chocolate, melted and
  cooled slightly
1 recipe quantity Chocolate Buttercream
  (see page 22)
icing sugar, for dusting

1   Preheat the oven to 180°C/350°F/gas 4. Grease and line a 30 x 20cm/12 x 8in Swiss
    roll tin.
2   Put the eggs and sugar in a mixing bowl and whisk together using an electric hand mixer
    or a whisk until the mixture is creamy and pale yellow and the whisk leaves a trail when
    lifted up. Sift in the flour and baking powder and add the melted chocolate, then fold
    them in, using a large metal spoon. Scrape the mixture into the tin using a spatula.
3   Bake for 10–12 minutes until the cake springs back when pressed lightly. Remove the
    cake from the oven and leave for a few minutes.
4   Put a sheet of baking parchment on a clean work surface. Turn the cake out on to the
    paper, cover with a damp tea towel and leave to cool for 10 minutes. Remove the tea
    towel and lining paper and cut away the edges of the cake to neaten it. Roll up the cake
    from a short end using the paper to help you and leave to cool completely. (The paper
    will end up rolled inside the cake.)
5   When the cake has cooled, unroll it. Spread a third of the buttercream over the cake.
    Roll the Swiss roll up again using the paper to help you but this time not rolling it inside
    the cake and place on a serving plate. Cover with the remaining buttercream and use a
    fork to make patterns in the buttercream resembling bark. Dust with icing sugar.

307 Christmas Cloud Cake

PREPARATION TIME 40 minutes **COOKING TIME** 1 hour 5 minutes **SERVES** 8

butter, for greasing
4 large egg whites
½ tsp cream of tartar
250g/9oz/1 cup caster sugar
225g/8oz/¾ cup mincemeat
2 tbsp almond liqueur, such as amaretto

1 eating apple, peeled, cored and grated
400g/14oz/2 cups preserved cherries
400ml/14fl oz/1½ cups double cream,
  whipped to stiff peaks
seeds of 1 pomegranate

1 Preheat the oven to 140°C/275°F/gas 1. Grease and base-line a 20cm/8in springform cake tin.
2 Put the egg whites in a clean, dry bowl and whisk with an electric hand mixer or a whisk until they form stiff peaks. Add the cream of tartar and whisk again, then add the sugar, a little at a time, whisking to form a glossy meringue. Pour the meringue into the cake tin, pushing it up the sides to make a well in the centre to contain the filling.
3 Bake for 1 hour until crisp. Remove the meringue from the oven and leave to cool in the tin.
4 Heat the mincemeat with the amaretto, grated apple and a quarter of the cherries in a saucepan over a gentle heat for 5 minutes. Leave to cool completely, then fold into the whipped cream. Remove the cake from the tin and place on a serving plate. Fill with the mincemeat mixture and top with the remaining cherries and the pomegranate seeds.

308 Cinnamon Orange Stollen

PREPARATION TIME 30 minutes, plus soaking and rising **COOKING TIME** 25–30 minutes
SERVES 10

55g/2oz/⅓ cup raisins
55g/2oz/⅓ cup sultanas
55g/2oz/¼ cup glacé cherries, chopped
55g/2oz/⅓ cup toasted flaked almonds
55g/2oz/⅓ cup mixed peel
100ml/3½fl oz/scant ½ cup orange
  liqueur, such as Cointreau
150ml/5fl oz/scant ⅔ cup warm milk
3 tbsp clear honey
2 tsp fast action dried yeast

450g/1lb/3 cups plain flour, plus extra
  for dusting
4 tsp cinnamon
finely grated zest of 1 orange
115g/4oz butter, melted and cooled,
  plus extra for greasing and brushing
1 large egg, lightly beaten
150g/5½oz marzipan
2 tsp icing sugar, for dusting

1 Put the raisins, sultanas, cherries, flaked almonds and mixed peel in a bowl with the Cointreau. Cover and leave to soak overnight.
2 The next day, put the warm milk, honey and yeast in a cup and leave for 10–20 minutes until foamy. Sift the flour and 2 teaspoons of the cinnamon into a large mixing bowl, add the orange zest, melted butter and egg and mix with your hands to form a dough. Add the soaked fruit and nuts.
3 Sift flour on to a clean work surface and turn the dough out of the bowl. Knead vigorously with your hands until you have a soft, pliable dough. Put the dough back in the bowl and cover with a damp tea towel. Leave to rise in a warm place for 1–1½ hours or until the dough has doubled in size.
4 Tip the dough on to the floured work surface and punch it a few times to knock the air out of it, then roll it out into a 30 x 15cm/12 x 6in rectangle. Roll the marzipan into a 30cm/12in long sausage shape with your fingertips and place in the centre of the dough. Fold the sides of the dough together over the marzipan, pressing them together well to seal the dough. Grease a 30cm/12in square baking tray and place the loaf on the tray. Cover with a damp tea towel and leave to rise in a warm place for 30 minutes until it has doubled in size.
5 Preheat the oven to 190°C/375°F/gas 5. Bake for 25–30 minutes until the bread sounds hollow when you pick it up with an oven glove and tap it underneath. Remove the loaf from the oven and brush with a little melted butter. Mix the icing sugar with the remaining cinnamon and dust over the stollen. Serve warm or cold.

309 Twelfth Night Cake

PREPARATION TIME 25 minutes, plus soaking   **COOKING TIME** 1½–1¾ hours   **SERVES** 10

55g/2oz/⅓ cup mixed peel
115g/4oz/heaped ½ cup raisins
115g/4oz/heaped ½ cup sultanas
115g/4oz/½ cup dried apricots, chopped
100g/3½oz/½ cup glacé cherries,
   chopped
3 tbsp orange liqueur, such as Cointreau
225g/8oz butter, softened, plus extra
   for greasing

225g/8oz/scant 1 cup caster sugar
4 large eggs, lightly beaten
250g/9oz/1⅔ cups self-raising flour
1 tsp cinnamon
1 tsp mixed spice
1 tsp ground ginger
1 whole blanched almond
icing sugar, for dusting

1 Put the mixed peel, raisins, sultanas, apricots and cherries in a bowl with the Cointreau. Cover and leave to soak overnight.
2 Preheat the oven to 160°C/325°F/gas 3. Grease and line a 20cm/8in springform cake tin.
3 Put the butter and caster sugar in a mixing bowl and beat using an electric hand mixer or wooden spoon until the mixture is light and creamy. Add the eggs gradually, beating after each addition. Sift in the flour, cinnamon, mixed spice and ginger and gently fold them into the mixture with the soaked fruit and whole almond, using a large metal spoon. Scrape the mixture into the tin using a spatula.
4 Bake for 1½–1¾ hours until the cake springs back when pressed lightly and a skewer inserted into the middle of the cake comes out clean. Remove the cake from the oven and leave to cool in the tin, then turn out.
5 When you serve the cake on Twelfth Night, tradition has it that whoever gets the almond (originally a bean) in their slice, becomes the king or queen of the festivities for the day.

310 Amaretto Gingerbread Nut Ring

PREPARATION TIME 30 minutes, plus soaking   **COOKING TIME** 60–70 minutes   **SERVES** 10

100g/3½oz/½ cup raisins
100g/3½oz/½ cup glacé cherries, halved
125ml/4fl oz/½ cup almond liqueur,
   such as amaretto
225g/8oz butter, softened, plus extra
   for greasing
125g/4½oz/scant 1 cup plain flour,
   plus extra for dusting
125g/4½oz/heaped ½ cup dark soft
   brown sugar
2 large eggs, lightly beaten
2 tbsp golden syrup

2 tbsp treacle
100g/3½oz/⅔ cup self-raising flour
1 tsp bicarbonate of soda
125ml/4fl oz/½ cup milk
4 pieces of stem ginger preserved in
   syrup, finely chopped
400g/14oz/2⅔ cups combined pistachio
   and brazil nuts
250g/9oz/1 cup caster sugar
150g/5½oz cream cheese
400g/14oz/2⅔ cups icing sugar, sifted
2 tbsp of the stem ginger syrup

1 Put the raisins and cherries in a bowl with the amaretto. Cover and leave to soak overnight. Preheat the oven to 160°C/325°F/gas 3. Grease a 23cm/9in ring tin and dust with flour.
2 Put 125g/4½oz of the butter and the dark brown sugar in a mixing bowl and beat using an electric hand mixer or wooden spoon until the mixture is light and creamy. Add the eggs gradually, beating after each addition, then add the syrup and treacle and beat again. Sift in the plain and self-raising flours and the bicarbonate of soda and fold them into the mixture with the milk, soaked fruit, amaretto and chopped stem ginger, mixing well. Scrape the mixture into the tin using a spatula.
3 Bake for 50–60 minutes until the cake springs back when pressed lightly and a skewer inserted into the cake comes out clean. Remove the cake from the oven and leave to cool in the tin, then turn out on to a serving plate.
4 Dry-fry the nuts in a frying pan for 3–5 minutes. Grease a large baking tray with butter and sprinkle the nuts over the tray. Heat the caster sugar in a heavy-based saucepan for about 5 minutes until the sugar has dissolved and starts to turn golden. Remove from the heat immediately and pour the caramel over the nuts. Leave to cool.
5 Whisk together the cream cheese, icing sugar, remaining butter and ginger syrup in a bowl to form a smooth icing. Cover the cake with the icing, using a round-bladed knife. Break the caramel nuts into shards and use to decorate the top of the ring.

311 Snowflake Cookies

PREPARATION TIME 25 minutes, plus chilling   **COOKING TIME** 12–15 minutes   **MAKES** 10 cookies

115g/4oz butter, softened, plus extra
  for greasing
55g/2oz/¼ cup light muscovado sugar
175g/6oz/heaped 1 cup plain flour,
  plus extra for dusting

1 tbsp cinnamon
1 tbsp milk (optional)
1 tbsp icing sugar, sifted
edible glitter (optional), to decorate

1   Put the butter and muscovado sugar in a mixing bowl and beat using an electric hand
    mixer or wooden spoon until the mixture is light and creamy. Sift in the flour and
    1 teaspoon of the cinnamon and mix together with your hands to form a soft dough,
    adding the milk if the mixture is too dry. Wrap in cling film and refrigerate for 1 hour.
2   Preheat the oven to 180°C/350°F/gas 4. Grease two 30cm/12in square baking trays.
3   Sift flour on to a clean work surface and roll the dough out to about 1cm/⅜in thick using
    a rolling pin. Cut out 10 snowflake shapes using different-sized snowflake cutters,
    gathering up the trimmings and re-rolling as necessary. Alternatively, for more elaborate
    snowflakes, cut out the centre of each cookie with a smaller snowflake cutter to leave you
    with snowflake outlines; the cut-outs make small biscuits. (If you do not have snowflake
    cutters, use a 10cm/4in star cutter for the cookies and a 6cm/2⅓in star cutter for the holes,
    if making, or use cardboard templates and a knife.) Place the cookies on the baking trays.
4   Bake for 12–15 minutes until golden brown and just firm. Remove the cookies from the
    oven and leave to cool on the trays for a few minutes, then transfer to a wire rack with a
    palette knife to cool. Mix the remaining cinnamon and the icing sugar together and dust
    them over the cookies. Decorate with edible glitter, if using.

312 Ribboned Christmas Tree Cookies

PREPARATION TIME 25 minutes, plus chilling COOKING TIME 12–15 minutes MAKES 10 cookies

115g/4oz butter, softened, plus extra
  for greasing
55g/2oz/¼ cup light muscovado sugar
175g/6oz/heaped 1 cup plain flour,
  plus extra for dusting

1 tsp cinnamon
1 tbsp milk (optional)
6 tbsp icing sugar, sifted
edible silver balls, to decorate
2m x 3mm/6ft 6in x ⅛in wide ribbon

1 Put the butter and muscovado sugar in a mixing bowl and beat using an electric hand mixer or wooden spoon until the mixture is light and creamy. Sift in the flour and cinnamon and mix together with your hands to form a soft dough, adding the milk if the mixture is too dry. Wrap in cling film and refrigerate for 1 hour.
2 Preheat the oven to 180°C/350°F/gas 4. Grease two 30cm/12in square baking trays.
3 Sift flour on to a clean work surface and roll the dough out to about 1cm/⅜in thick using a rolling pin. Cut out 10 large festive shapes, such as reindeer and stars, using cutters or cardboard templates and a knife, gathering up the trimmings and re-rolling as necessary. Place the cookies on the baking trays and, using a skewer or cocktail stick, make a 5mm/¼in hole in the centre of the top of each cookie.
4 Bake for 12–15 minutes until firm. Remove the cookies from the oven and, while the cookies are still on the baking trays, use the skewer or cocktail stick to reopen any holes that have closed during cooking while the cookies are still warm. Transfer to a wire rack with a palette knife to cool.
5 Mix the icing sugar with 1 tablespoon water to make a stiff icing. Spoon into an icing bag fitted with a 3mm/⅛in plain nozzle and pipe lines on to the reindeer to make a saddle and bridle and a white line around the edge of each star. Decorate with silver balls and leave to set. Cut the ribbon into 20cm/8in lengths, thread one length through the hole on each cookie and tie in a knot. Hang the cookies from your Christmas tree for no longer than 5 days if you intend to eat them.

313 Christmas Glazed Fruit Cake

PREPARATION TIME 50 minutes, plus soaking COOKING TIME 2½–3 hours SERVES 15

1kg/2lb 4oz/5½ cups mixed fruit
  (sultanas, raisins, currants)
200g/7oz/1 cup glacé cherries, halved
100g/3½oz/¾ cup flaked almonds
125ml/4fl oz/½ cup brandy, plus extra
  for feeding the cake
225g/8oz butter, softened, plus extra
  for greasing
175g/6oz/1 cup lightly packed dark
  muscovado sugar
55g/2oz/¼ cup caster sugar

4 large eggs, lightly beaten
175g/6oz/heaped 1 cup plain flour
55g/2oz/⅓ cup self-raising flour
1 tsp cinnamon
1 tsp mixed spice
¼ tsp freshly grated nutmeg
finely grated zest of 2 oranges
1 tbsp treacle
3 tbsp apricot jam
juice of 1 lemon
400g/14oz/1¾ cups mixed glacé fruits

1 Soak the mixed fruit, cherries and flaked almonds in the brandy in a bowl overnight.
2 Preheat the oven to 150°C/300°F/gas 2. Grease and line a 23cm/9in loose-bottomed square cake tin. Wrap the sides in a double layer of brown paper and tie with string.
3 Put the butter, muscovado sugar and caster sugar in a large mixing bowl and beat using an electric hand mixer or wooden spoon until the mixture is light and creamy. Add the eggs and whisk again. Sift in the plain and self-raising flours and the spices and gently fold in with the orange zest, treacle, soaked fruits and nuts and brandy. Scrape the mixture into the tin using a spatula.
4 Bake for 2½–3 hours until a skewer comes out clean with no cake mixture on it. (If the top of the cake starts to brown too much, cover it with a piece of baking parchment.) Remove the cake from the oven and leave to cool in the tin, then turn out.
5 Wrap the cake in greaseproof paper and cling film and store in a sealed tin. Open it once a week, prick the surface with a skewer and pour over 1–2 tablespoons brandy. The more weeks you do this for, the richer the cake will become. One month is ideal.
6 When you are ready to serve the cake, heat the jam with the lemon juice in a small saucepan and brush some over the top of the cake with a pastry brush. Arrange the glacé fruits in a decorative pattern on top of the cake and brush with some more of the glaze.

314 Christmas Glazed Spice Biscuits

PREPARATION TIME 30 minutes   **COOKING TIME** 14–18 minutes   **MAKES** 18 biscuits

115g/3½oz butter, chopped, plus extra
   for greasing
250g/9oz/1⅔ cups plain flour
1 tsp baking powder
1 tsp bicarbonate of soda
1 tsp cinnamon
1 tsp ground ginger
¼ tsp grated nutmeg

100g/3½oz/scant 1 cup ground almonds
2 tbsp golden syrup
2 tbsp clear honey
finely grated zest of 1 orange plus
   1–2 tbsp of the juice
150g/5½oz/1 cup icing sugar, sifted
1 egg white, beaten

1   Preheat the oven to 180°C/350°F/gas 4. Grease two 30cm/12in square baking trays.
2   Sift the flour, baking powder, bicarbonate of soda and spices into a mixing bowl and stir together with the ground almonds using a wooden spoon. Put the butter, syrup and honey in a saucepan and heat gently until the butter melts. Cool slightly, then stir into the dry ingredients with the orange zest.
3   Divide the dough into 18 walnut-sized balls and place on the baking trays, leaving about 5cm/2in gaps for spreading. Press each biscuit down slightly using your fingers.
4   Bake for 12–15 minutes until golden brown and firm. Remove the biscuits from the oven and leave to cool on the trays for a few minutes, then transfer to a wire rack with a palette knife to cool.
5   Mix together the icing sugar, orange juice and egg white and spoon the icing over the biscuits. Leave the icing to set, then apply a second coat. The icing will be quite translucent. Leave the second coat to set before serving.

315 Gold Leaf Cookies

PREPARATION TIME 20 minutes   **COOKING TIME** 14–18 minutes   **MAKES** 20 cookies

85g/3oz butter, plus extra for greasing
85g/3oz/⅓ cup caster sugar
300g/10½oz white chocolate, melted
   and cooled slightly
250g/9oz/1⅔ cups self-raising flour

100g/3½oz/⅔ cup plain flour
2 large eggs, lightly beaten
3 small sheets edible gold leaf,
   to decorate

1   Preheat the oven to 180°C/350°F/gas 4. Grease two 30cm/12in square baking trays.
2   Heat the butter and sugar in a large saucepan until the butter has melted and the sugar has dissolved. Add two-thirds of the melted chocolate and leave to cool. Sift the self-raising and plain flours into the saucepan, add the eggs and beat well with a wooden spoon.
3   Place 20 large spoonfuls of the mixture on to the baking trays, leaving about 5cm/2in between them to allow for spreading.
4   Bake for 12–15 minutes until golden brown and just firm. Remove the cookies from the oven and leave to cool on the trays for a few minutes, then transfer to a wire rack with a palette knife to cool. Spread each cookie with a little of the remaining melted chocolate and top with a small piece of gold leaf to decorate.

316 Chinese New Year Lucky Buns

PREPARATION TIME 40 minutes   **COOKING TIME** 15–20 minutes   **MAKES** 12 buns

115g/4oz butter, softened
115g/4oz/scant ½ cup caster sugar
2 large eggs, lightly beaten
115g/4oz/¾ cups self-raising flour, sifted
1 tsp red food colouring

1 recipe quantity Vanilla Buttercream
  (see page 22)
gold chocolate coins and red sugar
  sprinkles, to decorate

1   Preheat the oven to 180°C/350°F/gas 4. Put 12 cake cases in a 12-hole bun tin.
2   Put the butter and sugar in a mixing bowl and beat using an electric hand mixer or wooden spoon until the mixture is light and creamy. Add the eggs gradually, beating after each addition. Add the flour and food colouring and gently fold them into the mixture, using a large metal spoon. Spoon the mixture into the cake cases.
3   Bake for 15–20 minutes until the buns spring back when pressed lightly and a skewer inserted into the middle of a bun comes out clean. Remove the buns from the oven, turn out on to a wire rack and leave to cool.
4   Spread buttercream over the buns using a round-bladed knife and decorate with the chocolate coins and sprinkles. Make sure children unwrap the coins before eating them.

317 Scandinavian May Day Doughnuts

PREPARATION TIME 20 minutes   **COOKING TIME** 15–25 minutes   **MAKES** 15 doughnuts

2 large eggs, plus 4 large egg whites
400g/14oz/1⅔ cups caster sugar
175g/6oz/heaped 1 cup plain flour
4 tsp cinnamon

½ tsp freshly grated nutmeg
finely grated zest of 1 large lemon
1½ litres/52fl oz/6 cups vegetable oil,
  for deep-frying

1   In a bowl, whisk together the whole eggs and 175g/6oz/scant ¾ cup of the sugar until light and foamy. Sift in the flour, 2 teaspoons of the cinnamon and the nutmeg and fold in with the lemon zest. Put the egg whites in a clean, dry bowl and whisk with an electric hand mixer or a whisk until they form stiff peaks, and fold into the mixture. Spoon the mixture into an icing bag fitted with a 13mm/½in star nozzle.
2   Heat the oil in a deep saucepan to 190°C/375°F or until a cube of bread dropped into the hot oil browns in 30 seconds. Pipe five lines or circles of mixture into the hot oil and cook for 5–8 minutes, turning once, until the doughnuts are golden brown on both sides. Remove the doughnuts from the oil with a slotted spoon and drain on kitchen paper to remove the excess oil, then keep warm while you fry the remainder.
3   Mix the remaining sugar and cinnamon on a plate and coat the warm doughnuts in it.

318 Mardi Gras Cupcakes

PREPARATION TIME 40 minutes   **COOKING TIME** 15–20 minutes   **MAKES** 24 cakes

225g/8oz butter
225g/8oz/scant 1 cup caster sugar
4 large eggs, lightly beaten
225g/8oz/1½ cups self-raising flour, sifted
3 tbsp natural yogurt
3 tbsp rainbow sugar sprinkles

2 recipe quantities Vanilla Buttercream
  (see page 22)
a few drops each of red and yellow
  food colouring
brightly coloured sweets, popping candy
  and edible glitter, to decorate

1   Preheat the oven to 180°C/350°F/gas 4. Put 24 cake cases in two 12-hole bun tins.
2   Put the butter and sugar in a mixing bowl and beat using an electric hand mixer or wooden spoon until the mixture is light and creamy. Add the eggs gradually, beating after each addition. Add the flour, yogurt and sprinkles and gently fold them into the mixture, using a large metal spoon. Spoon the mixture into the cake cases.
3   Bake for 15–20 minutes until the cakes spring back when pressed lightly. Remove the cakes from the oven, turn out on to a wire rack and leave to cool.
4   Divide the buttercream between 2 bowls. Stir one food colouring into each of the bowls until the colour is uniform. Spoon the icing into a piping bag fitted with a 13mm/½in star nozzle, putting the red icing on one side and the yellow on the other. Pipe a swirl of 2-tone icing on each cupcake and decorate with the sweets, popping candy and edible glitter.

319 4th of July Starry Cupcakes

PREPARATION TIME 40 minutes   **COOKING TIME** 15–20 minutes   **MAKES** 24 cakes

225g/8oz butter, softened
225g/8oz/scant 1 cup caster sugar
4 large eggs, lightly beaten
225g/8oz/1½ cups self-raising flour,
   sifted
3 tbsp natural yogurt
1 tsp vanilla extract
125g/4½oz ready-to-roll icing

red and blue food colouring pastes
icing sugar, for dusting
2 recipe quantities Vanilla Buttercream
   (see page 22)

TO DECORATE
red and blue sugar sprinkles
edible glitter

1   Preheat the oven to 180°C/350°F/gas 4. Put 24 cake cases in two 12-hole bun tins.
2   Put the butter and caster sugar in a mixing bowl and beat using an electric hand mixer
    or wooden spoon until the mixture is light and creamy. Add the eggs gradually, beating
    after each addition. Add the flour, yogurt and vanilla extract and gently fold them into the
    mixture, using a large metal spoon. Spoon the mixture into the cake cases.
3   Bake for 15–20 minutes until the cakes spring back when pressed lightly and a skewer
    inserted into the middle of a cake comes out clean. Remove the cakes from the oven,
    turn out on to a wire rack and leave to cool.
4   Divide the ready-to-roll icing in half and colour one half red and the other blue using the
    food colouring pastes (see recipe 269 for the method). Sift icing sugar on to a clean work
    surface and roll the red and blue icings out to 5mm/¼in thick, using a rolling pin. Cut out
    12 red and 12 blue stars, using a 2.5cm/1in star cutter.
5   Spoon the buttercream into an icing bag fitted with a 15mm/⅝in plain nozzle and pipe a
    swirl on to each cupcake. Decorate with the red and blue sprinkles and top each cake
    with a red or blue star. Sprinkle over the edible glitter to make the stars sparkle.

320 Veg Patch Retirement Cupcakes

PREPARATION TIME 1 hour   **COOKING TIME** 15–20 minutes   **MAKES** 24 cakes

225g/8oz butter
225g/8oz/scant 1 cup caster sugar
4 large eggs, lightly beaten
225g/8oz/1½ cups self-raising flour
4 tbsp cocoa powder
2 tbsp natural yogurt
90g/3¼oz/½ cup milk chocolate chips

140g/5oz ready-to-roll icing
red, green and orange food
   colouring pastes
1 tsp green food colouring
2 recipe quantities Vanilla Buttercream
   (see page 22)
55g/2oz milk chocolate, finely grated

1   Preheat the oven to 180°C/350°F/gas 4. Put 24 cake cases in two 12-hole bun tins.
2   Put the butter and sugar in a mixing bowl and beat using an electric hand mixer or wooden
    spoon until the mixture is light and creamy. Add the eggs gradually, beating after each
    addition. Sift in the flour and cocoa and gently fold them into the mixture with the yogurt
    and chocolate chips, using a large metal spoon. Spoon the mixture into the cake cases.
3   Bake for 15–20 minutes until the cakes spring back when pressed lightly. Remove the
    cakes from the oven, turn out on to a wire rack and leave to cool.
4   Divide the ready-to-roll icing into 4 equal pieces and colour one red, one green and one
    orange (see recipe 269 for the method). Leave the remaining piece white. Roll the red
    icing into small balls for tomatoes. Roll half the green icing into small balls and press them
    flat with your fingertips to make leaves. Fold one leaf in half as the lettuce heart, then wrap
    a further 3 or 4 leaves around the heart to make lettuces. To make cauliflowers, use the
    same process for the lettuces but use a ball of white icing in the centre and wrap the
    green leaves around it. Mark dots in the white ball with a cocktail stick. Divide the
    orange icing into 4 pieces and roll into balls. Press the balls to flatten the top and bottom
    slightly. Make indents vertically around the sides with a knife to form pumpkins.
5   Stir the food colouring into the buttercream until the colour is uniform. Spread a thick
    layer of the buttercream over each cake using a round-bladed knife. Sprinkle the grated
    chocolate over each cupcake and place a sugar vegetable in the centre. Spoon the
    remaining buttercream into an icing bag fitted with a 15mm/⅝in plain nozzle and pipe
    small green dots on the tomatoes and pumpkins as stalks and stems. To make your
    cakes extra special, print out or draw pictures of small seed packets, cut them out and
    fix them to cocktail sticks with glue or adhesive tape, then poke one into each cake.

321 Thanksgiving Spiced Pumpkin Cake

PREPARATION TIME 30 minutes   **COOKING TIME** 40–50 minutes   **SERVES** 10

175g/6oz butter, softened, plus extra
 for greasing
175g/6oz/scant ¾ cup caster sugar
3 large eggs, lightly beaten
225g/8oz/1½ cups self-raising flour
1 tsp ground ginger
½ tsp ground cloves
2 tsp cinnamon
125ml/4fl oz/½ cup soured cream
200g/7oz tinned unsweetened
 pumpkin purée

85g/3oz/heaped ⅓ cup raisins
finely grated zest of 1 large lemon
115g/4oz/heaped ⅔ cup pecan nuts,
 chopped

FOR THE ICING
150g/5¼oz cream cheese
85g/3oz butter
400g/14oz/2⅔ cups icing sugar, sifted
1 tbsp lemon juice

1 Preheat the oven to 180°C/350°F/gas 4. Grease and line a 20cm/8in springform cake tin.
2 Put the butter and caster sugar in a mixing bowl and beat using an electric hand mixer or wooden spoon until the mixture is light and creamy. Add the eggs gradually, beating after each addition. Sift in the flour and spices and gently fold them into the mixture with the soured cream, pumpkin purée, raisins, lemon zest and half the pecans, using a large metal spoon. Scrape the mixture into the tin using a spatula.
3 Bake for 40–50 minutes until the cake springs back when pressed lightly and a skewer inserted into the middle of the cake comes out clean. Remove the cake from the oven and leave to stand for 5 minutes, then turn out on to a wire rack and leave to cool.
4 Put the icing ingredients in a mixing bowl and beat using an electric hand mixer or wooden spoon to form a smooth icing. Cover the cake with the icing, sprinkle with the remaining pecans and leave to set before serving.

CHAPTER 6

CHILDREN'S CAKES & COOKIES

Encouraging children to cook from a young age gives them an essential understanding of food and the confidence to cook for themselves in later life. This chapter is aimed at getting children to put on an apron, get out a mixing bowl and wooden spoon and learn to bake. Most of the recipes are simple and suitable for you to cook with your children. There are also some lovely ideas for children's parties, such as Ladybird Cakes, Fairy Toadstool Meringues and Magnifying Glass Biscuits, with clear peppermint that children can look through. At Christmas time, delight your children with Christmas Tree Biscuits to decorate the tree or Snowman Cupcakes to leave out for Santa. Why not let them help you bake treats for their lunchbox, such as Granola Bars, Lemon Fairy Cakes or Apple Flapjacks? And, after school, let them settle down to homework with a slice of warm Banana Bread or freshly baked cookies and a glass of milk. Whatever your children love, there will be something to tempt them here.

SAILING BOAT CUPCAKES (SEE PAGE 207)

322   Rainbow Cake

PREPARATION TIME 25 minutes   **COOKING TIME** 25–30 minutes   **SERVES** 8

225g/8oz butter, softened, plus extra
  for greasing
225g/8oz/scant 1 cup caster sugar
4 large eggs, lightly beaten
200g/7oz/1⅓ cups self-raising flour
4 tbsp cocoa powder

1 tsp vanilla extract
1 recipe quantity Chocolate Buttercream
  (see page 22)
sugar-coated chocolate beans,
  to decorate

1   Preheat the oven to 180°C/350°F/gas 4. Grease and base-line two 20cm/8in sandwich cake tins.

2   Put the butter and sugar in a mixing bowl and beat using an electric hand mixer or wooden spoon until the mixture is light and creamy. Add the eggs gradually, beating after each addition. Sift in the flour and cocoa and gently fold them into the mixture with the vanilla extract, using a large metal spoon. Divide the mixture between the tins using a spatula.

3   Bake for 25–30 minutes until the cakes spring back when pressed lightly and a skewer inserted into the middle of each cake comes out clean. Remove the cakes from the oven and leave to stand for 5 minutes, then turn out on to a wire rack and leave to cool.

4   Sandwich the cakes together with half the buttercream and cover the top of the cake with the remaining icing. Place the coloured chocolate beans on the cake in rings following the rainbow colours: a red ring around the edge of the cake, then a smaller ring of orange beans, then yellow and so on.

323   Banana Bread

PREPARATION TIME 15 minutes   **COOKING TIME** 50–60 minutes   **SERVES** 8

115g/4oz butter, softened, plus extra
  for greasing
175g/6oz/¾ cup dark soft brown sugar
2 large eggs, lightly beaten
3 ripe bananas, peeled and mashed with
  a fork

225g/8oz/1½ cups self-raising flour
1 tsp baking powder
55g/2oz/⅓ cup sultanas
115g/4oz/scant 1 cup chopped
  pecan nuts

1   Preheat the oven to 180°C/350°F/gas 4. Grease and line a 24 x 12cm/9½ x 4½in loaf tin.

2   Put the butter and sugar in a mixing bowl and beat using an electric hand mixer or wooden spoon until the mixture is light and creamy. Add the eggs gradually, beating after each addition, then beat in the mashed bananas. Sift in the flour and baking powder and gently fold them into the mixture with the sultanas and pecans, using a large metal spoon. Scrape the mixture into the tin using a spatula.

3   Bake for 50–60 minutes until the loaf springs back when pressed lightly and a skewer inserted into the middle of the loaf comes out clean. Remove the loaf from the oven and leave to stand for 5 minutes, then turn out on to a wire rack and leave to cool.

324 Coconut Swiss Roll

PREPARATION TIME 20 minutes   **COOKING TIME** 10–15 minutes   **SERVES** 6

butter, for greasing
3 large eggs
85g/3oz/⅓ cup caster sugar
85g/3oz/heaped ½ cup self-raising flour,
    sifted

55g/2oz/heaped ½ cup desiccated
    coconut
3 tbsp icing sugar, sifted
250ml/9fl oz/1 cup double cream,
    whipped to stiff peaks
300g/10½oz/2 cups raspberries

1   Preheat the oven to 180°C/350°F/gas 4. Grease and line a 30 x 20cm/12 x 8in Swiss roll tin.

2   Put the eggs and caster sugar in a mixing bowl and whisk together using an electric hand mixer or a whisk until the mixture is creamy and pale yellow and the whisk leaves a trail when lifted up. Add the flour and half the desiccated coconut and fold them in, using a large metal spoon. Scrape the mixture into the tin using a spatula.

3   Bake for 10–15 minutes until the cake springs back when pressed lightly. Remove the cake from the oven and leave for a few minutes.

4   Put a sheet of baking parchment on a clean work surface. Dust with the icing sugar and sprinkle with the remaining coconut. Turn the cake out on to the sugar- and coconut-covered paper, cover with a damp tea towel and leave to cool for 10 minutes. Remove the tea towel and lining paper and cut away the edges of the cake to neaten it. Roll the cake up from a short end using the sugar- and coconut-covered paper to help you, then leave to cool completely. (The paper will end up rolled inside the cake.)

5   Unroll the cake, spread the whipped cream over and cover with the raspberries. Roll the Swiss roll up, using the paper to help you but this time not rolling it inside the cake, and place on a serving plate. As the Swiss roll contains fresh cream, it should be eaten straight away or stored in a lidded container in the fridge.

325 Strawberry & Blueberry Muffins

PREPARATION TIME 15 minutes   **COOKING TIME** 20–25 minutes   **MAKES** 10 muffins

250g/9oz/1⅔ cups self-raising flour
1 tsp baking powder
1 tsp bicarbonate of soda
100g/3½oz/heaped ⅓ cup caster sugar
150g/5½oz/1 cup blueberries
finely grated zest of 1 lemon

150ml/5fl oz/scant ⅔ cup milk
4 tbsp natural yogurt
100g/3½oz butter, melted and cooled
3 tbsp strawberry jam
2 large eggs, lightly beaten

1   Preheat the oven to 180°C/350°F/gas 4. Put 10 muffin cases in a 12-hole muffin tin.

2   Sift the flour, baking powder and bicarbonate of soda into a mixing bowl, add the sugar, blueberries and lemon zest and stir well with a wooden spoon.

3   In a separate bowl, whisk together the milk, yogurt, melted butter and jam with an electric hand mixer or a whisk, add the eggs and whisk again. Pour the liquid into the bowl containing the dry ingredients and fold in with a large metal spoon. Do not overmix: the mixture should be thick and slightly lumpy. Spoon the mixture into the muffin cases.

4   Bake for 20–25 minutes until the muffins spring back when pressed lightly and a skewer inserted into the middle of a muffin comes out clean. Remove the muffins from the oven, turn out on to a wire rack and leave to cool.

326 Lollipop Cupcakes

PREPARATION TIME 20 minutes **COOKING TIME** 15–20 minutes **MAKES** 12 cakes

115g/4oz butter, softened
115g/4oz/scant ½ cup caster sugar
2 large eggs, lightly beaten
115g/4oz/¾ cup self-raising flour, sifted
2 tbsp natural yogurt
12 lollipop sticks

200g/7oz plain chocolate, melted
  and cooled slightly

TO DECORATE
sugar sprinkles
edible silver balls

1   Preheat the oven to 180°C/350°F/gas 4. Put 12 cake cases in a 12-hole bun tin.
2   Put the butter and sugar in a mixing bowl and beat using an electric hand mixer or
     wooden spoon until the mixture is light and creamy. Add the eggs gradually, beating after
     each addition. Add the flour and yogurt and gently fold them into the mixture, using a
     large metal spoon. Spoon the mixture into the cake cases.
3   Bake for 15–20 minutes until the cakes spring back when pressed lightly and a skewer
     inserted into the middle of a cake comes out clean. Remove the cakes from the oven,
     turn out on to a wire rack and leave to cool.
4   Remove the cakes from their cases and press a lollipop stick into the top of each one.
     Put a sheet of greaseproof paper on the work surface. Hold each cake by the stick over
     the bowl of melted chocolate and spoon over several spoonfuls of the chocolate so that
     each cake is covered. Lay the lollipops on their sides on the greaseproof paper and cover
     the chocolate with sprinkles and silver balls. Leave the chocolate to set before serving.

327 Chocolate Fudge Cupcakes

PREPARATION TIME 20 minutes   **COOKING TIME** 15–20 minutes   **MAKES** 24 cakes

225g/8oz butter, softened
225g/8oz/1 cup dark soft brown sugar
4 large eggs, lightly beaten
175g/6oz/heaped 1 cup self-raising flour
55g/2oz/⅓ cup cocoa powder

1 recipe quantity Chocolate Buttercream
  (see page 22)
100g/3½oz white chocolate buttons
55g/2oz milk chocolate, melted and
  cooled slightly

1   Preheat the oven to 180°C/350°F/gas 4. Put 24 cake cases in two 12-hole bun tins.
2   Put the butter and sugar in a mixing bowl and beat using an electric hand mixer or
    wooden spoon until the mixture is light and creamy. Add the eggs gradually, beating after
    each addition. Sift in the flour and cocoa and gently fold them into the mixture, using a
    large metal spoon. Spoon the mixture into the cake cases.
3   Bake for 15–20 minutes until the cakes spring back when pressed lightly and a skewer
    inserted into the middle of a cake comes out clean. Remove the cakes from the oven,
    turn out on to a wire rack and leave to cool.
4   Spoon the buttercream into an icing bag fitted with a 13mm/½in star nozzle and pipe a
    large star on the top of each cake. (If you do not have an icing bag, cover each cake with
    a layer of buttercream using a round-bladed knife.) Place several chocolate buttons on
    each cake and drizzle over the melted chocolate in thin lines using a fork. Leave to set
    before serving.

328 Chocolate Chip Buns

PREPARATION TIME 20 minutes   **COOKING TIME** 15–20 minutes   **MAKES** 24 buns

225g/8oz butter, softened
225g/8oz/scant 1 cup caster sugar
4 large eggs, lightly beaten
200g/7oz/1⅓ cups self-raising flour
55g/2oz/heaped ¼ cup cocoa powder
3 tbsp natural yogurt
100g/3½oz/heaped ½ cup white
  chocolate chips

100g/3½oz/heaped ½ cup plain
  chocolate chips
200g/7oz milk chocolate, melted and
  cooled slightly
mini sugar-coated chocolate beans,
  to decorate

1   Preheat the oven to 180°C/350°F/gas 4. Put 24 cake cases in two 12-hole bun tins.
2   Put the butter and sugar in a mixing bowl and beat using an electric hand mixer or wooden
    spoon until the mixture is light and creamy. Add the eggs gradually, beating after each
    addition. Sift in the flour and cocoa and gently fold them into the mixture with the yogurt,
    using a large metal spoon. Add the white and plain chocolate chips and mix again.
    Spoon the mixture into the cake cases.
3   Bake for 15–20 minutes until the buns spring back when pressed lightly and a skewer
    inserted into the middle of a bun comes out clean. Remove the buns from the oven, turn
    out on to a wire rack and leave to cool.
4   Spread some melted chocolate over each bun using a round-bladed knife and decorate
    with the mini chocolate beans. Leave to set before serving.

329 Ladybird Cupcakes

PREPARATION TIME 40 minutes   COOKING TIME 15–20 minutes   MAKES 12 cakes

115g/4oz butter, softened
115g/4oz/scant ½ cup caster sugar
2 large eggs, lightly beaten
115g/4oz/¾ cup self-raising flour
4 tbsp cocoa powder
2 tbsp natural yogurt

200g/7oz plain chocolate, melted and
 cooled slightly
icing sugar, for dusting
250g/9oz red ready-to-roll icing
2 heaped tbsp plain chocolate chips

1 Preheat the oven to 180°C/350°F/gas 4. Put 12 cake cases in a 12-hole bun tin.
2 Put the butter and caster sugar in a mixing bowl and beat using an electric hand mixer or
   wooden spoon until the mixture is light and creamy. Add the eggs gradually, beating after
   each addition. Sift in the flour and cocoa and gently fold them into the mixture with the
   yogurt, using a large metal spoon. Spoon the mixture into the cake cases.
3 Bake for 15–20 minutes until the cakes spring back when pressed lightly and a skewer
   inserted into the middle of a cake comes out clean. Remove the cakes from the oven,
   turn out on to a wire rack and leave to cool.
4 Reserve a small amount of the melted chocolate to use for the decoration and spread the
   rest over the cakes, using a round-bladed knife.
5 Sift icing sugar on to a clean work surface and roll the ready-to-roll icing out to 5mm/¼in
   thick using a rolling pin. Cut out circles the same size as the top of your cupcakes using
   a round cutter. Remove a strip from each circle that is about 1cm/⅜in wide at its widest
   point, and discard. Cut what remains of each circle in half from the flat end. Place the
   halves on top of each cupcake at an angle, so that their rounded ends stick out beyond
   the cake case, to resemble an open pair of wings, with the flat edges set slightly in from
   the edge of the cake to leave space for the eyes. Stick 2 chocolate chips in place for eyes
   and attach 2 or 3 more to each wing with melted chocolate for the spots.

330 Piglet Cupcakes

PREPARATION TIME 40 minutes   COOKING TIME 15–20 minutes   MAKES 12 cakes

115g/4oz butter, softened
115g/4oz/scant ½ cup caster sugar
2 large eggs, lightly beaten
115g/4oz/¾ cup self-raising flour, sifted
2 tbsp natural yogurt
2 tbsp raspberry jam

a few drops of red food colouring
1 recipe quantity Vanilla Buttercream
 (see page 22)
12 pink marshmallows
2 heaped tbsp plain chocolate chips
55g/2oz pink ready-to-roll icing

1 Preheat the oven to 180°C/350°F/gas 4. Put 12 cake cases in a 12-hole bun tin.
2 Put the butter and sugar in a mixing bowl and beat using an electric hand mixer or wooden
   spoon until the mixture is light and creamy. Add the eggs gradually, beating after each
   addition. Add the flour, yogurt and jam and gently fold them into the mixture, using a
   large metal spoon. Spoon the mixture into the cake cases.
3 Bake for 15–20 minutes until the cakes spring back when pressed lightly and a skewer
   inserted into the middle of a cake comes out clean. Remove the cakes from the oven,
   turn out on to a wire rack and leave to cool.
4 Stir the food colouring into the buttercream until the colour is uniform, then cover the
   top of each cake with the buttercream, using a round-bladed knife to make a smooth
   surface. Place a pink marshmallow in the middle of each cake and 2 chocolate chips
   above it for eyes. Using a little of the buttercream, attach 2 chips in the centre of the
   marshmallow for the nostrils.
5 Cut the ready-to-roll icing into quarters, then cut each quarter into six pieces to give
   24 pieces. Roll each piece into a small ball approximately 1cm/⅜in in diameter. Press
   each ball flat between your fingers and then pinch together at one end to form an ear
   shape. Add 2 ears to each cake. Leave the buttercream to set before serving.

331 # Bumblebee Cupcakes

PREPARATION TIME 40 minutes   **COOKING TIME** 15–20 minutes   **MAKES** 12 cakes

115g/4oz butter, softened
115g/4oz/scant ½ cup caster sugar
1 tbsp clear honey
2 large eggs, lightly beaten
115g/4oz/¾ cup self-raising flour
2 tsp cinnamon
100g/3½oz/heaped ½ cup white
  chocolate chips

a few drops of yellow food colouring
1 recipe quantity Vanilla Buttercream
  (see page 22)
icing sugar, for dusting
125g/4½oz black ready-to-roll icing
1 tbsp plain chocolate chips
6 sheets edible rice paper

1   Preheat the oven to 180°C/350°F/gas 4. Put 12 cake cases in a 12-hole bun tin.
2   Put the butter, sugar and honey in a mixing bowl and beat using an electric hand mixer or
    wooden spoon until the mixture is light and creamy. Add the eggs gradually, beating after
    each addition. Sift in the flour and cinnamon and gently fold them into the mixture with the
    white chocolate chips, using a large metal spoon. Spoon the mixture into the cake cases.
3   Bake for 15–20 minutes until the cakes spring back when pressed lightly and a skewer
    inserted into the middle of a cake comes out clean. Remove the cakes from the oven, turn
    out on to a wire rack and leave to cool.
4   Stir the food colouring into the buttercream until the colour is uniform, then cover each
    cupcake with the yellow buttercream using a round-bladed knife.
5   Sift icing sugar on to a clean work surface and roll the black icing out to 5mm/¼in thick.
    Cut 24 strips of icing measuring 8 x 1cm/3¼ x ⅜in and place 2 parallel on each cake to
    make the bee's stripes. Add 2 chocolate chips for the bee's eyes. Divide each sheet of rice
    paper into 4 and cut out wing shapes. Press 2 wings into the buttercream between the
    stripes. Leave the buttercream to set before serving.

332 Sugar Mice Cupcakes

PREPARATION TIME 20 minutes   **COOKING TIME** 15–20 minutes   **MAKES** 12 cakes

115g/4oz butter, softened
115g/4oz/scant ½ cup caster sugar
2 large eggs, lightly beaten
115g/4oz/¾ cup self-raising flour
4 tbsp cocoa powder
2 tbsp natural yogurt

a few drops of pink food colouring
1 recipe quantity Vanilla Buttercream
  (see page 22)
12 sugar mice
edible silver balls, to decorate

1   Preheat the oven to 180°C/350°F/gas 4. Put 12 cake cases in a 12-hole bun tin.
2   Put the butter and sugar in a mixing bowl and beat using an electric hand mixer or wooden
spoon until the mixture is light and creamy. Add the eggs gradually, beating after each
addition. Sift in the flour and cocoa and gently fold them into the mixture with the yogurt,
using a large metal spoon. Spoon the mixture into the cake cases.
3   Bake for 15–20 minutes until the cakes spring back when pressed lightly and a skewer
inserted into the middle of a cake comes out clean. Remove the cakes from the oven,
turn out on to a wire rack and leave to cool.
4   Stir the food colouring into the buttercream until the colour is uniform, then cover the top
of each cake with the icing using a round-bladed knife. Place a sugar mouse in the
centre of each cake and decorate the rest of the cake with silver balls.

333 Chocolate Butterfly Cakes

PREPARATION TIME 20 minutes   **COOKING TIME** 15–20 minutes   **MAKES** 24 cakes

225g/8oz butter, softened
225g/8oz/scant 1 cup caster sugar
4 large eggs, lightly beaten
175g/6oz/heaped 1 cup self-raising flour

55g/2oz/⅓ cup cocoa powder
1 recipe quantity Vanilla Buttercream
  (see page 22)
2 chocolate flakes, crumbled, to decorate

1   Preheat the oven to 180°C/350°F/gas 4. Put 24 cake cases in two 12-hole bun tins.
2   Put the butter and sugar in a mixing bowl and beat using an electric hand mixer or wooden
spoon until the mixture is light and creamy. Add the eggs gradually, beating after each
addition. Sift in the flour and cocoa and gently fold them into the mixture, using a large
metal spoon. Spoon the mixture into the cake cases.
3   Bake for 15–20 minutes until the cakes spring back when pressed lightly and a skewer
inserted into the middle of a cake comes out clean. Remove the cakes from the oven,
turn out on to a wire rack and leave to cool.
4   Cut a shallow, cone-shaped piece out of the top of each cake and fill the hole left with a
spoonful of buttercream. Cut each removed piece in half and place 2 halves on each cake
a little apart and at an angle to make wings. Sprinkle over the chocolate flake to decorate.

334 Lemon Fairy Cakes

PREPARATION TIME 20 minutes   **COOKING TIME** 15–20 minutes   **MAKES** 24 cakes

225g/8oz butter, softened
225g/8oz/scant 1 cup caster sugar
4 large eggs, lightly beaten
225g/8oz/1½ cups self-raising flour, sifted
3 tbsp lemon curd

juice and finely grated zest of 1 lemon
300g/10½oz/2 cups icing sugar, sifted
edible silver balls and sugar sprinkles,
  to decorate

1   Preheat the oven to 180°C/350°F/gas 4. Put 24 cake cases in two 12-hole bun tins.
2   Put the butter and caster sugar in a mixing bowl and beat using an electric hand mixer
or wooden spoon until the mixture is light and creamy. Add the eggs gradually, beating
after each addition. Add the flour, lemon curd and lemon zest and gently fold them into
the mixture, using a large metal spoon. Spoon the mixture into the cake cases.
3   Bake for 15–20 minutes until the cakes spring back when pressed lightly and a skewer
inserted into the middle of a cake comes out clean. Remove the cakes from the oven,
turn out on to a wire rack and leave to cool.
4   In a bowl, mix the icing sugar. lemon juice and 1–2 tablespoons water to make a smooth,
thick icing, and spread over the cakes. Sprinkle over the silver balls and sprinkles.

335 Sailing Boat Cupcakes

PREPARATION TIME 40 minutes   **COOKING TIME** 15–20 minutes   **MAKES** 10 cakes

115g/4oz butter, softened
115g/4oz/scant ½ cup caster sugar
2 large eggs, lightly beaten
115g/4oz/¾ cup self-raising flour, sifted
50g/2oz/⅓ cup plain chocolate chips

1 recipe quantity Vanilla Buttercream
   (see page 22)
a few drops of blue food colouring
10 sheets edible rice paper
10 cocktail sticks

1   Preheat the oven to 180°C/350°F/gas 4. Put 10 cake cases in a 12-hole bun tin and
    10 mini foil cases in a 12-hole mini-muffin tin.
2   Put the butter and sugar in a mixing bowl and beat using an electric hand mixer or wooden
    spoon until the mixture is creamy. Add the eggs gradually, beating after each addition. Add
    the flour and chocolate chips and fold them into the mixture, using a large metal spoon.
    Put a large spoonful of mixture into each cake case and 2 teaspoonfuls into each foil case.
3   Bake for 12–15 minutes (small) and 15–20 minutes (large) until the cakes spring back
    when pressed lightly. Remove from the oven, turn out on to a wire rack and leave to cool.
4   Reserve 2 tablespoons of the buttercream and stir the food colouring into the remainder
    until the colour is uniform. Cover the large cakes with the blue buttercream and then dot
    with small amounts of the reserved white buttercream. Use a fork to form the buttercream
    into peaks to make waves. Place a small cake in its foil case in the middle of each cake.
    Cut the rice paper into 20 small triangles and thread 2 sails on to each cocktail stick. Put a
    mast and sails into the middle of each mini-muffin. Leave the icing to set before serving.

336 Spiced Sugar Cookies

PREPARATION TIME 20 minutes, plus chilling   **COOKING TIME** 10–15 minutes   **MAKES** 10 cookies

115g/4oz butter, softened, plus extra
   for greasing
55g/2oz/¼ cup caster sugar
140g/5oz/1 cup plain flour, plus extra
   for dusting

4 tbsp cocoa powder
1 tsp cinnamon
100g/3½oz/heaped ½ cup chocolate chips
1 tbsp milk (optional)
2 tbsp demerara sugar

1   Put the butter and caster sugar in a mixing bowl and beat using an electric hand mixer or
    wooden spoon until the mixture is light and creamy. Sift in the flour, cocoa and cinnamon,
    add the chocolate chips, and mix together with your hands to form a soft dough, adding
    the milk if the mixture is too dry. Wrap in cling film and refrigerate for 1 hour.
2   Preheat the oven to 180°C/350°F/gas 4. Grease two 30cm/12in square baking trays.
3   Sift flour on to a clean work surface and roll the dough out to 1cm/⅜in thick with a rolling
    pin. Cut out 10 squares using a 7.5cm/3in fluted cutter, gathering up the trimmings and
    re-rolling as necessary. Place the cookies on the baking trays and sprinkle with demerara.
4   Bake for 10–15 minutes until firm. Remove the cookies from the oven and leave to cool
    on the trays for a few minutes, then transfer to a wire rack with a palette knife to cool.

337 White Chocolate Cookies

PREPARATION TIME 15 minutes   **COOKING TIME** 14–18 minutes   **MAKES** 20 cookies

125g/4½oz butter, plus extra for greasing
200g/7oz/¾ cup caster sugar
350g/12oz/heaped 2 cups plain flour
1 tsp bicarbonate of soda

2 tbsp golden syrup
1 tsp vanilla extract
1 large egg, lightly beaten
200g/7oz white chocolate, chopped

1   Preheat the oven to 180°C/350°F/gas 4. Grease and line two 30cm/12in square
    baking trays. Put the sugar in a mixing bowl and sift in the flour and bicarbonate of
    soda. Mix together with a wooden spoon. Put the butter and syrup in a saucepan and
    heat gently until the butter melts. Cool slightly, then beat into the dry ingredients with the
    vanilla extract, egg and chopped chocolate.
2   Divide the dough into 20 walnut-sized balls and place on the baking trays, leaving about
    5cm/2in between them to allow for spreading. Press each cookie down slightly with a
    fork. Bake for 12–15 minutes until golden brown. Remove from the oven and leave to
    cool on the trays for a few minutes, then transfer to a wire rack to cool.

Chocolate Checkerboard Cookies

PREPARATION TIME 20 minutes, plus chilling   **COOKING TIME** 12–15 minutes   **MAKES** 15 cookies

115g/4oz butter, softened, plus extra
  for greasing
55g/2oz/¼ cup caster sugar

175g/6oz/heaped 1 cup plain flour,
  sifted, plus extra for dusting
4 tbsp cocoa powder, sifted
1 tbsp milk

1   Put the butter and sugar in a mixing bowl and beat using an electric hand mixer or wooden spoon until the mixture is light and creamy. Add the flour and mix together with your hands to form a soft dough.
2   Divide the dough in half in the bowl, and remove one half. Add the cocoa and milk to the remaining half and mix them into the dough with your hands.
3   Dust the work surface with flour. Divide the plain and cocoa-flavoured dough pieces in half and roll each one with your fingers into equal-sized sausage shapes about 2cm/¾in thick and 15cm/6in long. Place 1 plain sausage next to a chocolate sausage and then top with the remaining 2 in reverse order to make a checkerboard effect. Press the dough together firmly with your hands. Wrap in clingfilm and refrigerate for 1 hour.
4   Preheat the oven to 180°C/350°F/gas 4. Grease two 30cm/12in square baking trays. Cut the dough into 15 slices and place on the baking trays.
5   Bake for 12–15 minutes until golden brown. Remove the cookies from the oven and leave to cool on the trays for a few minutes, then transfer to a wire rack with a palette knife to cool.

339 Thumbprint Cookies with Raspberry Jam

PREPARATION TIME 15 minutes   **COOKING TIME** 15–18 minutes   **MAKES** 24 cookies

175g/6oz butter, softened
85g/3oz/heaped ½ cup icing sugar, sifted
225g/8oz/1½ cups plain flour, sifted

1 tsp vanilla extract
1 tbsp milk (optional)
8 tbsp raspberry jam

1 Preheat the oven to 180°C/350°F/gas 4. Put 24 cake cases into two 12-hole bun tins.
2 Put the butter and sugar in a mixing bowl and beat using an electric hand mixer or wooden spoon until the mixture is light and creamy. Add the flour and vanilla extract and mix together with your hands to form a soft dough, adding the milk if the mixture is too dry.
3 Put large spoonfuls of dough into each cake case. Press down in the middle of each one with your thumb to make a dent and fill with 1 teaspoon of the jam.
4 Bake for 15–18 minutes until golden brown. Remove the cookies from the oven and leave to cool on the trays for a few minutes, then transfer to a wire rack with a palette knife to cool.

340 Melting Moments

PREPARATION TIME 15 minutes   **COOKING TIME** 15–18 minutes   **MAKES** 20 biscuits

115g/4oz butter, softened, plus extra
   for greasing
2 tbsp golden syrup
85g/3oz/⅓ cup caster sugar
1 large egg, lightly beaten

1 tsp almond extract
300g/10½oz/2 cups self-raising flour
85g/3oz/scant 1 cup porridge oats
10 glacé cherries, halved

1 Preheat the oven to 180°C/350°F/gas 4. Grease two 30cm/12in square baking trays.
2 Put the butter, syrup and sugar in a mixing bowl and beat using an electric hand mixer or wooden spoon until the mixture is light and creamy. Beat in the egg and almond extract. Sift in the flour and mix together with your hands to form a soft dough.
3 Divide the dough into 20 walnut-sized pieces and roll into balls with your hands. Roll each ball in the oats to cover it. Place on the baking trays, leaving about 5cm/2in between them to allow for spreading. Press each ball down flat with the back of a fork and top each with half a glacé cherry.
4 Bake for 15–18 minutes until crisp and golden brown. Remove the biscuits from the oven and leave to cool on the trays for a few minutes, then transfer to a wire rack with a palette knife to cool.

341 Lemon Sandwich Cookies

PREPARATION TIME 20 minutes, plus chilling   **COOKING TIME** 12–15 minutes   **MAKES** 8 cookies

175g/6oz butter, softened, plus extra
   for greasing
55g/2oz/¼ cup caster sugar
175g/6oz/heaped 1 cup plain flour,
   sifted, plus extra for dusting

juice and finely grated zest of
   1 small lemon
1 tbsp milk (optional)
200g/7oz/1⅓ cups icing sugar, sifted
2 tbsp condensed milk

1 Put 115g/4oz of the butter and the caster sugar in a mixing bowl and beat using an electric hand mixer or wooden spoon until the mixture is light and creamy. Add the flour and lemon zest and mix together with your hands to form a soft dough, adding the milk if the mixture is too dry. Wrap in cling film and refrigerate for 1 hour.
2 Preheat the oven to 180°C/350°F/gas 4. Grease two 30cm/12in square baking trays.
3 Sift flour on to a clean work surface and roll the dough out to about 1cm/⅜in thick using a rolling pin. Cut out 16 rounds using a 5cm/2in fluted round cutter, gathering up the trimmings and re-rolling as necessary. Place the cookies on the baking trays.
4 Bake for 12–15 minutes until crisp and golden brown. Remove the cookies from the oven and leave to cool on the trays for a few minutes, then transfer to a wire rack with a palette knife to cool.
5 In a bowl, mix together the remaining butter with the icing sugar, lemon juice and condensed milk using an electric hand mixer or a wooden spoon to form a smooth icing. Sandwich the cookies together in pairs with the icing.

342 Duck Pond Cookies

PREPARATION TIME 40 minutes, plus chilling   **COOKING TIME** 12–15 minutes   **MAKES** 16 cookies

115g/4oz butter, softened, plus extra
  for greasing
55g/2oz/¼ cup caster sugar
175g/6oz/heaped 1 cup plain flour,
  sifted, plus extra for dusting
1 tbsp milk (optional)

150g/5½oz yellow ready-to-roll icing
a few drops of red food colouring
300g/10½oz/2 cups fondant icing sugar,
  sifted
a few drops of blue food colouring

1   Put the butter and caster sugar in a mixing bowl and beat using an electric hand mixer
    or wooden spoon until the mixture is light and creamy. Add the flour and mix together
    with your hands to form a soft dough, adding the milk if the mixture is too dry. Wrap in
    cling film and refrigerate for 1 hour.
2   Preheat the oven to 180°C/350°F/gas 4. Grease two 30cm/12in square baking trays.
3   Sift flour on to a clean work surface and roll the dough out to about 1cm/⅜in thick using
    a rolling pin. Cut out 16 circles using a 5cm/2in round cutter, gathering up the trimmings
    and re-rolling as necessary. Transfer the cookies to the baking trays using a palette knife.
4   Bake for 12–15 minutes until golden brown. Remove from the oven and leave to cool
    on the trays for a few minutes, then transfer to a wire rack with a palette knife to cool.
5   Pinch off about a 1cm/⅝in cube of the ready-to-roll icing and form the remainder into
    small duck shapes with your fingers. Colour the pinched-off bit with the red food
    colouring to make orange icing and use this to make beaks for the ducks.
6   Mix together the fondant icing sugar with 2–3 tablespoons water and the blue food
    colouring to form a smooth icing. Spoon the blue icing over the cooled cookies, covering
    them completely. Place a sugar duck in the middle of each cookie and leave the icing to
    set before serving.

343 Fried Egg Biscuits

PREPARATION TIME 20 minutes, plus chilling   **COOKING TIME** 12–15 minutes   **MAKES** 16 biscuits

115g/4oz butter, softened, plus extra
  for greasing
55g/2oz/¼ cup caster sugar
175g/6oz/heaped 1 cup plain flour,
  sifted, plus extra for dusting

1 tbsp milk (optional)
300g/10½oz/2 cups fondant icing sugar,
  sifted
125g/4½oz yellow ready-to-roll icing

1   Put the butter and caster sugar in a mixing bowl and beat using an electric hand mixer
    or wooden spoon until the mixture is light and creamy. Add the flour and mix together
    with your hands to form a soft dough, adding the milk if the mixture is too dry. Wrap in
    cling film and refrigerate for 1 hour.
2   Preheat the oven to 180°C/350°F/gas 4. Grease two 30cm/12in square baking trays.
3   Sift flour on to a clean work surface and roll the dough out to about 1cm/⅜in thick using
    a rolling pin. Cut out 16 fried-egg shapes using a knife, gathering up the trimmings and
    re-rolling as necessary. Transfer the biscuits to the baking trays using a palette knife.
4   Bake for 12–15 minutes until golden brown. Remove the biscuits from the oven and
    leave to cool on the trays for a few minutes, then transfer to a wire rack with a palette
    knife to cool.
5   In a bowl, mix the fondant icing sugar with 2–3 tablespoons water to make a smooth
    icing. Spoon the icing over each biscuit so that the top and sides are covered.
6   Divide the ready-to-roll icing into 8 pieces and roll them into balls, then cut the balls in
    half. Place half a ball in the centre of each biscuit to form the yolk while the icing is still
    wet. Leave the icing to set before serving.

344 Gingerbread Men

PREPARATION TIME 20 minutes   **COOKING TIME** 12–15 minutes   **MAKES** 16 biscuits

70g/2½oz butter, softened, plus extra
   for greasing
185g/6½oz/1¼ cups plain flour, plus
   extra for dusting
1 tsp bicarbonate of soda
1 tsp ground ginger
1 tsp mixed spice
finely grated zest of 1 small orange

1 large egg, lightly beaten
85g/3oz/⅓ cup light soft brown sugar
2 tbsp golden syrup
55g/2oz milk chocolate, melted and
   cooled slightly
mini sugar-coated chocolate beans,
   to decorate

1 Preheat the oven to 180°C/350°F/gas 4. Grease two 30cm/12in square baking trays.

2 Sift the flour, bicarbonate of soda, ginger and mixed spice into a mixing bowl and add the orange zest. Rub the butter into the flour with your fingertips until it resembles fine breadcrumbs, then add the egg, sugar and syrup and mix together with your hands to form a soft dough.

3 Sift flour on to a clean work surface and roll the dough out to about 1cm/⅜in thick using a rolling pin. Cut out 16 biscuits using a 13cm/5in gingerbread-man cutter. Transfer the biscuits to the baking trays using a palette knife.

4 Bake for 12–15 minutes until golden brown. Remove the biscuits from the oven and leave to cool on the trays for a few minutes, then transfer to a wire rack with a palette knife to cool.

5 Use the melted chocolate to attach the chocolate beans for eyes and buttons. Leave to set before serving.

345　Magnifying Glass Biscuits

PREPARATION TIME 20 minutes, plus chilling　**COOKING TIME** 12–15 minutes　**MAKES** 8 biscuits

20 clear boiled peppermint sweets
115g/4oz butter, softened, plus extra
　for greasing
55g/2oz/¼ cup caster sugar

175g/6oz/heaped 1 cup plain flour,
　sifted, plus extra for dusting
1 tbsp milk (optional)

1　Remove the wrappers from the peppermints and blitz them to a fine dust in a blender or
　food processor.
2　Put the butter and sugar in a mixing bowl and beat using an electric hand mixer or wooden
　spoon until the mixture is light and creamy. Add the flour and mix together with your
　hands to form a soft dough, adding the milk if the mixture is too dry. Wrap in cling film
　and refrigerate for 1 hour.
3　Preheat the oven to 180°C/350°F/gas 4. Grease and line two 30cm/12in square baking
　trays, or use a silcon mat to make absolutely sure these delicate cookies won't stick.
4　Sift flour on to a clean work surface and roll the dough out to about 1cm/⅜in thick using
　a rolling pin. Cut out eight 10cm/4in rounds with a handle to look like magnifying
　glasses, using a knife. Transfer the biscuits to the baking trays using a palette knife.
5　Using a round cutter smaller than the circle of the magnifying glass, cut out a round
　from the centre of each biscuit. (You can reroll these cut-outs to make more biscuits, if
　wanted.) Fill each hole with a layer of the peppermint dust, ensuring there are no gaps.
6　Bake for 12–15 minutes until the biscuits are golden brown and the peppermint dust
　has melted. Remove the biscuits from the oven and leave to cool completely on the trays
　so that the sugar 'glass' solidifies.

346　Dinosaur Biscuits

PREPARATION TIME 20 minutes, plus chilling　**COOKING TIME** 12–15 minutes　**MAKES** 10 biscuits

115g/4oz butter, softened, plus extra
　for greasing
55g/2oz/¼ cup caster sugar
175g/6oz/heaped 1 cup plain flour,
　plus extra for dusting
1 tsp cinnamon

finely grated zest of 1 orange
1 tbsp milk (optional)
1 tbsp icing sugar, sifted
mini sugar-coated chocolate beans,
　to decorate

1　Put the butter and caster sugar in a mixing bowl and beat using an electric hand mixer or
　wooden spoon until the mixture is light and creamy. Sift in the flour and cinnamon and
　add the orange zest. Mix together with your hands to form a soft dough, adding the milk
　if the mixture is too dry. Wrap in cling film and refrigerate for 1 hour.
2　Preheat the oven to 180°C/350°F/gas 4. Grease two 30cm/12in square baking trays.
3　Sift flour on to a clean work surface and roll the dough out to about 1cm/⅜in thick using
　a rolling pin. Cut out 10 biscuits using dinosaur cutters or a cardboard template and a
　knife, gathering up the trimmings and re-rolling as necessary. Transfer the biscuits to
　the baking trays using a palette knife.
4　Bake for 12–15 minutes until golden brown. Remove the biscuits from the oven and
　leave to cool on the trays for a few minutes, then transfer to a wire rack with a palette
　knife to cool.
5　Mix the icing sugar with 1 teaspoon water to make a smooth, thick icing. Use the icing
　to attach the chocolate beans as eyes on each dinosaur.

347 Domino Biscuits

PREPARATION TIME 20 minutes, plus chilling   **COOKING TIME** 12–15 minutes   **MAKES** 18 biscuits

115g/4oz butter, softened, plus extra
   for greasing
55g/2oz/¼ cup caster sugar
175g/6oz/heaped 1 cup plain flour,
   sifted, plus extra for dusting

1 tbsp milk (optional)
300g/10½oz/2 cups icing sugar, sifted

TO DECORATE
18 matchstick chocolates
chocolate chips

1   Put the butter and caster sugar in a mixing bowl and beat using an electric hand mixer or wooden spoon until the mixture is light and creamy. Add the flour and mix together with your hands to form a soft dough, adding the milk if the mixture is too dry. Wrap in cling film and refrigerate for 1 hour.
2   Preheat the oven to 180°C/350°F/gas 4. Grease two 30cm/12in square baking trays.
3   Sift flour on to a clean work surface and roll the dough out to about 1cm/⅜in thick using a rolling pin. Cut out eighteen 7.5 x 4cm/3 x 1¼in rectangles using a knife or cutter, gathering up the trimmings and re-rolling as necessary. Transfer the biscuits to the baking trays using a palette knife.
4   Bake for 12–15 minutes until golden brown. Remove the biscuits from the oven and leave to cool on the trays for a few minutes, then transfer to a wire rack with a palette knife to cool.
5   Mix the icing sugar with 2–3 tablespoons water to make a smooth, thick icing. Spoon the icing over each biscuit so that the top and sides are covered. While the icing is still wet, cut the matchstick chocolates to the width of each biscuit and place in the centre to divide your biscuits into 2 halves. Decorate each side of the biscuit with up to 6 chocolate chips to represent the dots on the dominoes.

348 Stained Glass Biscuits

PREPARATION TIME 20 minutes, plus chilling   **COOKING TIME** 12–15 minutes   **MAKES** 12 biscuits

12 cola-flavoured boiled sweets
115g/4oz butter, softened, plus extra
   for greasing
55g/2oz/¼ cup caster sugar

175g/6oz/heaped 1 cup plain flour,
   sifted, plus extra for dusting
1 tbsp milk (optional)

1   Remove any wrappers from the boiled sweets and blitz them to a fine dust in a blender or food processor.
2   Put the butter and sugar in a mixing bowl and beat using an electric hand mixer or wooden spoon until the mixture is light and creamy. Add the flour and mix together with your hands to form a soft dough, adding the milk if the mixture is too dry. Wrap in cling film and refrigerate for 1 hour.
3   Preheat the oven to 180°C/350°F/gas 4. Grease and line two 30cm/12in square baking sheets, or use a silcon mat to make absolutely sure these delicate cookies won't stick.
4   Sift flour on to a clean work surface and roll the dough out to about 1cm/⅜in thick using a rolling pin. Cut out 12 biscuits using a 7.5cm/3in heart-shaped cutter, gathering up the trimmings and re-rolling as necessary. Transfer the biscuits to the baking trays using a palette knife. Using a smaller star- or heart-shaped cutter, cut away a star or heart from the centre of each biscuit. Fill each hole with 1 teaspoon of the sweet dust, ensuring there are no gaps.
5   Bake for 12–15 minutes until golden brown and the sweet dust has melted. Remove the biscuits from the oven and leave to cool completely on the trays so that the sugar 'glass' solidifies.

349 Face Biscuits

PREPARATION TIME 20 minutes, plus chilling   COOKING TIME 12–15 minutes   MAKES 18 biscuits

115g/4oz butter, softened, plus extra
    for greasing
55g/2oz/¼ cup caster sugar
175g/6oz/heaped 1 cup plain flour,
    sifted, plus extra for dusting
1 tbsp milk (optional)

300g/10½oz/2 cups icing sugar,
    sifted

TO DECORATE
sugar-coated chocolate beans
liquorice or sugar sprinkles

1   Put the butter and caster sugar in a mixing bowl and beat using an electric hand mixer
    or wooden spoon until the mixture is light and creamy. Add the flour and mix together
    with your hands to form a soft dough, adding the milk if the mixture is too dry. Wrap in
    cling film and refrigerate for 1 hour.
2   Preheat the oven to 180°C/350°F/gas 4. Grease two 30cm/12in square baking trays.
3   Sift flour on to a clean work surface and roll the dough out to about 1cm/⅜in thick using
    a rolling pin. Cut out 18 biscuits using a 5cm/2in round cutter, gathering up the trimmings
    and re-rolling as necessary. Transfer the biscuits to the baking trays using a palette knife.
4   Bake for 12–15 minutes until golden brown. Remove the biscuits from the oven and
    leave to cool on the trays for a few minutes, then transfer to a wire rack with a palette
    knife to cool.
5   In a bowl, mix the icing sugar with 2–3 tablespoons water to make a smooth icing. Spoon
    the icing over each biscuit so that the top and sides are covered. Use the sweets to make
    faces, with chocolate beans for eyes and mouths and chopped liquorish or sprinkles for hair.

350 Ice Cream Sandwich Biscuits

PREPARATION TIME 20 minutes   COOKING TIME 10–12 minutes   MAKES 8 biscuits

140g/5oz butter, softened, plus extra
    for greasing
125g/4½oz/heaped ½ cup light soft
    brown sugar
100g/3½oz/heaped ⅓ cup caster sugar
1 large egg, lightly beaten

1 tsp vanilla extract
250g/9oz/scant 2 cups plain flour
1 tsp baking powder
100g/3½oz/heaped ½ cup milk
    chocolate chips
500ml/17fl oz/2 cups vanilla ice cream

1   Preheat the oven to 180°C/350°F/gas 4. Grease two 30cm/12in square baking trays.
2   Put the butter, light brown sugar and caster sugar in a mixing bowl and beat using an
    electric hand mixer or wooden spoon until the mixture is light and creamy. Beat in the
    egg and vanilla extract. Sift in the flour and baking powder and add the chocolate chips.
    Mix together with your hands to form a soft dough.
3   Divide the dough into 16 walnut-sized balls and place on the baking trays, leaving about
    5cm/2in between them to allow for spreading. Press each biscuit down slightly with your
    fingers or a fork.
4   Bake for 10–12 minutes until golden brown. Remove the biscuits from the oven and
    leave to cool on the trays for a few minutes, then transfer to a wire rack with a palette
    knife to cool.
5   Remove the ice cream from the freezer 5 minutes before you want to assemble the
    biscuits so that it has softened a little and is easy to use. When the biscuits are
    completely cold, sandwich together pairs of biscuits with a few tablespoons of ice cream
    in each. Serve the biscuits immediately.

351 Sunflower Biscuits

PREPARATION TIME 30 minutes, plus chilling   **COOKING TIME** 12–15 minutes   **MAKES** 8 biscuits

115g/4oz butter, softened, plus extra
 for greasing
55g/2oz/¼ cup caster sugar
175g/6oz/heaped 1 cup plain flour,
 sifted, plus extra for dusting

1 tbsp milk (optional)
300g/10½oz/2 cups icing sugar, sifted
a few drops of yellow food colouring
100g/3½oz/heaped ½ cup plain
 chocolate chips

1   Put the butter and caster sugar in a mixing bowl and beat using an electric hand mixer or wooden spoon until the mixture is light and creamy. Add the flour and mix together with your hands to form a soft dough, adding the milk if the mixture is too dry. Wrap in cling film and refrigerate for 1 hour.

2   Preheat the oven to 180°C/350°F/gas 4. Grease two 30cm/12in square baking trays.

3   Sift flour on to a clean work surface and roll the dough out to about 1cm/⅜in thick using a rolling pin. Cut out 8 biscuits using a large flower cutter or a cardboard template and a knife, gathering up the trimmings and re-rolling as necessary. Transfer the biscuits to the baking trays using a palette knife.

4   Bake for 12–15 minutes until golden brown. Remove the biscuits from the oven and leave to cool on the trays for a few minutes, then transfer to a wire rack with a palette knife to cool.

5   In a bowl, mix the icing sugar with 2–3 tablespoons water and the food colouring to make a smooth, thick icing. Spoon the icing over each biscuit so that the top and sides of each biscuit are covered and place some chocolate chips in the centre of each biscuit to make the anthers. Leave the icing to set before serving.

Fairy Toadstool Meringues

PREPARATION TIME 30–35 minutes **COOKING TIME** 1–1¼ hours **MAKES** 20 meringues

butter, for greasing
3 large egg whites

175g/6oz/scant ¾ cup caster sugar
a few drops of red food colouring

1   Preheat the oven to 140°C/275°F/gas 1. Grease and line two 30cm/12in square
    baking trays.
2   Put the egg whites and sugar in a heatproof bowl set over a pan of simmering water.
    It is important that the bottom of the bowl does not touch the water. Using an electric
    hand whisk, whisk the egg whites and sugar over the heat for 5 minutes until they form
    stiff peaks. Remove the bowl from the heat and whisk for another 5–10 minutes until
    the meringue is stiff.
3   Spoon a third of the meringue into a separate bowl. Colour the remaining meringue with
    the red food colouring, stirring until the colour is uniform.
4   Spoon the red meringue into an icing bag fitted with a 2cm/¾in plain nozzle and pipe
    large ovals of meringue on to the trays a little distance apart for the mushroom caps.
    Spoon the white meringue into another piping bag fitted with a 1cm/⅜in plain nozzle
    and pipe the toadstool stalks under the caps and also small white dots on the caps.
5   Bake for about 1–1¼ hours until dried and crisp. Remove the meringues from the oven
    and leave to cool on the trays before serving.

353 Granola Bars

PREPARATION TIME 15 minutes **COOKING TIME** 30–35 minutes **MAKES** 14 bars

150g/5½oz butter, chopped, plus extra
   for greasing
150g/5½oz/⅔ cup light soft brown sugar
3 tbsp golden syrup
70g/2½oz/scant 1 cup desiccated
   coconut
150g/5½oz/1 cup self-raising flour, sifted
200g/7oz/2 cups toasted muesli

2 large eggs, lightly beaten
100g/3½oz/½ cup chopped mixed
   unsalted nuts
200g/7oz/2 cups porridge oats
55g/2oz/¾ cup pumpkin seeds
55g/2oz/⅓ cup chopped dried apricots
finely grated zest of 2 lemons

1 Preheat the oven to 180°C/350°F/gas 4. Grease and line a 30 x 20cm/12 x 8in Swiss roll tin.
2 Put the butter, sugar and syrup in a saucepan and heat gently until the butter has melted.
3 Put all the remaining ingredients into a mixing bowl and pour in the butter mixture. Stir well to make sure that everything is well coated, then spoon the mixture into the tin.
4 Bake for 25–30 minutes until golden brown. Remove from the oven and leave in the tin to cool, then cut into 14 bars to serve.

354 Jam Tarts

PREPARATION TIME 20 minutes, plus chilling **COOKING TIME** 12–15 minutes **MAKES** 20 tarts

115g/4oz chilled butter, chopped,
   plus extra for greasing
225g/8oz/1½ cups plain flour, sifted,
   plus extra for dusting

2 tbsp caster sugar
200g/7oz raspberry or strawberry jam
   or lemon curd

1 Preheat the oven to 180°C/350°F/gas 4. Lightly grease two 12-hole shallow bun tins.
2 Put the flour in a mixing bowl. Rub the butter into the flour with your fingertips until the mixture resembles fine breadcrumbs. Stir in the sugar and add 3–4 tablespoons cold water, a little at a time, until the mixture comes together to form a soft dough. Wrap the dough in cling film and refrigerate for 30 minutes.
3 Sift flour on to a clean work surface and roll the dough out to about 5mm/¼in thick using a rolling pin. Cut out 20 rounds using a 7.5cm/3in round cutter, gathering up the trimmings and re-rolling as necessary. Place the rounds in the bun tins and put 1 heaped teaspoon of the jam or lemon curd into each pastry case.
4 Bake for 12–15 minutes until the pastry is golden brown. Remove the tarts from the oven and leave to cool in the tins for a few minutes, then transfer to a wire rack to cool.

355 Raisin & Cinnamon Pinwheels

PREPARATION TIME 15 minutes **COOKING TIME** 15–20 minutes **MAKES** 8 pastries

15g/½oz butter, melted and cooled, plus
   extra for greasing
flour, for dusting
250g/9oz block puff pastry
2½ tbsp light soft brown sugar

1 tsp cinnamon
55g/2oz/¼ cup raisins
1 medium egg, beaten
3 tbsp icing sugar, sifted

1 Preheat the oven to 180°C/350°F/gas 4. Lightly grease two 30cm/12in square baking trays.
2 Sift flour on to a clean work surface and roll out the pastry into a 20cm/8in square using a rolling pin. Brush with the melted butter, using a pastry brush, and sprinkle over the brown sugar, cinnamon and raisins. Starting at one side, roll the pastry up like a Swiss roll and press down firmly.
3 Cut the roll into 8 slices and roll each slice out into a round about 1cm/⅜in deep. Place the rounds on the baking trays and brush with the beaten egg.
4 Bake for 15–20 minutes until crisp and golden. Remove the pastries from the oven and transfer to wire racks with a palette knife to cool. In a small bowl, mix the icing sugar with 1–2 teaspoons water to form a smooth icing. Drizzle the icing in thin lines over the pinwheels. Leave the icing to set before serving.

356 Chocolate Crispy Squares

PREPARATION TIME 20 minutes, plus chilling   **COOKING TIME** 2–3 minutes   **MAKES** 16 squares

55g/2oz butter, chopped, plus extra
   for greasing
200g/7oz orange milk chocolate,
   broken into pieces
3 tbsp golden syrup

1 tbsp cocoa powder, sifted
250g/9oz/8⅓ cups rice crispies
100g/3½oz/heaped ½ cup white
   chocolate chips
55g/2oz/⅓ cup pistachio nuts, chopped

1   Grease a 20cm/8in loose-bottomed square cake tin.
2   Put the butter, orange chocolate, golden syrup and cocoa in a saucepan and heat gently until melted. Remove from the heat and stir in the rice crispies until they are well coated.
3   Press the mixture into the tin using the back of a spoon and leave to cool for a few minutes. Sprinkle over the chocolate chips and nuts and refrigerate for 2 hours until the chocolate has set. Cut into 16 squares using a sharp knife and place in cake cases.

357 Cornflake Sprinkle Cakes

PREPARATION TIME 15 minutes   **COOKING TIME** 2–3 minutes   **MAKES** 20 cakes

55g/2oz butter, chopped
3 tbsp golden syrup

250g/9oz/8⅓ cups cornflakes
sugar sprinkles, to decorate

1   Put 20 cake cases in two 12-hole bun tins.
2   Put the butter and syrup in a saucepan and heat gently, stirring, until melted. Remove from the heat, add the cornflakes and stir well, making sure they are well coated.
3   Put a large spoonful of the cornflake mixture into each cake case and decorate with the sprinkles. Leave to set for 1 hour before serving.

358 Chocolate Egg Nests

PREPARATION TIME 15 minutes, plus chilling   **COOKING TIME** 2–3 minutes   **MAKES** 20 nests

15g/½oz butter, chopped
2 tbsp golden syrup
250g/9oz caramel-filled chocolate, broken

2 tbsp cocoa powder, sifted
250g/9oz/8⅓ cups cornflakes
60 sugar-coated mini chocolate eggs

1   Put 20 cake cases in two 12-hole bun tins.
2   Put the butter, syrup, chocolate and cocoa in a saucepan and heat gently, stirring, until melted. Remove from the heat and stir in the cornflakes until they are well coated.
3   Put a large spoonful of the cornflake mixture into each cake case and place 3 mini eggs in the centre of each nest. Refrigerate for 1 hour before serving.

359 Chocolate Refrigerator Cake

PREPARATION TIME 20 minutes, plus chilling   **COOKING TIME** 2–3 minutes   **MAKES** 16 squares

115g/4oz butter, chopped, plus extra
   for greasing
500g/1lb 2oz plain chocolate, broken
   into pieces
300g/10½oz ginger biscuits, roughly
   broken

100g/3½oz/½ cup glacé cherries, halved
55g/2oz/scant 2 cups cornflakes
55g/2oz/⅓ cup flaked almonds
55g/2oz/⅓ cup pistachio nuts
100g/3½oz white chocolate, melted and
   cooled slightly

1   Grease a 20cm/8in loose-bottomed square cake tin.
2   Melt the butter and chocolate together and leave to cool slightly.
3   Put the broken biscuits in a plastic bag and crush into small pieces with a rolling pin. Put the biscuit bits, cherries, cornflakes, almonds and pistachios in a mixing bowl, add the melted butter and chocolate mixture and stir well, making sure everything is coated in chocolate. Scape into the tin and smooth the top with a spatula. Refrigerate for 30 minutes.
4   Drizzle the melted white chocolate over the cake, using a fork to make thin, decorative lines. Refrigerate for a further 30 minutes to set, then cut into 16 squares.

360 Lemon & Raspberry Slice

PREPARATION TIME 20 minutes   **COOKING TIME** 25–30 minutes   **MAKES** 20 slices

225g/8oz butter, softened, plus extra
  for greasing
225g/8oz/scant 1 cup caster sugar
4 large eggs, lightly beaten
225g/8oz/1½ cups self-raising flour, sifted

finely grated zest of 2 lemons,
  plus 2–3 tbsp of the juice
200g/7oz/1½ cups raspberries
300g/10½oz/2 cups icing sugar, sifted
a few drops of pink food colouring

1   Preheat the oven to 180°C/350°F/gas 4. Grease and line a 38 x 25 x 6cm/15 x 10 x 2½in baking tin.
2   Put the butter and sugar in a mixing bowl and beat using an electric hand mixer or wooden spoon until the mixture is light and creamy. Add the eggs gradually, beating after each addition. Add the flour and gently fold it into the mixture with the lemon zest, using a large metal spoon. Add the raspberries and fold in gently. Scrape the mixture into the tin using a spatula.
3   Bake for 25–30 minutes until the cake springs back when pressed lightly and a skewer inserted into the middle of the cake comes out clean. Remove the slice from the oven and leave to cool in the tin.
4   In a bowl, mix the icing sugar with the lemon juice to make a smooth, thick icing. (You may not need all of the lemon juice.) Cover the slice with three-quarters of the icing. Add the food colouring to the remaining icing and then drizzle the pink icing over the top of the slice, using a small spoon to form pretty patterns on the white icing. Leave the icing to set, then cut the slice into 20 slices to serve.

361 Apple Flapjacks

PREPARATION TIME 20 minutes   **COOKING TIME** 25–30 minutes   **MAKES** 10 flapjacks

115g/4oz butter, plus extra for greasing
3 tbsp golden syrup
85g/3oz/⅓ cup light muscovado sugar
250g/9oz/2½ cups porridge oats

1 large cooking apple, peeled,
  cored and grated
2 tsp cinnamon
115g/4oz/⅔ cup sultanas

1   Preheat the oven to 180°C/350°F/gas 4. Grease a 20cm/8in loose-bottomed square cake tin.
2   Put the butter, syrup and sugar in a saucepan and heat for about 5 minutes until the sugar has dissolved and the butter has melted. Cool a little, then stir in the porridge oats, grated apple, cinnamon and sultanas. Spoon the oat mixture into the tin.
3   Bake for 20–25 minutes until the flapjack is golden brown. Remove the flapjack from the oven and leave to cool in the tin, then cut into 10 slices to serve.

362 Chocolate Coconut Kisses

PREPARATION TIME 15 minutes   **COOKING TIME** 12–15 minutes   **MAKES** 18 cakes

butter, for greasing
200g/7oz/2½ cups desiccated coconut
200ml/7fl oz/scant 1 cup condensed milk
150g/5½oz/1 cup self-raising flour, sifted

1 tsp vanilla extract
100g/3½oz/heaped ½ cup
  plain chocolate chips

1   Preheat the oven to 180°C/350°F/gas 4. Grease two 30cm/12in square baking trays.
2   Put all the ingredients in a mixing bowl and stir well with a wooden spoon. Using 2 teaspoons, place 18 walnut-sized mounds of the coconut mixture on the trays a small distance apart.
3   Bake for 12–15 minutes until golden brown. Remove the cakes from the oven and transfer to a wire rack to cool.

363 Simple Chocolate Brownies

PREPARATION TIME 20 minutes   **COOKING TIME** 35–45 minutes   **MAKES** 16 brownies

250g/9oz butter, chopped, plus extra
  for greasing
400g/14oz plain chocolate, broken
  into pieces
250g/9oz/1 cup caster sugar
250g/9oz/1 cup dark soft brown sugar

5 large eggs
1 tsp vanilla extract
200g/7oz/1⅓ cups plain flour, sifted
100g/3½oz/heaped ½ cup white
  chocolate chips

1   Preheat the oven to 190°C/375°F/gas 5. Grease and line a 30 x 23 x 6cm/12 x 9 x 2½in baking tin.
2   Melt the butter and 350g/12oz of the plain chocolate together for about 5 minutes, then leave to cool. Chop the remaining plain chocolate and set aside.
3   Put the caster sugar, dark brown sugar, eggs and vanilla extract in a mixing bowl and whisk using an electric hand mixer or a whisk until the mixture is very light and has doubled in size. While still whisking, slowly pour in the melted chocolate and butter mixture until it is all incorporated. Fold in the flour, remaining plain chocolate and the white chocolate chips. Pour the cake mixture into the tin.
4   Bake for 30–40 minutes until the brownie has formed a crust and a skewer inserted into the middle of the cake comes out clean. Remove from the oven and leave to cool in the tin, then cut into 16 slices.

364 Snowman Cupcakes

PREPARATION TIME 40 minutes   **COOKING TIME** 15–20 minutes   **MAKES** 12 cakes

115g/4oz butter, softened
115g/4oz/scant ½ cup caster sugar
2 large eggs, lightly beaten
115g/4oz/¾ cup self-raising flour
4 tbsp cocoa powder
100g/3½oz mint chocolate,
  chopped
1 recipe quantity Vanilla Buttercream
  (see page 22)

TO DECORATE
55g/2oz orange ready-to-roll icing
mini sugar-coated chocolate beans
  or chocolate chips
red fizzy liquorice strips

1   Preheat the oven to 180°C/350°F/gas 4. Put 12 cake cases in a 12-hole bun tin.
2   Put the butter and sugar in a mixing bowl and beat using an electric hand mixer or wooden spoon until the mixture is light and creamy. Add the eggs gradually, beating after each addition. Sift in the flour and cocoa and gently fold them into the mixture with the mint chocolate, using a large metal spoon. Spoon the mixture into the cake cases.
3   Bake for 15–20 minutes until the cakes spring back when pressed lightly and a skewer inserted into the middle of a cake comes out clean. Remove the cakes from the oven, turn out on to a wire rack and leave to cool.
4   Cover each cake in buttercream, smoothing the surface with a round-bladed knife.
5   Use the ready-to-roll icing to make 2cm/¾in carrot shapes for the snowmen's noses and place one in the middle of each cake. Use the chocolate beans or chips to make eyes and mouths. Cut 2 strips of the liquorice and place crossed over on the bottom of each cake to make a scarf for the snowman. Leave the buttercream to set before serving.

365 Christmas Tree Biscuits

PREPARATION TIME 20 minutes, plus chilling   **COOKING TIME** 12–15 minutes   **MAKES** 10 biscuits

115g/4oz butter, softened, plus extra
for greasing
55g/2oz/¼ cup caster sugar
175g/6oz heaped 1 cup plain flour,
plus extra for dusting

2 tsp cinnamon
1 tbsp milk (optional)
200g/7oz/1⅓ cups icing sugar, sifted
a few drops of green food colouring
sweets, to decorate

1 Put the butter and sugar in a mixing bowl and beat using an electric hand mixer or
   wooden spoon until the mixture is light and creamy. Sift in the flour and cinnamon and
   mix together with your hands to form a soft dough, adding the milk if the mixture is too
   dry. Wrap in cling film and refrigerate for 1 hour.
2 Preheat the oven to 180°C/350°F/gas 4. Grease and line two 30cm/12in square
   baking trays.
3 Sift flour on to a clean work surface and roll the dough out to about 1cm/⅜in thick using
   a rolling pin. Cut out 10 biscuits using a Christmas-tree cutter or a cardboard template
   and a knife, gathering up the trimmings and re-rolling as necessary. Transfer the biscuits
   to the baking trays using a palette knife.
4 Bake for 12–15 minutes until golden brown. Remove the biscuits from the oven and
   leave to cool on the trays for a few minutes, then transfer to a wire rack with a palette
   knife to cool.
5 Mix the icing sugar with 1–2 tablespoons water and the food colouring to make a
   smooth green icing. Cover each biscuit with green icing using a round-bladed knife and
   decorate with the sweets. Leave the icing to set before serving.

INDEX